DAVID HUME OF GODSCROFT'S
THE HISTORY OF THE HOUSE
OF
DOUGLAS

DAVID HUME OF GODSCROFT'S

THE HISTORY OF THE HOUSE

OF

DOUGLAS

Volume 2

EDITED BY

DAVID REID

The Scottish Text Society
27 George Square
Edinburgh

1996

ISBN 1 897976 135

Printed in Scotland by BPC-AUP Aberdeen Ltd

Distributed by
Scottish Cultural Press

Plate 12: James, 9th Earl of Douglas

[323] The Lyfe of 4 Archbald, Earle of[1] Wigtoun 14 Lord and 5 Earle of Douglas, 2 Duk of Turain.[2]

His mariage.

Vnto[3] Archbald callit Tynman succeidit[4] his eldest sone Archbald Earle of Wigtoun, as[5] 14 Lord and 5 Earle of Douglas, Lord of Galloway, Bothuel, and Annandail, 2 Duk of Turain, Lord of Longeville and Mareshal[6] of France. He mariet[7] a daughter of the Earle of Crafurds, whilk hes[8] bene the occasion of the Earle of Crafurds brothers going with him to France (as also was[9] said) and the ground of the freindshipe betwix Earle William, his brother sone, and the Earle of Crafurde; for the whilk[10] the said Earle William Douglas was slane in the Castle of Sterling, for Earle Williams wife was this Earle of Wigtouns daughter, and sa[11] that Earle of Crafurde ather[12] her grandfather or avuncle[13], or (at leist) Cousin[14] germane to her; thogh it seeme also there hes[15] bene continual freindshipe betwix these houses fra[16] the first Earles[17] tyme, wha procurit[18] the Earle of Crafurds peace efter the slaughter of Johne Lyon.

His childrein.

The childrein of the Earle of Douglas, (for we style him be a hammiet[19] style, and[20] verie honorable, rather then Duk[21] of Turain) [324] war[22] William, Dauid, and a doughter callit[23] Beatrix. The tyme that he possessit[24] the Earldome of Douglas from his fathers death, anno 1424 til[25] his awen 1439, is about fyftein zeirs, to wit[26] the hail[27] tyme of King James the first, in[28] the end of Duk Mordok, and about twa zeirs[29] of the beginning, and minoritie of King James the second, whereby the Estate of the Contrie in his dayes may be easelie seene, remembring what hes[30] bene said of the death of King Robert the Thrid in anno 1420[31], to whom

The Estate of the Contrie

[1]^Douglas and^ [2][14... Turain] etc [3]^this^ [4][callit Tynman] succeided [5][as] the [6]Mareshall [7]maried [8]which hath [9][also was] hath been [10]which [11]so [12]either [13]^her^ wncle [14]Cousen [15]hath [16]from [17]^of Douglas^ [18]who procured [19]by his homebred [20]^that^ [21]Duke [22]were [23]called [24]possessed [25]till [26]yeirs, [to wit *changed to* witt] even [27]holl [28][in] [29] two yeirs [30]hath [31]^and Robert the governour^

succeidit[1] Duk Murdok in[2] name of Governour rather nor[3] king for they are not[4] Kings indeid[5] (James being the iust aire) zit ruled[6] as kings during[7] his captivitie, whilk[8] (belike) they cared not how lang[9] it was; never mentioning his releife, nor dealing for it, til[10] out of their[11] iniquitie raise[12] the occasion of equitie towards him; and out of their pride their owne overthrow; for Duk[13] Murdok when he had governit[14] (or rather misgovernit[15]) for he had no governing[16] nay not of his awin[17] childrein[18] some thrie[19] or foure zeirs[20], irritat be[21] ane insolent fact of his eldest sone Walter (whilk[22] was the reaving[23] of a faulcon af[24] his hand, and thrawing[25] the nek of her asunder in dispyte of him;) to dispyte his sone agane, more[26] then for anie vther **[325]** cause[27], he determinit[28] (as he also menacit[29] his sone) to send and[30] relive the said King James out of captivitie in[31] England, and place[32] him in his kingdome. No vther[33] cause we read of, in our histories (be[34] whose faulte I know not) or if it be nones[35] faulte, but the verie true and sole cause, it is so remarkable[36] that I can not slipe vnremarking[37] it by the way. Nather[38] is it altogether by[39] my purpose but one thing whilk ensuit effects in the estate of the house of Douglas, and geves occasion therto[40]. And thogh it war[41] somwhat besyde the[42] purpose, zit[43] is[44] worthie for me to lay oppen, and for the reader to wonder[45] so rare a fact[46] betwix a father and a sone, as I think[47] not extant elswhere in anie vther monuments, of[48] historie, sen[49] the warld[50] was[51];

---

[1]succeided [2]by the [3]than [4][for… not] which name and charge, his father the Duke of Albanye had formerly bene in the king his fathers tyme. And in his brother Robert the 3. also *'which' to 'also' has been scored out* They being no righteous [5][indeid] ^but onely Gouernors, and^ [6]yett they ruling absolutly [7]^James^ [8]which [9]long [10]till [11]^owne^ [12]did arise [13]Duke [14]governed [15]misgoverned [16]^true^ government [17]owne ^familie and^ [18]^for the space of^ [19]three [20]yeirs ^hee being^ [21]by [22]which [23]taking [24]^violently^ of [25]pulling [26]rather [27]other **[325]** good motion in him [28]determined [29]menaced [30]^to^ [31]from [32]to posess [33]other [34]by [35]no [36]memorable [37]slipp ^the^ remarking [38]Neither [39]beside [40][but… thereto] [41]were [42]my [43]yett [44]^it^ [45]^at^ [46]an example [47]^the lik is^ [48]other monument, on [49]since [50]world [51]^first inhabited^

that a man in dispyte of his[1] sone sould quyte a kingdome that[2] he was possessit in[3], and[4] no vther[5] apparence but to have bruikit[6]. I confese there hes[7] bene meikle vnnaturalitie amang them[8] of that most natural[9] band in the world; to[10] the distruction, and to the[11] death of[12] whom they sould not; bot[13] that was for their awin[14] honour and dignitie, to obteine that[15] place, or to continue in it, that men aspyres so to[16], but that their vnnatural dispyte sould aryse[17] so fare[18] as to vndoe them selves, and to quyte a kingdome **[326]** (for obteining and reteining where of[19] men turnes al[20] vpsyde downe) onlie for satisfaction of his hart[21] aganes his sone; let[22] him that hes[23] read anie sik exemple tel[24] it, and joine this (I am sure)[25] for the second (at least[26]) among his records. jf it was for love of his Cousin[27], for respect to equitie, for duetie to god and to his contrie, whils he saw him self could not, and his sone wald[28] not governe rightlie, and therefor thought[29] fittist to renunce it to him that[30] could and wald[31], as it was[32] a gude[33], sober, wise and worthie thought, sa[34] our wryters dois[35] him wrange[36], that never once[37] signifies sik mynd[38]; mentioning onlie his awne[39] anger, and a bellies[40] of his Anger (proceiding from his awen hatred for iniurie done to him be his sone Walter) Colein Cambel (ane of the Principals in Argyl)[41]. Bot however[42] it be (if to prosecute his dispyte be iustice, or if to do justice be occasion of[43] dispyte) as he had threatnit[44] his sone, so he prosecuts[45]. He sendis Ambassadours

[1]^owne^ [2]whereof [3]possessed [in] [4]^sawe^ [5]other [6]enioyed it still [7]hath [8]much vnnatural vnkindnes amongs some [9]naturall [10]^the procuring of^ [11][to the] [12]^those^ [13][not] ^rather have wrought the safety^; but [14]owne [15]their [16]^do so much^ aspyre vnto [17]reache [18]farr [19]^ambitious^ [20]all ^things^ [21]there harts ^and mallice conceved^ [22]their owne chyld; lett [23]hath [24]such example tell [25][(I am sure)] [26]at most [27]Cousen [28]wold [29]^it^ [30]^both^ [31]^do it^ [32]had been [33]goode [34]^in him, then^ [so] [35]do [36]wronge [37][once] in the least [38]his mynd to have bene such [39]owne [40]the bellowes [41][proceiding... Argyl] Colein Cambel (ane of the Principals in Argyl whose hatred proceided likwaies from a privat iniurie done to him by the others sone Walter *See note.* [42]But howsoever [43]occasioned his [44]threatned [45]performed it. ^For^

Ambassadours sent for releif of King James the first

in[1] England for releive[2] of his Cousen[3] germane[4] James the first: the cheif of whom was this Earle of Douglas about the tyme of his verie first comming to the Earldome, for we may not stand precislie in maters of Chronologie, so incertainlie set[5] downe in the tyme; wha[6] with the rest of his associats[7] (William Hay [**327**] Constable and Henrie Bishope of Aberdene) behavit[8] themselvis saiglie[9] in this mater zit[10] they brought it to a gude[11] conclusion; having in some sort taken away the doubtes of his Captivers[12] wha doubtit leist[13] he sould be[14] a great Enemie to[15] them, because he had receivit[16] great[17] iniurie of[18] them be[19] his so lang, and wrangous[20] detention; and[21] having also, if not satiatit, zit[22] in some sort satisfiet their greidie[23] avarice, be[24] marying a wyfe taucherles[25] and paying a ranson saikles[26], never being[27] a lawful prisonner. And thogh these twa[28] things be eneugh to declare their vnreasonable and inhumane dealing[29] with him, zit[30] the English writers eikes[31] this thrid as compelling him to do that whilk[32] he might not[33]; to wit[34] to bind himself and his kindome to a sclaverie[35] to England, as halden[36] of that Crowne,[37] being ever as frie and more frie then themselves[38]. Our wryters grantis[39] that they war[40] shamles as to seik[41] it; but they eik also[42] he was so magnanim and couragious[43] as to refuse it; zit[44] the English sayes[45] he did it, and nameis[46] the place[47] at Windsore and the witnesses 3 Duks, 2 Archbishopes, 12 Earles, 10 Bishops, 20 Barons, 200 Knights and Esquyrs; besyds vthers[48] (a great nomber indeid) bot they designe them not.

Maior lib.6. Cap.14. fol. 135 pag.b Hol. Eng. in Henrie 6. second zeir

---

[1]into [2]releese? [3]Cousen [4]^King^ [5]sett [6]who [7]Collegues [8]behaved [9] so wisely [10][zit] that [11]goode [12]those that kept him Captive [13]who ^much^ doubted least [14]prove [15]vnto [16]received ^so^ [17]^an^ [18]from [19]by [20]wrongous [21]^these^ [22]satiated, yett [23]satisfied ^their^ [greidie] [24]by ^the King^ [25]taugherles *changed to* without any portion [26][saikles] that was but due [27]hee having been [28]two [29][and inhumane] deallings [30]yett [31]addes [32]which [33]could no wayes do [34]witt [35]servitude [36]^to acknowledge it to be^ holden [37]^It^ [38]free or more than their owne [39]grants [40]were ^so^ [41]vrge [42]saye withall that [43]magnanimous [and couragious] [44]^flatly^; yett [45]do alleage that [46]^they^ name [47]^to have been^ [48]others

I durst pleidge[1] **[328]** they ware al[2] Englishmen[3] and therefor pairtie therefor suspect; zit[4] that we sould not contend with them, sen[5] they are so careful to prove their barbarous[6] inhumanitie aganes a frie bairne keipit[7] vniustlie prisonner, and their foolishe feiblenes[8] to crave that[9] could do them no guid[10] of a Captive, and compelled persone[11]. Let ws grant both that they war so barbarous and so foolishe as to compel him, and that so he did on whatever necessitie being in their power: it is weil that[12] they dare[13] not say[14] this Earle of Douglas made[15] the alyke, hommage[16], or zit consentit[17] to that; whilk[18] (I am perswadit) al[19] England wald[20] not have causit[21] him[22] doe, more nor[23] his predecessor, Lord William[24] Hardie, wha[25] died[26] (as hath been said) in prison for the alike cause[27]; Nay they dare[28] not say that anie of the[29] Ambassadors[30] did it[31]; or consentit to it, whilk makis[32] the fact[33] voyde (if sa[34] had bene) cheiflie he not zit[35] being[36] King; But on what ever condition it war[37], King James the first was at last be[38] this Earles travels dimissit,[39] come in[40] Scotland, and was Crowned[41] the 21 of May, 1424. Now we have hard[42] hitherto the rysing of the house of Douglas,[43] the continual increasing be[44] their great deserts, with the allowance[45], and following of al[46] men[47] with the gud-wil[48] and liking[49] of their Princes, in a perpetual tennor be[50] the space of 120 zeirs and more: **[329]** their Princes delyting to

---

[1][designe… pleidge] name not anie one of them. But if any such there were [2]all [3]^and none of them Scotts Embassadors, or their company^ [4][pairtie therefor] the matter is iustly to be suspected; Yett [5]since [6][barbarous] [7]aganest a free borne Prince and a child keiptt [8][foolishe feiblenes] want of right iudgment [9]^or obteine^ what [10][do … guid] ^not stand with right nor the lawe of Nations^ [11][and… persone] extorted by compulsion [12][both that… weil that] all that they alleage, and it is no thing in effect; Sith [13]can [14]^that^ [15][made] being Cheef in the Comission from the state of Scotland did [16]lyke [hommage] [17]yett consented [18]^or any kind of homage at all^; which [19]perswaded) all [20]could [21]caused [22]^to^ [23]than [24]^the^ [25]who [26]^(as hath been saide)^ [27]a cause not much vnlike [28]Can [29]^other^ [30]^(who were ioyned with him)^ [31]the same [32]consented therevnto, which makes [33]^vtterly^ [34]any such [35][zit] [36]^as yett actually^ [37]But [on] whatsoever ^the^ conditions were [38]by [39]dismissed [40]^home^ into [41]^king^ [42]heard [43]^and^ [44]^thereof^ by [45]applause [46]all [47]^and^ [48]good-will [49]lyking [50]by

imploy them; they indevoring to serve their Prince[1], and[2] Contrie to the[3] vttermost with a gude[4] harmonie, and happie agreance to al[5].

The beginning of the troubles of the house of Douglas

Let ws now be content fra[6] this furth[7] to find the world to be a world; that is to say, to have a vicissitude;[8] as thogh this[9] house sal zit grow[10] (and greatter nor[11] ever), this concordance[12] not to[13] continue so fullie, bot to[14] begine to receave[15] Eclipses; their Princes jalous[16] of them; they in feare of their Princes; some tymes in favour, some tymes out of it; some tymes imployit[17], sometymes reiectit[18]. The affections of men siklyke[19], some tyme towards them some tymes from them[20]: some tymes praising[21], and sometymes pleining[22]. Then also on their pairt whils[23] content, whils not in al content[24]; whils medling, whils withdrawing[25] them selves from affairs[26]; and here of agane jarris[27], wardings, banishings[28], slaughters, whilk[29] things beginning in this mans tyme at the[30] warding, that malcontentednes[31] and lyings af ar continuit[32] in the nixt[33], proceeding[34] in his sones[35] to[36] slaughter; and in[37] his successors, with Jarres continuit as in his short tyme, and transferrit as hereditarie to his sones, in whom as[38] manie vicissitudes smyling[39] and frowning[40] of Court ending[41], in this tragedie[42] of their deaths; also prosecutit by and aganes[43] **[330]** his successor til[44] oppen Enimitie;[45]

---

[1]Prince [2]^their^ [3]there [4]goode [5]on all ^sydes^ [6]contented from [7]foorth [8]^So^ [9][thogh] that ^same^ [10]sall yett grow ^up^ [11]that to a higher pitch than ever), ^yett^ [12]^shall^ [13][to] [14]shall [15]receive [16]jealous [17]imployed, ^and^ [18]reiected *changed to* neglected [19]lykewise [20][from them] altered [21]likeing [22]compleining *changed to* dislykeing [23]being now [24][whils… al *changed to* all content] now descontented [25][whils… whils] now imployed and then [*illegible*] withdrawing *adopted* [26]^the^ effairs [27][agane] arysing jarres [28]banishments [29]which [30]this *altered to* his [31]the descontentments [32]^the^ [lyning] lynings *or* [lyuing] lyuings, *'lyings'*, *<u>1633</u>*, *adopted* off [ar] which arose from thence continued [33]next [34]^and^ proceeded [35]tyme [36]^his^ [37][in] was transferred as hereditarie to [38][Jarres… continuit *changed to* continued… transferrit *changed to* transferred… as] [39]^of^ smylings [40]frownings [41]^fortune and which^ ended [42]^fearfull^ tragedies [43][of their… aganes] The Princes desfavors wrought by the malice of others being often prosecuted against [44]successors till it grew to an [45]^to^

banishing[1], batels, and at last[2] captivitie, imprisonment, and wraik[3] of this so flurishing[4] a house in the 1483 zeirs.[5] the space of 59 or 60 „ zeirs fra[6] King James the first his returne in[7] „ Scotland, with whilk[8] begoude this varietie[9] spoken of. For first, the verie first zeir of his reigne this Earle[10] Douglas is committit[11] to warde; bot[12] soone dimissit[13] agane (as wald[14] seeme); and within some few zeirs[15] agane committit[16]. For his first committing[17] there is no cause theirof recordit[18]; the tyme may give some conjecture, with the rest of the circumstances. The tyme was when Duk Murdoks sones Walter and Alex*ander* and their mother, and her[19] father Duncan Stewart Earle of Lennox war committit[20]. The circumstances are, that he was not committit him[21] alone, bot[22] with him a great number[23] of the nobilitie; to the number of 24 Earles and Barons (and amongs them some of the Kings awin[24] special kinrid) as William Earle of Angus, wha[25] was his sisters sone; and sa Cousine to the Duk Murdok; the Earle of Douglas was also allya[26] with him; for the Duks father Robert Stewart Governour had bene in great freindshipe with[27] Archbald Tynman[28] and Archbald Grim, father and Gudshire[29] to this Earle of Douglas, whilk[30] was confirmit[31] also be allya[32] of Johne Earle of Buchan second sone **[331]** to the Governour, and brother to Duk[33] Murdok, wha[34] had maryet[35] this Earles sister, and with whom he had bene in great freindshipe in particular, and societie of armes in France; and his father, and he had died togeather at Vernoil[36]: the Earle of Marche also, wha[37] had bene restorit be[38] his father Robert the Governour, and had keepit

He is committit to warde

The[39] cause theirof.

Hol. Boe. An 1425

[1]banishments [2]^to the^ [3]^vtter^ wreike ^and overthrowe^ [4]floorishing [5]^and that dureing^ [6]from [7]into [8]which [9] these ^dysmell^ varieties ^to be herefter^ [10]^of^ [11]committed [12]but [13]desmissed [14]wold [15]yeirs [16]committed [17]commitment [18]recorded [19][his] her *adopted* [20]were committed [21]committed [him] [22]but [23]many [24]owne [25]who [26][allya *or* allyit?] allyde [27]^this^ [28][Tynman] father [29][father… Gudshire] the Grandfather [30]which [31]confirmed [32]allyance [33]Duke [34]who [35]maryed [36]Vernoille [37]who [38]restored by [39]No

gude[1] freindshipe with him, and his sone from[2] his restoring; Robert Stewart of Rothose, Stewart of Dordonald, Johne Stewart of Carden, war al[3] Stewarts, and touching the said Murdok or the Earle of Lennox in some proximitie of bluide[4], as the King him self was[5]. The rest as Hepburne of Hails, Hay of Zeaster[6], Ramsay of Dalhousie Halibourton of Dirltoun, we find to have bene dependars on the houses of Douglas and Marche; and the rest of the noble men their names are Walter Ogilvie, Alexander Setoun, Gordoun, Hay of Arrol, Scrimger Constable of Dundie hes[7] bene freinds and dependars of the house of Douglas, as of whom we find with them in dyvers battels, and hes[8] had perhaps some freindshipe with the Duk[9], or to his father in law, as commonlie the Nobilitie are allyeit[10], and of kin[11] with[12] vther, wha[13] therefore (thogh they war[14] willing to have their lawful Prince inioy his owine place) **[332]** wald[15] not agree so easelie to the slaughter of those whom the King (whether for revenging of the Governour Robert, there predecessor his misbehaviour to his brother and father, and neglegt of him self in captivitie; or thinking al[16] that governement to have bene ane vsurpation of his Crowne, and fearing the alyke zit[17]; or perhaps finding[18] some practise to his preiudice) resoluit[19] to rede[20] him self of sik[21] dangers, as he thought might importe him; and therefore to cute them of, thought best[22] to assure him self of these noble men, who[23] he supponit, wald[24] not be so[25] content therewith, as he desyrit, and[26] therefor committit[27] them, til[28] he had tryit[29] their mynds, and drawen them to the same[30] course; or at leist, tane order with them to be quyit; whilk[31] was not lang of[32] doing: for be[33] what meanes he hes constranit[34] them to be content, or what

[1]keeped goode [2]efter [3]being all [4]bloode [5]did [6]Yeaster [7]have [8]have [9]Duke [10][allyeit?] allyed [11]^one^ [12]^an^ [13]whoe [14]were [15]wold [16]all [17]lyke therefter [18]^of^ [19]resolued [20]ridde [21]such fears and [22]thought best to cutt them off ^And^ [23]whom [24]supposed, wold [25]^well^ [26]desyred, he did [27]comitt [28]till [29]tryed [30][the same] his [31]quyet; which [32]in [33]by [34]hath constraind

remonstrance, or what evidence he hes[1] geven them to make them find thir[2] men giltie of death; or what was the cryme they died for, if it was anie new conspiracie, or what els, I can not tel[3]; Nather dois[4] our histories recorde (whilk[5] is a very great defect in them): Bot[6] this I find that they war al[7] shortlie releivit[8] of ther wards, and some of them[9] put vpon their assise also[10]; as the Earles of Douglas, Angus, Marche, and Arrol. And therefor (this same[11] Maior sayes)[12] that it was liklie, **[333]** they have found some conspiracie aganes[13] the King in them and that vther[14] wayes they wald not[15] have condemnit sik[16] men; Princes of the blud[17] (as we may cal[18] them)[19] their awen[20] freinds to the death[21]. And this for the first warding, and[22] effect theirof.

Hol. Boe. 1430

His second warding the cause not shawen

Maior lib. 6. x.13.

Boe. Buch.

For the second warding Holinsyde, and Boetius sayes[23] in the nixt zeir[24] efter the Earle of Douglas sone was knightit[25], the King arrestit[26] him self, and held him long in captivitie and warde[27]; at last by supplication[28] of the Quene and Prelats, he and the Earle of Rosse war releivit[29]. Boetius callis[30] him Archbald Earle of Douglas, Duk[31] of Turain plainlie and Hol*insyde* geves him not[32] that style of Duk[33] of Turain; and sa[34] this is the difference betwixt them, in his style[35] in the 1430 zeir[36]: It was some zeirs efter his first warding, bot[37] what zeir[38], it is not condescendit[39]. Some sayes[40] it was in the 1431 but impertinentlie; for the zeir[41] 1430 is the zeir[42] of his delyverance, except we think he hes[43] bene thrise committit, whilk[44] is not[45] written. As lytle mention is there of the cause of his warding, whilk[46] Maior compleins; saying he wonders that our Annals tels not the cause of the execution of the Stewarts, and

---

[1]hath [2]those [3]tell [4]do [5]which [6]But [7]the foresaid prisners were all [8]releived [9]^also^ [10]the others Jurie [also] [11][same] [12]^and^ [13]aganst [14]other [15]wold never [16]condemned to death such [17]blood [18]call [19]^and^ [20]owen especiall [21][to the death] [22]^the^ [23]do argue that [24]next yeir [25]knighted [26]arrested [27][and warde] [28]mediation [29]were releived [30]calleth [31]Duke [32]But English Holinsyde is pleased out of some partiall humor (as wold seeme) to suppress [33]Duke [34]so [35][in his style] [36]yeir [37]but [38]yeir [39]condescended [40]saye [41]yeir [42]yeir [43]had [44]committed, which [45]nowhere [46]whereof

the **[334]** incarcerating of thir[1] noble men, the Earle of Douglas, and Johne Lord Kennedie, the Kings owne sisters sone (for they war wardit[2], the Douglas to Lochlevin,[3] Kennedie to Stirling) that it might be knawen, if iustlie and with a right ballancinge[4], they have[5] bene committit[6]; or if he have so handlet[7] noble men for triffils or[8] his owne pleasour onlie. Vthers mints at[9] a cause, but mints[10] onlie, and clearis[11] it not that fare, that[12] men may knaw[13], jf jtt was iustlie done or not; (whilk[14] Maior here requyres[15]), and[16] is indeid the light and lyfe, the end, and vse of ane historie. For they say it was, because they had spoken sinisterlie, or rashlie, and some what more frelie then behovit[17], of the Estate and governement of the Contrie. What vse can ane[18] mak of this generalitie; for (sinisterlie) is a fault, and (rashlie) may be ane[19], and zit[20] perhaps none to[21] them that it[22] is spoken of: siklyke[23] (frelier then became) is bot al involuit[24] in sik[25] generalitie, that the reader remaynes perplexit; Nather[26] can the posteritie (King or subiect) say then for[27] right or not right; nather[28] folow nor eshew the exemple[29]. It sould have bene set[30] downe what they spake, whom to, if to the King him self, or to vthers[31]; in what sort, **[335]** if be[32] admonishing, counselling, or advysing; or if by way of cavilling, detracting, mutining, and sik vther[33] circumstances, whereon depends the iudgment[34]. In this vncertaintie we can hardlie condemne, or absolve, praise or censure them; this maks further that he hes not bene of that mynd alane; if[35] Johne Kennedie was of that[36] same mynd, nather[37] appearantlie bare[38] in malice[39] that

Buchanan *sinistre, temere, et liberius quam oporteret*

---

[1]these [2]were both committed [3]^and^ [4]and for matters of weight [5]had [6]committed [7]handled [8]^for^ [9]Others insinuates [10]insinuates ^it^ [11]without clearinge [12][not… that] so farre, as [13]know [14]which [15]requyreth [16]^which^ [17]behoved [18]one [19]one [20]yett [21]^at all^ in [22]this [23]^they being prevy Counsellors^; likewise ^the phrase^ [24]but all involued [25]such [26]perplexd; Neither [27]conclud of this If it was [28]neither ^can men^ [29]example [30]sett [31]others [32]by [33]such other [34]the judgement ^cheefly^ depends [35][this maks… if] ^In that^ [36]the [37][nather] and the like Categorie with the Douglas [38][bare?] it hath not bene spoken [39]^if^

the Kings neirest[1] freinds, and[2] best (as thir[3] Kennedies war) approvit[4]; and that Noble men (sik[5] as they[6]) might not speike[7] their opinion[8] of things, to the King, or of the King (being without malice)[9] is very hard: for how sal[10] a King knaw[11], that wil[12] not heir[13]? he can not knaw al be[14] himself; and how ever he heir[15], if Noble men have not leive[16] to speike[17] frelie, he can not heire al be[18] him self. Sik[19] as this hes[20] oft done ewil[21] to Princes; And may be, hes[22] done that[23] same Prince no gude[24]; And whatever[25] it was that most greivit[26] the Earle[27] Douglas in the governement, if[28] it was ether for the contries sake, or[29] Kings awin[30] or for both, why might not the King think there might be errors, and why might he not heir[31] them? To have proceidit[32] so vehementlie (for there hes bene[33] great vehemence) to have cute[34] af his owne kine[35] and leave not but[36] him self to the Earle of Athol[37] to ayme at, was[38] **[336]** worthie[39] to be considerit if[40] it was best[41] so for him in policy. And[42] doubtles it hes[43] imboldned the Earle of Athol[44] to cute[45] of the Kings self[46], when al[47] the rest war cute af be[48] the King. And was it nothing to tyne the nobilitie, to tyne ther[49] harts, to irritat them be[50] warding, be forfalture[51], be reductions[52]? hes it not done il[53] (trow ze[54]) and imboldned[55] the said Earle luiking[56] for the favour of the nobilitie offendit[57]? or for their greatter slaknes to revenge the Kings death? We see the King him self retractes his taxations once or twise, at the greiting[58] of the people; and wyslie, in that he was careful to keipe the harts of the people. Bot[59] was there no respect to be had, to keipe the

---

[1]^owne^ neerest [2]^the^ [3]these [4]were) ^have^ approved ^thereof^ [5]such [6]^were^ [7]speake [8]^freely^ [9]^it^ [10]sall [11]know [12]will [13]heare [14]know all by [15]hear [16]leave [17]speake [18]all by [19]Such [20]hath [21]ewill [22]hath [23]this [24]goode [25]whatsoever [26]greived [27]^of^ [28][if] [29]^the^ [30]awne [31]heare [32]proceided [33]it was [34]cutt [35]kinesmen [36]none but [37]Atholl [38]^most^ [39]^and important^ [40]^well^ considered off ^whether or not^ [41]^in policye^ [42][in policye]^to do^. [And] For [43]this hath ^the rather^ [44]Atholl [45]cutt [46]King him self ^too^ [47]all [48]were ^first^ cutt of by [49]their [50]by [51]^and^ by forfaltures [52][be *changed to* by reductions]? hath [53]ill [54]yee [55]encouraged [56]^to go on in his damnable treason^ looking [57]offended nobilitie [58]weeping cryes [59]But

nobilitie also vngreivit[1] ⸮ Was it enough they wald[2] not, or durst not (perhaps), or could not (or what ze wil)[3] oppenlie rebel[4] ⸮ was it not some thing to want their affections ⸮ to want the[5] earnestnes of them[6] ⸮ to relent them ⸮ to cuile[7] them ⸮ Certainlie sik[8] as this hes encouragit the[9] Enemies in hope of impunitie, greatter then they gate; zit[10] in hope of it; and hes[11] furthered and haistit[12] to bring on that dolorous conclusion that insuet[13]. How ever it be, he acknawledges[14] the Earle of Douglases mynd not to have bene of the worst sort, in that he releivis[15] him

Releivit of ward and witnes to the Kings sones baptisme

[337] of his waird; and in pledge of his mynd fullie reconciled, made him a witnes to the baptisme of his twynes; both sones, borne him be[16] the Quene (whilk[17] was then ane[18] signification of honour and[19] inward freindshipe[20]). And[21] his sone William[22] who

His sone a child knight, and was the first amongs 50

succeidit[23] (a chylde of fyve zeirs[24] of age[25]) (as appeirs[26] being 14 zeirs[27] old at the death of his father)[28] knight of the order, sayes[29] the Manuscript. be whilk fact[30] as he honorit[31] the Douglas vsing him in that degrie[32] of familiaritie; so did he honour

Boe. Hol. 1430

him self in the eyes of his people, and of forranes[33], adorning his court[34] and that action be[35] the presence and countenance of sik[36] a noble man; far more then if he had bene accompaniet[37] only with the Chrichtoun[38] and Livingstoun, and sik base[39] men (base[40] in respect of him) at that tyme cheiflie[41]; for they war bot[42] then growing vnder his favour; for so it is indeid, the Prince honours his worthie nobilitie be[43] his favours to them; his worthie nobilitie decoris him be[44] their companie and attendance on him: And it is wyslie done so to esteeme, and vse

---

[1]vngreeved [2]wold [3][(what... wil *changed to* will)] [4]rebell [5]^edge and^ [6]thereof [7]coole [8]such ^proceedings^ [9]hath encouraged ^his^ [10]gott; yett [11]hath [12]haisted *changed to* haistened [13]which ensued [14]acknawledgeth [15]releives [16]by [17]which [18][then ane] in those dayes no small [19]^and pledge of^ [20]freindshipp [21]^he made^ [22]^Douglas^ [23]whoe succeided ^to his Earldome though but^ [24]yeirs [25]^at that time^ [26][appeirs] [27]yeirs [28]^a^ [29]sayeth [30]by which facts [31]honored [32]degree [33]forrraners [34]courte [35]by [36]such [37]accompanied [38][Chri... toun?] Chrichtoun *adopted* [39]such newe [40](but newe [41]cheeflie [42]ware but [43]by [44]by

them selves, and happie[1] on both syds, and also to the countrie where they concure[2]. This was in the 1430 zeir betwixt the tent and the sixteine of October, for sa they differ, some calling it the 11 some 13 some 14 some 16[3]. Some write that he was delyverit[4] at the earnest [**338**] sute of the Quene, and fyve vther[5] (whom they name not) of the greattest noble men of the Realme, vpon the remonstrance foresaid; and that his warding was that same zeir. Releivit[6] of his warde, and this solemnitie endit[7] he past into France, and was installit[8] in his Dukrie[9] of Turain. Whether[10] he went thither to that effect, or if he vsit[11] that fairest colour of his absence fra[12] seeing the governement whilk[13] he mislykit, or[14] where in he had no imployment. However it be, his going there gave vthers[15] occasion to growe in his absence, and[16] be imployit[17]; especialie to the house of Angus; and draw it at last to the overthraw[18] of his house; that[19] the honour and profite they had in France may be said to have bene their wraik[20] in Scotland; what be[21] the invy of the greatnes of it, what be the abstraction[22] (as is said). Sa incertaine ar[23] the affaires[24] of the warld[25]. Nather is there extant anie mention of his actions in France thogh at this tyme fra[26] the 1430 zeirs[27] the warres war[28] verie hote there. King Henrie the sixt being brought over in person, and crownit[29] at Paris. It is attributit[30] vnto the Earle of Douglas, that he movit[31] the King of France to requyre Margaret Stewart the King of Scotlands doughter in mariage to his sone (efterwards Lewis the ii) [**339**] whom he also met[32] at her landing at the Rochel[33], and was present at her mariage. He remainit[34] there til[35] the zeir[36] 1437, at what tyme on the 21 of February King James the

Hol. Manusc. Maior. Buch. Boetius

He passis in France, and was instald in the Dukrie of Turain.

Manusc.

Movith the King of France to seik Margaret Stewart the Kings doughter in mariage to his sone

[1]^to themselves^ [2]concurre [3][betwixt... 16.] in October [4]delyvered [5]other [6]yeir ^Thus^ Releived [7]ended [8]installed [9]Dukdome [10][Whither]Whether [11]vsed [12]from [13]which [14]mislyked, and [15]others [16]^to^ [17]imployed [18]overthrow [19]So as [20]^and overthrowe^ [21]by [22]by his absence [23]Soe vncertaine are [24]effaires [25]world [26]from [27]yeir [28]were [29]crowned [30]attributed [31]moved [32]mett [33]Rochell [34]remained [35]till [36]yeir

King James the first slane

first was slane in the Blak friers of St Johnestoun be[1] the hands of[2] Patrik Grame and Robert Stewart, at the instigation of Walter Stewart Earle of Athol[3], the Kings father brother be[4] the Earle of Rosses doughter; pretending him self to be[5] right aire; and defraudit be[6] the sones of Elizabeth Mure, whom he alledgit[7] to be onlie a concubine; whilk[8] posteritie of Elizabeth Mure he had causit[9] craftelie destroy everie ane another; as the Governour to destroy Dauid, and now Dauids brother James, to destroy the house of the Governour Duk[10] Murdok and his childrein, as hes[11] bene said: so that causing the King spoyle himself of his awin[12] freinds none left alyve bot[13] the king and his one[14] sone ane bairne[15] of sixt zeirs[16] old, he tuik imboldning[17] to cute[18] of the King also; the rather that he knew manie of the nobilitie to be discontent[19], what with warding, what with hurting them in their guids[20], lands and rents; what with the slaughter of their freinds; hoping there through the lese care of his death in them, zea[21] perhaps contentment theirof in sik vniversal[22] discontentment: whilk[23] things if the Earle of Douglas foresaw, and was greivit[24] therwith, and ather admonisit[25] the King (as is aboue said) or [**340**] causit[26] anie vther[27] to admonise[28] him, that[29] sorte of governement not to be[30] for his weil[31]; this event proves he did the pairt of a faithful subject, freind, and Counsellour; how ever it was tane be[32] the King for the tyme, as contrair to his humour and disposition; and[33] did wyslie withdrawe himself, seing he could not amend things.

He returns in Scotland 1436

Now that the King was thus slane, he returnit in[34] Scotland, and was (as some think) at the Coronation of the defunct Kings sone James the second, wha[35] was crownit[36] at Edinburgh the tent of

[1]by [2]^one^ [3]Atholl [4]by [5]^the^ [6]defrauded by [7]alledged [8]which [9]caused [10]Duke [11]hath [12]owin [13]but [14]onely [15]a chyld [16]sixe yeirs [17][tuik *changed to* took imboldning] was imboldned [18]cutt [19]discontented [20]goods [21]yea [22]such an vniversall [23]which [24]greeved [25]either admonished [26]caused [27]other [28]admonish [29]^that^ [30]was not [31]weill [32]by [33]^hee^ [34]the erle returned into [35]who [36]crowned

Marche 1437 zeirs, Not a moneth (or no[1] more) efter the slaughter of his father. Where it is to be noted, that ather[2] the slaughter of the king is wrangfullie said to be in the 1437 zeir[3] in Februar[4] in steid[5] of 1436; or els the count of the zeir[6] from the beginning of Januar, whilk[7] was not then the forme[8]. And zit[9] Buchanan seemes to say so: for he was slane sayes he, in the beginning of 1437 zeir[10] in Februar, whilk[11] makes me think[12] the Earle of Douglas hes[13] not commet[14] in tyme to it out of France, seing he could hardlie have vsit[15] anie sik[16] diligence[17] to have resavit[18] the advertisment out of Scotland, made him self ready, and comed out of France[19] thogh he had[20] wind, and al[21] things verie favourable. But whether he was present or not, the faction, that **[341]** had gotten themselves in possession of the handling of affaires[22] in the lait Kings tyme so handlit[23] the mater, that he was not regardit[24], nor anie count made of him, nor admittit[25] to the handling[26] of[27] anie pairt of the affairs[28] of the Common wealth; bot[29] the Chrichtoun and Levistoun made Chanceller and Governour. Our wryters saies[30] that the reason was, because the Nobilitie had[31] this greatnes of the Douglas (whilk was greivous even to Kings) suspect[32]. How pertinentlie it is ather written be them, or hes bene thought be the Parlament, I refer me[33]. He was fare[34] from the Crowne, never pretendit[35] title, his predecessors had[36] in the tyme of King Robert the second quyte al[37] pretence they had theirto; himself (from that furth)[38] and[39] predecessors[40] had modestlie vsit[41] them selves, modestlie submittit[42]

Neglectit

[1]litle [2]either [3]yeir [4]February [5]steed [6]yeir ^to be^ [7]January, which [8]^in that land^ [9]yett [10]yeir [11]February, which [12]^that^ [13]hath [14]commed [15]vsed [16]such [17]^as^ [18]resaved [19]^so speedily^ [20]^had the^ [21]all [22]^the^ effaires [23]handled [24]regarded [25]admitted [26]managing [27][affairs *changed to* effairs] *adopted* [28]effairs [29]but [30]saye [31]envyed [32][(whilk... suspect *changed to* suspected] (which was grown by this time to a more than ordinary pitch) [33][How... written be *changed to* by... refer me] [34]farr [35]pretended ^the^ [36]^but^ [37]quyted all [38][from... furth] [39]^his^ [40]^from that furth^ [41]vsed [42]submitted

them selves to al[1] rule, even to the rueling of them that war[2] governours onlie (and not kings) (Robert and Murdok) as obedientlie in everie thing, as anie of the meanest of the Nobilitie; and never geving occasion of anie suspition to anie man; nor taking anie[3] on them bezond[4] the rest, except it war gritter[5] paines in the defence of the libertie of their contrie; to the spending of their lyfes in that service, vnder their kings, and for their kings. And this same **[342]** man in the lait Kings tyme had behavit[6] him self most humblie, obeying wardings, obeying al[7] with out countenancinge[8] anie rebellion[9], that what opinion kings had taine, or anie man hes[10] put in the Kings heads of him, hes[11] bene without his deserving; wha[12] if he had bene malitiouslie disposit[13] how easelie he might have troublit[14] the Governours, and the hail[15] contrie. Bot[16] suppone they had greatnes[17] suspect (whilk[18] was without cause) what movit[19] them at the rest of the ancient nobilitie? Was there nane[20] of them aforesaid[21]? where was the Earle of Marche of ane ancient stoke[22] and a valiant man? Where[23] the Earle of Angus, the Earle of Cassils, and vther dyvers[24]? They wil[25] say the Chrichtoun[26] and Liuingstoun war[27] wyse men, bot war[28] they alone[29] wyse men? was there no moe[30] wyse men in the contrie? then if they war[31] wyse, war[32] they gude[33] also? war[34] they just? war[35] they sober, modeste and moderate? for without thir[36] their wisdome was il[37], cheiflie to be in authoritie. And I pray zow[38], what hes[39] this their wisdome bene? or wherein kythit[40] it vnder the lait king, they tel[41] not. And I trow, if it be tryit[42] sal be found it[43] that made him a short lyfe, that occasionit[44] his enemies to take courage agane[45] him, **[343]** seiking their awen[46] particulare

[1]all [2]were [3]^thing^ [4]beyond [5]ware gretter [6]behaved [7]^things else^ [8]^of^ [9]^in the least^ [10]had [11]hath [12]who [13]disposed [14]troubled [15]wholle [16]But [17]^in^ [18]which [19]moved [20]none [21]^in that ranke^ [22]stocke [23]^was^ [24]dyvers vthers [25]will [26]Chrightoun [27]were [28]but were [29]^the^ [30]more [31]were [32]were [33]goode [34]were [35]were [36]these ^vertues^ [37]ill [38]you [39]hath [40]kythed [41]tell [42]tryed ^it^ [43][it] to be the same [44]occasioned [45]aganst [46]owen

advancement; with offence and troublance of the Nobilitie, without regarde of the Kings weil[1], or the countries; and[2] must neids be so, if it be the same wisdome they kythe[3] now efter his death. therefor if we sal[4] speike in due termes of that mater, we sal[5] say that Alex*ande*r Livingstoun, and William Chrichtoun[6] both Barons onlie, and not of the ancient blud[7] of the nobilitie, Newe men set[8] for their owne profite only, without regarde to anie vther[9] duetie, wha[10] had[11] the credit vnder him,[12] gotten the cair[13] of the laite king, and had drawen sik[14] faction, that the Douglas being absent in France, before his returne they had gotten al[15] the affaires[16] in their hands. Alex*ande*r Livingstoun being made Governour, and William Chrichtoun[17] Chanceller (wha[18] is the first in that office we read namit[19] in Chronicles, for we never read of a Chanceller before him). At whilk[20] the Earle of Douglas tuik sik[21] indignation, taking it as a reproche and disgrace to the Nobilitie, and to him self cheiflie[22], that not finding his hart could acknawledge sik[23] men, and zit[24] not willing to impugne them, wha[25] had the authoritie, whereby to mak warres, and trouble the countrie, **[344]** he choisit[26] for the calmest and best behaviour[27] to withdraw him self from the handling of affairs[28], and from al cair[29] of the contrie; suffering them[30] to whom it was committit[31] (and wha[32] had taine it on them) to handle it as they pleasit[33], and could; And so resolvet, retirit[34] home to his owne house, making them no further troublance; but that he might keep them from infringing of his liberties and priviledgis grantit[35] to the house of Douglas of old, be[36] kings for their gude[37] services, commandit sik[38] as war[39] his to conteine them[40] within his regalitie,[41]

Discontentit

[1]weale [2]^it^ [3]showe [4]sall [5]sall [6]Chrightoun [7]blood [8]sett [9]other [10]who [11]^all^ [12]^had^ [13]guyding [14] such a [15]all [16]effaires [17]Chrightoun [18]who [19]named [20]which [21]took such [22]cheeflie [23]such [24]yett [25]who [26]choosed [27]course [28]effairs [29]caire [30]leaving that [31]committed [32]to such as [33]pleased [34]resolved, retired [35]priviledges granted [36]by ^former^ [37]goode [38]commanding such [39]were [40]^selves^ [41]^to^

answer thereto, and to no vther[1]; professing that he wald[2] keip his priviledgis[3]; and wha[4] wald vsurpe vpon them, sould be vsit[5] accordinglie. This was a bite[6] vnto thir[7] new Governours, and did curbe them verie short in this[8] syde of Forthe, his dominions[9] being large in these[10] pairts; where might soone be seene the foolishnes of them to take on them the authoritie in sik[11] a case, and the vnadvysednes of the gevers to sik[12] men, as war[13] not able to execute it, bot[14] at the pleasour of another. Hereon also fel[15] out great inconvenients; for the men of Annandail accoustomit[16] to thift and robberie seing the Earle of Douglas so discontent, and withdrawing him self from the affaires (wha[17] was the man onlie able to tak order **[345]** with them) contemning the authoritie of the Governours, begoud to vex the countries nixt[18] adiacent to them, dryving away prayes with plane hosting, as out of the Enemies ground; whilk[19] when the Governours war[20] not able to represse, the evil[21] increist daylie as a Canker, that it overrane almost the haile[22] region on this[23] syde of Forthe. In the meane while thir guide[24] Governours war[25] so cairful[26] of the commone weil[27] of the Contrie, and[28] charge committit to[29] them, that in steide[30] of pansing how to pacifie them, they[31] fal at out ilk[32] one with vther[33]; sending out contrarie proclamations; the Governour that none sould acknawledge the Chanceller; the Chanceller that none sould obey the Governour; so that if anie came to them to lament his estate, and seike redresse; he was vsit[34] as ane enemie be[35] the vther[36] syde; and both pretendit[37] the kings authoritie: for the Chanceller had him in custodie in the Castle of Edinburgh; the Governour had the name of authoritie and was in Stirling with the Quene

[1]other [2]wold [3]priviledges [4]who [5]vsed [6]bitt [7]these [8]the south [9]lands and command [10]those [11]such [12]such [13]were [14]but [15]fell [16]accoustomed [17]^from the^ *adopted* effaires who [18]next [19]which [20]were [21]evill [22]halle [23]vpon that [24]hese goode [25]were [26]cairfull [27]well [28]^the^ [29]committed vnto [30]steede [31]fall [32][out ilk] variance each [33]^the^ other [34]vsed [35]by [36]other [37]pretended

mother; til[1] at last vnder colour to visite her sone she fand[2] a moyen to convey him away in a kist[3] out of the Castle, then to Forthe, and so to Stirling: whereon the Governour (having gotten the Kings name, and the countenance of his persone as weil[4] as[5] authoritie) went with ane armie, and laid seige to the Castle of Edinburgh, where the Chanceller **[346]** was. He to make him self a pairtie, sendis „ to the Earle of Douglas, offers to come in his wil[6], „ desyrs to be taine vnder his protection, „ remonstrats to him the crueltie, greidines and „ ambition of the Governour; that he was deceivit[7], „ if he thought they war[8] to stay be[9] the „ extinguishing of the Chanceller, and[10] the „ Chancellers overthrow was bot[11] a stepe[12] to „ overthrawe him. The Earle of Douglas made „ ane[13] answer;[14] The Governour and Chanceller „ war[15] both alyke fals men, alyke greidie, and „ avaricious:[16] their contentions war[17] not of vertue, „ nor for the weil[18] of the contrie, bot onlie for their „ owne particular quarels[19] and commodities; in „ whilk[20] contention it was no great mater whilk[21] „ of them overcame; if both sould perishe, the „ contrie was the better; nather[22] could there be a „ better spectacle for al[23] honest men, nor[24] see sik[25] „ a couple of Scrimars zokit[26] togeather. Whilk[27] „ answere was so true, as none can, nor dois[28] ganesay. Their falset[29] he hes knawen[30]; and that is it that men cal[31] wisdome in them, be[32] a faire name. It apearis weil[33] (we sal see, in the persone of this Governours sone); it kythit in everie one of them aganes vther[34] striving who sould deceive vther[35]. Their factiousnes likwyse, ever when they durst for feare of the thrid, and that their contentions war bot[36] for particulars, on ambition, and avarice; and

Chanceller Chrichtoun cravis his protection. Buch

His answere

The judgement of the wryters there anent

[1]till [2]found [3]chest [4]weill [5]^the^ [6]will [7]deceived [8]were [9]by [10]^that^ [11]but [12]stepp [13][ane] [14]^that^ [15]were [16]^that^ [17]were [18]well [19]querels [20]which [21]which [22]neither [23]all [24]^than ^to^ [25]such [26]fensers yoked [27]Which [28]doth [29]falsehood [30]hath knowen [31]call [32]by [33](^as^ [34]aganst other [35]deceave other [36]were but

without anie care of the common weil[1]; the warld saw then, and it may be seene zit[2]. Likwyse **[347]** that the contrie had bene better to have bene red[3] of sik[4] ambitions and avaritious governours, seiking noght bot[5] them selves; and that it was not for no[6] honest man to imbrulzie[7] him self in their so vnhonest[8] debaits; bot a plaisant[9] spectacle, and to be desyrit[10] to see everie one of them (iniustlie both) zit[11] do justice on[12] another. It was a frie[13] speache also, no man can deny; bot[14] it is said, it was not a profitable speiche, for it causit[15] two pairties agrie[16], to his preiudice; and procurit[17] him the hatred of An. 1439 them both, as[18] no doubt he had their hatred of before. Nather[19] now wald[20] this man have[21] done ought but servit[22] his turne with him to some particular vse of his awne, ather[23] overthrowing the Governour, that he might the more surelie satisfie his avarice; or perhaps made a shew of his help to agrie[24] with the Governour on the easier conditions. It was for no common gude[25] to the Contrie, no question: What could he have done then? Why sould he have medlet[26] with them? Weil[27] they say, to have met[28] him in his awen craft, and vsit[29] the one of them, to the wraik of the vther: weil![30] wil we never leive[31] that? sal[32] we never leive sik[33] fals trikes; sik[34] bastarde wisdome; and not think[35] there is a way besyde it? that there is a true honest wisdome, that honest men may keip without falset[36], or anie point of falset[37]; without deceiving of anie bodie, even of the deceivers? zit[38] might he **[348]** have geven ane vther[39] answere, wil[40] they say: Bot[41] (I pray zow[42]) what answer? What answer deservit[43] it? Was it not fite[44], that sik petie[45] companions as they, (wha abusit[46] the contrie as

[1]well [2]^as^ yett [3]ridde [4]such [5]but [6]any [7]imbroolzie [8]deshonest [9]pleasant [10]desyred [11]^though^ both iniustlie yett ^to^ [12]^one^ [13]free [14]^it^; but [15]caused [16]agree [17]procured [18]though [19]Neither [20]wold [21]^have^ *adopted* [22]served [23]owne, either ^for^ [24]agree [25]goode [26]medled [27]Well [28]mett [29]vsed [30]other; well! [31]leave [32]sall [33]leave such [34]such [35]^that^ [36]falsett [37]falsett [38]yett [39]other [40]will [41]But [42]yow [43]deserved [44]fitt [45] such petit [46]who abused

they did, to their particular fansies,) sould heire[1] the naikit[2] truthe without disguysing, out of a noble mans mouth? sould sik[3] a noble man have glosit[4], with sik[5] as them; flatterit[6] and dissemblit[7]; and (as they say) straikit[8] creame in their mouths[9]? Nay, it is a pairt of punishment of wikednes to heire[10] the awin[11] name of it; and very fit[12] it sould be so,[13] that his speache can not be iustlie quarellit[14], but commendit[15] as true, frie[16], iust, magnamine[17] and sik[18] as becomes his place, house, and birth; without fraude or dissimulation, calling (as the Macedonians[19]) a spaid a spaid, vice vice be[20] the awen[21] name of it. Whilk[22] apearis weil be[23] this, and perhaps that whilk[24] he spake before of the governement (if we knawe[253] what it was) to have bene his very natural[26], far fra al frivile[27] flatterie, and dissimulation, ather of[28] kings or vthers; whilk[29] is now croppin in and countit[30] a wisdome in preiudice of the true ancient generositie[31] of thir[32] great spirits, far better, and far more worthie to be adorned with their ful[33] and due praise, nor nippit[34] obliquitlie by half words, as not being wyslie and profitablelie anough[35] said, when there can be no true blame gotten to them; and zit[36] for the[37] profite (questionles,[38]) **[349]** out of the same courage and magnanimitie, that he spake the truthe[39] he hes despysit[40] the personnes[41], not counting of their feid[42], nor anie harme they could do vnto him; and we see no apparence, bot[43] that he did it out of a right weying of his and their power;[44] not out of anie arrogancie, and idle confidence; and that during his lyfe, they durst not, nor could not harme him, for al[45] their agreance; Nather zit[46] his successor efter

---

[1]heare [2]naiked [3]such [4]glosed [5]such [6]flattered [7]dissembled [8]stroeked [9]mouthes [10]heare [11]owne [12]fitt [13]soe. ^In such sorte^ [14]quarelled [15]commended [16]free [17]magnanimous [18]such [19]^did^ [20]by [21]owen [22]Which [23]weill by [24]which [25]knewe [26]naturell [27]from all frivolous [28]either with [29]others; which [30]counted [31]generousnes [32]those [33]full [34]than nipped [35]enough [36]yett [37]ther [38]*should read* questi- **[349]** onles [39]before [40]hath ^now^ despysed [41]^of those men^ [42]fevd [43]but [44]^and^ [45]all [46]Neither yett

He dieth in Restarige 1439 Buchanan

His onlie fault

His praise

him without a treasonable[1] course, as ever[2] was, sence the warld stude, of ane; sa[3] that there was not (even in this pairt) anie vnprofitablenes. Alwyse his death ensuet[4] shortlie efter in that 1439 zeir in[5] Restarige be[6] ane hote[7] fever (verie opportunlie, and in a gude[8] tyme (sayes[9] our wryters) and[10] was indeid, for them; and sik[11] as them; that they might make the better praye of the commone Wealth,[12] spoyle it[13], and vse it to their awen[14] commoditie) bot vntymouslie[15] to the house of Douglas, that[16] was left in the hands of a zouth[17] without experience, and therefor[18] vncircumspect; zea[19] vntymouslie for the nobilitie to be a praye to the avarice and ambition of these twa[20]; and vntymouslie to[21] the countrie, to leive[22] these twa frie[23] from feire[24] of anie man, whom they stude[25] awe of, that might have repressit[26] their appetits, or somwhat have brydlit[27] them. This **[350]** onlie, I count reprufe[28] worthie in him, that he suffert[29] Annandail to overrune the adiacent contrie, and did not hinder them from wronging the innocent people. He sould not have countit[30] that not to perteine to him, whilk[31] if he had done and keipit[32] justice within him self, wald[33] have acquyrit[34] him also[35] favour and honour, if not[36] contempt of the Governours, that could not do sa[37] in a peacible[38] Contrie, and among them selves. For how excellent a thing is it, be gude[39] meanes to seike honour? It wald[40] have tane away the occasion of the calomnies of his Enemies, wha zit[41] did[42] worse them selves. Vtherways[43] a valiant wise man, a lover of his contrie, and frie[44], plaine, gude[45]

[1]but by a most treacherous [2]^any^ [3]stoode [of ane]; soe [4]ensued [5]yeir at [6]by [7]burning [8]goode [9]saye [10][and] as it [11]such [12]^and^ [13][it] [14]owen [15]but vnseasonablie for [16]which [17]youth [18]therefore [19]yea [20]two [21]for [22]leave [23]two free [24]feare [25]stoode ^in^ [26]repressed [27]^at least^ have somwhat brydled [28]reproofe [29]sufferd [30]counted [31]which [32]keeped [33]wold [34]acquyred [35][also] at least both [36]^a^ [37]so [38]peaceble [39]by goode [40]wold [41]who yett [42]^much^ [43]Otherways [44]^of a^ free [45]^and^ goode

generouse, Natural[1]. He was buriet[2] in the Kirk[3] of Douglas callit[44] St Brigides[5] Kirk, whose Elogie is there zit[6] extant, thus:

His Elogie

> *Hic jacet Dominus Archibaldus Douglas Dux Turoniae, Comes de Douglas, et Longaville Dominus Gallovidiae, Et Wigtoun et Annandiae, locum tenens Regis Scotiae. Obiit 26 die mensis Junij. An Dominj Millesimo, quadringentesimo tricesimo secundo.*

---

[1]Nature [2]buried [3]Church [4]called [5]Brides [6]yett

[**351**] The Life of[1] William, 6[2], slane in Edinburgh Castle; the 15 Lord, and 6 Earle of Douglas, 2 Earle of Wigtoun, Lord of Galloway, Bothuel and Annandail, 3 Duk of Turain, Lord of Longaville.[3]

His douce and sweit natural

The mishant treasonable dealing of his Enemies

Vnto Archbald Earle of Wigtoun succeidit[4] his sone William as[5] 15 Lord, and 6 Earle of Douglas, 2 Earle of Wigtoun, Lord of Galloway, Bothuel[6], and Annandail, 3 Duk of Turain, and Lord of Longeville[7] *etc*; a zouth[8] of no great age, a heigh and rare spirite, and natural[9] sweit, traitable, and douce; In whom we can bot[10] detest and execrat[11] the mishantnes[12] of the treasonable dealing[13] of his enemies, that sa[14] vnworthelie cuttit af a birth[15] in the verie budding, whereof could not have bene expectit bot[16] a passing guid[17] fruite; to[18] great vse of the Common Weil[19] and Contrie, if malitiousnes of treason[20] had sufferit[21] it to come to maturitie. Let ws alwayes be content[22] to see this vicissitude, begune in the father be[23] warding, and displacing[24] from the rowme of his father[25], from handling of affairs, prosecute to[26] him in the tyme of his lyfe;[27] vicissitude (I say) that is in al[28] thngs[29], to be also in this house, even to the inverting of al[30] due, and right order of things, to the judgment of men; that innocencie sould be overthrawen be[31] crueltie; honestie and vprighnes of hart, be[32] craft, falset and treason; and zit[33] reverence [**352**] the[34] worker, and overreuler of al[35] things; wha[36] in this misorder[37] certainlie directs al[38] things be[39] a great wisdome, and with gude[40] order doubtles; thogh vnsearchable

[1]^the 6.^ [2][6] ^Lorde of Douglas etc^ [3][the 15… Longeville *changed to* Longueville] [4]succeided [5][as] the [6]Bothuell [7]Longueville [8]youth [9] of disposition [10]but [11]execrate [12]meshantnes *changed to* wickednes [13]treacherous dealings [14]so [15]cutted of such a blossome [16]expected but [17]good [18]^the^ [19]Weill [20]and treachery [21]suffered [22][alwayes be] notwithstanding rest contented [23]by [24]^him^ [25] predecessors [26]^the^ effairs ^of the Kingdome^ prosecuted against [27]^a^ [28]all [29]^else^ [30]all [31]overthrowen by [32]by [33]yett ^lett ws^ [34]^Souerane^ [35]all [36]who [37]desorder [38]all [39]by [40]goode

to man. Bot sen[1] nothing[2] ever hes bene[3] so enorme[4] that may not receive[5] some colour ather[6] of vertue to mak it seeme gude[7]; or at leist[8] extenuation to mak it seeme not so il; and[9] this among vthers[10], I[11] perceive is of the same sorte; be[12] some thought gude[13] (very ignorantlie or malitiouslie); by[14] some excusable, both in forme and[15] fact, be[16] a necessitie and pretence of the common gude; be al[17] that hes[18] wreittin, more[19] slenderlie handlit[20], and doubtinglie; leaving it almost vncertaine vnder what judgment to bring it, of il[21] or gude[22]; that some tymes ze[23] wald think they condeme it, some tymes they allow[24] it; and deals[25] none of them[26] with it so fullie, as reason wald[27], for the information of the posteritie, and[28] right law[29] of historie; bot[30] as a netle that they wald gripe zit dar[31] not handle it hartfullie[32] and hardilye[33]. That this so mishant[34] a fact may the better appeire[35] in the awen bright[76] colours of it[77], I wil preise[38] to take away al fairds[39] where with the actors wald[40] so faine (bot[41] so falslie) couller it, or[42] the judgments of men (bot[43] half wise oftymes[44], and half perceiving of[45] things, not plumbing them so throughlie[46] to the deipe, and ground as neid war[47]) may[48] be deceivit[49] by vthers[50], or may by fantesie[51] to them **[353]** selves, for excusing it; to learne ws to detest, and abhore so detestable and abominable facts with a true detestation, and abhorring in earnest, and[52] effect; that the posteritie may knawe[53], and condeme[54], and be fare[55] from the lyke. And for this effect[56] (before we come to the declaration of the fact it self) I will speik[57] some thing of the actors, Livingstoun and

---

[1]But since [2]^hath bene^ [3][hes bene] [4]enormous [5]receave [6]either [7]goode [8]least ^of some^ [9]ill ^as it is^; [and] So [10]amongs others [11]^do^ [12]by [13]^to be^ goode [14] by [15]^in^ [16]by [17]goode; by all [18]have [19]too [20]handled [21]ill [22]goode [23]yee [24]^of^ [25][deals] [26]^deals^ [27]wold [28]^according to the^ [29]lawe [30]but [31]wold gripp yett dare [32]hartillie [33]hardelye [34]meshant [35]appeare [36]owen [bright] [37][of it] [38]will preisse [79]all the fairde [40]wold [41]but [42][or] to [43]but [44]oftentymes [45]perceaving [of] [46]thoroughlie [47]need were) ^and^ [48]^so the more easily^ [49]deceived [50]others [51][by fantesie?] fansie ^things amisse^ [52]^with^ [53]knawe [54]condemne [55]farr [56]purpose [57]speak

Chrichtoun[1], and their actions in the Earle of Douglases tyme.

The ambition and avarice of the Governour and Chanceller and particular stryfs therof

The Governour had taine the King from the Chanceller

We have hard[2] before (and we must[3] not forget[4]) how weil[5] they gydit the contrie, what care they tuik[6] of the Commone Weil[7], or (to say directlie) how litle care they tuik[8] of it; bot[9] only of their awen particulars; vnder colour of it stryving in disgracing vthers be[10] their privat speiches be[11] their oppin proclamations; so greidie and ambitious, that thogh they had al[12] the contrie betwixt them, zit[13] it was not anough[14] to satisfie their greidines[15]; they could not so meikle[16] as gree among[17] them selves to pairt it betwixt them peaceblie, (whilk[18] even brigands and goode[19] companions in thift wil[20] do.) They had not sa meikle[21] modestie nor iustice whilk[22] thieves wil[23] have, to pairt the praye equalie in some proportion: how heir[24] vpon they war[25] at variance, fighting and spoyling and seiging vther; whil[26] that remembring them selves of the thrid doge[27], that might come and gette the bane,[28] they war that[29] wise as to agrie[30] **[354]** in[31] preiudice, and il[32] of him (the Earle of Douglas)[33] more nor[34] for anie weile[35] of the Contrie, or love they had[36] to vther[37], as appearit[38] soone vpon his death: for incontinent they returne to their auld maners[39], and the aggreance that was made for feare of him, lastit[40] no longer nor[41] he livit. Depairtit[42] of this lyfe (as hes[43] bene said) in Restarige,[44] they beginne to draw asunder, especialie the Livingstoun being Governour, and having the King also (as hes[45] bene said) delyverit for[46] feare of the Douglas, respectit[47] no more for[48] the Chrichtoun,[49] begane to despyse him,[50] thoght there was no band to bind him anie longer to him;

---

[1]Chrightoun [2]heard [3]are [4]to forgett [5]well [6]took [7]Well [8]took [9]but [10]to disgrace others by [11]speaches ^and^ by [12]all [13]yet [14]eneugh [15]avarice [16]much [17]agree amongs [18]which [19][goode] [20]will [21]much [22]as [23] will [24]here [25]were [26]asseiging ^one an^ other; till [27][doge] [28]^from them both^ [29]were so [30]agree ^amongs themselves^ [31]^the^ [32]ill [33]^which they did^ [34][nor] in that regard then [35]welle [36]bare [37]other [38]appeared [39]ould byas [40]lasted [41]than [42]lived. Depairted [43]hath [44]Restalrige [45]hath [46]delyvered of the [47]respected [48]of [49]^But^ [50]^and^

he wald geve him no pairt of his pray, and spoyle of the Contrie; he wald keipe al[1] to him self; there was his Ambition, and zit groundit on[2] avarice (perhaps;) for gyding al[3], he might take al; had[4] he made the vther[5] partaker of the gyding, as[6] he behovit[7] to make him partaker of the pray; therfor he wald[8] have none of his assistance in gyding. Bot[9] how gydis he it himself, let[10] see? The Governour he wardes noble men at his pleasour vpon light causes, and light suspitions onlie; zea[11] castes them in fetters. he had done sa[12] on the 3 of August <u>1439</u> with the Lord of Lorne, and his brother William wha[13] had mariet[14] Quene mother; on suspition onlie of their dealling with the Earle of Douglas: he had wardit[15] the Quene in a straite[16] Chamber; there is his iniquitie, zea[17] tyrannie; and absurde abuse of Noble men. **[355]** He had geven remissions and impunities to men giltie of great crymes. The Chanceller therefor wha[18] thought he sould have pairt of the buittie[19], seing him self thus deboutit[20] by him, and not able to mend[21] it; Nether having patience to beare quyetlie with it, retyrit[22] himself af[23] Court, and gettis him self for[24] strenth to Edinburgh Castle; there to lye in waite for the first occasion he could find, to cowpe[25] the Livingstoun: Nather[26] was he lang[27] in doing[28]: for before the zeir[29] be rune out[30], he takes the occasion of the Governours being at Perth, gois[31] to the feilds about[32] Stirling, where the zoung[33] King vsit[34] to hunte; lyes[35] in waite for him gattes[36], him and caryis him to Edinburgh[37]. be this meane[38] the dyce is changit[39]; he had[40] now gotten the Durk (as our word[41] is) he wil[42] pairt the pray over agane; wil[43] have his large pairt of al[44], and gyd al[45] his course

The Chanceller takith the King agane from the Governour.

[1]all [2]yett grounded vpon [3]all [4]all. If [5]other [6][as] [7]behoved [8]wold [9]the government. But [10]^ws^ [11]yea [12]so [13]who [14]maried ^the^ [15]warded [16]close [17]yea [18]who [19]boottie [20]desplaced [21]amend [22]retyred [23]from [24]^his^ [25][cowpe*?*] supplant [26]Neither [27]long [28]^it^ [29]yeir [30]about [31]goth [32]neere [33]young [34]vsed *changed to* was accustomed [35]lyeth [36]gettes [37]^Castle^ [38]by thise meanes [39]cace is altered [40]hath [41]sayeing [42]will [43]will [44]all [45]direct all

about, as weil[1] as the Livingstoun did: wha[2] finding him self in this straite, may lament his case, bot can not mend him self; Neid hes no law. The Chrichtoun had zeildit[3] to him before, when he (or the Quene to him) stawe[4] the king; now he hes[5] gotten ane[6] meiting mides dishe[7]; he moit zeild[8] to him agane, and sa[9] he dois[10]; bowis his banie[11] hart, gois[12] to Edinburgh, gattes[13] mediators, bringes on a meeting, and finalie agreis. Bot wald ze[14] see the[15] face of a Clerke[16] play, deceivers, deceiving, dissimuling[17], and **[356]** and putting a fair[18] face on their foule falsets, and proceidings? read me their haragnes[19] on both sydes that ze[20] may ather[21] laugh, or disdane them in the histories that are written[22]. I may not take leasour to set[23] them downe at lenth „ here. Zit[24] in effect ze sal[25] find nothing bot „ pretences of the Common Weil[26], of the publike „ peace, the weil[27] of the King, the weil[28] of al[29] „ honest men, whilk al[30] is ioynit[31] with their weil „ (forsuthe[32].) that hes[33] bene aye[34] their butte; that „ hes[35] bene their intention; no particular, no „ avarice, no ambition, no greidines, for love of „ these common things; and because in them lyis „ al[36]; in their standing, honest mens standing; in „ their wrake honest mens wrake; the wrake of the „ King, the wrake of the Contrie; the hopes of „ ambitious men, and their increasing and „ advancing, *etc*. For this cause, (and for none „ vther[37]) that the Contrie may be weil[38], that „ wickednes may be brydlit[39], they forgive ilk ane[40] „ another. And because their discordes was[41] seene to be, and could not have bene sik[42], if they[43] both[44] had had[45] mynd of[46] the Common Weil[47], and not more of[48] their[49] avarice and ambition, they deny

They meit for agreance

Their ridiculous oraisons

[1]weill [2]who [3]yeilded [4]stole away [5]hath [6]a [7][mides *changed to* midd dish] [8][moit?] must yeild [9]so [10]doth [11]bonie [12]goeth [13][gattes?] gettes [14]agrees. Bot wold ye [15]^right^ [16]Stage [17]dissembling [18]faire [19]Speeches [20]yee [21]either [22]that are written in the histories [23]sett [24]Yett [25]yee sall [26]Weale [27]weale [28]weale [29]all [30]which all [31]ioyned [32]^owne^ weale (forsoothe) [33]hath [34]still [35]hath [36]lyeth all [37]other [38]well [39]brydled [40]each one [41]were? [42]such [43][they] [44]^of them^ [45][had] caryed such a [46]to [47]Weill [48]to [49]^owne^

this hindemost[1] plainlie, and sayes[2] their discordes raise not of them, bot[3] of diversities of opinions and iugments[4] onlie, while both seiking the Common Weil[5] allanerlie, he thinkes ane[6] forme[7] best for it; the vther[8] thinkes ane vther[9] forme. Whilk[10] if it was so indeid, let this that is said above[11] beare witnes. It wald[12] cause a man to **[357]** loath[13] speiking vertuouslie to see sik[14] by them sa fare abusit. Zit[15] the old proverb[16] (*oportet mendacem esse memorem*) and whils[17] a lier wil[18] speik truthe. They confesse their ambition in stryving for honour and authoritie, (they eshame to say geir[19] and riches; bot[20] it was no les true, and both war[21] alyke faultes) and exhorts vther[22] and promisis to mend therefter be[23] a better strife, wha sal[24] be most moderate and just. But they war[25] as true in that promise keeping, as they war[26] in discourse of what was past. When the fox preachis[27] take tent[28] to the[29] henis (sayes[30] our proverbe.) We wil[31] see, indeid, a notable moderation and iustice, sik[32] as the warld hes[33] skairce seene, ane exemple of ane[34] more treasonable tyrannie: this is the effect of thir[35] jolie mens harangues[36]; the conclusion is a new freindshipe (if freindshipe be falset[37]) it is a new conspiracie aganes[38] the Contrie, and directlie aganes[39] the Noble men, whom their Conscience tels them haits[40] them, as new men (they grant) liftit[41] vp to the heigest degrie, and that was reproche enough to the nobilitie, and ane argument of their vnworthines. Bot[42] they might have said as trulie for abuse of the King and Contrie to their particular, vnder pretence of[43] Common Weil, whilk if[44] **[358]** the hail[45] nobilitie resentit or not[46], we can not tel[47], for there is no mention[48]; and it is a wonder

Quod prauo studio certaminis vter honoribus et auctoritate auctior esset; Ita imposterum contendamus, vter moderatione justitia alterum antecedat

They conclude a new conspiracie aganis the nobilitie

Homines novos in summo gradu collocatos

[1]last point [2]saye [3]but [4]iudgments [5]Weill [6]one [7]^to be the^ [8]other [9]other [10]which [11][said] above saide [12]wold [13]loathe [14]such ^virtue^ [15]so farr abused. Yett [16]^should warne them^ [17]sometimes [18]will [19]goods [20]but [21]were [22]other [23]by [24]who sall [25]were [26]were [27]foxes preache [28]heed [29]thy [30]sayeth [31]will [32]such [33]world hath [34]a [35]thise [36]orations [37]falsett [38]aganst [39]aganst [40]haites [41][they grant] lifted [42]But [43]^the^ [44]Weal which ^whither or not^ [45]wholl [46]resented [or not] [47]tell [48]^thereof^

if they did not. Zit[1] it wald[2] seeme[3] not; they had joukit[4], and taine on ane vnworthie zoke[5] of their sclaverie. Bot[6] how ever the rest did, ther was one was a sore thorne in their fuite[7], and mot[8] in their eye. It behovit[9] to be plukit[10] out; the Earle of Douglas is of the old spirit, of the ancient Nobilitie, he can not serve nor obey bot[11] whom he sould, and the lawful Commanders, lawfullie commanding to his honour and[12] vtilitie, whereof they war nather. Sik[13] a spirit, was not[14] sufferable vnder those now conspyring tyrannes. he wil[15] not ken[16] their authoritie: his father had told them their Holydays name[17]: him self tuik[18] them for his Enemies. how sal[19] they do with him? he is not easie to be dealt withal[20]: they must have muffils that wald take sik[21] a Cate[22]. Indeid he caryet[23] him self as one that wald[24] not be in their danger: he interteinit ane[25] great household; he raid[26] ever weil accompaniet[27] so oft as he went in publike: 1000, 2000 horse was his ordinarie tryne: he had great freindshipe and dependants[28] of old; he had bene careful to intertein them; he had accressit[29] them, and conciliat many new dependars with his beneficence and liberalitie, zea[30] with a magnificence according to the place [**359**] he caryet[31] as Earle of Douglas, and Duk[32] of Turain (whilk Dukrie[33] he had obteinit[34] him self investit[35] into, as aire to his father) having sent Malcolme Lord Fleminge, and S*ir* Johne Lauder of Bas (or Hotoun as others say) to France, for that effect; and[36] was weil acceptit[37] in remembrance of his father, and Gudshire, wha[38] for their gude[39] service done to Charles the sevint had inioyit[40] that honour: he had al[41] his affairs[42] in a singular gude[43] ordour; and had his ordinarie Counsel,[44] and

His ordinarie tryne

Is installit in his Dukrie of Turain

Hol. An. 1439

[1]yet [2]wold [3]^they did^ [4]stowped [5]yoke [6]But [7]foote [8]^a^ mote [9]behoved [10]pluked [11]but [12]^the publike^ [13][whereof.. nather] wherein he had an speciall interest. Nather was such [14][was not] [15]will [16]acknowledge [17][told... name] [18]took [19]sall [20]withall [21]such [22]Catte [23]caryed [24]wold [25]interteined a [26]roid [27]weill accompanied [28]dependars [29]accressed [30]yea [31]held [32]Duke [33]which Dukdome [34]obteined [35] invested [36][and] There he [37]weill accepted [38]Grandfather, who [39]goode [40]inioyed [41]all [42]effairs [43]goode [44]Counsell

Counsellers for the gyding of his affairs[1]: he institute[2] knightes also[3] as he thought[4] men worthie. Whilk[5] power and priviledges he had not be[6] vsurpation or of pryde, taking on to imitate or contrefite[7] the King (as some wald[8] innuate) bot be[9] vertue of both these twa places,[10] Earle and Duk: and though he was bot[11] 14 zeirs of age at the deathe of his father in 1439 zeir, and is slane him selfe in the 1440 zeir, so that he hes never atteinet above the fyftein or sixtein zeirs of his age at the farrest, zit in this his pairt, and this[12] his behaviour did not onlie the sparkes[13] of great spirit appeare; bot[14] also of so wyse and provident[15] as could be skairce luikit[16] for in sa zoung a Man. Whilk iappit[17] them so meikle[18] the more, to think **[360]** if that frute sould come to a rypnes at anie tyme, how poysonable, or rather how great a contrepoyson[19] it wald[20] prove to their greatnes. But here the skine of a Lion wald[21] not serve them (he was over[22] hard to[23] them to deale so with[24]), they sewe[25] on that of the foxe. The occasion falleth out thus, during the tyme of the Jarres foresaid betwix them selves stryving for authoritie, and vther[26] their particular profits, the common affairs ware neglectit[27] betwixt hands[28], and pairtlie because they could not, (being bot[29] meane men[30] of smal force)[31] pairtlie because they carit[32] not to prevent, or[33] to mend[34] things, manie insolencies war done without redresse; as the Islesmen had made ane excursion in the maine land; and had put al[35] to fyre and sword, men and wemen, bairns[36] and aget, fare[37] and wyde; omitting no kind of exemples[38] of avarice and crueltie, and

Boe. Buch.

They put on the foxes skine agains him. Buch.

Great enormities committit and not repressit

[1]effairs [2]dubbed [3]^such^ [4]found to be [5]thereof. Which [6]by [7]contrafete [8]wold [9]but by [10]^as^ [11]but [12][14... zit *changed to* yett... zeirs *changed to* zeire... this] a very youth in yeares yett he was of so hopefull an expectation that in all [13]sparkles [14][bot] [15]prudent ^a mynde^ [16]looked [17][sa... Man] a youth that had been so litle versed *[in]* effares. This vexed [18]much [19][poysonable... contrepoyson] great a countrepoise [20]wold [21]Lyon wold [22]too [23]for [24]withall [25]sowe [26]other [27]effairs were neglected [28]both [29]but [30]^and^ [31]small power ^and^ [32]cared [33]nor [34]amend [35]putt all [36]infants [37]aged, farr [38]examples

that not onlie in the pairts neir the see[1] Coastes, bot[2] in the Lennox also, out of ane Isle of Louchloumond, callit Marin[3]; they had callit[4] a gentil man to name Johne Colchan Laird[5] Lus to a tryst[6], the 23 day of September, and had slane him, and manie sik[7] foule facts had bene done in dyvers pairts of the Contrie. Likwyse Allane Stewart of Darnlie was slane at Paislay be[8] S*ir* Thomas Boyde, and S*ir* Thomas Boyd was slane by Alex*ande*r Stewart of Belmet **[361]** and his sones. Where throgh there aryses[9] great troubles in the West pairts of Scotland; and siklyke amongs vthers[10], the borderers had not bene idle, whilk[11] being ather[12] vnder the Earle of Douglases charge, and his dependars[13], or some of his[14], their factes were interpretit[15] to be[16] his allowance, and at a Convention at Edinburgh, manie complaints[17] geven in. There is never a word of the fact of the Isles men; never word of the facts of the Livingstoun and Chrichtons awin[18], who had ilk[19] one wrakit vther[20]; never a word of anie sik vther[21] mens blud[22], and slaughter; bot[23] as thogh nothing had bene wrang[24] in the Contrie, bot[25] that whilk[26] was done be[27] the Earle of Douglasis dependars. Whether it was be[28] the instigation of these his Enemies, or not, the histories makis[29] no mention: Nather wil[30] I affirme; bot[31] it is strange[32] there was complants of no moe, when[33] there was so[34] manie more enorme[35] faults (for the Isles men was[36] more enorme[37]) at leist there is no moe[38] taine regard of; they ar exaggeratit, multipliet[39], and made odious, and the invye dryven on[40] the Earle of Douglas, as actor of al[41]. Here vpon S*ir* Alex*ande*r Livingstoun Governour, having hatred in his hart, bot

Complaints at the Convention onlie of the Earle of Douglases dependars ther facts

Buchanan

[1]sea [2]but [3]called ^Inch^ [4]called [5][Colchan Laird] Colhoune of [6]meeting [7]such [8]by [9]arose [10]lykewise amongs others [11]which [12]either [13]dependents *changed to* dependers [14][some of his] retayners [15]interpreted [16]^be^ by [17]^were^ [18]owne [19]each [20]^of them^ wraked other [21]such other [22]blood [23]^as was before mentioned^; but [24]amisse [25]but [26]which [27]by [28]by [29]make [30]Neither will [31]but [32]^that^ [33]^as^ [34]soe [35]enormous [36]mens were ^much^ [37]enormous [38]more [39]exaggerated, multiplied [40]thereof laide vpon [41]all

dissimulating[1] it for a tyme, with a false deceitful minde perswadis the rest, the Earle of Douglas to be that[2] man, **[362]** wha[3] was fitter to mitigate[4] by faire meanes, then to[5] irritat by suspicions; as he wha[6] was of that puissance, that if he opponet him self, might stay the Decreit of them al[7], and if he might be movit[8] to ioyne with them[9] might him[10] alone remeid al[11]. Therefore he procurit[12] a letter to be written to him in a[13] honorable maner, in name of them al[14], gentlie to intrait[15] him, that myndful[16] of the[17] place, myndful[18] of his forebears, whose ,, benefits were extant most ample, and most ,, notable to the Realme of Scotland; he wald come ,, to the convention of the Estats (whilk[19] could not ,, be convenientlie halden[20] without him and his ,, friends); if he was plentuous[21] of anie thing, they ,, wald[22] satisfie him as fare as was possible: if ,, there was anie oversight committit be[23] him, or ,, his freinds, they wald remit[24] it, and wald ,, forgyve[25] manie things to his most noble house, ,, and so weil[26] deserving of the Contrie: manie ,, things to the tyme, manie things to his age, and to ,, that great hope they had of him. Let him come ,, therefor, and take on[27] what pairt[28] of the common ,, weil[29] he best pleasit[30]; and as his predecessors ,, had oftymes delyverit[31] the Realme of Scotland ,, from perils be the[32] armes of the Douglases[33], so ,, he wald[34] now be[35] his[36] presence lift it vp and ,, confirme it, almost succumbing[37], and ,, overthrowen with intestine discordes. The letter ,, as it was honest **[363]** in wordes, and verie right[38], carying that right course, that sould have bene vsit[39] with him, and the duetie that al[40] these reasons conteinit[41] in it, cravit[42] to have bene done to[43] him,

The Governour procureth the nobilitie to writ to him.

[1]but dissembling [2]the [3]who [4]^be^ mitigate [5]^be^ [6]who [7]all [8]moved [9]^hee^ [10]^self^ [11]remedy all ^that was amisse^ [12]procureth [13]an [14]all [15]intreat [16]myndfull [17]his [18]myndfull [19]Estates (which [20]holden [21]did complaine [22]wold [23]committed by [24]wold remitt [25]wold yeild [26]weill [27]vpon ^him^ [28]^in the maniement^ [29]weill ^which^ [30]pleased [31]delyvred [32]by ^their feates of^ [33][of... Douglases] [34]wold [35]by [36]^peaceable^ [37]sinking [38][verie right] [39]vsed [40]all [41]conteined [42]craved [43]by

He acceptit it out of the honest disposition of his hart

if it had bene[1] in sinceritie; so being in falset[2], and with a treasonable[3] hart, onlie vsit[4] to intrape[5] him, makes their dittie[6] the clearer. For he out of the honestie of his awin[7] hart, interpreting their meaning to be according to their wordes; and being of no il[8] disposition, bot[9] of a sweit, and tractable natural[10], desyrous of glorie, and be gude[11] meanes to have folowit[12] the futstops[13] of his predecessours, in al[14] gude offices to his Contrie; nather having in his awen[15] mynd so great malice[16], nor thinking anie could have in his mynd sa[17] great malice agains[18] him, as to seik his life (for there had bene no sik[19] occasion[20]). Their contentions with his father had not past to that degrie[21], but had bene conteinit[22] within the bounds of words onlie; and therefor not imagining, that so great disloyaltie[23] could have harbourit[24] in their harts,[25] willinglie imbracis[26] this occasion of peace to his contrie, and imploying[27] him self to the weil[28] thereof, addressis[29] him self to Edinburg[30]: his freinds is said to have furderit[31] him to the resolution, in hope everie one of their awen[32] particular advancements, whilk[33] is said to have blindit[34] their eyes, that they saw not the perils. And certainlie I can **[364]** not see, how they could see them except we say the Governour and Chanceller were[35] knawen to be treasonable men, and had geven some proofe of as great disloyaltie before, (whilk[36] is not mentionit[37] in anie place, that I read of): for thogh they war[38] knawin to be subject to that fault[39] of falsnes[40] (as his father had obiectit[41] to them before) zit[42] it was so covert a falsnes[43], that it was not countit[44] falset, bot[45] wisdome; for there is[46] degreis[47], and there is[48] manie that wil[49] dispense with them selves to pas[50] some thing from the

[1]saide [2]falsett [3]^and double^ [4]vsed [5]intrapp [6]treacherie [7]owne [8]ill [9]but [10]nature [11]by ^all^ goode [12]folowed [13]footstops [14]all [15]owen [16]^against any^ [17]there mynds so [18]against [19]such [20]^given them^ [21]degree [22]conteined [23]desloyaltie [24]harboured [25]^he^ [26]imbraceth [27]^of^ [28]weill [29]addresseth [30]Edinburgh [31]furthered [32]owen [33]which [34]blinded [35]had been [36]which [37]mentioned [38]were [39]faulte [40]falshood [41]obiected [42]yet [43]falshood [44]counted [45]but [46]are [47]^of it^ [48]be [49]will [50]pass

precise reule of vprightnes (whilk[1] they count simplicitie to be[2] precise in[3]) that wil[4] be ashamit[5] of so heigh a degrie[6] of manifest treasone, as this was; so that[7] not the lesse of that falset, they could not have luikit[8] for sik[9] a[10] treasone[11]. Besyde[12] this, it might have seemit[13] to anie[14] man in discourse of reasone, that if they carit[15] not for blotting of their name with the foulnes of sik[16] a fact; zit[17] could[18] have no great purpose, wherebe[19] to do it in profite[20]: for what could it availe[21] to cut[22] him away, sen[23] another wald[24] succeid in his rowme, as il[25], perhaps, as he; so that be[26] his slaughter, al[27] their profite wald be ane irreconciliable deidlie feid[28] with that house; whilk[29] hetherto was not comed to that degrie[30], and was[31] but grudges, and mendable[32]. So that sence the discourse of men for ought we can knaw[33], could never have risen so fare[34] as to have meanit[35] that whilk folowit bot be[36] the contrair; I **[365]** see not, how this fact can be blamet[37] for credulitie, can be blamet[38] in him[39] as a faulte of his zouthfulnes,[40] and want of experience: or[41] what he[42] could[43] have done vther[44], if he had never bene so old, and expert; Nather zit to[45] his freinds, to think that[46] their hopes blindet[47] them from seing anie perril, whilk[48] discourse of reasone could not[49] apprehend. It is most true, men sould[50] be circumspect; bot[51] also it is ane[52] fault, and proceidis of il[53] nature to be suspicious[54] as he might weil[55] have seemit,[56] if he had refusit[57] this. The event declares, there was cause; bot[58] I deny that reason could foresee that event, or[59] anie considerance[60] of

Not to be imputit as youthful simlicitie.

---

[1]which [2]^too^ [3]into [4]^yett^ will [5]ashamed [6]degree [7]as [8]looked [9]such [10]^notable^ [11]^as this^ [12]Besydes [13]seemed [14]anye [15]cared [16]such [17]yet [18]^they^ [19]whereby [20]profitte [21]^them^ [22]cutt [23]sence [24]wold [25]ill [26]by [27]all [28]feede [29]which [30]hight [31]were [32]amendable [33]know [34]farr [35]^thought they^ meaned [36]which did folowe but by [37]blamed [38][can… blamet] [39]^or imputed^ [40]youthfulnes [41]for [42][he] else [43]^he^ [44][vther] [45]^is it^ yett ^to be reproched^ [46][to… that] as though [47]^had^ blinded [48]perrill, which ^noe^ [49][not] ever [50][apprehend] *adopted* [51]but [52]a [53]^an^ ill [54]without sufficient cause [55]weill [56]seemd [57]refused [58]but [59]^that^ [60]consideration

the circumstances[1] have luikit[2] for it, and no man can save him self fra sik[3] treason. Nather could it be imputit for[4] simplicitie to[5] the sufferer, bot[6] monstrousnes in[7] the doers.

The Chanceller invits him to his house.

To returne to our purpose; their disloyal[8] practise stayed not in this smuthe[9] letter, they doubled fraude vpon fraude: for so soone[10] the Chrichtoun had knawledge[11] he was in his journey, he went manie miles to meit[12] him, and invitit[13] him to his Castle of Chrichtoun (whilk[14] was neir to his way[15] not fare[16] from Edinburgh) where he feastit[17] him, and cherisit[18] him. he interteinis[19] him freindlie, cheirfullie and magnifiklie; and not ane[20] day, bot twa[21] dayes kyndlie and amiablie, with al[22] the taikens[23], that could be geven[24] of a freindlie mynd; and to remove al suspicion [**366**] of disloyaltie, and the more to circumvein him, he familiarlie

Advysis him freindlyk, bot traiterouslie

„ admonisis[25] him, that he wald[26] remember the „ Royal dignitie of his Prince, and his awen[27] duetie „ towards him; that whom the condition of his „ birth, the lawes of the contrie, the consent of the „ Estats had set at the rudder[28] of the Common „ Weil[29], he wald[30] acknawledge for his Lord and „ Superior; that his so great patrimonie acquirit be[31] „ the vertue and bluide[32] of his progenitors he sould „ transmit[33] to his posteritie, even so as he had „ resavit[34] it; that the Name of Douglas being no „ lesse illustrous be[35] their faithfulnes then be[36] „ their great facts, he sould be careful not onlie to „ keip it from the foule blote[37] of treasone[38], bot also „ fra al[39] blemish of anie suspicion theirof; that he „ wald abstein him self[40], and cause his men „ absteene from indomaging the poore people; that „ he wald[41] put from him thievis and limmers;[42]

[1]^could^ [2]looked [3]from such [4]imputed to [5]in [6]but ^to a^ [7]monstrous doublenes and onheard of by [8]disloyall [9]smoothe [10]^as^ [11]knowledge ^that^ [12]meet [13]invited [14]which [15]^and^ [16]farr [17]feasted [18]cherished [19]interteines [20]one [21]twa [22]all [23]toekens [24]given [25]admonisheth [26]wold [27]owen [28]ruther [29]Weile [30]wold [31]acquired by [32]bloode [33]might transmitt [34]resaved [35]illustrious by [36]than by [37]blott [38]rebellion [39]from all [40]wold him self abstein [41]wold [42]^And^

finalie that in tyme to come he wald set[1] him self,, to defend justice; that if he had offendit[2] in any,, tyme past it wald[3] be imputit[4] not to his natural,, but[5] to il[6] Counsel; that in that infirmitie of his,, zouth[7] penitencie might and wald be taine for,, innocencie. Venemous Vipere that could vnder so,, faire shewis[8] cover so dispytful[9] a poysone. Vnworthie tounge, except it war[10] to be cut out for exemple[11] to al[12] ages. Let not the poets be thought fabulous that transformes[13] men in[14] beastes; Lo[15] a beast composit[16] **[367]** of manie beastes, a monstre of al[17] sort of wickit[18] beastes; a Lyon, a Tiger for crueltie of hart; a Vespe, a Vipere of dispyte and poysonablenes; a Foxe, a Camelion for falset and doublenes; a Cokatrice, a Crocodile, and what so nature hes[19] made bearing malice in the hart of it; a Siren singing sweit[20] with hony to the mouth, and the outwarde sensis, so meikle[21] the more odious that it was in the shape of a man; and the more detestable that it dare[22] so pollute that jmage[23], so abuse that glorie of man, (the speiche of the tounge) therefor bezond[24] beastes geven him to imploy weil[25], to informe right, to speik gude[26], to vse to gude[27]. The honest hart of the heirer[28], that knew the speiches[29] to be right, that intendit[30] to folow so gude counsel[31], accepts al[32] in gude[33] pairt, beleevis the true speiche[34] for it awne[35] sake, the man for his speichis[36] sake. And who could have done vther[37] wayes? Wha[38] wald not have thought, bot he who knew so weil[39] what was the[40] right, wald have[41] some regarde to do the[42] right? sal[43] we count[44] it bairnlines[45], that he countit[46] so of him, and suffert[47] him self to be so deceivit[48]? Nay, he could not keip him self vndeceivit; agit[48] men, and wyse men hes[49]

[1]wold sett [2]offended [3]^it^ *adopted* wold [4]imputed [5]^disposition^, but [6]ill [7]youth [8]showes [9]dispytfull [10]were [11]example [12]all [13]have transformed [14]into [15]^there^ [16]composed [17]all [18]wicked [19]hath [20]sweet [21]much [22]dares [23]^of god^ [24]beyond [25]weill [26]goode *changed to* Truth [27]goode ^ends^ [28]hearer [29]speeches [30]intended [31]goode counsell [32]all [33]goode [34]speeche [35]the truthes [36]speeches [37]other [38]Who [39]soe weill [40][the] [41]^had^ [42][the] [43]sall [44]counte [45]Chyldishnes [46]accounted [47]sufferd [48]deceaved [49]vndeceived; aged [49]have

bene deceivit[1] both in sacred and prophane historie; we must not impute ane bairnlines to[2] Abner, that Joab slew him vnder trust; bot[3] to the traiterousnes of Joab, [**368**] whilk[4] Dauid sayes; He dieth[5] not as a foole dieth, howbeit his hands war[6] not bound; bot[7] as a gude[8] man falleth before a wickit[9] man; that is be[10] treasone, whilk[11] no man can eshew[12]. It is said that his freinds seing sa[13] extraordinarie interteinment, sa faire language above measure, sa[14] humble behaviour, and sik[15] a bussines; sa[16] manie messages at everie moment almost, running betwixt the Governour and Chanceller, tuik[17] some suspicion of il[18] meaning; and that there arose first a stil[19] murmure throgh the hail[20] companie; therefter some begane to admonise[21] him, that if he wald[22] not desist himself, at leist[23] he sould send bake his brother Dauid; myndeful[24] of a precept of his fathers; that they sould not go both togeather in one „ place, where them selves war[25] not maistre: that „ they sould not put the hail[26] familie in danger at „ once. The vnware zouth, vnware[27] indeid (but „ what warnes[28] could he have (pure[29] innocent!) „ and verie weil[30] inclyned?)[31] even angrie with his „ freinds, stayes these murmurs be[32] a plaine „ commandement, and answerit[33] his freinds thus; „ that he knew weil[34], it was ane[35] perpetual pest[36] to „ great houses, that they had ever about them some „ men impatient of peace; who made gaine of the „ perils and travels and miseries of their Patrons; „ and because in peace they war restrainit be[37] the „ brydil[38] of[39] lawes, they war ever stirrers vp [**369**] „ of stryfe and sedition; that might in troublit[40] „ affairs have the greatter libertie of their „ wikednes: As for him self, he reposit[41] more on „ the knawen[42] Wisdome, and Prudencye of the

His freinds suspect.

He puts them to silence be a proclamation[43]

[1]deceaved [2]as childishnes in [3]but [4]of whom [5]died [6]were [7]but [8]goode [9]wicked [10]by [11]which [12]eschew [13]so [14]so [15]such [16]so [17]took [18]ill [19]still [20]wholl [21]admonish [22]wold [23]least [24]myndefull [25]were [26]wholl [27]vnwary youth, vnwary [28]warines [29]poore [30]weill [31]^he was^ [32]murmures by [33]answered [34]weill [35]a [36]peste [37]restrained by [38]brydill [39]^the^ [40]troubled [41]reposed [42]knowen [43]candide answer

Governour and Chanceller, nor[1] to give eare to „ their suspicious surmises. This speich thus vtterit[2] „ testifieing both ane acknawledging of the ewils[3] past, and resolution of amending, was it not sufficient to have purgit whatsomewer[4] errours had bene, or might have bene thought to have escapit[5] him before? as certainlie it wald if thir[6] men had regardit[7] iustice, or the weil[8] of the Common Wealth, and desyrit[9] to have reclamit[10] the zoung[11] man from his errours, and wone him to his Contrie. Bot[12] his so ful[13] confidence;[14] This reposing on ther[15] credit was it not ynough to have tyed them to have keipit[16] their credit, if there had bene anie spunke[17] of humanitie, or nature of man left in them? And if they had[18] bene worse then savage beasts? Lippening[19] to ws deservis[20] worthines of that lippening[21]; and credit, procurs keiping of credit; where al[22] humane nature is not extinguishit[23]. And verelie[24] simplicitie deservis[25] favour. Nather[26] can a man that is not geven over, and sauld[27] to wickednes bot[28] favour it; zea[29] thogh he had bene vther[30] wayis disposit[31] **[370]** in the beginning. It wald[32] even move anie mans hairt (indeid a mans, and not transformit[33] in a beast) to favour it, and to have compassion on it; and tamed anie miscontentment, and thrawin[34] out of their[35] hands[36] anie intention of evil whilk[37] they might perhaps, before have conceivit[38]. Alwayes he gois[39] on in the innocencie of his hart, and[40] the more quicklie to cute[41] af[42] occasion of sik speiches[43]; and with his brother and a few of the principal[44] of his freinds gois[45] directlie to the Castle of Edinburgh; A fatalitie (as it war[46]) so drawing them, both enters in the power of these their traiterous Enemies, fainzit[47]

Entreth the Castle with his brother

[1]than [2]vttered [3]evils [4]purged whatsomever [5]escaped [6]these [7]regarded [8]weill [9]desyred [10]reclaimed [11]young [12]But [13]full [14]^And^ [15]their [16]keeptt [17]sponke [18]^not^ [19]Trusting [20]deserves [21] trust [22]all [23]extinguished [24]even [25]^itself^ deserves [26]Neither [27]sauld [28]but [29]yea [30]other [31] disposed [32]wold [33]^one^ transformed [34]throwne [35]^harts, there^ [36]^at least^ [37]evill, which [38]conceived [39][he] this noble youth goes [40]^that^ [41]cutt [42]^all^ [43]such speeches [44]principall [45]goes [46]were [47]^but^ fained

Dyneth with the king

Presentit with a Buls head

freinds). At the verie instant comes our Governour (as was before appointit[1] betwixt them) to play his pairt of this tragedie that they might be the lyke[2] imbarkit[3] in the action, and bear the horrour of so[4] vglie a fact, that the weight theirof sould not ly on[5] no one of them alone. Zit[6] to play out their trecherous pairts[7] they welcome him most courtiouslie, settis him to denner[8] with the king, at the same table, bankets him royallie, intertenis him cheirfullie, and[9] a long tyme; at last about the end of the denner[10] they compas him about with armed men, and presents a Bul[11] head before him on the boarde; the Bul[12] head was in these[13] dayes a taiken[14] of death (sayes our histories) **[371]** how it hes[15] had that representing[16], how it hes[17] comed in that[18] vse so to signifie, nather tel[19] they, nor heir[20] we els where, nor[21] anie mention[22] (that I remember) save in this one place; Nather[23] can we coniecture what affinitie can have their with; except it war[24] to exprobat grosnes, as is the French and our awin[25] saying, (whilk[26] is alwise[27], a veilles head[28], and not a Bulles[29] head) jnsulting so over that inocencie they had snared[30]; and advancing their awen[31] wisdome and sharpnes of wit[32] that had so compassit[33] him, a tryme ruise[34] and ane vnhonest! Zit[35] I wonder what they meanit be[36] so fair interteining[37] him; there was some reason of[38] it be[39] the way, that tratours might worke the treason til[40] he was within their compase; and[41] now within their[42] Castle, and fullie within[43] their danger, I wonder what it did meane to welcome[44] him sa fairlie, to banket him so carefully, to set him at the table with the King, and from it to draw him to the skembels[45]: It wonders me what hes[46] bene their

[1]appointed [2]^both^ alyke [3]imbarked [4]soo [5]lye vpon [6]Yett [7]^the better^ [8]dinner [9]for [10]dinner [11]Bulls [12]Buls [13]those [14]toeken [15]hath [16]representation [17]hath [18][that] [19]nether tell [20]heere [21][nor] [22]^of it^ [23]Nether [24]were [25]awne [26]which [27]not the les [28]vealles [head] [29]Bullocks [30]ensnared [31]owen [32]witt [33]compassed *changed to* circumveend [34]braue ruisse ^indeed^ [35]honest! Yett [36]meand by [37]^of^ [38]for [39]by [40]^the more securely^ till [41]But [42]the [43]in [44][welcme] *emended* [45]shambles [46]hath

intention: Might they not have convoyit[1] him to anie privat chambre? Might they not have taine them to the place of[2] execution immediatlie, without al[3] this proces, and never lettin[4] them see the King? It wald[5] seeme they have not bene weil advysit[6] vpon it, nor resolvit[7] of before; and their **[372]** purpose hes[8] not bene treasonable; bot[9] treason hes[10] tane occasion or[11] the facilitie: to that the wryters are contraire[12]: or[13] that they wald[14] communicat the mater, or transferre it al[15] vpon the King (wha[16] was ever zoung[17], and purgit[18] him self be[19] disapproving). Sa[20] I see no reason of it, bot[21] as a lyon with his praye, or a more basse (zit[22] a more familiar exemple[23] and heigh ynough for so base a fact) the Cate[24] with her praye[25] the mouse, whilk[26] she might devore immediatlie, zit[27] it pleasis[28] her to play a little with it;[29] for[30] satisfaction of their mynd[31] to play out their farce more stranglie, that ane[32] proces and vncouth forme[33] of doing may[34] represent some deipper[35] wisdome; whilk[36] I confesse is so deip[37] a follie and mishantrie[38], that I can not sound it, except that I think the place of the man, the worth of him, forcit[39] their wiked harts to acknawledge it (not the lesse of[40] their wickednes), and thogh it could not extinguishe wickednes[41], and make it to leive af il[42] altogeather, zit[43] it threw[44] it in some sort, and threw out some[45] confession of his worth, as[46] the actions of wickednes and al wickednes in the[47] wickednes[48] is ful[49] of contradictions, as[50] this same[51] is most cleare. For if this man was giltie of death, why was he[52] taine in[53] the Kings presence? why set[54] at his table? if he was not giltie, why was he slaine? why was he

[1]convoyed [2]^of^ *adopted* [3]all [4]lett [5]wold [6]weile advysed [7]resolved [8]hath [9]but [10]hath [11]of [12]contrairy [13]^rather^ [14]wold [15]all [16]who [17]too young [18]purged [19]by [20]^it^). So [21]but [22]yett [23]example [24]Catt [25][her praye] [26]which [27]yett [28]pleaseth [29]^So^ [30]^the^ [31]mynds ^they delyte^ [32]such [33]formes [34]might [35]deepper [36]which [37]deep [38]meshancetie [39]forced [40]^all^ [41]the same [42]leave of ill [43]yet [44]qualifyed [45]extorted this [46]^all^ [47][al… the] even [48]^it self in the abstract^ [49]full [50]^by^ [51]^example^ [52]^he^ *adopted* [53]into [54]sett

executit[1]? so dificile a thing it is in a[2] lie to keip a conformitie, ather in a lie of actions[3] (so to speik) or[4] in a lie of words! [**373**] In words it is dificil, that the attentive heirer sal[5] not perceive contrarietie: In actions it is impossible, as[6] they can be dissembled. This action of this zoung[7] mans slaughter is a lie; for it sayes he is giltie of death, bot[8] the welcoming of him, the setting of him at the table with the King, and this banketting of him, sayes[9] he was a[10] innocent, worthie, noble man. Indeid[11] onlie truth in word[12] and actions can accord with it self; as it is vniforme,[13] flowis from vnitie, tends to it, and endis in it, and keipes the taist[14] of the fontane it came fra[15]. Alwyse having geven this confession of his worth, and agane be this[16] signe gainsaid the[17] confession, representit[18] death, as vnworthie. And he ather vnderstanding it, as a common thing, or stupefied with it as a[19] vncouth thing, vpon the sight of the Bul[20] head, as he is about to ryse, he is apprehendit be[21] their armet[22] men in the Kings presence, at the Kings table, whilk[23] (if there had bene no more) sould have bene Girth[24] to him; and without regarde of King, or anie duetie, or without anie farther[25] proces[26] without anie order, syse[27] or law, without anie cryme objectit[28], or evictit[29], a zoung man of that[30] age that could not have sufferit law[31]; a noble man of that[32] place, a worthie zouth[33] of[34] great expectation; a ghast[35] of that acceptation, a lippener[36] reposing on that[37] credit,[38] that had committit[39] him self to them[40]; a freind in mynd, [**374**] and luiking[41] for freindship, to whom al[42] freindshipe was promisit; agains[43] duetie and law (convict of no cryme, giltie of none) agains

---

[1]executed [2]^a^ *adopted* [3]^or^ [4][or] [5]hearer sall [6]that [7]young [8]but [9]sayeth [10]an [11]Indeed [12]words [13]^it^ [14]taest [15]from [16]by that ^ominous^ [17]that [18]represented [19]an [20]Buls [21]apprehended by [22]armed [23]which [24]a sanctuarie [25]further [26]^proces^ *adopted* [27]Jurye [28]objected [29]evicted [30]youth within [31][that... sufferit *changed to* suffered law] [32]^ranke and^ [33]young gentleman [34]^rare and^ [35]ghest [36]Truster [37]their [38]^and^ [39]^voluntarly^ committed [40]their ^hands^ [41]looking [42]all [43]promised; against

freindshipe, agans[1] fayth, aganes[2] honestie, aganes[3] humanitie, aganes[4] Nature, aganes[5] humane societie; aganes[6] gods law, Mans law, Natural law, is cruellie execute[7] and put to death; they (in dispyt as it were) spitting on the face of al[8] duetie and honestie; proclaming as far as in them lay, there was no god, there was no duetie to God or[9] man to be regardit[10], and to eik an zit[11], the Comble[12] of their wickednes[13] is (as it wald[14] seeme) to be aganes[15] the wil[16] of the King; wha weippit[17] at their execution, and forbade them to medle with his Cousine[18]; the shamles men[19] chyding him for weipping at the death of his Enemie (as they callit[20] him,) during whose lyfe (said they) he neidit[21] never to luik[22] for peace, where them selfs war[23] his cheife[24] Enemies, and traitours to[25] him; and besyds him to God and Nature; and to the office of justice that they caried; bringing a blot on the one and the other, and a blude[26] vpon his Crowne, as far as in them laye. This is that detestable fact never ynough execrat, whilk[27] I[28] preissit[29] indeid to set downe in the awen[30] simple Colours of it, strype[31] it nakit[32] of the faird it wald[33] tak on (thogh I confesse no words are able to equal the wickednes of it) that men [**375**] may learne to detest sik[34] things. Wherein may be seene, what respect they have cariet[35] ether to justice, to equitie, to common peace, or common weil[36], that thought it better to cute[37] af sik[38] a plante, nor[39] to maniure it; to wrake sik[40] a[41] house, nor[42] to winne it. Whilk[43] they wald[44] never have done, if their particular pryde and avarice had not had the greatest sway with them. I think al[45] honest mynds sould disdaine to reade what they have before

Murdered

The King weipping

[1]lawe [convict… none] against [2]aganst [3]aganst [4]aganst [5]aganst [6]against [7]executed [8]all [9]nor [10]regarded [11][to… zit *changed to* yet] which addeth yett vnto [12]heapt vp measure [13]All [14]wold [15]aganst [16]will ^and consent^ [17]who weipped ^bitterly^ [18]Coosine [19]Bloodie butchers [20]called [21]neided [22]look [23]were [24]cheifest [25]vnto [26]bloode [27]^to be^ execrated, which [28]^have^ [29]preissed [30]owen [31]^and to^ stripp [32]naked [33]wold [34]such [35]caried [36]weill [37]cutt [38]such [39]than [40]such [41]^noble^ [42]than [43]Which [44] wold [45]all

This fact to be detestit not extenuat.

geven out of their intention in[1] publike weil[2]; having there[3] so terriblie[4] belied it. Nather sould anie man speik[5] of it in indifferencie, without a note of detestation; Nather extenuat it be[6] this Earls simplicitie (whilk seemes[7] to diminish the half of the fault)[8] jf this was the wisdome, where of they had acquyrit[9] vnder the former King (James the first) and if they had practisit sik[10] as this, it hes[11] bene a bitter roote, and hes[12] brought furth[13] a[14] bitter fruit; and hes[15] bene[16] pairt of the cause of the hastening of his death, and the emboldning of his Enemies to[17] it: as[18] indeid I find pairt of our wryters seemes to say that the same King sould have allurit[19] the Lord of the Isles and the Earle of Rosse, and the Countese his mother, daughter to Walter Leslie Earle of Rosse and manie vthers great men in a stronge Toure **[376]** one and one, and then inclosit[20] them in waird, ower whom, when he had gatten them so inclosit[21], he insultit[22] to his awin folkes be[23] some latin verse that he made af hand:

Maior lib. 16. Cap. 14

Ad turrim fortem ducamus caute cohortem
Per Christi sortem, meruerunt hi quoque mortem.

That amongs thir war[24] Angus, Dufe, Kennedies, Iohne Rosse, William Leslie, Angus of Morton, and Makeinzies, of whom pairt he slew, pairt he wardit[25]. Whilk[26] if he did[27] hes bene ane ympe[28] of this same trie, sprung of sik[29] mens breistis as thir[30] and perhaps the[31] same, wher of hes[32] risen meikle il[33], hatred and feare (the causes aye of il) and a commone opinion in the harts of the people, whilk[34] the same wryters tellis of, to wit, that the King had

[1]to ^the^ [2]well [3][there] in this action [4]terriblye [5]speak [6]by [7]which wold seeme [8]^if any were^ [9]acquyred ^the name^ [10]practised such [11]hath [12]hath [13]foorth [14]^verye^ [15]hath ^(in all appearance)^ [16]^no small^ [17]vnto [18][as… and not imployet in affaires, as indeid] *Alterations in this long excision will be noted separately below.* [19]allured [20]inclosed [21]inclosed [22]insulted [23]by [24]these were [25]warded [26]Which [27]^it^ [28]a scyon [29]such [30]these [31]^very^ [32]hath [33]much ill [34]peeple, which

ane intention to cute[1] af al the Nobilitie of Scotland, and that he sould have said to the Quene, he sould cause al[2] the Nobilitie of Scotland ly in her armes, meaning he sould cute[3] them al af bot[4] him self, whilk[5] not the lesse the author denyis that the King had sa meikle[6] as dreamed of; for then (sayis[7] he) how could he have keipit[8] the Contrie from forrainars, and that it was but a report sawen be his Enemies in malice. Zit[9], it may[10] be that sik[11] men hes[12] geven sik[13] counsels, whilk hes come[14] abrode, and hes[15] done il[16], seing them made vp[17] and the Nobilitie wardit[18], **[377]** troublit[19] and not imployit[20] in affaires,[21] as indeid sik[22] new men gois[23] about to perswade princes, that[24] noble men are Enemies to[25] them, and barres to their greatnes; and that is it that these[26] men meanis now in saying, that the Earle of Douglas was ane Enemie to the King; not that he bearit[27] anie il wil[28] to the King (for that they could not prove, nor mak appeare) bot[29] because he was so great a man, be[30] the general[31] rule; as thogh to be a great man, be the same that he is great, were a point of Enimitie aganes[32] a king. Whilk[33] Maxime I feare, they have dunge[34] in his head efterwards, not to strenthen and provyde for the Kings securitie, bot[35] to draw the King to their pairty; to strenthen them selves: for we see al[36] their intents are but particulars; and so they do in this, coullours[37] their particulars vnder pretense of the Kings service, to do[38] so mishant[39] a fact. Alwyse vthers wreittis[40] of no fraude to have bene vsit be[41] King James the first[42], and I war weil[43] content to vendicate a Prince so accomplishit fra so[44] foul a fault[45]; as also al[46]

The practice of new men aspyring

Ane il maxime to put in Princes heads

[1]cutt [2]all [3]cutt [4]but [5]which [6]so much [7]sayeth [8] keiped [9]^And^ Yett [10]^well^ [11]such [12]have [13]such ^perverse^ [14]that have comd [15]have [16]ill [17]themselfs to be advanced [18]warded [19]troubled [20]imployed [21]effaires [22]such [23]goeth ^commonly^ [24]^ancient^ [25]vnto [26]theise [27]beare [28]ill will [29]but [30]by [31]generall [32][be the same... aganes *changed to* aganst] were by an infallible consequence to be an Enimye to [33]Which [34]beaten [35]but [36]all [37]^they^ coullour [38]perpetrat [39]meshant *changed to* wicked [40]others wryttes [41]vsed by ^the^ [42][James ... first] [43]am weill [44]accomplished from such a [45]facte [46]all

Princes fra[1] this vther il[2] opinion, that al[3] great men are enemies to[4] them. Where as indeid they are the truest servands, and most able to do gude[5] service, and may be best[6] made[7] willing to serve; and best services hes ever bene[8] done by them. Nather with out them anie great[9] service[10]. Dauid Douglas[11] brother to the Earle was also execute[12] with him, **[378]** and Malcolme Fleming of Combernalde, his special[13] Counsellour; al beheadit[14] in the bake close of the Castle, that luikit[15] westward. This augmentes zit[16] the wickednes of the fact, that they slay his brother also, whose age the other[17] not being great (as hes[18] bene said) behovit[19] to be lesse. Zit[20] I can hardlie be inducit[21] to think[22] their ages hes[23] not bene[24] more nor[25] it is geven out, to whilk[26] there is commonlie Curatoris geven: Nether vse they to administer things be[27] them selves, as this man seemes to have done: Nether could he have administrat[28] it with sik[29] dexteritie and authoritie, as he seemes to have had; and his brother is callit[30] participant of al[31] his counsels and deids[32], whilk[33] (alace puire boyes[34]) what could they be[35] in that age, the one 14 zeir old, when he begoude, and bot 15 now, the other could be but 13 or 14 at the most. Zit[36] his[37] errour (that I[38] see) is onlie this that he left not this Dauid[39] out of danger; whilk wyse sal we cal bairnlines and[40] simplicitie? In how wise and agit[41] men wil it[42] be found, the best hes[43] bene circumveinit? bot cal[44] it what ze wil[45]; if fatalitie, it is commone to al[46]; if simplicitie, it fallis to[47] wyse men: be nather[48] of thir[49] names let[50] it be reproched, bot[51] rather regratit[52]: Nather accuse this man; bot[53]

His brother Dauid and Malcolme Fleming of Cumbernalde

Their age aggravats the fact

So dois their simplicitie

Fatalitie extenuats it not

---

[1]from [2]other ill [3]all [4]vnto [5]^them^ goode [6]easeliest [7]^most^ [8]have bene ever [9][great] *a second 'great' scored out; adopted* [10]^hath bin done^ [11]^the younger^ [12]putt to death [13]speciall [14]all ^three^ beheaded [15]looked [16]yett ^further^ [17]others [18]hath [19]behoved [20]Yet [21]induced [22]^that^ [23]hath [24]^somewhat^ [25]than [26]which [27]by [28]administred [29]such [30]called [31]all [32]deeds [33]Which *changed to* But [34]poore youthes [35][be… 15. ^as^… most] doe or devise [36]Yett [37]^greatest^ [38]^can^ [39]^his brother^ [40]which [wyse… bairnlines and] not the les we may tearm too confident [41]aged [42]these [43]have [44]circumveined. but call [45]yee will [46]all [47]falleth into [48]by neither [49]these [50]lett [51]but [52]regrated [53]but

excuse him; Nather extenuat the fault[1] of the committers, bot[2] aggravate it, as it weil deservis[3]: for if it was fatalitie, they ceise not to be giltie; and if it was simplicitie, they ceise not to be treasonable. Nather dois[4] **[379]** it diminish anie degrie theirof[5] that the vther was zoung[6]: I[7] think also (to speake zit be[8] the way) there seemes some vncertaintie of the Kings age: the calculation of the historie wil[9] mak him to have bene above ten zeirs of age, for he was borne in the 1430, and this fact is countit[10] to have fallen in the 1440. Zit[11] his hanting the feilds, and hunting then on horsbake (as he did when the Chanceller tuik[12] him) wald make him older. and now he was beginning to be a zoung man (or adolescent) whilk[13] we interprete fourtein zeirs of age at leist. Whilk[14] of the twa soever it was they war gude[15] bringers vp of him, to bait him in the blude of[16] his Nobilitie, and[17] imprent this lesson in his tender mynd, that they war[18] his Enemies. Be sik as this may be considerit what count we may make of our Chronologie. Bot[19] for conclusion of this mater anent[20] these zoung men[21]; as there was no law laid aganes[22] them, so bearis no historie witnes[23] they war[24] giltie of anie Capital[25] cryme. And Mr Johne Maior[26] expreslie: *Apud annales legi, quod viri illj non erant rei mortis, sed consilio vel dolo Gulielmi Chrichtoni Scotiae Cancellarij haec perpetrata sunt*: that is, I reid in our Annales[27], that these men war[28] not gyltie of death; bot[29] this mater atchivit was be[30] the counsel[31] and fraude of William Chrichton Chanceller of **[380]** Scotland. It is sure the people[32] abhors the fact, execrating the verie

The Kings age

Buch. *Regem iam adolescentium ingressum.*

The people execrat the fact

[1]faulte [2]but [3]weill deserveth [4]Neither doth [5]^But augment it rather^ [6]others were young [7][I... in the blude of] *corrections to this long passage will be noted individually* [8]yett by [9]will [10]counted [11]Yett [12]took [13]which [14]Which [15]were goode [16][of the twa... blude of] And concerning the Kings part herein, we have told already how hee detested and forbad it. But as to them It was a lewd training vp of his youth, to give him such an example of treacherous seuerity against [17]^To^ [18]were [19][Be sik *changed to* By such... considerit *changed to* considered... Chronologie]. But [20]touching [21]young ^noble^ gentlemen [22]aganst [23]^that^ [24]were [25]Capitall [26]^saieth^ [27]Annals [28]were [29]but [30]atchived by [31]counsell [32]peeple

place, where it was done in detestation theirof: whereof the memorie remaynes zit[1] to our dayes in these words:

Edinburgh Castle, Towre and Towne,
God nor thow sinke for sinne,
And that is for the blake denner,
The Douglas gate[2] therein.

Now sen[3] these zouthes war not giltie, wherof war they not giltie, that pute[4] them to death? and with what note to be reprochit[5]? That they seeme to blame the zoung man innocent (whilk[6] they can not deny) with half words, as gydit be[7] flatterie, geven to insolence, presumptuous in his porte[8] whereof no effect, nor affection is brought, importing ather[9] his being adictit[10] to flatterie, or insolent[11]; or[12] more presumptuous and arrogant, then became his ranke; bot[13] a gentil Natural[14]; a repulser of flatterie as he grew in age;[15] a due magnificence, sik[16] as became him. Let ws therefore accept[17] of him sa[18] very singular in these zeirs[19], and let[20] the blame be fullie on his enemies; wha sal have[21] some meeting[22] hereafter be[23] his Cousine, that they may find al[24] the house perishit[25] not with him; thogh indeid the punishment[26] nothing lyke to that[27] they deservit[28].

Buchanan

[1]remayneth yett [2]gott [3]since [4]putt [5]reproched [6]innocent young man (which [7]by [8]port [9]either [10]addicted [11]insolence [12]^being^ [13]place; but ^of^ [14]Nature [15]^of^ [16]such [17]accounte [18]as [19]yeirs [20]lett [21]who sall find [22]requytale [23]by [24]all [25]perished [26]^was^ [27]^which^ [28]deserved

[**381**] The Lyfe of[1] James callit Gros[2] Lord of Abercorne, the 16 Lord, 7 Earle of Douglas, 4 Duk of Turain, and thrid of the name of James[3]

Vnto William succeidit[4] his fathers brother callit[5] James, Lord of Abercorne, the 16 Lord and 7 Earle of Douglas, Lord of Bothuel, Balvennie and Evindail, 4 Duk of Turain, and Lord of Longeville *etc*. for there being alyve a sister of thir zoung[6] mens, slane in the Castle of Edinburgh to name Beatrix, she fel[7] air to them of sik[8] lands as war[9] not tailzeit, whilk war[10] manie (sayes[11] our wryters) specialie Galloway, Wigtoun, Balvenie, Ormond and Annandaile. This James (callit[12] Gros James, because he was corpulent of bodie) had to wyfe Beatrix Sinkler, daughter to the Earle of Orknay.[13] it is not set[14] downe, to try[15] we must consider, that from William Sinkler the first that came fra[16] France, and mariet[17] Agnes Dumbar, daughter to Patrik first Earle of Marche, 2[18] Henrie his sone mariet[19] Katherine daughter to the Earle of Stratherne 3. his sone Henrie mariet[20] Margaret Gairtnay daughter to the Earle of Mar. 4. This Henries sone past with Good S*ir* James Douglas and[21] the Bruces hart, callit[22] S*ir* William; he mariet[23] Elizabeth [**382**] Speir daughter to the Earle of Orknay, and Schitland. and so became Earle (first of that name) bot[24] this mans tyme is lang[25] before.[26] 5. persone, and second Earle callit[27] S*ir* William, sone to the former, maried Florentina doughter to the King of Denmark.[28] 6. persone, and 3 Earle was his sone callit[29] Henrie, wha[30] maried Giles Douglas daughter to the Lord of Nethsdail.[31] 7

Hol.

Beatrix Douglas his neece

Beatrix Sinkler his wyfe

1444.

[1]^the third^ [2]called Grosse etc [3][Lord… James] [4]succeided [5]called [6]these young [7]fell [8]such [9]were [10]entailed, which were [11] saye [12]called [13]^which of them^ [14]sett [15]^it^ [16]from [17]maried [18]^Earle^ [19]^who^ maried [20]maried [21][and] who carried [22]^and was^ called [23]maried [24]but [25]long [26]^The^ [27]called [28]^The^ [29]called [30]who [31]^The^

persone, and 4 Earle is S*i*r William that maried Elizabeth Douglas daughter to Archbald Tynman Duk[1] of Turain. Now this James his wyfe can not have bene this S*i*r Williams daughter, for then was scho his awne[2] sister daughter; and therefor she hes bene ather Henrie Sinklers daughter and Giles Douglasis, or els Henries sister, doughter to Florentina the King of Denmarks daughter, whilk[3] of the twa[4], I leave to coniecture. Her great spirite and heigh ambition wald say[5] she war[6] comed of kings, and neir[7] them. The moniment in the Kirk of Douglas callis[8] her daughter to Henrie; Sche bare to him[9] seven sones and four daughters; the eldest of them was callit[10] William; the second James, wha succeidit[11] also to the Earldome; the thrid Archbald, wha[12] maried the daughter of Johne Dumbar Earle of Murray, wha[13] was brother to George Earle of Marche; and[14] neice[15] to King Robert, by whilk[16] meanes he gate[17] the Earldome[18] of Murray **[383]** and was creat Earle of Murray[19]; the fourt namit[20] Hugh[21] efterward made Earle of Ormond, and had sindrie lands geven him be[22] the King in Tividail[23], and Rosse; the fyft callit[24] Johne, and was made Lord of Balvenie; the sext Henrie was Bishope of Dunkelden; the sevint George, wha diet[25] before[26] he was fyftein zeirs[27] of age, as our Chronicles wryteis[28]; but there is no mention of him in the monuments at Douglas; where the rest are set downe be[29] name. As for his foure daughters, Margaret the eldest was maried to the Lord of Dalkeithe; Beatrix the second to the Lord Aubigny or[30] Albany (as the monuments cal[31] him) Constable of Scotland, and Captane of fyftie men of armes in France; the thrid Jennot maried to the Lord Fleming of Combernald; the fourt was callit[32] Elizabeth,

His Childrein

[1][Tynman] the first Duke [2]owne [3]which [4]twoe [5]wold innuat that [6]was [7]neere ^to^ [8]calleth [9]this Earl James [10]called [11]who succeided [12]who [13]who [14][and] she was [15]neece [16]which [17]gatt [18]lands [19][Murray] thereof [20]named [21]^was^ [22]by [23]Tividaile [24]^was^ called [25]who died [26]*'before' repeated and scored out* [27]yeirs [28]beares [29]by [30][the Lord… or] John Stewart Duke of [31]call [32]called

wha[1] died vnmaried.

This Gros James his eldest sone[2] (pairtlie to reteine[3] the greatnes of the house of Douglas, pairtlie be[4] the gentilwomans awin[5] desyre, wha[6] expreslie refusit[7] to marie anie vther[8] of the name of Douglas) maried this his Cousine foresaid Beatrix Douglas callit[9] the fair[10] Maden of Galloway, and so reteinit these[11] pairts of the living to the Earldome of Douglas, whilk vther[12] ways war to be devydit fra[13] it, be[14] her partage: wherebe[15] it not onlie **[384]** reteinit[16] the awin[17] greatnes bot[18] had also the accession of Abercorne; whilk[19] was fare aganes[20] the opinion of the rest of the name of Douglas; whose mynd was[21] she sould rather have[22] bene maried in[23] some of the houses of Angus or Dalkeith; alledging, that his greatnes wald[24] be the decay of his house. Whilk thoght[25] it is a Maxime, that proves oft[26] true, that over great dominions vnder Princes, as also Princes them selves having[27] great Dominions, and vther[28] Republikes, and Commonwealthes fra[29] they come to that hudgnes, that they can not easelie[30] be governit perishis[31] and that[32] be their awen force[33] oftymes, be[34] the conspiracies of them[35] without fearing their greatnes; And in[36] subjects ather[37] by the Princes him self[38] of him self suspecting them; ather[39] drawen be vther Invyers[40] of them, to suspect them: whilk[41] may be imputit[42] indeid to their awne[43] greatnes. And therefor al[44] both Empyres and Lordshipes, are to be restrainit[45] to a mediocritie, as weil Princes and Commonwealths, as subjects, whilk al wil[46] confesse: but what this mediocritie is,

Ma-yeth his eldest sone William on Beatrix Douglas.

Of greatnes of houses

[1]who [2]^Williame^ [3]hold vp [4]by [5]owne [6]who [7]refused [8]other [9]called [10]faire [11]reteined those [12]which other [13]which otherways had been devyded from [14]by [15]whereby [16]reteined [17]owne [18]but [19]which thing [20]farr aganst [21]^that^ [22][had] have *adopted* [23]to [24]wold [25]Which thogh [26]often [27]excessiue [28]other [29]when [30]eeselie [31]governed doe perish ^oftentymes^ [32]^overthrown^ by [33]owen weight [34][oftymes], ^And^ by [35]their Nebours [36]Or by the [37]^within^ either [38][him self] Jealousies [39]either ^being^ [40]by others Invyous [41]which [42]imputed [43][greatnes *erasure adopted* awne] onely [44]^all^ [45]restrained [46]which all ^men^ will

they declare not; nather wil[1] they confesse[2]. Nether thinkes anie of them[3], that they are comed to that fulnes, that there is anie peril[4]. It is said of Augustus Caesar, that he sould have intendit[5] some moderation of the Empyre, and a counsel[6] to have propagat it[7] no further; zit[8] it is doubtit[9] of what mynd it was, **[385]** whether of this prudencie, or of invy of the[10] successors; that none sould have bene thought to go bezond[11] him. And indeid it is ane hard argument to perswade, and perhaps no lesse kittle[12] to prove: for al[13] agrie[14] these inferior things (al[15] of them) to be[16] in a perpetual motion; and that they can not stand lang stil[17] without going forward or bakward, increassing or decreassing: if therefor they go not forward, they most[18] go bake; if they increase not, they most[19] decrease; whilk[20] if it be[21] true, better it is[22] to seik the increassing so lang[23] as men may, nor[24] take them to a standing, fra the whilk[25] they most[26] decrease. Bot[27] whether out of that discours of reason they wald[28] thus have perswadit[29] him; or for anie particular of their awen[30]; or he out of this vther[31] reason, or rather this common mynd geven to men to go[32] ever increassing[33], so it is, that he choyse[34] the greatnes with the aventure[35]; And because they war[36] in degreis countit[37] not lawful[38] to mary without dispensation (to wit Cousine germanes) he sent for[39] Manuscr. dispensation to Rome, whilk[40] before it could come, fearing leist[41] the King, and the rest of the name of Douglas sould cast al[42] impediments they could to staye it (as the raport was) and not without cause, he causes them haist[43] the mariage before[44] dispensation came, and in[45] tyme[46] then forbidden Buch. (in Lent) and on the[47] Friday before Pasch **[386]**

---

[1]neither will [2]^it^ [3]^ever^ [4]perrill [5]intended [6]had consulted [7]propagated it [8]yett [9]doubted [10]his [11]beyond [12]tickle [13]all [14]^that^ [15]^even^ all [16]are [17]long at a staye [18]must [19]must [20]which [21]were [22]were [23]long [24]then to [25]from which [26]must [27]But [28]his frends of the name of Douglas wold [29]perswaded [30]owen [31]other [32]press [33]rather forward [34]choose [35]adventure [36]were [37]counted [38]lawfull [39]^a^ [40]which [41]least [42]^in his waye^ all ^the^ [43][them] haiste [44]^the^ [45]^a^ [46]^as^ [47]^very^

callit guid[1] Friday, countit[2] ominous be[3] the common peoples opinion;[4] confirmed (as they accountit[5]) be[6] the vnhappie event theirof. They war[7] maried in the Kirk of Douglas. Some wryte this mariage to have bene purchest[8] and consumat be[9] the zoung[10] man him self, efter the deceise of his father. Howsoever these maters went, this was a[11] cause of dissention[12] amongs the Name of Douglas.

Anent[13] the actions of this Gros James we have no particulars recordit[14] in histories. In his brothers tyme also (the Earle of Wigtoun) nather[15] in his Cousins[16] tyme no mention[17] of him;[18] not now efter he comes to the Earldome[19] on ather[20] pairt; ather for the revenge of the slaughter of his Cousine[21] or ought els: belike as he hes[22] bene corpulent, so hes[23] his corpulencie causit[24] a dulnes (as commonlie it dois[25]). Some wryt[26] he was warden of al[27] the Marches, and his monument at Douglas callis[28] him sa[29], and a great justicier. Vthers wryt[30] that he was no il[31] man; he interteinit[32] no disorderit[33] wicked men, zit[34] he supprest them not sharplie ynough[35]; and therfor was suspect to the King, and hated by the people[36]. He died within twa zeirs[37], or not thrie (sayis[38] the Manuscript) efter the mariage of his sone, whilk[39] hes not bene lang in making we may gese[40], most equalie[41], to have bene not ful thrie zeirs[42], and so[43] to have died in the 1443 zeir[44] or 1444. He is **[387]** buried in Douglas, where he is callit[45] Magnus Princeps, and stylit[46] (amongs vther[47] his styls[48]) Lord of Liddisdail, and Jedward Forrest. We find in the Registers[49] he is callit[50] James Douglas of Balvennie, and takes now[51] infeftment of the Baronies of Avach, Edirdoun,

Ibidem.

Ibidem.

He dieth.

His burial

[1]Easter called good [2]counted [3]by [4]^and^ [5]accounted [6]by [7]were [8]purchesd *changed to* procured [9]consummat by [10]young [11]^speciall^ [12]^and diuision^ [13]For [14]recorded [15]neither [16]Cousens [17]^made^ [18]^Naye^ [19]^to have sided him self^ [20]either [21]Cousens [22]hath [23]hath [24]caused [25]doth [26]^that^ [27]all [28]styleth [29]so [30]others wryte [31]ill [32]interteined [33]disorderly [34]yet [35]enough [36][hated... people] misliked by many [37]two yeirs [38]sayeth [39]which [40]we may gesse hath not bene lang in making [41]probablie [42]full three yeirs [43]^he^ [44]yeir [45]called [46]styled [47]other [48]titles [49]^that^ [50]called [51]nowe

Brachtin, Botherny, Balvennie, Murchlach, Ratray, whilk war[1] geven him of before be vmquhil[2] Archbald Douglas Earle of Wigtoun his brother, the thrid pairt of Duffus, thrid pairt[3] Albasher, the lands of Evin[4]. 1426. His wyfe is stylit Domina Aueniae, Lady of Evindail. His Epitaphe there, is zit[5] to be seene thus:

His Elegie

Hic jacet magnus et potens Princeps Dominus Jacobus de Douglas, Comes de Douglas, Dominus Annandiae, et Gallovidiae Jedburgh Forrestiae, et Dominus de[6]
Magnus Wardanus Regni Scotiae versus Angliam etc. Qui obiit vicesimo quarto die mensis Martij, Anno Dominj millesimo quadringentesimo quadragesimo tertio.

And as[6] the Elogie of his wyfe.

Hic jacet Domina Beatrix de Sinklar, filia Domini Henrici Comitis de Orcadum, Domine de Sinkler, Comitissa de Douglas et Aveniae, Dominae Gallovidiae.

[388] And of their Childrein

Hae sunt proles (inquit) inter praedictos Dominum et Dominam generatae, Dominus Gulielmus primogenitus, et haeres praedicti Domini Jacobi successit ad totam haeriditatem praedictam. Jacobus secundo genitus, Magister de Douglas. Archibaldus tertio genitus Comes Murray. Hugo quarto genitus Comes Ormondiae: Joannes quinto genitus Dominus Balvennie. Henry sexto genitus. Margareta vxor de Albania, Janeta

[1]which were [2]by late [3]Aven [4]^of^ [5]yett [6]*a blank here; see note* [7]^to^

1 *vxor Dominini de Bigger, et Combernalde.*
Elizabetha de Douglas quarta filia erat.

[389] The Lyfe of[1] William slane in Sterling the 17 Lord and 8 Earle of Douglas, 5 Duk of Turain etc. and 7 of the name of William[2].

His Inclination

Buch.

Manuscr.

Ordereth his affairs

His greatnes

Vnto James succeidit[3] his sone William, as 17 Lord and 8 Earle of Douglas, 3 Earle of Wigtoun, Lord of Galloway, Bothuel and Annandail, 5 Duk of Turain, and Lord of Longeville[4] *etc.* A man of another mettel[5], and resembling more his Gudshire[6], and Cousin[7] germane slane in the Castle of Edinburgh then his father; and remembring more his diligence, then his fathers negligence;[8] more imitating it alwayes by al[9] meanes to interteine or augment the grandeur of the house; be[10] bands, be[11] freindshipes, be[12] dependances; reteining, renewing and eiking[13] them: and therefore some attributis to him self the marying of his Cousine Beatrix. Vpon his first coming to the Earle, his first care was to establish some certaine order for his affairs[14]. For whilk[15] effect he conveinit[16] his hail[17] freinds, and dependars at Dumfreis; choisis[18] his counsel; creatit[19] his officers for his rentes and casualities; and satlit[20] the order of his house; great (as hes[21] bene said before) and doubtles[22] not diminishit be[23] him, bot[24] rather augmentit[25] as the rentes war augmentit be[26] accesse of his fathers rentis to the old living, whilk[27] was ever growing from hand to hand, fra[28] S*ir* James **[390]** slane in Spaine continuallie, wha[29] had the lordshipe of Douglas, whilk hes[30] bene (questionles) a greatter[31] revenewe, according to[32] the ranke, we see he ever caryis, as second in the Kingdome. To it was eikit[33] efter, the Lordshipe of Galloway be[34] Archbald slane at

[1]^the 7.^ [2][the17… William] etc [3]succeided [4]Longueville [5]metell [6]Grandfather [7]Cousen [8]^and^ [9]^and^ by all [10]by [11]by [12]by [13]encreasing [14]effairs [15]which [16]conveined [17]wholl [18]chooseth [19]counsell; created *changed to* createth [20]setleth [21]hath [22]doubtled *changed to* doutles [23]diminished by [24]but [25]augmented [26]were augmented by [27]which [28]from [29]continuallie ^that was^ slane in Spaine who [30]which hath [31]great [32]in regard of [33]eiked [34]by

Halydonhil; be[1] Archbald Grim the first Earle Williams second sone, the Lordshipe of Bothwel; be[2] Archbald Tyneman[3] the Ducherie[4] of Turain and Lordshipe of Longeville; Annandail, and the Earldome of Wigtoun be[5] his lait vncle; and now the Lordshipe of Abercorne be[6] his father. His dependance and following may be judgit be[7] these his Dominions[8]; And for his vther[9] freindshipe, there was dyvers houses of the Douglas[10]; as the Earle of Angus; wha[11] was not fare[12] comed of[13] the house; for William Gudshire[14] to the Earle of Angus, was father to Archbald Grim this Earle of Douglas Grandshire[15]; the Earle of Mortoun and Lord of Dalkeithe, was comed af[16] long before, and was allyit[17] of new; had[18] maryed the Earls eldest sister Margaret. Dumlanrige was in vogue we see in Archbald Tynmans[19] tyme; remarkit[20] at the burning of Roxburgh. Be[21] his vther[22] sisters he had the Lord Aubigny Stewart, and[23] Lord Fleming of Combernalde; be[24] his mother, the Earle of Orknay; be[25] his wyfe Beatrix, the house of Crafurde, she being a sister doughter[26]; besyds [**391**] the old freindshipe that was ever betwixt them. And this by the diligent reader may be seine in histories, whereof more may be gathered be the[27] more exquisite diligence, and that whereof mention can not be found in histories (whilk[28] is greatter not the lesse[29] I[30] geve[31] a short view of it). Alwyse thus inrichit[32], thus waittit[33] on, thus servit[34], thus vnderproped[35], and susteined be[36] moyen, freindshipe, and dependance, allya[37] and kin apparentlie invincible, at leist not[38] to be matchit be[39] anie subject in Scotland.[40]

Dumlanrige.

Here is the malheure; the principal[41] of his awin[42]

---

[1]Halydonhill; by [2]Bothwell; by [3][Tyneman] the 3. [4]Duchie [5]by the 4. Archbald [6]by [7]judged by [8]Lordships and Estates [9]other [10]Douglasses [11]who [12]farr [13]off [14]Grandfather [15]Grandfather [16]aff [17]allyed [18]as hauing [19]the 1 Duke of Turains [20]^and^ remarked [21]By [22]other [23]^the^ [24]by [25]by [26]^thereof^ [27]by a [28]which [29][not the lesse] though [30]^do^ [31]^but^ [32]inriched [33]waitted [34]served [35]vnderpropped [36]by [37]allyance [38]kinsmen of such power and greatnes as he was not [39]matchable by [40]But [41]principalls [42]owne

Angus and Morton devydit from him.

name (the house of Angus and Morton) assistit[1] him not; bot devydit[2] themselves from him; and ather war[3] not freinds, or perhaps[4] vnfreinds, as wil appeir[5] heirefter. What was the occasion, is not directlie mentioned: some think[6] the miscontentement of his mariage with his Cousine; whether they countit[7] it vnlawful[8], or wald[9] some of them selves[10] have had her, which is most certaine[11]; or if[12] kinred with the King (wha became indeid (but was[13] not zit) his pairtie[14]), or if emulation of his greatnes[15] a hinder to their growth, by the counsel[16] of Bishope Kennedie (the Earle of Angus[17] half brother;) or whatever[18] occasion. But[19] so it fallis out oft[20] where a decay is to come vpon a house, it[21] devydes fra[22] the self. Zit[23] was that, at this tyme bot[24] ane insensible point; **[392]** his awen[25] greatnes was sik[26] as could skarse suffer[27] to find the losse; standing, as it war[28], not be[29] anie freindshipe, bot be his awen verie greatnes[30]. At his first entrie to the Earldome, he enterit[31] (as hereditarie) to the Enemitie of the two gyders for the tyme

His Enemitie with the Governour and Chanceller.

(Livingstoun and Chrichtoun;) with whome the hatred begane in his avuncles[32] tyme,[33] traterouslie, and cruellie exercisit be[34] them on his Cousins[35]; continued coldlie in his fathers,[36] is now quicklie revyvit be[37] him self in his tyme[38]. They wald[39] lay the blame of whatever[40] harmes happenit[41] in the Contrie vpon this Enimitie; not in the borders onlie, where he reulit[42], or might reule indeid; bot[43] in the Hielands. Not sa meikle[44] as Johne Gorme of Athol, wha faught[45] with the Lord Ruthven, and wald[46] have taine a theife fra[47] him, whom he as Sheriff had

[1]assisted [2]but divyded [3]either ^they^ were [4]became [5]will appeire [6]^it was^ [7]counted [8]vnlawfull [9][wald] [10]^wold^ [11]likely [12]^it was theire^ [13]who was indeed, (though [14]^as^ yett induced to think hardlie of him [15]^was thought to be^ [16]counsell [17]^his^ [18]whatsoever ^other [19]^there was^. But [20]falleth often out [21]^first^ [22]from [23]Yett [24]but [25]owen [26]such [27]^him^ [28]were [29]by [30]but meerly of himself [31]entered [32]wncles [33]^and was therefter^ [34]exercised *changed to* executed by [35]Cousens [36]^and^ [37]quickened ^and^ revived by [38][in... tyme] [39]wold [40]whatsoever [41]happened [42]reuled [43]indeed; but [44]so much [45]who faught [46]wold [47]from

apprehendit[1], was defait, and had 30. of his men slane; bot[2] they wald[3] insinuat[4] the[5] Douglas had a hand in it, at Leist was[6] thought sa: bot[7] al is weil that they say, it was bot[8] thought sa[9]: And thogh it had bene said sa to be[10] his Enemies, they had done him now[11] wrong, and more treacherouslie delth[12] with him[13] then to make sik[14] a report. For me, it soundes not in my eares, that it had so long a foote; and that Johne Gorme could not do sik[15] a thing without the Earle of Douglas; or that the Earle wald[16] medle with sik[17] a mater. **[393]** This indeid, I think, in his awen[18] bounds, he wald[19] let nane[20] acknawledge the Governours, whilk[21] was also his avncles[22] course (as we hard, since[23] he was to be answerable for them him self.) It was his fathers also (thogh more coldlie according to his Natural[24]) as may be gathered of that, where[25] is said: He repressit[26] not theivis, thogh he also interteinit[27] them not. Whilk[28] is as meikle as[29] to say[30] he was not the occasion of their thift; bot[31] being no magistrate him self, and vthers[32] having taine the governement on[33] them, he wald[34] let them beare the weight of their owne charge in executing thereof; the rather that having slane his Cousins[35] so wrongouslie, he could not with credit imploy him self to ease them with anie help. He did them no harme; he could not with honour do them gude[36]; so he lets them alone, doing them nather il nor good; then the whilk[37] (I wait[38] not) what[39] he could do lesse; and where Enimitie was, how it could be more modestlie vsit[40], except they wald[41] have had him efter sik[42] a fact[43] creiping[44] vnder their feit (as we say;) whilk[45] the meanest men wil[46] not do, efter the smalest iniurie. Zit[47] thogh there be no iniure, except they[48] have

Buch. *Quamuis non aleret tamen non satis acriter reprimeret.*

---

[1]apprehended ^but^ [2][bot *changed to* but] [3]wold [4]^that^ [5]^Earl of^ [6]least they wold have it to be [7]so: but [8]but [9]so [10]so too by [11][now] more [12]dealt [13]^and his^ [14]such [15]such [16]wold [17]such [18]owne [19]wold [20]none [21]which [22]wncle [23] ^haue^ heard, sithe [24]Naturall ^disposition^ [25]^it^ [26]repressed [27]interteined [28]which [29][meikle as] much [30]^as^ [31]but [32]others [33]vpon [34]wold [35]Cousens [36]good [37][then the] which [38]wote [39]how [40]vsed [41]wold [42]such [43]^to goe^ [44]creeping [45]which [46]will [47]yett [48]Men

some benefite, they wil[1] suffer men[2] to do their owne pairts, and not help them, onles[3] they have[4] interest;[5] some charge theirof, or some benefite thereby. It is true, **[394]** he onlie might do that service, and there was no sufficiencie in them that had the charge. Nather was he oblishit[6] to supplie[7] their insufficiencie, and why sould they have taine it on them? or why sould the Estates (if it was the Estates[8], and not a faction) have laid it on them, that had not abilitie to discharge it? This was not wyslie done, and it is the verie point of the errour in the Estaits (so callit[9]) and the ground of al[10] inconvenients that fel[11] out; sence they choose men not able to discharge the office; and they that war[12] able,[13] lets them do it their[14] alane; and withal[15], perhaps, disdains their preferrement, as without merite: for we see no merite be[16] true vertue. thereon rysis[17] discontents[18], then grudgis, then Crosses, then blames and reproches in words and deids; growing at last to[19] oppen Enimitie: of sik[20] importance is it to make choise of imployment[21], and sik[22] wysdome is requisit in the Electors (be it „ Estate, be it Prince) not to follow affection, bot[23] „ to wey worth and abilitie rightlie; and[24] imploy „ according therto; whilk[25] if it be not done, caryis „ infinit inconvenients, and hes[26] bene the trouble „ of manie Estates zea the ruine[27]; and most[28] neides „ be sa[29]. Happie Estate! Happie Prince! Zea[30] „ happie man wha[31] soever, that most[32] imploy „ vthers[33] (as wha most[34] not!) that imployes be[35] „ reason, and not be[36] his affection, or hes[37] his „ affections reuled **[395]** be reason; whilk[38] if he do „ not,[39] caryis disgrace to the imployer, disdane to „ the imployed;[40] contempt of both, to burst out

The errour of the state

---

[1]will [2]others [3]vnles [4]^thereat^ [5]^either^ [6]oblished [7]supplee [8]^as I think it was not^ [9]called [10]all ^the^ [11]fell [12]were [13][and] *adopted* [14][their] [15]withall [16]^in them^ by [17]arysis [18]arysis descontents [19]^an^ [20]such [21]^men for^ imployments [22]such [23]but [24]^to^ [25]which [26]hath [27]yea ^euen^ the ruine of manie Estates [28]^it^ must [29]so [30]Yea [31]whoe [32]must ^needs^ [33]others [34]who must [35]by [36]by [37]hath [38]which [39]^it^ [40]^and makes^

with the occasion; whilk[1] can not be hinderit[2] „ long, thogh it lurke for a tyme. It may be the Earle „ of Douglas hes proceidit[3] further nor[4] his father in the contempt of the iustice bearers; It may be, he hes[5] borne more with the border men, and[6] lesse sharpe in repressing of them (for his father repressit[7] them, thogh not sharple ynough)[8] having greatter intention to employ them, as he wha[9] was more sensible of the wronges done[10] his Cousins, and had a greatter eye to the revenge of it; and therefore was the lother to control thir[11] men of service, further then[12] verie necessitie of his place made crave of them[13]; where of the reule (in the eyes of the people) was, what ever he might do, to save al[14] men fra[15] that miserie; in his owne eyes it hes[16] bene to protect his owne freinds and dependars; and for[17] his adversaries (perhaps)[18] reioyce at their smarte, if not procure it; for newtrals leive[19] it to the Magistrat to redresse[20], not perceiving that be this[21] meane he[22] more hurt his Contrie then his Enemies; more his awen[23] credit, then their estimation; and therefor[24] tynt more therby, be incurring the[25] obloquie; and offending of[26] the harts of the people[27], and honest men[28] then he gained be[29] hurt of his adversaries, or[30] favours of broken men. Nothing is **[396]** more populare; zea[31] nothing is more profitable then iustice, sayes al[32] wryters; not to meane and privat men onlie, wha incurreth[33] danger of law be[34] iniustice; bot[35] even to great men, even to Princes; whilk[36] if they incure no danger of law (as plaicet[37] with out the reache of it); zit[38] tyne they, the most profitable instrument of al[39] their actions (whilk[40] they must neids work by, and can not work without[41]) the harts of men. It fears me manie think it ynough, if they have their hands, if

Not rightlie if he fosterit or toleratit thift

Iniustice ever and to al Estate vnprofitable

[1]which [2]hindered *changed to* avoided [3]hath proceided [4]then [5]hath [6]^been^ [7]repressed [8]hee [9]who [10]^to^ [11]controlle these [12]^the^ [13]did require of their hands [14]all [15]from [16]hath [17]tuching [18]^to^ [19]^as^ newtrall ^he doth^ leave [20]^what is amiss^ [21]by that [22]^doth^ [23]owen [24]^he^ [25]by giving some ground to their [26][of] [27]peeple [28][and… men] [29]by ^the^ [30]^by the^ [31]yea [32]saye all [33]who incurre [34]by [35]but [36]which [37]plaiced [38]yet [39]all [40]which [41]^it^

they have mens bodies at Command: bot[1] let no man think he can have their bodies, if they have not their harts; Nather the hart, if he have it not indeid[2] in heigh[3] measour of affection; No pairt of affection; no action of the bodie to anie importance; a slake affection, a slake action doubtles, as it hes[4] ever proven that in effect[5] policie is that[6] cheif obiect of the[7] work of it[8], the affections of men;[9] not to deceive them, or[10] force them: for nather of theis can work weil[11] and long. Nather[12] is it sufficient, that a man see not a present ewil[13]; as a Prince a present insurrection; a great man, a present losse of his folowers, and favourers; whilk[14] comes to passe some tymes, bot[15] not aye[16]; oftentymes[17] is a Canker working peice and peice insensiblie, from degrie to degrie vpon the affections, til[18] it have consumate the work of disgrace of the pairtie it seasis on, and windit[19] ther favours out of the harts of men; as commonlie mens actions **[397]** that procuris[20] it, are sik lyke[21], not al[22] at ane[23] instant, or[24] one tyme, bot ane[25] vngratious fact efter ane vther[26]; and a vther[27] agane[28] and so furth[29]. This therefor the more diligentlie is to be taine head of, and eshewit[30] in the beginning; or if anie errour escape, to be taine vp, and recompensit be[31] amandement; or some vther gratful[32] fact, importing as meikle[33] favour, as the errour did disdaine favour[34]; Nather[35] suffer the affections of men to be eaten vp at vnawares, or cuiled[36], and sufferit[37] to go languishing and decaying, til it[38] be quyte away[39]. This we may see here, hes[40] not bene advertit be[41] these of this house of Douglas, whilk[42] before war[43] the most esteimit[44], the best beluvit[45] and favourit[46]

---

[1]but [2]indeed [3][heigh] some [4]hath [5]in the best [6][is that] the [7][of the] and [8]^is^ [9]^and^ [10]nor [11]weill [12]Neither [13]evill [14]which ^yett^ [15]but [16]ever [17]^it^ [18]till [19]wynded [20]procures [21]in that sorte [22]all [23]an [24]^at^ [25]but one [26]other [27]an other [28]^vpon the neck off that^ [29]foorth [30]eschewed [31]recompensed by [32]other gratfull [33]much [34][favour] [35]^to^ [36]cooled [37]suffered [38]till they [39]gone [40]hath [41]adverted by [42]which [43]were [44]esteimed [45]beloved [46]favoured

vniversalie, almost be[1] the hail[2] contrie; bot[3] now be[4] this disdaine nurishit agans[5] the Governours whils[6] they wald trouble them, or let their inhabilitie to governe be seine, and for that effect ather[7] bare with theivis or sufferit[8] them at leist (thogh it may weil[9] be they did not hurde them, nor allow them) ar[10] not aware that be these[11] meanes they suffer a il[12] opinion of them selves to creipe in mens mynds; and that luve[13] of the people to diminish peice and peice for the space now of thrie[14] or four mens lyves; and where as they war[15] wont with their heritage to succeid to a general[16] favour of the people[17]; Now be[18] **[398]** the contrair they succeid to a grudge and il opinion, and so ane vniversal[19] disfavour, whilk at last it hes[20] wroght away al that wonted love, and turned al contrariwise into hatred; whilk farderit[21] greatlie the plots of their Enemies agans them, and made that their greatnes odious, that was accoustomit[22] to be favoured[23]. It is most true, that the men agains[24] whom he[25] delt, had vsit[26] no gude[27] meanes; abusit[28] their office; abusit[29] their Contrie, and the name of the King and Commonweil[30] to their awen particulars; zit[31] sould not il[32] meanes be vsit,[33] nay not aganes il[34] men; and the bare name of authoritie is of weight[35] in the eyes of men; as the name of thift[36] odious; from anie[37] countenancing whereof[38] Noble men sould be far[39], as also fra[40] seeming to rise aganis[41] any[42] authoritie, thogh authoritie[43] be bot[44] even in meane mens hands, as these war[45]; cheiflie[46] where they[47] made nothing[48] appeare bot[49]

---

[1]by [2]wholle [3]Bot [4]by [5]nurished aganst [6][whils… accoustomit to be favoured] *see notes for replacement; changes to the scored out passage will be noted individually.* [7]either [8]suffered [9]well [10]^they^ are [11]by those [12]an ill [13]love [14]three [15]were [16]generall [17]peeple [18]by [19]vniversall [20]hath [21]which furthered [22]woont [23]congratulated [24]against [25]this man [26]vsed [27]gcode [28]abused [29]abused [30]Commonwealth [31]owen particular ^ends^ yett [32]sinister [33]vsed [34]aganes ill [35]^enough^ [36]^or oppression is^ [37]the least [38]^I wish that all^ [39]very farr [40]from [41]against [42]^manner of^ [43]the same [44]but [45]^men^ were [46][cheiflie… broken men. Zit] *changes will be noted individually* [47]^who^ [48]^to^ [49]but

there[1] particular; and that blottit[2] with the[3] enormities of broken men. Zit[4] what sal[5] we geve vnto a[6] just anger[7]? What vnto the tyme? What vnto the zouth[8]? al[9] these plaids[10] pardon (if not approbation;) the rather[11] that he takes vp him self fra[12] that sort of doing, so soone as he can gete ane[13] just king, to whom he could have accesse, and to whom he could zeild[14] with his honour save[15]. Nather was it long [**399**] or[16] then.

He takith vp himself

The nixt zeir[17] efter[18] anno 1444 the King takes the governement on him self directlie; thether immediatlie the Earle of Douglas concludes to adresse him self, and be al gud[19] meanes to obteine his favour, to satisfie the people[20], to satisfie al[21] men that war offendit[22] and fullie[23] change his maners of[24] that course he had before folowit[25]. Certainlie repentance is worth misdeid. And it may be seine the force of Enimitie hes[26] throwen him to[27] these faults, whilk so soone as he can[28], he laide af. And comming with a great Companie to Sterling, deals[29] with the King be[30] intercession of sik[31] as war[32] about him; and finding he was appaisit, gois[33] and puts him self, and his Estate at[34] his Princes wil[35]; pairtlie purging the crymes[36] of his lyfe past, pairtlie ingenuouslie confessing them. What ever Estate he sould have fra[37] that furth, he sould[38] esteme it of the Kings clemencie,[39] not attribute it to his owne[40] innocencie; that if the King wald[41] suffer him self to be satisfiet be gud[42] offices, he sould[43] endevore not to be overcome by any in fidelitie, observance, diligence, and gud wil[44] towards him; that in repressing and punishing of theives[45] (whose facts his Enemies laid over vpon him) there sould no man be more [**400**] sharpe, nor more diligent; that he was comed of that house whilk[46] was

Cometh to the King

[1]^owne^ [2]blotted [3]^a nomber of^ [4]Yett *changed to* But [5]sall [6]the [7]^of this Earle^ [8]his youth [9]all [10]pleads [11]^in^ [12]from [13]gett a [14]yeeld [15]safe [16]ere [17]yeir [18]^in^ [19]by all good [20]peeple [21]all [22]were offended [23]^to^ [24]in [25]folowed [26]hath [27]into [28]errors, which he can be, so soone [29]deales [30]by [31]such [32]were [33]appeised, goeth [34]in [35]will [36]errors [37]from [38]would [39]^and^ [40]owne [41]wold [42]satisfied by gud [43]would [44]good will [45]theeves [46]which

growen vp, not be[1] doing[2] iniuries to the weaker, bot be[3] defending the weaker and Common people of Scotland be[4] armes. Certanelie a true conclusion, and not denyable be[5] his greatest Enemies. Bot[6] I thought gud[7] to set al[8] downe, as it is conceivit[9]: for if[10] fault[11] was, or no fault was[12], his submission was great; and his repentance sufficient to purge whatsoever. Sik[13] is his respect to his due[14] Prince, and sik[15] the force of authoritie placed in the awner[16] theirof! And sik[17] was also the force of the truthe in his speiche[18], that the King vnderstanding[19] it was true in his predecessors; and hoping it sould be true in him self; moved also with the secreit commendation of his Courteours, not onlie passit[20] by, and forgave what ever was amise[21] in his lyfe past; bot[22] also receivit[23] him in his most inward familiaritie, and[24] communicate to[25] him the secreits of his counsels. Nather was the Earle vnworthie theirof on his awen[26] pairt, but so weil behavit[27] him self, that within a short tyme he acquyrit[28] the favour of the King be[29] obedience; of his Courteours and servands be[30] liberalitie; of al[31] men be[32] gentilnes, courtisie and modestie; and put the people in[33] hope to prove a meik[34] and sober myndit[35] man. The wyser sorte (sayes[36] our wryters) Hol. Boe. **[401]** doubting whether so suddane a change sould turne. Whilk[37] for al[38] that, why sould we think a change? or if a change, very casual, very apparand[39], and nothing to be wondered at; for is not this it in effect? He had bene outward to base men, why not zeild[40] to his King? He had miskend the shadow of authoritie in them; why not acknawledge and reverence the beames of it in his Prince? He had bene thrawart[41] to his Enemies; why not gentle to his freinds? he had sought to

---

[1]by [2]^of^ [3]but by [4]^from iniuries^ by [5]by [6]But [7]good [8]sett all [9]conceaved [10]^a^ [11]^ther^ [12][was] [13]it, whatsoever it was; Such [14]Soverane [15]such [16]owner [17]such [18]speache [19]knowing [20]passed [21]amisse [22]but [23]received [24]^did^ [25]with [26][awen] [27]behaved [28]acquyred [29]by [30]by [31]all [32]by [33]^pregnant^ [34]meike [35]mynded [36]saye [37]Which [38]all [39]apparant [40]yeild [41]froward

smarte them, that wronged him; why not cherise them that benefits him ? He keipt[1] warre with them, that warred on him; why not freindshipe with them, that dealth[2] freindlie with him ? Certainlie thir[3] are not changes nather[4] of nature, nor of maners; bot commonlie we see are in one and the same natural[5], and proceids from one and the same cause (greatnes of courage, and regarde of due honour); the most dispyser of basnes, the greatter reverence of due[6] greatnes; the greattest repyner at throwing[7], the gentlist[8] dealer in courtese vsing[9]: the hardest Enemie, the fectfullest[10] and surest freind. So that I must suspect thir[11] wyse mens wisedome, that so farre miskend[12] true courage, and countit it[13] a change, whilk[14] was[15] a continuation of[16] maners. Two[17] ar designit[18] to have taine fray[19] at the mater whais conscience war[20] giltie of what they had deservit[21]; Alexander **[402]** Livingstoun, and William Chrichtoun, not for the change of his maners, bot[22] for the change of his credit. They had traterouslie slane thrie[23] innocent[24] men, his twa Cousins[25], and Malcolme Fleminge; they had keipit[26] him self bake from the Prince, and his Prince fra[27] him; and war[28] sorie that ever they sould meit[29] in freindlie sorte; they wald[30] have bene glaid to have blowen the bellies[31] of dissention;[32] iritate the one, and misinformit[33] the vther;[34] made their owne querrel[35] the Kings, and so have causit[36] the King and Contrie[37] esteme of it. They war disapoyntit[38] of that, and the Douglas had accesse to informe the King of their misdemanour[39] in their office[40]; and to move him to cognosce[41] of it[42]: they knew he wald[43] remember the wrong done[44] his Cousins: they knew how vnable they war[45] to geve

---

[1]keiped [2]deale [3]these [4]neither [5]naturell [6]rightfull [7]compelling [8]gentlest [9]vsage [10]feckfullest [11]these [12]mistooke his [13]counted that [14]which [15]^but^ [16]^his innate^ [17]^men^ [18]designed [19]fraye [20]whois consciences were [21]deserved [22]but [23]three [24]^noble^ [25]two Cousens [26]keiped [27]from [28]were [29]meete [30]wold [31]bellowes [32]^to^ [33]misinformed *changed to* misinforme [34]other; ^to haue^ [35]querrell [36]caused [37]^to^ [38]were disapoynted [39]misdemeanour [40]offices [41]to judge [42]^rightly^ [43]wold [44]^to^ [45]were

due answer for manie their facts, and therefor retirit[1] them selves from Court: The Livingstoun til[2] his awen house; the Chrichtoun to the Castle of Edinburgh, whilk[3] he had stil[4] in keeping. Nather[5] was the Earle of[6] Douglas negligent in this occasion that he had to seik iustice be[7] law; and be[8] justice[9] be avengit[10] on his Enemies, for the wrong done be[11] them agans[12] law; bot[13] diligentlie informit[14] the King of their misbehaviours in their office[15]; how they had abusit[16] him, abusit[17] his rents from publike to their awen[18] privat vses; and movit[19] him to cal[20] them to ane accompt **[403]** hereof[21]. Where vpon being sommond to ane[22] certane day, they durst not compeir; Bot[23] to set a faire face on the matter, sent their procurators[24], or be[25] letters answerit[26] they war readie to geve ane accompt of their governement;[27] had bene verie careful of the weil[28] of the King and Contrie;[29] desyrit nothing sa meikle[30], as to give ane accompt thereof, before equal judges; bot[31] for the present, when the mynds of men war preoccupiet[32] with favour of their Enemies; and al[33] accesse closit[34] with armet[35] men, the King behovit[36] to appardone them; that they did eshew not[37] to come in[38] judgement; but[39] to come in the danger of their deidlie enemies, and[40] keip their lyves aforehand to[41] better tymes, when the Captane of theivis being removit[42] from the Kings syde (whilk[43] they had oftymes done before) they sould approve their innocencie to the King, and al[44] honest men. These reproches and brags touchit and war meanit of[45] the Earle of Douglas: him it was they callit[46] Captane of Theives because of the border men, of whom manie war[47] his folowers; that they removit[48] him oft

---

[1]retired [2]to [3]which [4]still [5]Neither [6]^Earle of^ *in original script; adopted* [7]by [8]by [9]^to^ [10]avenged [11]by [12]against ^the^ [13]but [14]informed [15]^severall^ offices [16]abused [17]abused [18]owen [19]moved [20]call [21]thereof [22]a [23]but [24]Proxies [25]by [26]answered ^that^ [27]^that they^ [28]weile [29]^and^ desyred [30]soe much [31]but [32]were preoccupied [33]all [34]closed [35]armed [36]behoved [37]not eschew [38]into [39]but [40]^took that course to^ [41]till [42]removed [43]which [44]all [45][and... of] not only glaunced at, but were ^directly^ meantt by [46]called ^the^ [47]were [48]removed

Manuscr.

before from the Kings syde, was ydle bosting[1]: he had absteinit[2] to come to the King, sa lang as he was in their[3] custodie; so long as he was in the Castle of Edinburgh, where they might have murderit[4] him, as they did his Cousins[5]; **[404]** That he was their Enemie, he denyit[6] not, and had iust cause; bot[7] to take that excuse from them, he assurit[8] them, he sould not persue them anie wayes bot[9] by order of[10] Law, and offerit[11] for that effect to go af[12] Court, til they war at Court[13] in saiftie. And to meite their reproche (of Captane of Theives) and their brags of their just administration of their offices, he was readie to prove them[14] theives;[15] that they had stowen[16] the kings revenues, and distribute[17] it to their freinds, and[18] their[19] particular vses; and that they had traterouslie aganes[20] justice murderit[21] his Cousins[22]; where of he besought the King for justice. And there vpon ane new charge was geven out, another day appointed to them to compeir on; whilk[23] being also come, and they not compeiring, war denuncit[24] rebels,

Denuncit Rebels

Their guds intromettit with.

and put to the horne in a Convention halden at Stirling, the fourt of November; and their guds[25] and geir[26] confiscate; Therefter Johne Foster of Corstorfine a dependar of the Earle of Douglas is sent with a power of men to intromet[27] therewith; wha[28] having receivit[29] their houses, pairt[30] he razit, pairt[31] he mannes with new forces and provision; and so no man resisting he retiris[32] him self with a great spuilzie. He was skarse retirit[33], when the Chrichtoun[34] having conveinit his freinds and dependars in a[35] host so suddenlie, that none wald[36] have thought[37], furrowed[38] the lands **[405]** of Corstorfine, with the lands of Strabrok,

---

[1]^which they were never able to do^ [2]^indeed in his owne iudgement^ absteined [3]his enemyes [4]murdered [5]Cousens [6]denyed [7]^so to be^; but [8]assured [9]but [10][justice] *scored out on second thoughts* [11]offered [12]from [13][war *changed to* were at Court] should come vnto it [14]^selves to be the^ [15]^in^ [16]stollen [17]distributed [18]^to^ [19]^owne^ [20]aganst [21]murdered [22]Cousens [23]which [24]^they^ were denunced [25]goods [26]moveables [27]intromett [28]Who [29]received [30]some [31]razed, some [32]retires [33]retired [34]Chrightoun [35]an [36]wold [37]^it^ [38]forrowed

They spuile the Earle of Douglas lands

Abercorne and Blaknes; And among the rest of the guds, whilk[1] he spoylit, draiwe[2] away a stoode[3] of meirs[4], that the Earle of Douglas had brought from Flanders, and keipit[5] in Abercorne; doing greatter domage then he had receivit; whilk[6] may seeme strange to anie man; Nather dois[7] our histories sufficientlie explicate it, nather[8] where he gate thir[9] forces, or[10] where he put thir guds[11]: They signifie[12] that he was assistit[13] quyetlie be[14] James Kennedie Bishope of St Androis; be George[15] Douglas Earle of Angus; and Johne[16] Earle of Morton. The Earle of Angus was the Kings Cousin[17] germane, borne of his fathers sister, and be[18] her half brother to the Bishope: The Earle of Morton had maried the Kings sister; but of these, the Bishope lay[19] bezond Forthe, and the Earle of Angus farther, bezond Tay[20], that it seimes hardlie[21] to conceave ather[22] how they could have suddanlie conveinit[23] folkes; or that they could convein manie except sik[24] as the Earle of Angus had in the southsyde of Forthe, as Liddisdail, Jedward Forrest, and Bonkle: lykwyse the Earle of Mortons lande, and freindshipe was most pairt on the same syde of Fourthe[25] to give assistance aganes[26] the Earle of Douglas. Bot[27] how ever he[28] did it, he[29] did it aganes[30] order, aganes[31] **[406]** authoritie, and aganes[32] lawes; and if it had bene done by the Erle of Douglas,[33] wald[34] have bene callit[35] rebellion aganes[36] the King, thift[37], oppression, presumption, arrogancie, insolencie; as we[38] hard before in the persones of[39] the Governours onlie, and wil perhaps be heirefter[40]. And if men wil alledge[41] the King was gydit[42] by the Earle[43] Douglases counsel[44], and his name vsit[45] to a

[1]goods which [2]spoyled, drave [3]race [4]meers [5]keiptt [6]received; which [7]Neither doth [8][nather *changed to* nether] ^Never mentioning^ neither [9]gott these [10]nor [11]putt these goods [12]intimate [13]assisted [14]by [15]by James [16][Johne] the [17]Cousen [18]by [19]laye [20]further bezond Taye [21]hard [22]conceive either [23]conveined theire [24]such [25]Foorthe [26]aganst [27]But [28]they [29][he] apperantly it was not openly, and the Chrighton [30]aganst [31]aganest [32]aganst ^the^ [33]^it^ [34]^assuredly^ [35]called [36]against [37]theft [38]^have^ [39][in the… of] the like was saide by [40][onlie… heirefter] and their faction [41]^that^ [42]gyded [43]^of^ [44]counsell [45]vsed

particular onlie; tel (I pray them) was[1] anie thing more formallie done nor[2] this aganes[3] the Chrichtoun[4]⸮ and if the Earle of Douglas[5] particular was in it, what then⸮ how manie iustices are vther[6] wayes done, with out instigations of privat men⸮ without the mixture of their cause⸮ without their particular[7] sute and particular insisting⸮ and if it be lawful to[8] anie, to seik iustice for his particulars, the Earle of Douglas particulars war sik[9], as became him verie weil to insist[10]; the wrong so manifest, the murther so vyle, and traterous; let be inique and iniust. And if that whilk[11] is done aganes[12] law, sal[13] not be comptit[14] a wrong, nor to touche the King, because pairties hes[15] their particulars in that law, none or few things sal[16] be comptit[17] done aganes[18] the law or King, with whom the[19] particular is[20] ever joynit[21]. And this same hes[22] bene, and wil[23] be the Douglas case. this therefor can[24] be comptit no[25] innocencie;[26] no les then[27] violence, **[407]** and (being with a conveinit power) most[28] be oppen rebellion, and presumption aganes[29] the Earle[30] clad with justice and laws; and aganes[31] the King[32] protector, and doer[33] of justice. No mervel[34] then if the Earle of Douglas was offendit[35] herewith, both for his owne cause, whom the harme touchit[36]; and for the Kings, whom the[37] contempt touchit[38]; And that therefor[39] he seikis to be avengit[40] theirof. Bot[41] there was a dyverse forme to be vsit[42], according to the dyvers actors, of the whilk[43] we sie[44] there are twa[45] sorts; the one (the Chrichtoun[46] and Livingstoun) oppen Enemies, oppen actors; them selves obnoxious to the law; aganes him[47] the law wil[48] strike; and so he dois beseige him[49] in the

[1]^there ever^ [2]then [3]aganst [4]Chrightoun [5]^his^ [6]other [7]particulare [8][do] *adopted* [9]such [10]^in^ [11]which [12]aganst [13]sall [14]compted [15]have [16]sall [17]compted ^to be^ [18]aganst [19]some [20]^not^ [21]joyned [22]hath [23]will [24]^not^ [25]compted [no] [26]^yea^ [27]^open^ [28][conveinit power] power and convocation of the Kings lieges) must [29]aganst [30]^as^ [31]aganst [32]^as^ [33]patron [34]mervell [35]offended [36]touched ^so neere^ [37][whom the] so manifest [38][touchit] [39]therefore [40]avenged [41]But [42]vsed [43]which [44]see [45]two [46]Chrightoun [47]aganst them [48]lawe will [49][dois *changed to* doth… him] beseeges first the Chrighton

Castle of Edinburgh, and no question had spoyld him before of what some[1] ever was without it. The vthers war[2] not oppen actors them selves, but[3] quyet stirers[4] vp[5] and assisters of the vther[6]; and amongs them the Bishope[7] was principal mover; aganes[8] him the law could not weil[9] be had, he most[10] be mete[11] in his awne[12] forme: he had done besyds[13] law, he must be met besyds[14] law: he had done disawouedlie[15], he must be met[16] (as it war) disavowedlie[17]. The Earle therefor wrytes to the Earle of Crafurde, wha[18] with Alex*ande*r Ogilvie of Innerwharitie gatherit[19] a great host, enterit in[20] Fyfe, and without resistance spoylit[21] the Bishops lands in Fyfe; whether because **[408]** they could not get[22] him self, or having more mynd of[23] the pray, nor[24] the cause. The Bishope vsing his wapons[25], curses them; bot[26] they tuike[27] no accompt of it. Not the les short[28] efter a difference falling out betwixt the Earls sone[29] (Maister of Crafurde) and the Ogilvies for the bailzerie[30] of Arbrothe, whilk[31] the Monkes had geven from the Maister to the Laird of Innerwharitie; and[32] being gathered on both sydes, the Ogilvies assistit be[33] the Earle of Huntlie, Crafurde be[34] the Earle of Douglas (wha[35] had sent him <u>100</u> speirs out of Cliddisdail[36]) as the Earle of Crafurde having gotten advertisment, was about to compose the matter, and leaning to the opinion of his authoritie with both the parties, enterit[37] betwixt the two Enemies without armour, and having stayed his sones companie, was going towards the Ogilvies to have stayet[38] them also, he was striken[39] in the face with ane speir, and slane be ane[40] of them, not knawing[41] what he was, nor what was his intent. Where vpon the battels ioyning the victorie

Earle of Crafurde aganes Bishope Kennedie

Hol. 1444.

Earle Crafurde slane

[1]so [2]others were [3]bot [4]stirrers [5]^abbetters^ [6][the vther] his ennemyes [7]Bishop ^of St Androwes^ [8]^the^ principall devyser; aganst [9]weile [10]must [11]mett ^with^ [12]owne [13]^the^ [14]mett besydes ^the^ [15]disadvouedlie [16]mett ^with^ [17]were disadvowedlie [18]who [19]gathered [20]entered into [21]spoyled [22]gett [23]to [24]then [25]weapons [26]but [27]tooke [28]shortly [29](^the^ [30]bailyerie *changed to* baillerie [31]which [32]they [33]assisted by [34]by [35]who [36]Cliddesdail [37]entered [38]stayed [39]stroken [40]by one [41]knowing

was on the Maister of Crafurds syde (specialie be[1] the Cliddisdail[2] men)[3] being 500 of the Ogilvies syde slane, Alex*ande*r Ogilvie taken, and the Earle of Huntlie horsit[4] and escapit[5]. This is the Earle of Crafurde, of whom mention wil[6] be heirefter, callit[7] commonlie Earle Bairdye[8], with whom the Earle of Douglas is said efter to have enterit[9] [**409**] in ligue[10], thogh we see their freindshipe hes[11] bene in his fathers tyme, slane in this battle callit[12] of Arbrothe; whose doughter (or sister) was mother to Beatrix Douglas, the Earle[13] Douglas wyfe, besyde the freindshipe that was ever of old betwixt those houses from the first Earls tyme.

Chrichton beseigit in the Castle of Edinburgh. 1445

In the meane tyme the seige of the Castle of Edinburgh, wherein the Chrichton[14] was inclosit[15], had now continued some six or seven monethes, from the mids of July as appearis. At what tyme a parlament was appointit[16] to have bene halden[17] at Perth; and for the more straiting[18] of the Castle of Edinburgh be[19] seige, the parlament was transportit[20] to Edinburgh, whilk[21] was in the beginning of Februar 1445: the seige lastit[22] for twa or thrie moneths efter (being the hail tyme of the seige[23], Nyne moneths) and at last both the pairties,[24] seigers and beseigit[25] being wearied[26], the Castle was renderit[27] to the King on conditions, that the Chrichton[28] sould have pardon for al[29] the offences whilk[30] he had committit aganes[31] the King, and sould be suffert[32] to depairt[33] lyfe saife, whilk[34] he did. Our wryters cals it his[35] offences, whilk[36] he was said to have commitit aganes[37] the King; as if they wald say, there was no offence indeid done to the King; and more planlie a lytle efter; as in al[38] contention he who is [**410**] most

Renders on condition

Quae in Regem commississe dicebatur

[1]especialie obteined by [2]Cliddesdail [3]^there^ [4]horsed [5]escaped [6]will [7]called [8][Bairdake*?*] Bairdye *adopted* [9]entered [10]league [11]hath [12]called [13]^of^ [14]Chrighton [15]inclosed [16]appointed [17]holden [18]straeting [19]by [20]transported [21]which [22]lasted [23]the hail tyme of the seige being Nyne monethes [24]^the^ [25]beseiged [26]wearyed [27]renderd [28]Chrighton [29]all [30]which [31]committed aganst [32]sufferd [33]^his^ [34]which [35]the [36]which [37]committed aganst [38]all

In enim[46] omni certamine, qui potentior est, etiam innocentior studet videri

strong wald[1] seeme also most Innocent. Whilk[2] sayings are to be judiciouslie considerit[3], and accuratlie weyed, whereof hes[4] bene said before; where anent always[5] (if anie so plaise[6] to have it), I wil[7] not be contentious. Thus[8] the Chrichtoun[9] not so[10] hurt, as terrified, escapit[11] the due punishment be[12] the occasion[13] of the Castle, whilk[14] could not vther[15] ways be easelie obteinit. If be[16] the impatience of the Earle of Douglas, that wald[17] not byde[18] on the seige at leasure, til it might[19] bene forcit[20] with hunger; or if there hes[21] bene some quyet moyen[22] of his in court, wha[23] did vse that occasion to worke[24] his savtie[25] (as wil appeir heirefter) there is no mention. Bot[26] the Livingstoun leips[27] not so dry shode. Agans[28] him no les giltie of his Cousins[29] murther the Earle[30] Douglas had bendit[31] his iust indignation, and caused sommond to the Parlament at Edinburgh Alexander Lord Livingstoun the father (wha[32] had bene Governour, as is above said) and his sonnes James and Robert Livingstons (Robert had bene Thesaurer) and Dauid Livingston his Cousin[33]; and of his freinds Robert Bruce of Arthe,[34] James and Robert Dundases[35]. The Lord Livingston, and the twa Dundases war[36] convict, forfalted, and condemnet[37] to perpetual prisone, within the Castle of Dumbarton: the vther[38] thrie James and Robert Livingstons with Robert Bruce of Airth, war executit[39]. **[411]** What war[40] the crymes laid to their charge, where of this distinguishing their punishment[41] arose, it is not written[42] by the histories of old, nor of our tyme.[43] By this it may appeir, that it hes[44] not bene the particular[45] of the Earle of Douglas (whereof the father was most

Livingston condemnit 1445 Hol.

[1]wold [2]Which [3]considered [4]hath [5][always] notwithstanding [6]please [7]will [8][This] Thus *adopted* [9]Chrightoun [10]^much^ [11]escaped [12]by [13]meanes [14]which [15]other [16]obteined. Whither by [17]wold [18]abyde [19]^have^ [20]forced [21]hath [22]frend [23]who [24]worke *?* [25]saftie [26]But [27]leapt [28]Aganst [29]Cousens [30]^of^ [31]bended [32]who [33]Cousen [34]^with^ [35]Dundasses [36]two Dundasses were [37]condemned [38]other [39]were executed [40]were [41]punishments [42]sett down [43]tymes. ^However^ [44]hath [45]particulare [46]'n' *for* 'enim' *expanded from Buchanan*

giltie) nather gydit be[1] him, nor framed be[2] his particular anger, whilk wald[3] have bene most directit[4] to the harme of the olde man, as assistant to the death of his Cousins[5]; whereof we see he escapis be[6] imprisonment onlie: the zoung[7] men his sonnes are hardlier vsit[8], and put to death;[9] that it most[10] neids be on[11] some vther[12] cryme, where of the acts of Parlament, that are extant in print, makis no mention, or relation in particular[13], as the forme[14] is. And James Livingston in his speiche at his death, set downe in the Chronicles, seemes, what be[15] remission, what be gyltlinese[16], to purge al[17] true cryme; zit[18] mentions not, what was pretendit[19]: Some coniecture that it was[20] holding of houses agans[21] the King, conforme to an act made be[22] the Chrichton[23], before; and be[24] the whilk[25] he is forfaultit efter[26] him self: bot[27] we knaw no ground of that, and therefor most[28] leave it as vncertaine; as also the acte (whilk onlie[29] is extant, and may sound[30] to anie sik[31] mater) made in the second Parlament in the 1438 agans **[412]** Rebellious men reset in Castles, whilk[32] imports na[33] charging of houses, bot[34] onlie arreisting of their personnes, or[35] surtie for them that they do no harme. Nather is there mention of anie penaltie (let be[36] forfaulture) bot[37] onlie of compulsion, and streinzeing thereto[38].

1447. Hol. Sco.

This execution of the Livingstoun is cassen[39] in the zeir 1447, efter Quene Marie the Duk of Gelders daughters mariage vpon[40] the King. at whilk[41] tyme the Chrichton[42] is said to have bene forfaultit[43], not the les that he had bene Ambassador for that mariage; and the cause geven out, the keiping of the house of Chrichton[44], it being chargit be[45] ane herauld. vpon the foresaid acte, thogh the acte is as we have said, and we find no mention of anie

[1]gyded by [2]by [3]which wold [4]directed [5]Cousens [6]by [7]young [8]vsed [9]^So^ [10]must [11]for [12]other [13]particulare [14]manner [15]by [16]by gyltlesnese [17]all [18]yet [19]pretended [20]^the^ [21]against [22]by [23]Chrighton [24]by [25]which [26]efter forfaultit [27]but [28]must [29]which now [30][be] *adopted* [31]such [32]which [33]no [34]but [35][are] or *adopted* ^taking^ [36]much les [37]but [38]distreyning therevpon [39]casstten [40]to [41]which [42]Chrighton [43]forfaulted [44]Chrighton [45]charged by

Parlament that zeir[1]. Nather from the 1443 til the 1449. Whilk[2] I[3] mark, that judgment may be adhibitit[4] in the reading of these and sik[5] lyke things. Always the Chrichton thus dasht, the Livingstons execute, wardit, forfaultit[6], and condemnit[7], there seemit to be[8] some recompansing of[9] the slaughter of his Cousins[10]. Also their assister the Bishope of St Androis had receivit[11] his parte, as said is[12], to have had meikle[13] ado to save him self; having his guds[14] a pray to them, that likit[15] to take them. Zit[16] are[17] these things imputit[18] as faults to the Douglas; why I can not weil tel[19], except that we requyre of him that exacts[20] [**413**] the Philosophical disposition, frie[21] from al[22] avenging; whilk[23] few hes[24] brought with them to be verse in[25] affairs of a Commonweil; na[26], not those that hes[27] bene comptit[28] as philosophers (and that verie precise;) as ather[29] of the Catoes, whose common course was to be avengit[30] on their Enemies, be[31] publike accusations, and persute of law; wherein if there be fault[32], let there be no law that permits it; zea[33] that allowis and exhorts to it. And it is wryten of the elder Cato callit[34] Censorius, that having met ane zoung[35] man in the streit, wha[36] had accusit[37] ane Enemie of his fathers, and gotten him condemnit[38]; he cherisit[39] him, and imbracit[40] him, saying: *It was far righter so to celebrate the funerals of their fathers, with the tears and condemnations of their adversaries, then to sacrifice vnto them with kids, and lambs*. Natural it is to man to resent iniuries, as natural to seik the mending of them: and he is excusit[41] to recompance iniuries, wha[42] was

The Earl may not be blamit in these proceidings.

[1]yeir [2]Which [3]^do the rather^ [4]adhibited [5]such [6]execute, warded, forfaulted [7]condemned [8]seemed that the Douglas had [9]requytale for [10]Cousens [11]received [12]and is saide [13]much [14]goods ^made^ [15]liked *changed to* listed [16]Yett [17]^all^ [18]imputed [19]tell [20][that exacts] what [21]Philosophicall precepts exacts, or frienes [22]^maner of^ [23]which [24][few of *deletion adopted* hes] or none have [25]hat do converse in the [26]Wealth; No [27]have [28]compted [29]either [30]avenged [31]by [32]^anie^ faulte [33]yea [34]called [35]mett a young [36]streets, who [37]accused [38]condemned [39]cheriste [40]imbraced [41]excused [42]who

provokit theirto be[1] the doers of them first, and he comptit[2] just that dois[3] it be[4] order and modestie, that hes[5] patience so to sute it, and byd[6] the delays of that sute, as a meane to purge blud[7] out of the Contrie. Nather dois[8] anie ather[9] philosophie or Religion forbid it; bot be[10] the contrare bids[11] and allowis[12] it; Only[13] that the **[414]** mynd may be void of malice, and the eye set on iustice, of which al[14] onlie the searcher of mynds can be competent judge. if imperfection[15] of nature mix[16] it self in the action, we ar not to cast away nor condemne vtterlie the actor, for that; bot acknawledge[17] what is ryght as right, and appardon the imperfection (that na man wantis[18]) and not exclame aganes[19] it, as being al[20] particularitie; Nor aganes[21] the doer, as also[22] vindicative; cheiflie in a fact so verie enorme[23], as the slaughter of thir[24] his Cousins war[25]; that if we sal[26] without partialitie considder the hail[27] persute of the[28] mater, and gife[29] it the right name, we sal cal[30] it rather kyndnes of[31] his kinsmen, equitie, iustice, modestie and patience; nor wrongfulnes and[32] malitiousnes; and praise him for his kyndnes, and faithfulnes in freindshipe,[33] revenging thir[34] quarrels; whilk hes bene their verie[35] inclination (as wil[36] appeir heirefter). Zit[37] is not onlie this his just persute, bot[38] everie thing that fel[39] out in the Contrie, drawen for a reproche to him; as the slaughter of James Stewart be[40] the Boyds, and the lyke; the taking of the Castle of Hails, be[41] Patrik Dumbar, whilk[42] he is said to have taine, and slane the keiper theirof, because then[43] Hails had receivit[44] the Quene mother in[45] the Castle of Dumbar, fled thether to eshew[46] troubles; what perril that could be, is not easie **[415]** to vnderstand.

Other facts vniustlie imputit vnto him.

[1]provoked therevnto by [2]^is^ compted [3]doth [4]by [5]hath [6]abyd [7]blood [8]doth [9]either [10]but by [11]contrary ^doth^ bidd [12]allowe [13]^they wills^ [14]all which [15]infirmitie [16]mixe [17]but ^to^ acknowledge [18]which no man wantes [19]aganst [20]all [21]aganst [22][also] [23]enormous [24]these [25]ware [26]sall [27]this wholle [28]this [29]give [30]sall call [31]to [32]than wrongousnes or [33]^and^ [34]their [35]which implacable malice hath rather bene his Enemys [36]will [37]Yet [38]but [39]fell [40]by [41]by [42]which [43][then] [44]^then^ received [45]from [46]eschew

Alwyse the Earle of Douglas is sa[1] far there fra[2], that he within a few dayes efter, gate[3] the Castle of Hails agane, on condition to suffer the said Patrik Dumbar, and his men to depairt with their lyfes save[4]. The passing of S*i*r James Stewart, callit[5] the blak knight, the Kings good father[6] out of the contrie, is said to have bene compellit be[7] the Douglas, vpon some speiches[8] uttered be[9] S*i*r James aganes[10] the misgovernement of affaires: bot[11] nether is it set downe, what the words war[12]; nether what sorte of compulsion was vsit[13]. This S*i*r James his shipe[14] was taine be[15] the Flemings, and him self died soone efter.

Hol. Boe.

Hol. ibidem.

The nixt zeir[16] following, whilk[17] was the 1448 zeir, fel[18] out some warres with England, and incursions made on both sydes be[19] the borderers, where the Earle of Douglas begoud efter so lang tyme ceassing (to wit from the entrie of King James the first in anno 1423, the space of 25 zeirs) to take agane the handling of[20] warres vpon him, and his house; whilk[21] they sal zit discharge[22] to their honour, and[23] imitation of their predecessors. For Dumfreis being brunt by the Earle of Shrusberrie[24] (or Salsberrie); Dumbar spoyld be[25] the Earle of Northumberland. James Douglas the Earle of Douglas brother brunt Anwick in England, and thus there being driwen **[416]** away great preyes and buties[26], Manie personnes[27] taine in[28] both syds, be[29] the common agreance of Captanes being almost equal[30], they war interchangit[31], and al[32] set at libertie. Bot[33] this was a lytle essay afore[34] a gretter matter whilk followit, be[35] appearance this same zeir; zit[36] there was some intermission and truce taine for sevin yeirs[37]; in the whilk[38] tyme the Earle whom we sie hes[39] bene zealouse in the[40] revenge of

James his second brother burns Anwick

[1]so [2]from [3]gott [4]safe. ^Likewayes^ [5]called [6][good] father ^in lawe^ [7]compelled by [8]speaches [9]by [10]aganst [11]effaires: but [12]were [13]vsed ^therein^ [14]shipp [15]by [16]yeir [17]which [18]yeir, fell [19]by [20]^the^ [21]which [22]yett descharge [23]^the^ [24]Shreosberrie [25]by [26]booties ^and^ [27]prisoners [28]on [29]by [30]equall [31]were interchanged [32]all [33]But [34]before [35]which folowed, by [36]yeir; yett [37]yeirs [38]which [39]sie hath [40][the]

He kyndelie advancith his brother.

Archbald made Earle of Murray.

Hugh made Earle of Ormond. Johne made Lord of Balvennie

the wrong done be[1] his Enemie[2]; kythis another propertie no les commendable; whilk[3] is to be a zealouse[4] freind to his freinds, earnest and careful[5] to advance them; for this same zeir[6] James Dumbar (Holinsyd cals him Johne) Earle of Murray being dead, first he obteinis the foresaid Earls doughter (wha[7] was Neice to King Robert the second be[8] his doughter) to his thrid[9] brother Archbald,[10] then the title of Earle of Murray, at the Kings hands, to invest his brother therin; Not the les that his wyfe was[11] her fathers second doughter onlie[12], the first being mariet[13] before her fathers deceise vnto James Chrichton; of whom is discendit[14] the house of Frendrat; whether that to the titles of Earls men succeidis not be[15] mariage, bot[16] as they are geven be[17] Kings before[18], at their choise; or if there was anie respect had also to the kinred, or what ever vther[19] cause there was, it gave mater of speiches[20] to his invyers, and to our histories of censuring it, as a wronge done to [**417**] the eldest sister, to whome they think the title belongit[21]. He obteinit[22] also his fourt brother George (or Hugh) to be made Earle of Ormond, and his fift brother Johne Baron, and Lord of Balvenie, with manie riche and frutful lands; wherein men finding no ground,[23] of alledginge anie wrong to have bene done be[24] him, blames his immoderatnes in augmenting the power of his familie. I can not bot[25] praise his carefulnes and kyndnes to his freinds in advancing them be al[26] lawful meanes, whilk[27] is a mans duetie; standith with wisdome, and that a right wisdome; nether war[28] ever, or can be discommendit[29], when iniurie is away; where[30] not to do so (if a man can[31]) and not to seime to do so, proceidis ather[32] of carelesnes, or of worse, wickednes or selfnes[33], and in some of

[1]wrongs ^his Cosens had suffered^ by [2]Enemies [3]which [4]kind and carefull [5][careful *changed to* carefull] diligente [6]yeir [7]who [8]by [9]third [10]^and^ [11]^but^ [12][onlie] [13]maried [14]discended [15]by [16]but [17]by [18][before] [19]other [20]speaches [21]belonged [22]obteined [23]^at all^ [24]by [25]but [26]by all [27]which [28]was ^it^ [29]iustly discommended [30]^as^ [31]be able [32]either [33]self love

invyfulnes and malignitie even to ther awen[1] freinds: whilk doing[2] deservis no commendation, and zit[3] les when it is done of purpose, not onlie to advance, bot[4] to hald[5] bak their freinds on[6] a wisdome (whilk[7] they think verie deipe) that they may remaine servands to them, fearing that if they come to anie preferment, they might be not so readie to serve them, and perhaps grow vp bezond[8] them. Whilk[9] as it is of[10] malignitie and il natural[11], so is it not gud[12] wisdome, what subtilitie that[13] ever it seime to carie: for they advert not, that they hinder them, wha[14] sould stand them in steid[15], and cuttis **[418]** them short of power to do it; and so cuttis away the propes[16] of their[17] standing, and supports in a mister[18]. And whil[19] they fear[20] that their freinds overgrow them, geves place and mater to their Enemies to overgrow them both, thogh that fear[21] be verie far af, and if ever it come to passe (so they remayned in kyndnes) sould not be invyit[22], and even thogh they answerit[23] not to expectation[24] in kyndnes, except it war ioynit[25] with the extremitie of wickednes; And I wate not if even in that, to a right mynd; zit[26] war moe[27] tolerable, then to be over matchit[28] with Enemies, as it falleth oft[29] out, and can hardlie bot fal[30] out, where a house standis al be[31] it self, having no honest member theirof, and vnderprops to susteine it with. Besyds that whil[32] men so seikis to aservil freinds[33] vnto them, their freinds perceiving[34] it (as it can hardlie bot[35] be perceivit[36], vse what wisdome they wil[37]), are the lother to serve, as is the natural[38] of man; in whom love-service questionles is the best, zea[39] onlie fectful[40] service and therefor ather repyns the more, or at leist[41] withdraws[42] them selves, if they

[1]owen [2]which doings [3]yett ^farr^ [4]but [5]hold [6]^out of^ [7]which [8]beyond [9]Which [10]^a^ malignant [11]ill [natural *changed to* naturall] nature [12]good [13]soe [14]who [15]stead [16]proppes [17]^owne^ [18]need [19]while [20]feare [21]feare [22]invyed [23]nswered [24][exception] expectation *adopted* [25]were ioyned [26]yett [27]^it^ [moe?] more [28]matched [29]often [30]but fall [31]all by [32]while [33]make their freinds servile [34]perceiving [35]but [36]perceived [37]will [38]nature [39]yea [40]feckfull [41]least [42]withdraweth

be of anie spirit[1], and their doings anie thing worth; so that they tyne even that service, whilk[2] they so affect; and some tymes turnes it by vnkyndnes, to vnkyndnes, and Enimitie on the vther[3] syde, whilk[4] experience hes[5] ever proven. Nather flurishit[6] ever anie houses so weil, or anie man in a house as they wha[7] concurred with one mynd to the help **[419]** of vthers[8]; and he who vsit[9], and shew a care, not of holding bak his freinds, or neglecting them; bot[10] advancing them, and imbracing their adoes[11], even with a zeale, as his awen[12]. This is the true paterne of kyndnes, and certainlie a trew wisdome; let men subtilize as they liste, whilk[13] is eafaldlie[14] and earnestlie vsit be[15] this noble man, and verie worthie both of commendation and imitation. Nather wil it be found that this is it, whilk[16] did him il, bot[17] questionles made him il[18] and difficil[19] to be dealth with[20] (as we say) zea[21] so il[22] and so difficil[23], that they could find no vther[24] meane to overthrow him, bot[25] that whilk[26] they vsit[27]. Therefor to say his greatnes was the cause of his wrake, is more subtilie said, then feckfullie; That[28] it may be said in some sorte, bot as[29] a mans riches must be callit[30] the cutting of his throat, be[31] brigands; then[32] a mans vertue and gude[33] qualities are so oftymes; whilk sould[34] not[35] be eshewed for that. Bot[36] sal there then be na[37] moderation, wald[38] some say, and is it not fite[39], that subiects sould hold them[40] within certane bounds, that is not invyous or not[41] suspect be[42] Princes? I love moderation verie weil[43] both in subjects and Princes, and wish that al wald[44] moderat their greatnes, at leist[45] the appetite of it,[46] at leist[47] the meanes to atteine it, and the end why[48]

---

[1]spirite [2]which [3]other [4]which [5]hath [6]flourished [7]who [8]others [9]vsed [10]but [11]effaires [12]owen [13]lyste, which [14]vprightlie [15]vsed by [16]which [17]ill, but [18]ill [19]difficill [20]dealt withall [21]yea [22]ill [23]difficill [24]other [25]but [26]^same treacherie^ which [27]vsed [28]Even as [29][bot as] that [30][must… called] Is [31]by [32][then] ^or that^ [33]goode [34]his overthrowe; which are [35]^to^ [36]for ^all^ that ^to^ be eschewed. But [37]no [38]wold [39]fitt [40]^selves^ [41]^to be^ invyed nor [42]by [43]weill [44]all wold [45]least [46]^or^ [47]least [48]for which

they[1] seik it; and[2] have that wise conference institute[3] with Pirrhus before their eyes **[420]** whilk[4] if they wil[5] do, they sould les affectate[6], or[7] les erre in affectating[8]: bot[9] the ends luikit[10] to, the meanes right[11] framed, who seikis farther moderation and limitating[12], whether it be Princes of their Empyrs (as that of Augustus) or subjects of their greatnes (as in this man and manie vthers[13]?), what ever shew it caryis, and how histories speik[14] theirof (besyds the moderation that duetie and religion put[15] to al[16] mens appetits) in so far as touchis[17] policie, wil[18] be found bot[19] sophistrie in policie; and no gude[20] policie[21], when it is weil[22] examined.

No fault in al this

In al this therefor we can acknawledge[23] no fault, bot be[24] the contrare[25] Kyndnes and fectful freindshipe; a due and provident wisdome; streching[26] himself aganes[27] his Enemies, and vnderproping his house most wyslie and most circumspectlie. Where is then his faulte will ze[28] say? And what was the cause of his wrake? For we find that he wrakis in the end. Certainlie we must not count al[29] to have faultit,[30] that faileth. that is a great errour in mens[31] mynds, and over common[32] to be comptit wysest[33]. Zit is it not il[34] to find[35] if we wil[36] beleive the speiche of his Enemies, set downe in our histories: for thogh his freinds fear nothing, and see nothing, bot[37] his greatnes (whilk[38] is a weast fear[39]) his Enemies seis[40] further (as Enemies are quicker sightit[41] in faults) or wald[42] seeme **[421]** to spye farder[43].

Faults imputit by his Enemies

In their speiche ze sal[44] find the[45] grose and lourd faults; first, ane insatiable cupiditie, (say they) and explicate it as[46] avarice. 2. then[47] ane

1.

2.

[1]^do^ [2]^wold^ [3][institute] of Cynias [4]which [5]will *changed to* wold [6][affectat *changed to* affectate] affect [7]^farr^ [8]affecting an vnlimited greatness [9]but [10]^rightly^ looked [11]rightly [12]limitation [13]others [14]speak [15]putts [16]all [17]toucheth [18]will [19]but [20]goode [21]^indeed^ [22]weile [23]acknawledge [24]faulte but by [25]contrary [26]strenthing [27]aganst [28]ye [29]all [30]faulted [31]mends *changed to* mens, *adopted* [32]^to seeke^ [33]compted the wiser by the tart censuring of others. Yett [34]ill [35]^this cause^ [36]will [37]but [38]which [39][a... fear] too much securenes [40]see [41]sighted [42]wold [43]farther [44]yee sall [45][the] [46][explicate it as] [47][then] by

jmpotent tyrannie; twa[1] great faults[2]; Tyrannie and
avarice sufficient to bring downe, and hes[3] oft
brought downe[4] Kings, let be subjects. And that ze[5]
sould not think there war bot[6] ane ydle[7] disposition
in him[8] and a natural, whilk[9] he brydlit[10], and suffert
not to be debordit[11], they tel zow[12] the effects of
them; of the avarice, and that iniust (as it is ever,
3 where it is avarice properlie) 3.[13] he invadit[14] the
Patrimonie of the Nobilitie him[15] self be[16] law, and
4. by[17] law: of[18] his Tyrannie and oppression; 4.[19] he
gave the patrimonies of meine[20] men[21] vnto his
5. dependars; 5.[22] and zit[23] further, them that
withstoode his pleasure[24], he hearied or slew be
6. thevis[25] and Brigands. 6.[26] He advancit[27] new men to
heigest honours; placing them in the rowmes of the
7. ancient families. 7.[28] jf anie spake a frie[29] word,
taisting of libertie, it cost him no les nor[30] his lyfe.
Thir faults[31] (as may be seine) war[32] indeid great
faults[33], (if they war[34] true) and worthie where of the
end sould have bene as it was: Thir[435] are indeid
errours both in policie, and humanitie; in privat
man, or Prince; smal[36] or great, in what somever
persone; and worthie to be detestit[37] and abominat
be al[38] men (if they war[39] true) I say, if they war true
agane, and expreslie[40]. **[422]** For our authors sayis[41]
not[42] they ware[43] true, bot[44] repeits them only, as the
voyce of[45] Enemies; exaggerating things as
invyouslie, as they could; and that among vther
speichs[46] of theirs, to wit, 1. that al the riches of the
Contrie was cassin[47] in one familie, 2. that there was
great power and potencie in his hands. 3. great
Earls besyds Barons and Knights. 4 So that the
King reigned bot[48] by their licence[49] and Courtesie,

---

[1]two [2]faultes [3]hath [4]^great^ [5]yee [6]were but [7]onlie [8]^to these capitall vyces^ [9]which [10]brydled [11]deborded [12]tell yow [13][3.] [14]invaded ^saye they^ [15]it [16]bye [17]besydes [18]Touching [19][4.] that [20]meane [21]^in praie^ [22][5.] [23]yett [24]pleasour [25]by theivis [26][6.] that [27]advanced [28][7.] that [29]free [30]than [31]These faultes [32]were [33]faultes [34]were [35]These [36]small [37]detested [38]abhorred of all [39]were [40]agane if they were true [and expreslie] [41]saye [42]^expresly that^ [43]were [44]but [45]^his^ [46]other speachs [47]casten [48]but [49]favour

as it war[1]. And as for the authors awen[2] judgement of them (besyde these whilk[3] he said before,[4] they war amplified in the most odious sorte) he subjoynit those[5] and sik[6] speiches as thes, some war[7] true,[8] manie bezond[9] the truthe, augmentit[10] to acquyre them hatred. So he leavis[11] the judgement incertane[12], what these war[13], that war[14] true,[15] what these war[16], that war[17] fals, and augmentit; whilk[18] we most decerne[19], and separate: (if it be possible:) for this is indeid the craft of calomnie, to mixe truthe and falset togeather, that some being knawin[20] to be true, al[21] may be comptit[22] so. bot[23] prudencie wil[24] sift and separat them, and window them be[25] a ryght judgement, both these thinges whilk[26] are fals fra[27] these whilk[28] are true; and in everie one of them that which is truthe, fra[29] that whilk[30] is falset: for it may be that in everie one of them there be some truthe, some falset, as Calumniators ar[31] perfite craftesmen, mixing their composition to[32] falset and truthe accuratlie, and so exactlie, that it had mister[33] of[34] attentivnes to separate them. Zit[35] if we wald[36] **[423]** adhibite attentivenes[37], it may be they[38] appeir easelie. Our attentivenes most[39] be to consider the particulars, and what particular we find in anie of those, that[40] to acknawledg[41]; what is not so, reiect it as falset, and[42] of the number of these, that are bot amplifiet[43] and augmentit[44] for invy. Efter whilk[45] reule we sal[46] find in effect thir[47] last thrie[48] to be these, whilk[49] are true, 1. the riches, 2. the number, 3.[50] puissance of the name and house of Douglas: and zit[51] not simplie true, as they set[52] them downe, bot[53] amplified also to this invy, except we interpret it

Thrie of thir onlie true.

[1]were [2]owen [3]that which [4]^that^ [5]subioyned these [6]such like [7][men] some *adopted* were [8]^and^ [9]beyond [10]augmented [11]leaves [12]vncertane [13]those were [14]were [15]^and^ [16]those were [17]were [18]augmented; which [19]must discerne [20]knowne [21]all ^thereof^ [22]^also^ compted ^to be^ [23]but [24]will [25]by [26]which [27]from [28]which [29]from [30]which [31]are [32]of [33]neede [34]^great^ [36]Yett [36]wold [37]attention [38]^will^ [38]must [40]^to be true^, [that] [41]^it^ [42][and] as? [43]but amplified [44]augmented [45]which [46]sall [47]these [48]three [49]those which [50]^the^ [51]yett [52]sett [53]but

favorablie also: for not al[1] the riches of the contrie, nor al the honour was in the Douglas[2] hands, thogh[3] more then in anie vthers, zit hes[4] there bene more in some surnames before: for the Cumings is comptit[5] to be[6] greatter. And[7] their power bezond[8] the Kings, it was[9] fals. The rest are fals[10] being as bot ane[11] dependant power on[12] the Kings; and not to be supponit[13] so[14] great, nather[15] so vnitit[16] (thogh they ware[17] of ane[18] name) as it also kythit[19]. And however we find it was thought so before in the first Earls tyme, zit vsit[20] he it never to the kings preiudice, fra[21] he was informit[22] of his right, whilk[23] was now out of[24] question; bot[25] these caryis no fault in them. The rest which caryis faults[26], the first twa[27]; (Avarice, and Tyrannie)[28] are to be tryed be[29] ther effects. **[424]** The 3. taking to him self of Noble mens patrimonies be[30], or by[31] law; If be[32] law, it was not then theirs; by or besids[33] law, we heir no instance geven[34]. There is a fact may seime[35] so in the Earldome of Murray; whilk[36] was not to him self, bot[37] to his brother; nather was it the patrimonie, bot[38] the title, of whilk hes[39] bene said, and[40] was bot[41] a sober mater. The 4 and 5. (his slaying and hearying be Theives; and his dependars invading other mens patrimonies) are of the same qualitie: for we heir of no instance carying wronge; Nather zit[42] of the advancing of[43] new men wrangouslie[44]; or[45] slaying of anie man for frie[46] speiches. And cheiflie[47] advancing of new men was on[48] of the things he lykit[49] worst, and al[50] that hous; and the ground of al the discord with the Livingston and Chrichton, and I think no man wil cal[51] his brother a new man. Sa[52], that (to be short) when we

The 4 and 5 faults

The 6 and 7

[1]all [2]Douglases [3]^somewhat^ [4]others, yett hath [5]are compted [6]have been [7]^that^ [8]^was^ beyond [9]^flatly^ [10][The rest are fals] Theirs [11][as] but a ^subordinate and^ [12]vpon [13]supposed [14]^verie^ [15]neither [16]vnited [17]were [18]one [19]kythed ^thereafter^ [20]yett vsed [21]when [22]^once^ informed ^truely^ [23]which [24]^all^ [25]but [26]were faultie, are [27]twoe [28]^these^ [29]by [30]by [31]beside [32]by [33]and of these that were besids ^the^ [34]given [35]^to be^ [36]which [37]but [38]but [39]which hath [40]^that^ [41]but [42]yett [43]^any^ [44]wrongouslie [45]^the^ [46]free [47]^the^ [48]one [49]lyked [50]all [51]will call [52]So

have siftit al[1] these, we see nothing bot falset[2], and Calumnies in them al[3]; and augmentations for invy[4]; whilk makis[5] it[6] no truthe; for a truthe augmentit[7] or diminishit[8] is no langer truthe, thogh vther[9] wayes it war[10] true. Therefor leaving these things for the speichis[11] of his Enemies, that is to say, for calumnies; as they are callit[12], and as they are indeid; It is of gritter[13] weight that followis in the authors awen[14] name, that he (*animus per se insolens*) was of ane insolent mynd of him self. whilk[15] being **[425]** the iudgement of one of the most judicious wryters, I wil[16] not contest, bot[17] leave it in the mids; and soberlie crave, that men may wey[18] it, and see if there be anie necessitie to mak ws think[19] so; for it is historical only, whilk[20] I most[21] think he hes searchit[22] and fund in fact, (as we say) as having had leasour, and pervsit[23] histories (of whilk both we are skant) to wit[24]; that be the[25] succes he grew[26] to that impotencie of Commanding his affections, that he had his eares closit fra[27] the frie admonition[28] of his freinds. Nothing more pernicious, nor greatter prognostication of a wrake to ensue; then when men are so puffit[29] vp with the presumption of their owne wit[30] that they disdane and conteme[31] to heir[32], and even to wey the judgment[33] of vthers. Zit[34] this that followis, is a heigh[35] degrie of it and extremitie[36]; that men might not dissumulat[37] their mynd in silence, to hald[38] their peace of these[39] things[40] they could not approve; that it was not sure to them (whilk[41] sould be sure to al[42] men) to say nothing, and keipe[43] their mynds to[44] them selves and god, whilk[45] no vther[46] man (no not a mans self)

Faults imputit him be writers.

The first pryde to heir no admonition.

---

[1]sifted all [2]but falsett [3]all [4]invye [5]which makes [6]^to be^ [7]augmented [8]diminished [9]other [10]were [11]speaches [12]called [13]gretter [14]owen [15]which [16]will [17]but [18]weye [19]^it^ [20]which [21]must [22]hath searched [23]pervsed [24][both... are] myself is somewhat skanted; Namely [25]by his ^fortunat^ [26]hee might have grown [27]closed from [28]free admonitions [29]puffed [30]witt ^and iudgement^ [31]contemn [32]heare [33]opinions [34]others. Yet [35]heigher [36]and extremitie of it [37]safely conteine [38]and hold [39]at those [40]^which^ [41]which [42]all [43]keape [44]^god and^ [45][and god] which [46]other

can command altogidder[1]. He is obedient that obeyis[2] the rest; the mynd is his that made it, and can searche it; over whilk[3] no man sould vsurpe. The cause of al[4] this il[5] followis; the abundance of flatterers, and eare geving[6] to them; a natural, **[426]** bot[7] a pestiferous fault; Natural to al[8] men great and smal on[9] their owne sorte[10]; men geven to delyte in what they beleive[11]; and to beleive easelie most gud[12] of them selves, whom they love most of anie, and most lyke therefor, most of anie[13]. And for the abundance of flatterers, wha[14] wantis them? Diogenes said, he had his owne parasits; the mous was it, if men faillit. Zea[15] men never faillis, and perhaps faillit[16] not him. He whom al[17] the warld flatterit[18] (even King Alexander) flatterit[19] he not Diogenes? What was that speiche[20] of Alexanders, bot[21] a flatterie both of him self, and Diogenes; or els ane errour anent[22] them both? If he war[23] not Alexander, he wald[24] be Diogenes. So common is it, and so natural is it, bot[25] not the les hurtful, nor the les to be eshewit; bot[26] the more[27] carefullie to be taken head of. He hes[28] the fairest[29] of the play, that is most ware[30] of it; and countis it his greattest perfection to knaw[31] his imperfection; and he most accomplishit[32] that best knawes[33] his deffects[34], and wishes[35] for supports, and wattis[36] he hes neid of them. Out of doubt these war[37] ynough to bring downe more then ane Earle of Douglas. As for that whilk[38] is said of him further; his olde Enemies war drawin to law, and compelled to pleade their cause before that same man, both judge and pairtie; of whom manie war[39] spoylde of their guds[40], some of their lyfes; moe[41] to eshew[42] the vniust judgment, tuike[43] voluntarie exile **[427]** vnto them. And that

2. gave eare to flatterers.

3. Depression of al men.

[1]altogither [2]^in^ [3]which [4]all [5]ill [6]geving care [7]naturall, but [8]all [9]in [10]kinde [11]beleeve [12]good [13][and most *changed to* must… anie] [14]who [15]failed ^him^. Yea [16]failled [17]all [18]world flatterd [19]flatterd [20]speache [21]but [22]in [23]were [24]wold [25]but [26]eschewed; but [27]^more^ *adopted* [28]hath [29]fayrest [30]wary [31]know [32]accomplished [33]knowes [34][effects?] deffects *adopted* [35]wisheth [36]wottis [37]were [38]which [39]were [40]goods [41]more [42]eschew [43]tooke

whilk[1] is said of their dependars; they overshote[2] them selves, careles of al judgments (because none durst contend with them be[3] judgment)[4] to al[5] sorte of licentiousnes, reiving and ruginge[6] holy things, prophane things; striking, and slaying whom they might gete[7] their hands over; Nather keipit[8] anie brydle or measure, of al[9] wickednes. Of al[10] this (I say) anent[11] his dependars[12] being so generallie, and almost hyperbolicalie conceavit[13], I wald[14] wishe among so manie, there had bene some instances set[15] downe, that we might the better have knawne[16] it, and discernit[17] it. This I ame sure can not be without[18] hyperbole, that they did some gratuit[19] wickednes (that is for noght) and without gaine, pleasour, or profite theirof; having no causes in the world for them, bot[20] onlie to hald[21] their hand in vse of wickednes, leist disacustomet fra il[22], some honest thought sould come in[23] their mynd, that might tame them, and wine them from their wickednes and vyldnes[24]. So stronge a conclusion, wald[25] have had cleare and plane antecedents, and[26] not a few of them. It is hard to beleive this, or anie man[27] anent it on[28] his[29] word; cheiflie a man, that was not in these[30] tymes, and ane oculare witnes as it war[31] of[32] things; wha[33] might give ws perhaps be sik speiches[34] to conceive more then he could expresse, or war[35] expressable be[36] words. Bot[37] what anie vther[38] **[428]** that hes[39] it be historie[40], could have gatherit be historie[41], we could also have taken vp at his admonition be[42] the particular[43] narration of the same histories; bot[44] there being no traces of sik[45] enormities in the historie (as it is set downe) that can leid[46] ws to this, I wate[47] not if I sould sa[48] reverence anie mans persone, as to accept[49] it

This to be weyit[50].

---

[1]which [2]overshott [3]by [4]^fall^ [5]all [6]rugginge *changed to* spoileing [7]gett [8]keiped [9]all [10]all [11]touching [12]^the same^ [13]conceaved [14]wold [15]sett [16]knowne [17]discerned [18]^an^ [19]gratuate [20]but [21]hold [22]least disacustomet from ill [23]into [24]vylenes [25]wold [26]^that^ [27]mans assertion of [28]vpon [29]^bare^ [30]those [31]were [32]^those^ [33]who [34]by such speeches [35]were [36]by [37]But [38]other [39]hath [40]onely by hearesay or by reading historie [41]gathered thereby [42]by [43]simple [44]But [45]such [46]leade [47]wote [48]soe [49]believe [50]weyed

absolutlie[1]. And charitie wil[2] command the contrare[3]. It is of the same stufe[4], the judgment set downe hereon to amplifie the evils of those dayes: that it fel[5] weil out for Scotland, that England had their owne Civile Warres in those dayes; vther[6] ways Scotland had succombit[7] vnder the burdein. For first there Civile Warres from this tyme, whilk[8] was from 1444 zeir to the[9] 1448 was not great; and bot[10] quyet grudgis onlie: the commotion of Blewbairde was not til 1449. And[11] of Kent be[12] Johne Cade in the zeir[13] 1450. Then the forrane warres with England might have removit[14] the discord at home, as they had often done; and men geven to warres sould have had mater of better imployement aganes[15] the Enemie, wha[16] in tyme of peace can not employ them, and are oft therefor the cause of evil[17]. Last the event proveth vtherways[18], and that the Estate at home hinderit[19] not the Scotismen fra[20] a notable victorie, obteinit be[21] the same Douglases, countit[22] so inique in peace, and provit[23] ever honorable and duetiful in[24] warre; their Enemies not being **[429]** able[25] to detract the evidence of their worthe.

Buch.

The occasion of this victorie fel[26] out thus; we[27] harde how efter the burning of Anwike be[28] James Douglas second brother to the Earle, a truce was taine for seven zeirs; Not the les[29] wherof in this zeir[30] (as wald[31] seeme) or in the nixt[32] at fardest[33], the Englishmen without anie regarde thereto made incursions in[34] Scotland, spoylit, haryit[35] and brunt the villages farre and wyde, where they went; whilk[36] the Scots men finding wald[37] not suffer it lang vnrevengit[38]: for ryding in[39] England with a sufficient companie, they renderit[40] them as great harme, as they had receivit[41]: so their mynds being

Warre begone

[1]^and with implicite faith, because he hath said it^ [2]will [3]contrary [4]stuff [5]fell [6]other [7]succombed [8]which [9]yeir ^to the^ *adopted* [10]but [11]^that^ [12]by [13]yeir [14]removed [15]against [16]who [17]evill [18]otherways [19]hindered [20]from [21]obteined by [22]counted [23]^was^ proved [24]^time of^ [25]^therein^ [26]fell [27]^have^ [28]by [29]yeirs; Not with standing [30]yeir [31]wold [32]next [33]furthest [34]into [35]spoyled, haryed [36]which [37]wold [38]long vnrevenged [39]into [40]rendered [41]received

irritate on both syds, the ground was laid farre waist[1] on ether syde, bot[2] cheiflie the skaithe lightit on[3] Cumberland. Wherefra[4] had come[5] the beginning of the troubles; so that it was redactit[6] almost to a wildernes. When the newes of these things war[7] brought to Londone, they causit[8] a verie great armie of 40000 men (as some wryte) be decernit[9] to come to the borders agans[10] the Scotismen, and also to invade Scotland; thinking be[11] that number easelie to overthrowe, and redact vnder their dominion a Contrie wastit[12] and impoverishit[13]; and being at discord amongs them selves at home. Therefor having made a levie of choyse and the best soldiours, the Earle of Northumberland **[430]** is made cheif Captane of the armie, to whome they ioyne a certaine man callit[14] Magnus,[15] a gentilman onelie[16] borne, bot[17] who had geven great proves[18] of his valiantnes[19] manie tymes in France, where he had bene brought vp, and exercisit[20] in the warres from his zouthe[21]; this man being inflamed with a spytful[22] hatred aganes[23] Scotismen, is said to have transacted[24] with the King of England, that what soever lands he could wine from the Scotismen be[25] slaying them, or expelling them out of it he and his airs sould have it in perpetual[26] heritage. He was remarkable be[27] a long rid baird[28]; and therefor was callit be[29] the Englishmen Ridbairde; be[30] the Scotismen in derision Magnus with the Ridmaine[31]; as thogh his baird[32] had bene a horse[33] meane, because of the lenth and thiknes of it. The manuscript callis[34] him Magnus with the rid[35] hand, in taking the word maine[36] (whilk[37] is Scots) from the French word, maine, whilk is callit[38] a hand; bot[39] the attentive reader may see the difference; and it was bot[40] in

Manuscr.

English armie.

[1]waest [2]but [3]harme lighted vpon [4]from whence [5]comd [6]redacted [7]were [8]there was [9][be] decerned [10]aganst [11]by [12]wasted [13]impoverished [14]called [15]^onely^ [16][onelie] [17]but [18]profes [19]vallour [20]trayned [21]youthe [22]spytfull [23]aganst [24]transacted [25]by [26]perpetuall [27]by [28]reed beard [29]called by [30]English Reedbearde; by [31]Reedmaine [32]beard [33]horses [34]calleth [35]reed [36]mayne [37]which [38]which signifieth [39]but [40]but

derision. The King of Scotland heiring[1] of this preparation of the English, he also causes prepare

Earle of Ormond sent against them as general An. 1450

ane armie, where of George Douglas Earle of Ormond (or Hugh as vthers cal[2] him righter) was made general, wha incontinent passit[3] to Annandail whilk[4] way he vnderstude the English armie was to come. **[431]** Thus preparation being made on both syds, the Englishmen[5] preveinis, and first comes in[6] Scotland, and having passit[7] the Rivers of Silvay[8] and Annand, pitchis downe their Campe vpon the

Battel of Sark.

water of Sark, fra[9] whence having sent[10] Companies on al[11] hands, they spoylit[12] the Contrie fare[13] and wyde: bot heiring[14] of the Scotismen[15] approche, they sent out trompetters[16], and recallit[17] their furrowers[18], conveining al[19] their troupes in one. So soone as the two Enemies came within sight of vther[20], arrayed, and set[21] in ordre, they made no delay of fight. In the right winge of the English

Hol. Scot.

armie, was this Magnus with the rid[22] maine; In the left *Sir* Johne Ponentarie knight, to whom war joynit[23] the Walles men (relikes of the ancient Brittons); the mids battle was reulit be[24] the Earle of Northumberland himself. On the vther[25] syde the Earle of Ormond placit aganes[26] Magnus William Wallace of Cragie; aganes[27] *Sir* Johne Ponentarie, the Knight of Carlaverok callit[28] Maxwel; and Johnstoun of that ilk[29]; with manie inland gentilmen (sayes[30] the Manuscript) because they had no[31] confidence in their awin wha war bot[32] Theivis, and had nothing bot spuilzie[33] before their eyes. He him self tuike[34] the middle battle; where he exhortit[35] „ them shortlie[36] they sould have great hope of „ victorie **[432]** as having put on armes provokit[37]; „ a gud end could not faile sa[38] gud a cause; let

---

[1]hearing [2][vther *emended*] others call [3]passed [4]which [5]English [6]into [7]passed [8]Solway [9]from [10]^out^ [11]all [12]spoyled [13]farr [14]but hearing [15]Scotismens [16]trompetts [17]recalled [18]forrowers [19]all [20]other [21]sett [22]reed [23]joyned [24]reuled *changed to* directed by [25]other [26]placed aganst [27]aganst [28]called [29]Johnston [30]sayeth [31]^great^ [32]owne who were but [33]but spoile [34]tooke [35]exhorted [36]briefly ^that^ [37]^being^ provoked ^therevnto. That^ [38]so

them onlie do valiantlie and remember the pryd[1] „ of the Enemie with a notable defait; that so they „ sould receive a lang[2] lasting fruict of a short tymes „ travel[3]. When the English, who passit[4] in the number of Bowmen, did with their arrows a far of annoy[5] the Scotismen greatlie, William Wallace of Cragie, wha[6] had the leiding[7] of the left winge, cryed out with a loud voyce,[8] that he was hard be[9] his followers; Why sould they stand stil[10] thus to be woundit[11] a far „ af[12]; let them follow him, and joyne at hand „ straikes[13], where true vertue was to be seine; that „ was the due pairt of valiant men; and with that „ rushit[14] foreward him self, and with him the hail[15] battel with sik[16] violence that with speirs and lang wappons[17] assalting the Enemies battel[18], they had quicklie overthrowen the right wing theirof: whilk[19] Magnus perceiving, more myndful of his honorable past tyme, nor[20] of the present perril[21]; that he might ather[22] restore the battle with hardines, or lose his lyfe with the report of worthines be[23] a memorable fact, preissit[24] forward aganes[25] Cragie Wallace, with sic[26] violence, and seiking to approche him, that he might have put[27] furth his greif vpon him, was with a few of his freinds **[433]** that followit[28] him, inclosit[29] in the mids[30] of the Scotish troupes, and there slane. The slaughter of this man, in whom consistit[31] no smal[32] hope of the victorie on the English syde, put the residue of the armie in such feare, that they war[33] not able to resist anie Langer[34] the Scotismen[35] impression; bot[36] turned their bakes[37], and fled in great disorder; whom the Scotismen persewit[38] so feirclie that there was[39] greater nomber slane of them[40] in the chase, then in the battle; cheiflie at the brink of the river of Silway[41], where the tyde being come[42] in stayet[43]

Magnus with the rid maine slane.

The English defait.

[1]pryde [2]long [3]travell [4]passed [5]ennoy [6]who [7]leading [8]^so^ [9]heard by [10]still [11]wounded [12]of [13]stroekes [14]rushed [15]whalle [16]such [17]long weappons [18]battell [19]which [20]honor acquyred in the tyme past, than [21]perrill [22]either [23]by [24]preissed [25]aganst [26]such [27]putt [28]followed [29]inclosed [30]midst [31]consisted [32]small [33]were [34]longer [35]Scotismens [36]but [37]backes [38]persewed [39]^a^ [40]of them slane [41]Solway [42]come [43]stayed

their flight, or drowned them, that venterit[1] in the water. There died in the battle of Englishmen to the number of 3000, and amongs vthers[2] their so haitful Enemie, and presumptuous conqueror (as before ze[3] have hard;) ane[4] notable exemple[5] to represse presumption; and (as the proverb is) not to sel[6] the beirs[7] skine before he be slane. There was slane besyds him elevin knights of no smal comt[8], and estimation. Of Scotismen war[9] lost bot 600. There war[10] taken prisoners a great number, amongs whom[11] *Sir* Johne Ponintoun, *Sir* Robert Haringtoun knights, and the Lord Percie sone to the Earle of Northumberland, whils he helpit his father to horsebake[12], whereby he escapit, be[13] flight. There was also **[434]** gotten so great spuilzie[14], as men rememberit[15] not to have bene gotten in anie battle before: for the English men relying vpon the number of their armie, and valour of experimentit[16] soldiours, togeather with the Scotismen[17] variance at home; war come[18] furth with sik[19] confidence and securitie, that they seemit[20] not to come to a warre, bot[21] to a pompe and triumphe: sik[22] was the trust in them selves, and contempt of the Enemie. The Laird of Craggie Wallace sore woundit[23] in the battel was was caryit[24] home, and died a[25] thrie moneths efter.

The Earle of Ormond, ioyfully receivit at Court

The Kings speiche

The Earle of Ormond having gotten this honorable victorie convoyit[26] the cheifest[27] of the prisoners to Louchmaben[28], and efter repairit[29] to Courte, where he was of the hail[30] joyfullie met[31] and receivit,[32] and with al[33] sorte of honour interteinit[34], Invy not daring[35] oppin hir mouthe: the King himself commending gritlie the[36] facts acthivit[37] in warfare; exhortit[38] him and his brother; „ that as oftymes they had geven prove[39] of their „ valour aganes[40] the forrane Enemie, and defendit[41]

[1]venterd [2]others [3]yee [4]a [5]example [6]sell [7]bears [8]accomt [9]were [10]was [11]^were^ [12]helped to horse his father [13]escaped, by [14]spoile [15]rememberd [16]experimented [17]Scotismens [18]were comd [19]such [20]seemed [21]but [22]such [23]wounded [24]caryed [25]some [26]convoyed [27]cheefest [28]Loughmaben [29]repaired [30]holle [31]mett [32]received [33]all [34]interteined [35]^to^ [36]his [37]atchived [38]that expedition; ehorted [39]profe [40]aganst [41]defended

the state of Scotland with their travel[1] and vertue ,, in most perillous tymes, so they wald[2] at home ,, accustome them to modestie, absteine them ,, selves, and conteine their freinds from iniuries ,, towards the waker[3] sorte; their power and ,, puissance, whilk[4] they had acquyrit be[5] so **[435]** ,, manie their great deserts to his Predecessors the ,, Kings, and their contrie, they wald[6] imploy rather ,, in suppressing of theivis, nor[7] make shew of[8] it ,, be[9] cherising them: that[10] onlie on[11] thing was ,, laiking[12] to their ful[13] praise; whilk[14] if they wald ,, this[15] prosecute and do, they sould find by prove[16] ,, there was nothing more deare to him, then the ,, advancement of the house and name of Douglas. ,, To this when they had answerit[17] beninglie, and courteouslie, they war dimissed[18], and so returnit hame[19] to their owne houses with honour and applause, both of Prince and People[20]; to whom they had be[21] this victorie purchesit[22] great quyetnes. For nather war[23] the English borderers able to invade them anie more; nather the King of England (thogh he greatlie desyrit[24] it) to send downe ane[25] new armie be[26] reason of the Civil[27] Warres, whilk[28] shortlie efter insued, so that he choisit[29] rather to have peace with Scotland in that Estate; and for that effect directit[30] his Ambassadors, wha procurit[31] a truce, for the space of thrie zeirs[32] at the King and Counsel[33] of Scotlands hands, they thinking it no les meit[34] for them to have peace with England in the case not vnlik[35], brangling (thogh not with insurrection aganes[36] their King **[436]** as in England) zit[37] with dissention amongs them selves be[38] the factions fore said. For thogh the Douglas had thus pacified the contrie, zit[39] had they not pacified the hatred of their

The Douglas Enemies stil invy them.

[1]travells [2]wold [3]weaker [4]which [5]acquyred by [6]wold [7]then ^to^ [8]^giving way to^ [9]by [10]thatt [11]one [12]lacking [13]full [14]which [15]wold thus [16]proofe [17]answered [18]were dismissed [19]returned home [20]Peeple [21]by [22]purchesed [23]were [24]desyred [25]a [26]by [27]Civill [28]which [29]choosed [30]directed [31]who procured [32]three yeirs [33]Counsell [34]meite [35]vnlike [36]aganst [37]yett [38]by [39]yett

Enemies; and thogh they had throwen out[1] a confession of their worth; zit[2] had they not thrawen[3] the malice out[4] of their harts; and[5] invy they beare both to their greatnes, and to their vertue; bot be[6] the contrar[7] their quyet practices stil continuet[8], and their credit in Court seimit[9] to increase aganes[10] them.

The Kings mariage.

The Crichton wha[11] had bene before sent Ambassador to Charles the 7, King of France for procuring a wyfe to the King of Scotland, had by his meanes concludit[12] the same with Marie daughter to Arnold Duk[13] of Gelder, the Duk of Burgundies sister, and be[14] that meanes touching the blude[15] Royal of France; and about this tyme[16] was returnit in[17] Scotland with her; having be that service and her moyen increasit[18] greatlie his credit with the King; whilk[19] the Earle of Douglas perceiving, and nothing contentit[20] therewith, having sought and obteinit[21] licence from the King, retirit[22] from Court; finding his errour, in being contentit[23] the Chrichton[24] sould be imployed in that honorable message: so to be red[25] of him be[26] absence, as he countit[27] it; whilk[28] practice of Court succeidit[29] **[437]** some tymes happelie, as it did aganes[30] the Boyds in the verie lyke case heirefter, in the tyme of this Kings sone and successor, King James the thrid; zit[31] did it not so now, but turned to his greatter advancement; whereof the Earle of Douglas impatient, contentit[32] himself to declare his miscontentments be[33] this his calme retreat, no les to the contentment of the Chrichton[34]; counting it his gaine to be so red[35] of him, from the Kings eare and presence. Whils thus they concordit[36] in sik[37] a discord; both willing on[38] thing, in so contrarie mynds[39]; to wit, the absence of the Douglas; fel[40] out

Douglas discontent retirs from Court

---

[1]extorted from them [2]yett [3]throwen out [4][out] [5]^the^ [6]but by [7]contrary [8]still continued [9]seemed [10]against [11]Chrighton who [12]concluded [13]Duke [14]by [15]bloode [16]^he^ [17]returned into [18]increased [19]which [20]contented [21]obteined [22]retired [23]contented [24]Crighton [25]ridd [26]by ^his^ [27]counted [28][in] *adopted* which [29]succeided [30]aganst [31]yett [32]contented [33]by [34]Chrighton [35]ridde [36]they thus concorded [37]such [38]one [39]myndes [40]^There^ fell

ane occasion that agane occasionit[1] his longer absence, not[2] out of the Courte, bot[3] out of the Contrie. Richard Colvin, or Melvin (as some cal[4] him) of Okiltrie, was in Enemitie with Johne Auchinlek of that ilk, ane[5] freind and dependar on the Earle of Douglas; for whom the Earle of Douglas having sent for to repare towards him to the Castle of Douglas, for sik affairs[6] as he had to do with him; the said Richard informit[7] of his journey (not the les that he knew that he went towards the Earle) whether stirit[8] vp be[9] the adverse faction in Court[10] so to disgrace him; or leaning to their credit for impunitie[11], or what ever[12] his impatience, presumption, **[438]** or contempt of the Earls want of Court, not having regarde to him, or[13] feare of his anger, vmbesets his way[14] with a number of armit[15] men, and efter a smal[16] conflict slayis[17] him, and divers of his servands and freinds with him. The Earle of Douglas having receavit[18] advertisement heirof, and counting the fact touching him so neirlie in the persone of his freind,[19] of his servand in his service, coming to him,[20] sent for be[21] him, was so incensit[22] therewith, that whether mistrusting the ordinarie course of justice, as wherein he might be eludit be[23] his Enemies[24] (gyders of[25] Court); or impatient of so long delay; or not counting it most honorable for him, nor most awful[26] in exemple to vthers, to seik, concludit[27] immediatlie to be avengit; wowing[28] he sould so be[29] before he ather[30] eate or dranke; and accordinglie incontinent he tooke horse, and with the readiest of his freinds raid[31] to the Castle of Okiltrie, beseigit, forcit[32] it, and slew the said Richard, and sa[33] manie as ware come to the age of man that ware[34] found within the Castle. This fact thus done oppenit[35] mens mouthes

Manuscr. Anno 1450

Slayeth Richart Colvin.

[1]occasioned [2]^onely^ [3]Courte, but [4]call [5]of Auchinlek, a [6]such effairs [7]informed [8]stired [9]by [10]Courte [11][importunitie] impunitie *adopted* [12]whatsoever ^else^ [13]nor [14]^the said Colvine^ besets the others waye [15]armed [16]small [17]slayeth [18]receaved [19]^and^ [20]^and^ [21]by [22]incensed [23]eluded by [24](^the^ [25]^the^ [26]awfull [27]others, [to seik] concluded [28]avenged; vowing [29]be so [30]ether [31]road [32]beseiged, forced [33]so [34]were [35]oppened

in dyvers speiches, according to their dyvers humours; some condemming his crueltie, some comending his courage, some that he had done over meikle[1], some that he had rather[2] les; that he had iust cause, that he was il vsit[3], his freind slane, **[439]** his honor so interest, that[4] sorte of justice best became him.[5] His Enemies always[6] in Court tuke gud[7] hold of it, aggravating it to the King as a enorme[8] fact, aganes[9] law and custome, and however deservitlie (whilk[10] they could not denye) zit[11] perrillous in exemple; prejudicial to al[12] order, and to the King; to whom the ordering of such things belongit[13]; Nether was the King a litil incensit[14] therewith. Whilk[15] the Earle of Douglas vnderstanding pairtlie to geve place theirto, and[16] the King a tyme to sattle his Cholere; pairtlie on some remorse (as all blud hes[17] with it) of the fact,

Zeir of Jubile

the zeir[18] of Jubile[19] being the nixt zeir[20], he purchest licence from the King to goe to Rome; pretending

Manuscr.

he wald[21] do pennance for the said slaughter; bot[22], as was interprete be[23] his Enemies, and is the iudgment of men to this daye[24] to shewe[25] his grandeur to forrane nations. Before he depairtit[26], having a care of his house, and out of hope to have Children of his awen[27] bodie (as being 7 or 8 zeirs[28]

Confirmeth his brother James Earle failzeing him self

maried without Children) he procured his second brother James to be receavit be[29] the King, and confirmed in the Earldome failzeing[30] him self. There went with him in Companie,[31] great number

Boe. Hol. 1450

of noble[32] and gentilmen; sik[33] as war[34] the Lords Hamilton, Gray, Salton, Setoun Oliphant and Forbes; also Calder, Vrwharte Cambel **[440]** Fraser, and Lauders of Crumartie, Philorthe and Bas

Goeth on his journey to Rome

knights, with manie vther[35] gentilmen of great[36] accomt. He went first to Flanders, and from thence

---

[1]too much [2]could do no [3]ill vsed [4]^that^ [5]Howsoever [6][always] [7]took good [8]an enormous [9]aganst ^the^ [10]deservedlie (which [11]yett [12]all [13]belonged [14]litill incensed [15]Which [16]^to give^ [17]which all blood hath ^ever^ [18]yeir [19]Jubilee [20]next yeir [21]wold [22]But [23]by [24]dayes *changed to* daye *adopted* ^it was cheefly^ [25]showe [26]depairted [27]owen [28]yeirs [29]receaved by [30]failleing ^of^ [31]^a^ [32]noblemen [33]such [34][war] [35]other [36]good

be[1] land to Paris, where he was honorablie receavit be[2] the King of France, whom some cal[3] Lewis the Elevinth; bot most neids[4] be Charles the Sevint, wha livit til[5] the zeir[6] 1460, some ten zeirs efter the Jubile; whilk behovit[7] to be in Anno 1450. The remembrance of the gud[8] service done be[9] his avuncle[10] at Baugé and his Gudshire[11] at dyvers tymes; and at last his liberal spending[12] his lyfe for the libertie of France at Vernoile war zit[13] grein in his memorie; in respect wherof, and for the place the Earle caryit[14], and the publike ligue[15] betwixt the Contries, he[16] left no kind of honour vndone to[17] him: from thence he tuke[18] his journey towards Rome, whilk[19] he fillit[20] with expectation of his coming. He had tane out of Paris his zoungest[21] brother George, a zoung man who[22] was there at the scoolis[23]; and of whom was great expectation, bot[24] dyed by the way, to his great[25] greif. He is said be[26] the Manuscript to have bene nominate Bishope of Dunkel[27], and that he was to have bene inaugurate at Rome; whilk[28] Buchanan also sayes,[29] perhaps folowing him; bot[30] they both forgot[31] **[441]** that his elder brother Henrie is said by the Manuscript in the lyfe of their father to have bene Bishope of Dunkel[32], and that this George died before he was fyftein zeirs[33] of age. Also I take it to be ane oversight in the same Buchanan, that he sayes, that he was destinat[34] to the Earldome, with the Kings permission, be[35] his brother having no children, whilk[36] is aganes al[37] reason, he being the zoungest[38] of manie brethren,[39] worthie men, whom no reason wald[40] defraude for him, zit[41] a child at the schole.[42] Always whils the Earle was thus in his pilgrinage[43], his Enemies sleipit[44] not at hame; bot[45] taking the opportunitie of his absence, did both be al

His brother George dieth

1. oversight of our was wryters anent this man.

Buch. 2

Manusc.

---

[1]by [2]receaved by [3]call [4]must needs [5]who lived till [6]yeir [7]Jubilee; which behoved [8]good [9]by [10]wncle [11]Grandfather [12]^of^ [13]were yett [14]caryed [15]league [16]the King [17]vnto [18]tooke [19]which [20]filled [21]youngest [22]youth that [23]scooles [24]but ^he^ [25]exceeding [26]by [27]Dunkeld [28]which [29]sayeth [30]but [31]forgott [32]Dunkell [33]yeirs [34]destinate [35]by [36]which [37]aganst all [38]youngest [39]^all^ [40]wold [41]yett [42][cheiflie]*a slip* [43]^or voyage^ [44]sleiped [45]but

His enemies movit the King aganes him

invention[1] they could devyse, blame him at the Kings hands; and stirit[2] vp such of the Common people, as had receavit[3] anie tort of anie man[4] to complein to the King; alledging they had receavit[5] of the Earle of Douglas, his freinds, or servands; and be[6] these meanes movit[7] the King to cause seike[8] the Laird of Symontoun[9] (then his bailzie[10] in Douglasdail) to answer to sik[11] crymes, as war[12] laid to the Earls charge; wha[13] not knawing[14] how to behave himself in sik[15] a new sorte of sute, laid to his Maisters charge, for the facts perhaps of his dependars; and however sik[16] as his Maister **[442]** had nather commandit[17] nather happelie hard[18] of; and luiking[19] for no equitie at their hands, wha movit sik[20] a citation;[21] choise not to come[22] in judgment; suffering things rather to pase[23] for non compeirance, nor[24] to compeir not knawing the Estate of things, nor how to answer[25], having nather[26] knawledge of them be[27] himself, nor[28] direction, nor[29] information from his Maister. Vpon whilk[30] occasion his Enemies taking hold,[31] interpret this his non compearance in the most odious sorte; and calling it contumacie, and what greivous name they could devyse,[32] first movit[33] the King to send his servands, and[34] apprehend him, and wald[35] gladlie have proceidit[36] in al[37] extreme sorte aganes[38] him, crying out aganes[39] his „ presumptuous contempt of the King; that his „ Royal authoritie was become a dispysinge and „ mokerie to everie base fellow; that by his lenitie „ he did but foster the malapertnes of the wiked „ sorte; that by the impunitie of the misdoers new „ men ware oppenit[40] to new misdeids; with sik vther[41] speiches in the most vehement sorte[42] they could[43] to have dippit[44] the King in blud[45], and cute

---

[1]by all ^the^ inventions [2]stirrd [3]receaved [4]^whosoever^ [5]receaved ^the same^ [6]by [7]moved [8]cyte [9]Symintoun [10]baillie [11]such [12]were ^to be^ [13]who [14]knowing [15]such [16]such [17]commanded [18]heard [19]looking [20]who moved such [21]^made^ [22]appeere [23]pass [24]than [25]^them^ [26]nether [27]by [28]^anie^ [29]or [30]which [31]^they^ [32]^they^ [33]moved [34]to [35]wold [36]proceided [37]all [38]aganst [39]aganst [40]were promoved [41]such other [42]^that^ [43]^desyre^ [44]dipped [45]blood

af al[1] hope, as far as[2] in them lay[3], of reconcilment betwixt them. bot[4] the King not being that far[5] as zit alienat[6] from the Earle of Douglas, thogh the compleants[7] of sa[8] manie as they had stirit[9] vp, had made some impression in his mynd, nothing movit[10] with these speiches, persistit[11] in his opinion, to recompanse the Compleaners in the **[443]** lose of money maters; bot[12] not to satisfie the accusers, desyrous of revenge, with the blude[13] of anie man; and therefor he causit[14] the Laird of Symontoun (Bailzie[15] fore said) to be set[16] at libertie; commanding him onlie to answere to complaints, or satisfie the Compleaners[17]. He on the vther[18] pairt, wha[19] could nather without information answere, nor without direction satisfie, humblie besought the King, that sence[20] he had no information, and could not answere being bot[21] a servant, and vnacquent with things; that sence also he was not Collector of his Maisters rents, bot[22] only commander of his servands, it wald[23] please his Maiestie to delay the mater til[24] his Maisters returne, whom he expectit[25] within few moneths; and wha[26] (he doubtit not) both could and wald[27] answere to whatsomever[28] complainte,[29] satisfie sufficientlie at his Princes pleasour, whatsomever[30] he sould be found to have trespast in aganes[31] anie man. This seemit[32] most reasonable, that the Earle himself sould be hard first[33], and not condemnit vnhard[34] in his absence; and[35] there could be no great preiudice in a short delay; so that the King him self did also[36] condiscend thereto: Not the les importunit be[37] the multitude of new compleants he sent William Sinkler Earle of Orknay,[38] neir **[444]** Cousine to the Earle of Douglas (Cousine germane as wald[39] seeme); for the Earle of Douglasis mother

---

[1]cutt of all [2][*illegible*] as in *adopted* [3]laye [4]but [5]farr [6]yett alienated [7]complaints [8]so [9]stird [10]moved [11]persisted [12]but [13]bloode [14]caused [15]Baillie [16]sett [17]Compleeners [18]other [19]who [20]since [21]but [22]but [23]wold [24]till [25]expected [26]who [27]wold [28]whatsoever [29]^and^ [30]whatsoever [31]into aganst [32]seemed [33]first heard [34]condemned vnheard [35]^that^ [36][also] graciously [37]importuned by [38]^Chancellor and^ [39]wold

Earle of Orknay sent to intromet with his Rents.

namet[1] Beatrix Sinkler, was daughter to the Earle of Orknay, wha[2] appearantlie was this mans gudshire[3]; also[4] the Earle of Orknay, was sone to Giles Douglas daughter to the lord of Nethsdail, by whilk[5] meanes they are thrids of kine: last of al, he had maried the Duk of Turains daughter, that is to say, Gros James this Earls fathers sister, and so there hes[6] bene double or triple mariage[7] betwixt their[8] houses)[9] being Chanceller for the tyme, to intromet[10] with the Earle of Douglas his guds[11] and rents in Galloway, and Douglas[12] for satisfaction of Compleaners[13]: but it was to no effect; for he was eludit[14], and almost mokit be[15] the tennents. He alledgit[16], and reportit[17] to the King, that it was be[18] the instigation of the Earle of Ormond, that his travels war[19] so frustrate[20]. For to him had the Earle of Douglas committit[21] the handling of his affairs

Hol.

during his absence; and he greatlie disdainit[22] that Orknay being so neir of blude[23] and allya[24] to them sould vndergoe that charge. The King irritate herevpon[25], as a contempt of his authoritie, causit[26] charges[27] be directit[28] to sommond[29] the hail[30] Douglases and their favourers to compeire at ane[31] certane day; And the Earle **[445]** himself within thriescoire dayes; whilk[32] being come, and they not

The King goeth in persone with ane armie.

compeiring, ware denoncit[33] rebels:[34] raisis ane armie, and gois[35] in persone to Galloway; where at his first his first entrie having forcit[36] their Captanes to retire them to strenthes, a smal number of his host whils they followet[37] the rebels vncircumspectlie throgh strait places war[38] put bake

Hol.

to the King, not without ignominie: wherefor[39] taking great indignation[40] that a[41] number of misruled[42] men durst be so bold; that he might

---

[1][named] [2]who [3]Grandfather [4][also… Chanceller for the tyme] *corrections of this scored out passage will be noted individually* [5]which [6]hath [7]mariages [8]those [9]^hee^ [10]intromett [11]goods [12]Douglasdale [13]Compleeners [14]eluded [15]moked by [16]alledged [17]reported [18]by [19]were [20]frustrated [21]committed [22]disdained [23]blood [24]allyance [25]herewith [26]caused [27]^to^ [28]directed [29]^all^ [30][hail] [31]a [32]which [33]^they^ were ^all^ denonced [34]^And he^ [35]went [36]forced [37]whiles they followed [38]were [39]whereatt [40]^in^ [41]^fewe^ [42]desorderly

remove the contempt of him self, he invadit[1] the places of their receyts[2]; and first tuke[3] the Castle of Louchmaben without great travel[4]; Efter having with great weirying of his men gotten the Castle of Douglas, he razed it to the ground; the fermerers[5] and tennants (labourers of the ground) wha[6] had renderit[7] themselves to him, he commandit[8] to pay their dueties to his Collectors vnto sik[9] tyme as Compleiners war satisfiet[10] with the Douglases guds[11]. These things reportit[12] thus, as they war[13] done, to the Earle of Douglas, whils[14] he was zit[15] at Rome; movit[16] him greatlie, and greatlie astonishit[17] them, that war[18] in his[19] Companie with him; so that manie with drew them selves, fearing what it might turne to; and he with **[446]** the few that remaynit[20] with him, made the haist they could homeward. As he came through England, he was honorablie interteinit[21] by the King, and Quene there; bot[22] when he approchit[23] neir to the borders of Scotland, he stayit[24] a tyme; and sent his brother James before to try[25] the Kings mynde towards him; whilk[25] finding to be placable, he returnit[27] home, was gentillie receivit[28], and lovinglie admonishit[29] to separate theives[30] from him, speciallie them in[31] Annandail; wha[32] had in his absence done manie wicked and cruell[33] facts; whilk[34] when he had faithfully promisit[35], he was not onlie reteinit[36] in his former place of favour, bot[37] also was made Lieutenant general[38] of the hail[39] Kingdome of Scotland. Thus was the fructe bitter of his perillous pilgrinage, as having lousit[40] the brydle to his Enemies, zea[41] geving them power so fare[42] to prevaile, as to imbark the King in oppen quarel aganes[43] him; and thus[44] fare ingadgit[45] him to the casting downe of his houses, and intrometting with

Razed the Castle of Douglas

Earle Douglas returneth, and is weil receivit.

Hol.

Is maid Lieutenant. Anno 1450

[1]invaded [2]recepts [3]tooke [4]travell [5]fermers [6]who [7]rendered [8]commanded [9]vntill such [10]were satisfied [11]goods [12]reported [13]were [14]whiles [15]yett [16]moved [17]astonishd [18]were [19][his] [20]remayned [21]interteined [22]but [23]approched [24]stayed [25]trye [26]which [27]returned [28]received [29]admonished [30]the vnruly borderers [31]especiallie them of [32]who [33]cruell [34]which [35]promised [36]reteined [37]but [38]generall [39]wholle [40]loused [41]yea [42]farr [43]quarell aganst [44]this [45]ingadged

his revenues. This not the les was ather[1] his Princes wisdome, or[2] accounte of authoritie[3] and respect borne[4] him with[5] the King who, how be it he[6] had done the Earle that ather[7] harme or disgrace, could[8] be content[9] so to forget it, receaving him so fare in favour, and advancement, that **[447]** whatever[10] defect might be imputit[11] to the iourney sa[12] taine on, and[13] had sa[14] dangerous a sequel; zit[15] can not this retraite frome that storme bot[16] be commendit[17], gyding[18] throgh sik surges[19] to so peacible a port whatever[20] dexteritie; whereof it war[21] to be wishit[22] the wryters had set[23] downe the meanes, for the more perfyte vnderstanding of the historie. but we most[24] beare with that amongs manie vther[25] defects, and sik[26] wants. Now whatever[27] wisdome (thogh vndescryvit be[28] the particular[29]) may appeare in this, as meikle[30] vnadvysednes is evident[31] in the fact incontinent subioynit[32] hereto;[33] of his journey to[34] England, whilk not[35] acquenting the King there with, he interprysit[36], passing to the[37] Court of England[38] and having privie conference with the King and Quene of England.[39] he pretendit some[40] restitution of some guds[41] taine out of Scotland, and not redrest be[42] the Wardans of England; bot the[43] cause the lighter it was, the greatter suspition did[44] it move[45] in the King of Scotlands mynd; wha[46] could not thinke it appearant[47], that he being of that place, of that courage, of that Natural, wald[48] for sik a[49] occasion take sike[50] a iorney. The true cause is thoght to be, that it was to treate of certane conditions for his assistance to be geven[51] the King of England

His privie conference with the King and Quene of England.

[1]either [2][ather *changed to* either] or *adopted* ^the^ [3][of authoritie] [4]^to^ [5]by [6]^how be it he^ *adopted* [7]either [8]^not the les^ [9]contented [10]whatsoever [11]imputed [12]so ^vnadvisedly^ [13]^which^ [14]so [15]sequele yett [16]but [17]commended [18]^him^ [19]such [surgeons] surges *adopted* [20]^by^ whatsoever [21]were [22]wished [23]sett [24]must [25]other [26]such [27]whatsoever [28]vndescryved by [29]particulare [30]much [31]^was^ [32]subioyned [33]^I meane that^ [34]^back^ into [35]which without [36]^rashlie^ interprysed [37]that [38]Courte [of England] [39]^The cause^ [40]pretended was the [41]goods [42]by [43]But that [44][did] [45]moved [46]mynde; who [47][appearant? *changed to* appairant] probable [48]Nature wold [49]such an [50]such [51]^to^

aganes[1] his Nobilitie, with whom he **[448]** was then in hard tearmes, the warres with the house of Zorke[2] beginning to springe vp; whilk[3] efterwards increast mightelie, and prevailit[4] to the eiecting of him out of the Kingdome; whilk[5] the Quene of England ather[6] foreseeing, or fearing some vther[7] the like interpryse aganes[8] him, had delt with the Earle of Douglas at his coming home throgh England frome Rome, the zeir[9] before, to strenthen them be[10] his help; and appoyntit[11] that[12] his returne for performance, and perfyting theirof. these conditions we find not to have taine anie effect whether because that conspiracie of the Duk[13] of Zorke[14] was not zit come[15] to maturitie, and the Douglas therefor not imployed, bot[16] prevented by death shortlie efter (as we sal heire[17]); or because they war[18] not fully agried[19]: nather is there anie specialitie,[20] what they war, bot[21] are coniectured to be sike[22] as the same King Henrie grantit[23] efter to the Earle of Angus in King James the thrids[24] „ tyme; to wit of lands worth 2000 merks stirling „ erected in a Ducherie[25] to be halden[26] of England; „ without preiudice to his serving the King of „ Scotland at al[27] tymes, and so furthe (as we sal see „ then[28]) not preiudicial to the King of Scotland in „ anie sorte: zit[29] being done without his „ knawledge[30], gave occasion ather[31] to natural jalousie[32] of Princes to think hardlie of it **[449]** be[33] his awne[34] motion; or be[35] his Enemies so to construe it to the King, and steir vp be[36] their speiches that suspicion[37] he inclynit[38] to; of the whilk[39] both he ought to have bene ware[40], and not to have geven sik[41] grounds to the ane, or[42] the vther[43]; by interprysing sik[44] a journey without his

[1]aganst [2]Yorke [3]which [4]prevailed [5]which [6]either [7]other [8]aganst [9]yeir [10]by [11]^had^ appoynted [12]^same^ [13]Duke [14]Yorke [15]yett comd [16]but [17]sall heare [18]were [19]agreed; neither [20]specialltie [21]the ^conditions^ were, but [22]such [23]granted [24]thirds [25]Duchie [26]holden [27]all [28]then see [29]yett [30]knowledge [31]either [32]^the^ ordinarie jealousie [33]by [34]owne ^meere^ [35]by the Earles [36]by [37]^which^ [38]inclyned [39]which [40]wary [41]such [42]nor [43]other [44]such

Manuscr.

Hol. ibidem

kings knawledge[1]. Whether he did acquent the King with the true cause at his returne, it is not certaine; and our wryters seeme to say the contrare. Zit[2] in so fare as he brought letters from the Quene of England to the Quene of Scotland, and she there vpon interceidit[3] for him, it is not vnapparant, bot[4] that he hes acquentit[5] her (and therefor[6] the King also) with the truthe of things, whilk[7] whether the King did not believe; or if his jalousie remaynet[8] not the les; and that he had no wil[9] of that increase[10] of the Earls greatnes, whom he thought was greatter already nor[11] was sure for him, he pardonit[12] him the fact at the intercession of the Quene, and dyvers Noble men; bot spoylit[13] him of the office of Lieutenantrie; and al vther[14] publike charge; whereby he might be made invtile, to the King of England, or les vtile[15], and so be frustrate of the Conditions foresaid at his hands. Nather[16] only did he denude him bot restorit[17] his ancient Enemie William Chrichton[18] to the office of Chancellerie.[19] The Lieutenantrie was geven to the Earle of Orknay. [**450**] This not onlie disapoynting of his hopes, bot[20] disgrace at his Princes hands; both by depressing of him self, and advancing of his Enemies, incensit[21] him aganes[22] the hail[23] Courtiours; taking the Kings action to be done herein[24] by their instigation; bot[25] speciallie his anger was bendit aganes[26] the Chrichton[27]; both as aganes the ancient Enemie of his house, and also the authour of al[28] his present disfavour, by his surmissinge; where throgh transportit[29], he gave place to his passion to carie him a course[30] more then civile, whilk[31] to that tyme he had tempered, reteining it with the brydle of equitie, and him self within the compas of the lawes. Now wheather

The lieutenatrie taine from him

Chrichton restorit to the Chamcellerie

---

[1]allowance [2]contrary. Yett [3]interceeded [4]but [5]hath acquented [6]therefore [7]which [8]jealousie remayned [9]will [10]encrease [11]than [12]pardond [13]but spoyled [14]all other [15]or ^at least^ les vtile to the King of England [16]Neither [17]^(as said is)^ but restored [18]Chrighton [19]^And^ [20]but [21]incensed [22]aganst [23]whalle [24]herein to be done [25]but [26]bended aganst [27]Chrighton [28]all [29]transported [30]^somewhat^ [31]which

altogeather for these causes foresaid, or if irritate be a[1] new cause of malicious speiches vttered be[2] the Chrichton[3]; that the Kingdome of Scotland wald[4] never be at rest, so lang as the house of Douglas was on fute[5]; that in the wrake of it, stude the weil of the Realme, and the peace of al[6] Estats; that necessare[7] it was[8] a man so turbulent of natural[9], so puissant in power, and strange be[10] kynred and allya, wha[11] could be[12] no benefits be appeasit[13], nor by honours satiat, sould be cute af[14], and the publike peace establishit[15] by his death. Or if the Chrichton contryvit[16] these speiches to make him the more odious, and his querrel appeare the iuster aganes[17] him (for both are written) sa[18] it is that the Earle **[451]** causit[19] certane[20] his servands and freinds[21] ly in waite for him, as he was ryding from Edinburgh towards Chrichton; bot[22] he escapet[23] being foreseine theirof (as some wryte) weil accompanied, and excellentlie weil horset[24]; bot not vnbeing woundit[25] himself, and having slane some of them in his escapade. Vthers[26] attribute his escaping to no foresight, and say that he was set[27] on in the night at vnaware, and astonishit[28] at the first; bot[29] being a man of gude[30] courage he recollectit[31] him self, and slew the foremest he met[32] with; and having receivit[33] some wounds, brake throgh them, and reparit[34] to his house of Chrichton[35], where he remainet[36] not lange, when having skarse curit[37] his wounds he conveinit[38] a companie of[39] freinds, and coming suddanlie to Edinburgh had neirby surprysit[40] the Earle of Douglas at vnawars; wha[41] was then in quyet maner luiking[42] for no sik[43] thing, bot[44] that he also getting some advertisment theirof, did advertis the King, that

Buchanan.

Manuscr.

Hol.

Chrighton vnbeset be the Douglas men.

[1]by anie [2]by [3]Chrighton [4]wold [5]foote [6]all [7]necessary [8]^that^ [9]nature [10]stronge by [11]allyance, who [12]by [13]appeased [14]cutt of [15]established [16]Chrighton contryved [17]aganst [18]so [19]caused [20]^of^ [21]^to^ [22]Chrighton; but [23]escaped [24]weill horsed [25]without being wounded [26]escape. Others [27]sett [28]astonished [29]but [30]goode [31]recollected [32]mett [33]received [34]repairit [35]Chrighton [36]remained [37]cured [38]conveined [39]^his^ [40]surprysed [41]who [42]looking [43]such [44]but

Earle Douglas retirit from Court

Bandith with the Earls of Crafurde and Rosse

he could not anie langer indure the Chrichtons hide[1] malice, and practises aganes[2] his lyfe and Estate; and now[3] oppen attempt also, whereof he desyrit[4] the King to excuse him that he could not anie more repaire to Court, so long as the Chrichton[5] was there. And so retyrit[6] him self to his house to remaine as a malcontent for a season. In the meane tyme finding his Enemies thus increase in credit at Courte, and with their credit (as commonlie cometh to passe) in number **[452]** and force; he to strenthen him self also on the vther[7] syde aganes[8] them, enterit[9] in a new confederacie with the Earles of Crafurde and Rosse, men of greattest puissance and force nixt[10] to the Douglases that war[11] in Scotland in those[12] tymes; or rather renewit[13] their old freindshipe; for their houses were in old tyme in great freindshipe with the house of Douglas (as hes[14] bene said) and the house of Crafurde speciallie oblishit[15] to them be dyvers benefits, from the dayes of King Robert the second, and in this same mans tyme had receivit[16] help aganes[17] the Ogilvies; and his father imployed aganes[18] the Bishope of St Androis; and this same Earls wyfe Beatrix Douglas (callit[19] the faire Maden[20] of Galloway) was comed of the house of Crafurde, her mother being a daughter of ane[21] of the Earls, and could not be fare af from this same Earle. The tennor of their band was, that they sould everie ane assist and defend vthers[22], their freinds and dependars aganes al[23] men; have common freinds and Common Enemies; with reservation always and exception of their duetie to their Prince. Bot[24] wheather this band was of new made (as some write); or if it hes[25] bene of old continued from hand to hand; or if it was of ane old band new renewit, as thoght[26] it war intendit[27] in

[1]Chrightons hidd [2]aganst [3]^his^ [4]desyred [5]Chrichton [6]retyred [7]other [8]aganst [9]entered [10]next [11]were [12][*illegible*] those *adopted* [13]renewed [14]hath [15]oblished [16]received [17]aganst [18]aganst [19]called [20]Maiden [21]one [22]others [23]aganst all [24]But [25]hath [26]newly renewed as thogh [27]were intended

Buch.

special aganes[1] the Chrichton[2] and his partiseans[3], and due exception of the King expreslie conteinit[4] in it, zit[5] had the King so **[453]** addictit[6] him self to that syde, as they so occupyet[7] and possest him be[8] feare of the Douglas, or be[9] what somever[10] meanes[11] that he interpret al[12] as done aganes[13] himself; and therefor maters being come to ane oppen hostilitie betwixt the Douglas, and the Chrichton[14], and the Contrie devydit[15] in dyvers factions, when the Earls of Crafurde and Rosse had sent to the Chrichton[16], and dischargit[17] freindshipe with him, as Enemie to their darrest freind be[18] vertue of the fore said leigue[19], he with al[20] vehemencie exaggerating the said leigue[21] as conspiracie aganes[22] the King of sa[23] manie great men, of sa[24] great houses, the King was content to apprehend no lesse. And vpon that ground once satlit[25] his mynd to bige[26] the interpretation of the Earle of Douglas his haile[27] actions, and frame his awen[28] accordinglie aganes[29] him. Nather was he so fortunat, nor so circumspect as to eshew[30] the occasions of fostering that[31] opinion in the King; bot[32] (as it comes to passe) when wrake is to come on men, al[33] things worke that way. So fortuned it with the Earle of Douglas in twa[34] facts; first in the persone of the Lord Hereis, weil[35] hardlie vsit[36] by him (as appearis[37]); then in the persone of the Tutor of Bombie (more iustlie indeid) zit[38] seeming to teast[39] of that, whilk[40] his Enemies alleadgit[41]; more absolutlie vsing his power and priviledgis **[454]** nor[42] the King was content with.

Hol.

Johne Hereis of Tarrigilis.

The occasion of the first, and forme theirof was, that S*ir* William Hereis of Tarrigles, having bene the Earls ancient dependar, led[43] now in this diversitie of these factions, (wheather following the humours of

[1]aganst [2]Chrighton [3][partiseans*?*] partakers [4]conteined [5]yett [6]addicted [7][so] preoccupied [8]by [9]by [10]so ever [11]^else^ [12]interpreted all [13]aganst [14]Chrighton [15]devyded [16]Chrighton [17]discharged [18] by [19]league [20]all [21]league [22]aganst [23]so [24]so [25]setled [26]build [27]whalle [28]owen [29]aganst [30]eschew [31]^hard^ [32]But [33]all [34]two [35]weill [36]vsed [37]appeares [38]indeed) yett [39][teast*?*] taeste [40]which [41]alleadged [42]then [43][led]

Court, and because he countit[1] it justest to follow it; or because he indeid mislikit[2] things done be[3] the border men, wha followit[4] the Douglas) withdrawes himself from his dependance[5], and if he followit[6] not the vther[7] pairt oppenlie (whilk[8] he could hardlie do lying in these[9] pairts where the Douglas greattest power was) zit[10] did he not follow with the Douglas nather, and ather be[11] a verie Enimitie in privat, or a kynd of newtralitie in publike had incurred the like behaviour of the Douglas to him, to behave himself as newtral[12] in his affairs; and as he had abstractit[13] his attendance from the Earle of Douglas, so the Earle abstractit[14] his protection from him. Whilk[15] the theivis of Annandail perceiving (readie ever in sik occasion[16]) made a raid[17] on him, and furrowed[18] his lands: whereof he compleaning to the Earle of Douglas, and receaving[19] according to this their cold disposition foresaid on ather[20] syde; wald[21] neids attempt some what by him self, and therevpon conveining a companie of his freinds, raid[22] in Annandail to have renderit[23] them the lyke, ather be[24] recovering his awen[25], or taking of their guds; bot[26] he was overthrowen be[27] them, and made **[455]** prisoner, and brought to the Earle of Douglas, wha[28] as his awen[29] servand, and taken within his bounds, where his jurisdiction be[30] regalitie, or vtherways was[31], put him to ane assyse, whereby (because he was taine efter he had saisit[32] the guds[33] with rid hand (as they say[34]) was easelie convict of thift, reif,[35] condemned, and execute; being hanged as a theife; not the les for the Kings earnest requesting for him, be letters[36]. A pitieful mater, and greatlie to be lamentit[37], and though vnder the colour of iustice, not taisting sa meikle[38] of justice, as of malice; nor[39]

He hangs the Lord Hereis

Hol.

[1]counted [2]misliked [3]by [4]who followed [5]dependancy [6]followed [7]other [8]which [9]those [10]yett [11]by [12]newtrall [13]abstracted [14]abstracted [15]Which [16]vpon all such occasions [17]raed [18]forrowed [19]^answer^ [20]either [21]wold [22]roid [23]renderd [24]by [25]owen [26]goods; but [27]by [28]who [29]owne [30]by [31]otherways extended [32]saised [33]goods [34]transmit [35]^and^ reef ^and^ [36]by ^his^ letter [37]lamented [38]so much [39]^of the^

indifferencie, whilk[1] sould be in a justicer; having eye to the due circumstances, as partialitie; not without contempt of the King, and his equitable requeist; al[2] circumstances considerit[3] in this behalf. Whilk[4] was also so construed, and gave more just occasion to the misreports of his Enemies,[5] to the increasing of the Kings indignation; whilk be zeilding[6] a lytle of his priviledgis, and having some respect of[7] the Kings request he might have convictit[8] in some measour without anie danger, that he had bene able to have incurrit be[9] the said Lord Heries his Enemitie, if[10] he wald have bene[11] Enemie; and perhaps might have regainet[12] him to his freindshipe, be[13] wyse convoy[14] therin. **[456]** The vther[15] fact, whilk[16] insued on this (not so inique, bot[17] made as odious, as carying the odiousnes of this with it) was that Maklanen Tutor of Bombie, the cheif of that name, and amang the principal houses in Galloway, falling ather in feid or in querrel with a servand of the Earle of Douglases, had slane him; and was theirfor (with his brother partaker of the slaughter) apprehendit[18] and put in prison in the Treive. His freinds made moyen to the Courteours, and be[19] them to the King, informing him that the Earle of Douglas was to execute that man, not so meikle[20] because of the fact, as because he was a favorer, and folower of the best syde (so they callit[21] their awen[22]) desyring him he wald not suffer a noble man, and vtherways[23] a gud[24] man (though that slaughter had happened in his hand[25]) to be drawen not so meikle[26] to judgment, as to a certaine death, before ane[27] and the same man both judge and pairtie; And be[28] this and sik[29] information, whereby oftymes the eares of Princes are deceavit[30] thinking so to withdraw him

[1]which [2]requeest all [3]considerable [4]Which [5]^and^ [6]which by yeelding [7]to [8][convictit *changed to* convicted] mitigated [9]incurred by [10]altho [11]^his^ [12]regained [13]by ^a^ [14]carriage [15]other [16]which [17]but [18]apprehended [19]by [20]much [21]called [22]owen [23]otherways [24]good [25]hands [26]much [27]one [28]by [29]suchlike [30]deceaved

fra[1] the due punishment of justice, perswadit[2] the King to send for him, and if the Earle had anie thing to lay to his charge, that he wald[3] follow him, and persue him before him. Among[4] the furtherers of that sute was Patrik Gray of Fouls (avuncle[5] to the said Tutor) wha[6] was also directit[7] with the Commission to the Earle; as he wha[8] wald both **[457]** be earnest therein being so neir to the pairtie; and wald[9] be respectit[10] being some what of kine to the Earle; The Earle having vnderstude[11] of his Commission, and perceaving therbe[12] that they meanit[13] no vther[14] thing bot[15] to defraude him of justice for the slaughter of his servand, whilk[16] he thought he could not do with his honour; nor wald not permit[17], that he might do it[18] the more calmely, and with the lesse offence (as he thought), having humainlie receivit[19] the said Patrik Gray, interteinit[20] him with dyvers purposes, causet[21] the Tutor in the meane tyme to be put to a[22] assyse, and being condemned, was[23] quicklie convoyet[24] ane myle from thence to ane[25] place callit[26] Carlingworke, and there executed. Efterwards when the Lord Gray (ignorant what was done) had delyverit[27] his commision from the King, the Earle of Douglas answerit[28] he was sorie he was come so lait, shewe[29] him what was done, and desyrit[30] him to excuse him to the King. Whilk[31] the Lord Gray heiring[32], and seing him self eludit[33] in a great chafe and rage presentlie renuncit al[34] kinred and freindshipe, and what ever[35] band[36], where with he might seeme to be oblishit[37] to the Earle of Douglas, wowing[38] that fra[39] that tyme furth, he sould be his deidlie[40] Enemie in al sorte, and be[41] al the meanes he could. Whilk[42] the vther[43] lytle regarding

Executs the Tutor of Bombie

Lord Gray dischargis freindshipe with him.

[1]from [2]^then^ perswaded [3]wold [4][him] his justice. Amongs [5]wncle [6]who [7]directed [8]who [9]wold [10]^also^ respected ^as^ [11]vnderstude [12]therby [13]meant [14]other [15]but [16]which [17][nor... permit] and yett [18][it] what he had determind [19]received [20]interteind [21]causeth [22]an [23]to be [24]convoyed [25]a [26]called [27]delyvered [28]answered [29]laite, shewd [30]desyred [31]Which [32]hearing [33]deluded [34]renunced all [35]soever [36]^besides^ [37]oblished [38]vowing [39]from [40]deadlie [41]by [42]Which [43]other

dimissit[1] him. Bot[2] regard **[458]** as lytle as he lykit[3], the French proverb proveth true, and worthie to be regardit be al[4] men; that there is no lytle Enemie: for he had[5] power to be his death efterwards with his[6] hands, and with counsel[7] compast it; or poussit[8] it fordward, being compasset[9] and devysit[10] by vthers[11]. For being come to the King and declaring the succes of his message al was be[12] him, and the rest of the Courtiours aggravatit[13] in the most haynous sorte; that the Kings commandements ware contemnit, eludit[14] and mokit[15]; that it was lykliest the Earle of Douglas was King; that doubtles he intendit sa[16] to be; zea[17] he behavit[18] him self already as sa[19]; that that was the end and meaning of that quyet conference with the King of England; on that ground raise the licence of the slaughter of sa[20] manie honest men; of spoyling and hairshipe; that innocencie now was contemned for[21] beistlines; faithfulnes towards the King punishit for[22] vnfaithfulnes; that be the Kings indulgence[23] the commone Enemie was become insolent; Let him once tak vpon him his place as King, and once do things be[24] his[25] authoritie, and be his[26] power, then wald[27] appeire wha war[28] freinds, wha war[29] foes. These, and sik[30] as these war[31] the speiches of the Courtiours, and in interpretation of the facts of the Earle[32] Douglas, sik[33] as it pleasit[34] them to make, folowing their humour **[459]** of faction, or of judgment; not considering nather[35] the equitie of what was done (punishing blud[36] by blud[37]); nor the authoritie it was done by (for he had authoritie and jurisdiction sufficient of old tyme grantit be[38] Kings before, to the worth of his predecessors); nather the ordour and formalitie being rightlie and formallie vsit[39] in the procedure; nather his honour in

---

[1]dismissed [2]But [3]lysted [4]regarded by all [5]^the^ [6]^owne^ [7]counsell [8]poust [9]compassed [10]devysed [11]others [12]by [13]aggravated [14]were contemned, eluded [15]moked [16]intended so [17]yea [18]behaved [19]^being^ so [20]so [21]as [22]punished as [23]indulgency [24]by [25]^royall^ [26][be his] [27]wold [28]who were [29]who were [30]such [31]were [32]^of^ [33]such [34]pleased [35]neither [36]blood [37]blood [38]granted by [39]vsed

revenging his servands slaughter; nather what skorne it was to him on the vther[1] pairt, if he had send him; his priviledgis to have bene infringit[2], his servands slane, and no amends of it, bot[3] to be eludit[4] vpon the purchesing of his Enemies; iustice defraudit[5], and the giltie throwen[6] out of his hands; and be[7] their credit with the King procuring him to hinder justice, wha[8] sould have bene the furtherer of it; onlie vpon their particular privat motion and factious[9] inclyning[10]. In thir[11] respects what had bene more extraordinarilie done, wald[12] have bene excusit be thir[13] same men in another, Now in him (thogh done orderlie[14]) is thus traducit[15], aggravat, exaggerat, amplifiet[16], and namit[17] contempt of the King, and affecting of the Crowne: sik[18] is the miserie, (when Princes are movit[19] by pairties to command, or request inique[20] things) there being perril and inconvenients (ather in obeying or refusing their requests) to receive skaith[21] in their rights, skorne **[460]** of their pairtie, or[22] offend whom they wald fain serve[23]. And happie[24] that man that can gyde right betwixt the[25] difficulties; happie wha[26] falleth in sik[27] a Princes handes, as moderats be[28] equitie his commands and requests; or in their iniquitie (when anie happens) (as in what Prince may it not happen) moderats[29] his mynd in the just refusal[30] theirof, taking it rightlie; and countis not his authoritie condemnit[31], when a iniust[32] command is refusit[33]by his subjects. Zea[34] his pleasour to be in what is right and[35] him self obeyit[36]. Wheather it was on the displeasour of this fact, or[37] a Jalousie apprehendit[38] in vther[39] facts of the Douglas, is hard to discerne; bot[40] so it comes to pase[41] his Enemies vsing to their purpose the credulous suspicion of the Prince, they prevailit[42] sa fare[43] as to move the

[1]other [2]infringed [3]but [4]eluded [5]defrauded [6]pulled [7]by [8]who [9]factions ^so^ [10]^him^ [11]these [12]wold [13]excused by these [14]orderlie done [15]traduced [16]amplified [17]named [18]Such [19]moved [20]vniust [21]wrong [22]^to^ [23]fainest please [24]^is^ [25]these [26]who [27]such [28]by [29]moderates [30]refusall [31]condemned [32]an vniust [33]refused^ [34]Yea ^makes^ [35]^thinks^ [36]obeyed ^when that is performed^ [37]^of^ [38]apprehended [39]other [40]But [41]^that^ [42]prevailed [43]so farr

King to resolve[1] the Douglases slaughter, and that (since it[2] could not be gotten be[3] oppen force)[4] in what[5] ever sorte it could[6] be done[7]; whereof when they had advysit[8] on al[9] the meanes[10], this they fand[11] for the most expedient; that he sould be sent for to Court[12] vpon faire promises, and being come[13] the King sould enter[14] with him in termes of querelling[15]; and thereon they that war appoyntit[16] for the purpose[17] sould dispatch him[18].

Earle Douglas slaughter resolvit.

To this effect they causit[19] a certane Courteour of their faction (bot frie[20] from suspicion of Enimitie aganes[21] the Douglas) to addresse him self **[461]** to a gentilman his freind, shewing vnder great privatie, how the Chrichton was retirit[22] to his awin[23] house; that in his absence it war fit[24] the Earle sould take that gude[25] occasion to come and find the King; with whom he might be assurit[26] to find favour, if he wald humblie crave it. The gentilman beleiving his feinzit[27] report, went to the Earle, and delt earnestlie with him to this[28] effect; bot[29] he (having in doubt the craft of the Chrichton[30], and the murther of his Cousins by him, before his eyes) refusit[31] expreslie to go to Court; in whilk[32] there was so manie[33] his Enemies, sa[34] potent, and of sa[35] great credit; and by some of whom he had bene, not long sence, lyen in wait[36] for; except he saw[37] surtie for his lyfe, and libertie. Herevpon he was directlie sent for to come to Court vnder promises of al friedome[38], and assurance by the Kings gret Seale. And to remove al doubt[39] that he could conceive[40], the noble men that war[41] present at Courte, war movit[42] to send ane[43] warrand to him subscryvit[44] with al[45] their hands[46], and sealit[47] with al[48] their

Sent for to Court vnder saif Conduct.

---

[1]give waye to [2]his life [3]not be gotten by lawe; and hardly by [4]^they do resolve to have it^ [5]^so^ [6]can [7]had [8]advysed [9]all [10]^they could^ [11]found [12]Courte [13]^that vpon^ [14]Kings contesting [sould enter] [15][termes of querelling] words [16]appoynted [17]his slaughter [18]tak that occasion to putt hands on him [19]caused [20]but free [21]aganst [22]retired [23]owne [24]were fite [25]goode [26]assured [27]feined [28]that [29]but [30]Chrighton [31]refused [32]which [33]^of^ [34]so [35]so [36]waite [37]^good^ [38]all freedome [39]all doubts [40]conceave [41]were [42]were moved [43]a [44]subscryved [45]all [46]^also^ [47]sealed [48][al]

seals, with their great[1] oathes interponit theirto[2]. Nather[3] that onlie, bot wroite[4] severallie everie man his particular[5] letter, assuring him of the Kings gud wil[6]; and further promising him, if sa war[7] the King wald be sa faithles, as to interprise anie thing aganes[8] him, his lyfe lands or libertie, [**462**] they sould send him home not the les. Quhat[9] could he seik[10] more at their handes? or what could he devyse more[11]? and wha[12] wald have doubtit[13] efter sik[14] assurances? Zit[15] that he sould not repose al[16] his saiftie on his Enemies credit; he accompanies him self to his honour and surtie, with al as[17] might make him frie[18] from anie mans danger. So relying (for the Kings pairt) vpon a saif conduct, and the noble mens credit interponit[19] their with, he gois[20] to Stirling, where the King was, accompaniet[21] with a gude[22] number of his subiects and servands, bot[23] in a peaceble maner; thinking[24] him self be these meanes[25] to be in surtie inought fra vthers[26]. When he was comed, the King efter some sorte of[27] admonition to lieve[28] a more peaceble and orderit[29] lyfe, seemit[30] to apardone[31] him[32] what[33] ever was past; and kyndlie invitit[34] him to supper in the Castle; whilk[35] being cheirfullie and merrelie[36] past, Manuscr. the King takes him asyde to the[37] Inner Chamber, them selves alone, and[38] Patrik Gray the Earls Cousine (bot[39] his[40] Enemie since the execution of the Tutor of Bombie). There the King taking the beginning of his speiches from the valour and faithfulnes of his predecessors, came shortlie to his Quarellit awin[41] indulgencie towards the hail[42] familie[43], and towards him self in particular; then sharplie

[1]greatest [2]^also^ interponed ^for his further confirmation^ [3]Nather [4]but ^they^ wroote [5]particulare [6]good will [7][sa war] by [8]Kings authoritie anie thing were interprysed aganst [9]would notwithstanding guarde him safely home again. What [10]seike [11]beyond this [12]who [13]doubted [14]such [15]Yett [16]all [17]all that [18]free [19]interponed [20]goeth [21]accompanied [22]goode [23]but [24]whereby he thought [25][be *changed to* by these meanes] [26]inough from enemys [27]shorte [of] [28]^him to^ live [29]ordered *changed to* orderlie [30]seemed [31]pardone [32]^for^ [33]^so^ [34]invited [35]which [36]merrilie [37]an [38]with [39]but [40]^mortell^ [41]owin [42]wholle [43]familie

vpbraiding him, how oft he had pardonit[1] him[2] what insolencies [**463**] he had committit[3]. To the whilk[4] the Earle of Douglas answerit[5] verie modestlie, craving his Maiesties pardone of what he had offendit aganes[6] him self in anie sort; that his intention was not aganes[7] him, bot aganes[8] his Enemies: that as for vthers[9] that wald[10] compleine on him, he was readie to satisfie them according to justice, and at the Kings awen[11] pleasour. There restis zit ane[12] thing (answers the King) the league betwixt zow[13] and the Earles of Crafurde and Rosse. I wil[14] have zow[15] presentlie to brek it. At that word the Earle was som what astonishit[16] at the first; zit[17] gathering his spirits togeather, answerit[18] that for him[19] he knew nothing wherein that league could[20] preiudge or offend his Maiestie; in so fare as their duetie to him was therein especiallie reservit:[21] The King replyit[22], I wil have zow[23] presentlie to brek the samin. The Douglas answerit[24], that if he so wald[25] geve him leive[26] to advertis the said Noble men[27], he sould do it; bot vntil[28] their consents war[29] had their vnto, he wald[30] be countit[31] a faith breaker, if having enterit[32] in freindshipe with them, he sould forsaik[33] them, not shawing them a cause why; and theirfor he besought him to have patience. The King replyit[34] in ane angrie maner [**464**] speiking aloude, jf ze will[35] not break it, I sal break it; and with those words strikes him on the breist with ane whinger[36]. at the same instant Patrik Gray strikes him on the heade with ane Pole axe; the rest wha war[37] attending at the doore, heiring[38] the dinne, enterit[39] and slew him out of hand; at leist[40] (to shew their affection towards the King) gave him everie

Slane.

[1]pardond [2]^and^ [3]committed [4]which [5]answered [6]offended against [7]never aganst [8]aganst [9]others [10]wold [11]owen [12]yett one [13]yow [14]will [15]yow [16]astonishd [17]yett [18]answered [19]himself [20]^in reasone^ [21]reserved: ^But^ [22]replyed [23]yow [24]answered [25]so he wold [26]leave [27][man] men *adopted* [28]but vntill [29]were [30]wold [31]counted [32]entered [33]forsaek [34]replyed [35]will [36]a dagger [37]who were [38]hearing [39]noise, entered [40] least

The hand of the King made the instrument of privat mens particulars.

man ane straik[1] efter he was deade. Thus died he, by the hand of the King, by the moyen[2] of his Enemies, they being the cheif movers[3] the King zeilding[4] to their motions, as being his quarrel (so they wald[5] have it to seeme) bot[6] in effect[7] their awen[8] particular; Or if the quarrel[9] was the Kings, it was this fare[10] the Kings, that he tuke[11] it on him as his; spousit[12] theirs for his; and imbarkit[13] him self „ theirin. A common practise to Courtiours, wha „ hes[14] Princes eires[15]; whatever is contrare[16] their „ wil[17], is al aganes[18] the King, is al[19] presumption, „ is al[20] heigh treason; where as they are indeid „ themselves oftymes[21] his greattest Enemies, what „ ever shew of service and affection they seime to „ make[22]; and they[23] whom they cal[24] his Enemies, „ fare[25] more hartilie affectit[26] to him. Their „ quarrels alwyse they make him spous; their „ errours they cause him beare, and the hail[27] hatred „ and jnvy of their enormities; and oftentymes „ drawes[28] him to great absurdities besyds; and „ **[465]** contrare[29] his awen[30] natural[31] to his great „ disgrace; or diminishing of his grace[32] in the eyes „ of his subjects;[33] not without perril[34] of his lyfe, „ and his[35] Estate. Happie[36] Prince that can rightlie „ tak vp, rightlie discerne the quarrels, whilk[37] are „ indeid his awen[38] frome the quarrels, whilk vthers „ wald[39] have him to think[40] his; and so vnderstand „ the disposition of his subjects, that al that is from „ him[41] he count not to be aganes him[42]. These „ Courteours had obtinit[43] this poynt of the King, and be[44] that meanes brought him to do that hard fact, aganes[45] this worthie noble man; as his awen[46] Enemie, an ane aspyrer to his Crowne, where (in

---

[1]a blowe [2]practise [3]^and^ [4]yeilding [5]wold [6]but [7]truth it was [8]owen [9]quarrell [10]farr [11]tooke [12]espoused [13]imbarked [14]Courteours, wha have [15]eares [16]contrary ^to^ [17]will [18]all against [19]all [20]all [21]indeed themselves oftentymes [22]have [23]those [24]call [25]farr [26]affected [27]wholle [28]^they^ drawe him oftentymes [29]contrary ^to^ [30]owen [31]^disposition^ [32]^at least^ [33]^and^ [34]perrill [35][his] [36]^the^ [37]which [38]owen [39]which others wold [40]^to be^ [41]all that are against others [42]aganst himself ^or all that is don for the Courteors to be don for him^ [43]obtined [44]by [45]aganst [46]owen

effect) never anie sik[1] thing appeares to have bene motionit be[2] him; bot[3] onlie aganes[4] his[5] Enemies; or[6] if he aspyrit[7], that aspyring was not so meikle[8] of his intention, as drawen on by the King, geving eare to his Enemies, and spousing[9] their cause, as his awin cause. And for the vther[10] crymes that his Enemies alleadgit on[11] him, smal[12] presumptions, cold conjectures, and no apparance. Bot[13] above al[14] this is the greattest pitie, that they hade power to bring sik sik[15] a King to commit sik[16] a fact contrare[17] his fidelitie solemnellie seallit[18], and sworne be[19] him self, be[20] his Nobiltie to breake the bands[21] of al humaine societie: It is **[466]** worthie[22] considering to see their pretenses and arguments set downe be[23] the wryters; whereby to make him accept of[24] this streange and vnnatural[25] fact. A paradoxe in truthe (thogh a Maxime in Machivelisme). Ane[26] is necessitie: for they make him beleive first, that the Douglas had aspyrit[27], then that he was so stronge[28] that there was no vther remede. Bot[29] for his aspyring, they are[30] weake presumptions that are leaned[31] on: And as for[32] his strenth, he was stronge[33] indeid to defend him self aganes[34] his Enemies, or ane iniust[35] force: Bot it had bene ane vther[36] mater injustlie to have invadit[37] the Kingdome, whilk[38] his force was not stronge[39] for, as iustice and a iust title to a Crowne is a great[40] force, and meikle[41] force vther[42] ways wil[43] prove[44] nothing, aganes[45] it: bot[46] (God having geven his image of authoritie with it in the harts of men) not easelie to be abolishit bot[47] by[48] enorme factes[49]; and skarse by enorme faults[50]; that it was[51] errour to

Be what meanes the King is drawen to it.

Buch.

I. they make the King to beleive the Douglas aspyrit to be King
2. there was no vther remeid to resist him

Manuscr.

---

[1]such [2]motioned by [3]but [4]aganst [5]^privat^ [6][or… awen cause] *corrections of individual items will be noted separately* [7]aspyred [8]much [9]^of^ [10]other [11]alleadged against [12]small [13]^there was^. But [14]all [15]such [16]authorise or countenance such a fact [17][contrary… societie] *individual corrections of this scored out passage will be noted separately* Much more to be an actor thereinto [18]sealled [19]by [20]by [21]bonds [22]^the^ [23]by [24]approve [25]extraordinary [26]One [27]aspyred [28]strong [29]remedy. But [30]^but^ [31]the same doth leane [32]to [33]strong [34]aganst [35]any vniust [36]other [37]invaded [38]which [39]^so^ stronge [40]an vnmatcheable [41]much [42]other [43]will [44]^but^ [45]aganst [46]but [47]abolished even [48]^the most^ enormous [49]faults [50][and ^even^… faults] [51]^an^

Hol. 1452

think, there was no remede[1] in a iust authoritie to defend it self without quyting it self, and becoming iniustice; and that in sik a hateful[2] maner; bot be[3] the contrare[4] it was not onlie the meane to defend him self, bot[5] almost the meane to be depryvit[6] of that whilk[7] he wald have had men thinking[8] he preservit[9] by it; to wit, of[10] his Crowne: for the fact being so filthie[11], it not onlie movit[12] the freinds and folowers of the Douglas **[467]** to rebellion[13], bot also incensit[14] the hail[15] Commone People; that if the Earle of Douglas his brother, wha succeidit[16] him, had bene as skilful[17] and politike, as he had power sufficient, the King might have bene set besyde his Throne[18]; and as it was he was once in[19] great brangle, and resolvit[20] to quyt the Countrie, had not bene the counsel[21] of James Kennedie[22] Bishope of S. Androis; So fare[23] was this fact from the establishing of his Throne, as[24] they made[25] him to think! Therefor the honestie and lawfulnes of it, is to carefullie weyed[26]. It is lawful (say they) to take fraude in the awen[27] craft of it. And indeid that saying is most true, gud[28], and conforme to al[29] wisdome, being rightlie taine; that is to say, Let fraud work on fraudfullie, til[30] in his awen[31] fraude he having[32] intangled, and entrappit[33] him self, and[34] become as[35] giltie;[36] so obnoxious to a lawful, and orderlie iust judgment. Bot[37] that for to meit[38] fraude, men may iustlie vse fraude; and that aganes al[39] promises, ather[40] seales or[41] subscriptions, to the extremitie of murther; changing iustice to iniustice, in the verie seat of iustice,[42] is not, nor ever was, nor can[43] vnder vnder anie pretence (as it whilk[44]

3. that it was lawful to take fraude in the awen craft of it.

How that is to be taine.

[1]remedy [2]such an extraordinary [3]But by [4]contrary [5]but [6]depryved [7]which [8]think [9]preserved [10][of] [11][so filthie] such [12]moved [13]defection [14]incensed [15]whalle [16]who suceided [17]skilfull [18]in danger of his Crowne [19]^a^ [20]resolved [21]counsell [22]^the^ [23]farr ^off^ [24]which [25]would have had [26][Therefor... to *changed to* too carefullie weyed] Yett such kind of doeings never want such men as these to make Apologies for them [27]owen [28]good [29]all ^true^ [30]till [31]owen [32]the fraudfull have [33]entrapped [34][and] till he [35][as] flatly [36]^and^ [37]But [38]meet [39]aganst all [40]both [41]and [42]^It^ [43]^be iustified^ [44]that which

breakes the bands[1] of[2] humaine societie) be allowit in reason. It is ane vnworthe Kingdome, that can not vther ways defend **[468]** it self, and an vnkindlie, and base mynd, that can demit it self to sik base meanes[3]. It hes[4] also bene pretendit[5] by some for colour of sik[6] a fact, that by it meikle bludshed[7] is eshewit[8], that wald be committit[9] before sik ane war vther[10] ways cut af (whilk[11] I mervel they have omittit) bot[12] that is frivolous among[13] the rest; for it is the cause of meikle bludshed[14], taking away trust, and so peace, ending warres no vther[15] wayes, than be[16] the destruction of the one pairtie. Besyds this they insinuatit[17] it for a poynt of want of Courage, and Cowardise[18] in the King, if he durst not sa meikle[19] as deceive him. Whereby they wald meane[20] it was[21] Courage to deceive. Ane vnhappie darring[22], to dare[23] do a wrange[24], and verie fare misnamit[25]. And last of al[26] they half menace to abandon, and desert him, and provyde for them selves at the hands of the Douglas as the stronger partie; whom if the King wald[27] not slay[28], they wald[29] follow; and that ther was no vther[30] remeid[31] left them. Sik[32] boldnes had they taken to half menace their maister[33] and King; and sik[34] is the weaknes of that place, where it dimitteth[35] it self to servands. Be[36] these meanes was this gude[37] King fare contrair[38] to his awne[39] natural[40], drawen on be[41] them who had his eare to this vnnatural[42] fact, as most lawful and flat necesarie. Zit[43] was nether his pretendit[44] necessitie, nether his alledgit[45] lawfulnes **[469]** sufficient to defend the fact, even to[46] the judgment of the doers them selves: and therefor the Courteours fand[47] out

4 that bludshed was eshewit sa.

5 that it was of Cowardise not to do it. *Si ne id quidem auderet.*

Quid superesse nisi ut sibi considerent

[1]bonds [2]^all^ [3][be allowit *changed to* allowed... sik *changed to* such base meanes] [4]hath [5]pretended [6]such [7]much bloodshed [8]eschewed [9]might have bin committed *changed to* shead [10]such a one were other [11]cutt of (whilk [12]omitted) but [13]amongs [14]much bloodshed [15]other [16]by [17]insinuated [18][and Cowardise] [19]so much [20]declare that [21]^an act of^ [22]dareing [23]^to^ [24]wronge [25]farr misnamed [26]all [27]wold [28]dispatch [29]wold [30]other [31]remedy [32]Such [33]maester [34]such [35]demitteth [36]By [37]goode [38]farr contrairy [39]owne [40]^disposition^ [41]by [42]vnlawfull [43]Yett [44]pretended [45]this alledged [46]in [47]found

another meane to put[1] some faire face, at leist[2] some coullarable[3] excuse on[4] it (as they thought); for ashamit[5] of these alledgeances, or mistrusting[6] they wald[7] be acceptable[8] for iust causes of faith breaking; and fearing they sould be by al[9] men detestit[10], they gave it[11] out the slaughter was not committit[12] of set purpose, bot[13] fallen out by venture[14]; and that the King had not[15] intent to slay[16] him; bot[17] him self by his indiscretion had procurit[18] it; having irritate the King by his presumptuous answers. Bot[19] this is ane[20] weake excuse to commit murther contrare[21] promise (if it had bene sa) and not having[22] apparence to be sa; Nather was it beleivit[23] in these[24] dayes; and the wryters since witnesse the contrare[25], (as may be seine in the perswasions foresaid, whilk[26] the Courteours gave him) and sayes[27] plainlie, that the Courteours wald[28] have had it appearing, that it came by his arrogancie in his answers, bot[29] not that it was so indeid. He had geven over meikle[30] mater to his Enemies to worke on, be[31] his rashe voyage to[32] England and privie conference with the King and Quene there: bot this (is[33] ane oversight onlie,[34] appeirantlie **[470]** so tryed and knawen be[35] the King) had bene forgevin him. He had bene vehement in the revenge of the slaughter of his Cousin and servand Johne Auhinlek, bot[36] that (thogh vehement) zit[37] not as iniust;[38] we never find as imputit[39] to him. He had aganes[40] equitie[41] execute the Lord Hereis, zit[42] by a forme of law, whereof the particulars not being perfytlie knawen[43], the judgment is difficile; zit sa[44] (as for aught we can see) no wayes to be excusit[45]. The execution of the Tutor of Bombie, was verie

Siue responsi (vt videri volebant Aulici) contumacia offensus

---

[1]putt [2]least [3]^an^ [4]vpon [5]eshamed [6]^that^ [7]wold ^not^ [8]held [9]all [10]detested [11]^that^ [12]committed [13]but [14]adventure [15]^the^ [16]slaye [17]but ^that^ [18]procured [19]But [20]^other^ [21]contrary ^to^ [22]so) whereof there was no [23]that it was so; neither was the same believed [24]those [25][the wryters since ^do^ witnesse the contrare *changed to* contrary] [26]which [27]^the writers since witnes the contrary^ saying [28]wold [29]but [30]too much [31]vpon, by [32]into [33]as [34]^and^ [35]knowen by [36]but [37]yet [38]^for^ [39]it to be imputed [40]aganst [41]^caused^ [42]yet [43]knowen [44]Yett so [45]excused

gude[1] justice, and vnreprobable; thogh it bred him[2] most hatred and il wil[3] at Courte. Other particulars, are not mentioned,[4] saying[5] generallie, that he beire[6] with thievis[7], to have their assistance. Ane il[8] vnwyse course, and ever pernicious, to the vsers[9] of them[10], to harme them he hated[11]; a fare[12] worse and vnworthie[13] fact, vnfit[14] for a generous mynd to companion it selfe with them, whom it sould punish; and to participate of the giltines, it sould correct. Bot how far ather[15] of these twa meanes hes[16] bene vsit[17] by him,[18] is not very certaine; at leist is[19] not speciallie set[20] downe. And for the speiches[21] of his Enemies reproching him[22] in the hatefullest sorte, they man[23] not be taine al as truthes[24]. Al[25] agrie[26] he was a man of great **[471]** power, great policie, great execution[27], greatter expectation; in whom the name of Douglas rose[28] to that greattest tope[29] of height; and with[30] whom it begoude to fal; whilk[31] efterwards was accomplishit[32] in his successor, as sal[33] be said[34]. The slaughter was committit[35] the 13. of Februar, 1452 esteemit to have bene Fastingseven efter the Romane supputation, or in the 1451 Fastingseven, as Maister Johne Maior calleth it, according to the Compt of Scotland. Efter he had bene Earle the space of nyne zeirs[36], or thereby, having left no Children efter him. Where he was buried, what was done with his bodie, no mention is in historie.

[1]goode [2]^the^ [3]ill will [4]^they^ [5]^onely^ [6]beare [7]theevis [8]ill ^and^ [9]mak vse [10]such [11]whom one hates [12]farr [13][and vnworthie] [14]vnfitt [15]either [16]two faultes have [17]vsed *changed to* practised [18]^it^ [19]least [is] [20]sett [21]speeches [22][them] him *adopted* [23]all must [24][al as truthes] for truth which they saye [25]All men [26]^that^ [27]activity and [28]arose [29]topp [30]in [31][it begoude... fal *changed to* fall; which] that same exceding greatnes, drew neere, the vtmost period. Which [32] accomplished [33]sall [34]^herefter^ [35]committed [36]yeirs

[472] The Life of[1] James 4 of that name[2], the 18 Lord, 9, and last Earle of Douglas, 6 Duk of Turain *etc*[3]

William Earle of Douglas being thus slane be[4] instigation of these Courteours his Enemies, and be[5] the meanes foresaid, to the end (as they wald have it seine) that the King might be establishit[6] in his Crowne; by the taking away of him, whom they made the King[7] think was so great a[8] Enemie to[9] him; sa[10] far[11] was it from working that effect, that be[12] the contrare[13], there was nothing neirer nor[14] it had bene the verie occasion to have spoylit[15] him theirof. For the[16] Douglass wha[17] before tuike[18] the Chrichton[19], and his faction onlie for their Enemie[20], now takes[21] the King for their Enemie: they wha[22] before thought not their greifes[23] the Kings doing, now takes them for the Kingis doing: they wha[24] before war[25] onlie malcontents[26] within the bounds of obedience, and had[27] a gud[28] opinion of the King; now becomes Enemies with an il opinion of him as a wicked man[29]: they wha[30] before had conteinit[31] themselves in Civil[32] termes; now becomes oppenlie rebellious; and they who had gud[33] hope, and luikit[34] for reconcilment, now castis[35] af al hope theirof; and (maters becoming vnreconcileable) **[473]** castes af al[36] love, al[37] regarde, al[38] reverence; Al[39] their harts being loaden[40] with the iniurie, with the dishonestie, with the horrour of it; bursts out al in[41] outragious words, and deids; things coming to

---

[1]^the 4.^ [2][of that name] [3][6 Duk of Turain] [4]by ^the^ [5]by [6]established [7]^to^ [8]an [9]vnto [10]so [11]^of^ [12]by [13]contrary [14]neerer than [15]spoyled [16]^Earle of^ [17]^his successor^ who [18]tooke [19]Chrighton [20]his Enemies [21]betakes ^him to^ [22]himself, hee who [23]his predecessors Greevances to be [24]directly to be his. hee and his friends who [25]were [26]^but^ [27]^still^ [28]good [29][Enemies… as ^of^… man] ill affected to his Majestie himself [30]who [31]conteined [32]Civile [33]good [34]looked ^hitherto^ [35]cast [36]^withall^ all [37]all [38]all [39]All [40][*illegible*] loaden *adopted* [41][the iniurie… dishonestie *changed to* deshonestie… in] heavy displeasure and indignation of what was don. Bursting fourth into vnfitting and

that poynt[1], that[2] could not be endit bot[3] by the[4] destruction of the one pairtie, ather they to wrake the King, or to be wraked by him[5]. Where the hardest lotte[6] at the first (by al[7] apparence) was the Kings; the power of his[8] adverse pairtie being so great, their mynds so enflammed, their yre[9] so incensit aganes[10] him. Nather the pairtie onlie, bot[11] the hail[12] people, (in a maner)[13] detesting the horriblenes of[14] the fact, in sik[15] sorte that he was put by al[16] his shiftes, and[17] driven to sik point of dispaire[18], as to have left[19] the Contrie, and fled[20] by sea to[21] France. For thogh the Earle himselfe was dead, zit[22] had he[23] behind him in the Towne of Stirling that were come[24] thether with him four[25] brethrein, of whom the eldest callit[26] James thrie zeirs[27] before, vpon the defunct Earls iourney to Rome to the Jubile be[28] the Kings consent[29], was provydit[30] to the living, in case of his brothers discease: He with the rest of the Nobilitie their favorers having hard[31] the report of his[32] slaughter, first astonishit[33] by the suddane newes[34] rane to armes with great tumult, **[474]** bot[35] having continit[36] them selves, and commanding their companies to be at quyet, everie man halding[37] him within his awen[38] lodging, on the morne being conveinit[39] in Counsel[40], according to the defuncts Ordinance, and the Kings consent therto[41] of before, he was declared lawful air[42] and successour to his brother Earle William, and so[43] was the Eightein Lord and Nynt Earle of Douglas, thrid Earle of Wigtoun, Lord of Galloway, Bothuel and Annandail, Sixt Duk of Turain, and Lord of

[1]hight [2]^they^ [3]ended but [4]^apparent^ [5][ather… by him] [6][latte?] lotte [7]all [8]the [9]ire [10]incensed aganst [11]but [12][hail] [13][(in a maner)] in generall [14][the horriblenes of] [15]such [16]all [17][put… al *changed to* all… and] was [18]such a strait and exigent [19]think of leaving [20]of goeing [21]see into [22]yett [23]^left^ [24]comd [25]foure [26]called [27]three yeirs [28]Jubilæ by [29]license [30]provyded [31]heard [32]the Earles [33][first] ^being^ estonished [34]^first^ [35]but [36]contined [37]holding [38]owen [39][on… conveinit *changed to* conveined] the next morning they all meeting together [40]Counsell [41]^had^ [42]they acknowledged him lawfull aire [43]^he^

Longaville. Therefter[1] with manie bitter words aganes the treasonable periurie of the King and Courteours, exhortes[2] them wha war[3] present on his „ pairtie to lay seige[4] to the Castle;[5] sent for their „ freinds and dependars from al[6] quarters, and drew „ out of their lurking holes these men valiant onlie „ to perfidie[7]; whils as zit[8] they wawerit[9] vncertaine „ of their Counsels, and trimbling with the giltines „ of so horrible a fact[10]. They wha war[11] present „ praisit[12] his pietie towards his defunct[13] brother, „ and his courage also; zit[14] because they war „ come[15] in a peaceble maner, and vnprovydit[16] of „ thinges necessarie for so great a worke[17], they „ absteinit[18] from the seige; whilk[19] if they had according to the Earls mynd bidden at (as the moments of tyme are of great weight in sik[20] caises) whils the odiousnes of the[21] fact was zit grein[22]; the King **[475]** and his followers being vnprovydit[23], and vnforesein in anie certaine course of their affairs[24], as nather able to consult, nor meit for consultation[25], the Castle being inclosit[26] whilk being also (as is to be supposed) not[27] weil wittualet[28] for a seige, hardlie could the King have escapit[29] their hands: Nather[30] was the matter so difficile for them to have remainit[31], and sending[32] for the rest of their freinds, and anie vther[33] provision whilk[34] they laikit[35], who war[36] able to returne efter fyve weekes leasour geven the King, and to do that[37] they did. Nather[38] could the King having al[39] that space and tyme to draw his ende[40] (as we say;) to consult, advyse and provyde for his best; find anie meanes sufficient to match them. For[41] having vpon this their deliberation

Buch.

[1]Longuevile. And then hee [2]passionat and vehement words, doth exhorte [3]who were [4]seige [5]^They^ [6]all [7][and drew… perfidie] to assault the Enemyes [8][as zit *changed to* yett] [9]wavered as yett [10][of their… a fact] what to resolve in such a cace [11]who were [12]praised [13]dead [14]yett [15]were comd [16]vnprovyded [17]an interprise [18]absteined [19]seege which [20]such [21][odiousnes… the *sic*] detestation [22]yett greine [23]vnprovyded [24]effairs [25][as… meit *changed to* meet… consultation] [26]^once^ inclosed [27][being… not] and not [28]wittualed [29]escaped [30]Neither [31]remained [32]^to have^ sent [33]other [34]which [35]lacked [36]were [37]what [38]^then^ performed. Neither [39]all [40]breath [41]^they^

resolvit[1] on the worst pairt (be al[2] apparence) and depairted to their houses, and taine ful[3] advyse of al[4] their affairs, they returnit[5] the Twenty fyve of Marche, and be[6] the way[7] James Hamiltoun[8] trailling[9] the Kings saife conduct (whilk[10] had bene sent to the Earle that was slane) with the great seale hinging[11] at it, at the tail[12] of ane il favored meire (the most deforme they could gette[13]) throgh the streits[14] of al[15] the Townes and Villages, as they went;[16] absteining fra na[17] contumelie of words against **[476]** the King, his Counsellors and Courteours,[18] Came to Stirling to[19] the Mercat Crosse, and there sounding with fyve hundreth blowing hornes and trumpets, be[20] the voyce of ane Herauld proclamit the King and them that war with him mansworne traitours to God and man; and to be abhorred by men. Vthers wreite[21] that they went to the Castle gate, and made that proclamation, the King heiring and seeing, and luiking on them[22]; and that it was done on the[34] morne efter the slaughter. Therefter they spoylit[24] the towne, and angrie even at the jnnocent[25] place, sent bak James Hamiltoun Laird[26] of Kadzow[27], and brunt it. Where it is to be considerit[28] what is the cause that these men, wha[29] before war on the advysement of seiging[30] the Castle, nather stayet, bot because[31] they were vnprovydit[32]; being now comed agane, and provydit, absteinit[33] not the lesse from the seige[34] of

Returns Marche 25.

Trailes the Kings great seale.

Proclames King and Courtiours traitours. Manuscr.

Brunt Stirling Hol.

---

[1]resolved [2]^for themselves^ (by all [3]full [4]^of^ *adopted* all [5]returned [6]by [7]^vsed a newe and exorbitant kinde of revenge^ [8]^of Cadyow^ [9]trailleing [10]which [11]hanging [12]taile [13][ane il... meire *changed to* meere... gette)] an ill favoured Mare [14]streets [15]all [16]^And^ [17]from no [18][against... Courteours] Came [19][to] where they did the like, and att [20][and there sounding... trumpets be] with the sound of many hornes and trumpetts by [21][proclamit *changed to* proclamed... ware *changed to* were... men] of their own making made a proclamation with many contumelious words expressing their indignation and desire of revenge, with the causes thereof. Others write [22][the King... luiking *changed to* looking on them] in the Kings hearing [23]^next^ [24]spoyled [25]sakles [26][Laird] [27]Kadyow [28]considered [29]who [30][ware *changed to* were... seiging] advised to beseige [31][nather stayet bot *changed to* stayed bute because] and forbar onely for that [32]vnprovyded ^at that instant^ [33]provyded, absteined [34][the seige... king was] beseigeing ^therof^

the Castle wherein the King was[1], having nothing to let[2] them; and whilk[3] if they had obteinit[4], they had inioyet ful[5] victorie, being Maisters of the feilds, the King inclosit[6], and excludit[7] from his favorers[8]: No vther[9] (by appearance) could[10] have made them[11] heade against the Douglas; for nather[12] could anie have taine it **[477]** vpon them; nather wald[13] the people[14] have followit[15] them; at leist[16] not so frielie[17]. Wheather[18] because they had no hope to force it, being strong; Nather soone to famish it, being weil provydit[19] for a long tyme, that[20] they thought not fit[21] to tyne; or if they choose to spoyle[22] him first of his favorers[23], forcing them to leave him; wha[24] they thought wald then[25] be easelie overtaken, having onlie a single house to confide in: Or what[26] ever[27] occasion[28] was theirof[29]; our histories (verie defective in this special[30] point) tells[31] not. Bot[32] so it was, that they leaving the Principal, (the King himself)[33] wherein might have consistit[34] the hail[35] sume of a ful[36] victorie, and to whilk[37] they sould cheiflie[38] have directit[39] their courses; contentit[40] onlie to have blasfemit[41], and reprochit[42] him, turnit towards his favorers[43], spoyling and hearying sik as remaynit on his syde[44].

The King disparing determinit to goe to France. Hol. Manuscr.

Whereby[45] the King was so put to his shiftes, that he determinit to leave[46] the Countrie, and to flee in[47] France, had not James Kennedie[48] Bishope of St Androis causit[49] him to stay, and hope for a[50] better; shewing[51] him, that if he could keipe[52] himselfe a

[1][wherein... was] [2]lett ^or hinder^ [3][and whilk] which [4]obteined [5]inioyed ^a^ full [6]inclosed [7]^so^ excluded [8]favorites [9]other [10]^ever^ [11][them] [12]neither [13]neither wold [14]^(as was thought)^ [15]followed [16]least [17]freelie [18]^it was^ [19]weill provyded [20]which [21]fitt [22]deprive [23]^abroad^ [24][who] And [25]^that those that were within^ wold [then] [26]^so^ [27]^other [28]^there^ [29][theirof] [30][special] [31]^was^ [32]But [33]Principall [(the... himself)] [34]consisted [35][hail] [36]full [37]which [38]might safely [39]directed [40]^being^ contented [41][to... blasfemit] with the bafling [42]reproches ^aforesaid^. [43]they turned onely against the enemies abroad, by [44]harrying them and their parttakers [45]^notwithstanding^ [46][so put... determinit *changed to* determined... leave] brought to such a straite, as it was thought he wold have left [47]have gon over into [48]^the^ [49]caused *changed to* aduised [50][a] [51]schowing [52]keepe

Confortit by Bishope Kennedie

fore hand[1], have patience, and linger a while, tyme wald[2] worke[3] dissolving of that **[478]** faction. Amongs them wha war on the Kings syde[4], was some of the principals of the Name of Douglas, nixt[5] to the Earle, and his brethrene; to wit[6], the Earle of Angus brother vterine[7] to this James Kennedie by their[8] mother, daughter to King Robert the thrid, and sister to King James the first, be whilk[9] meanes they war[10] Cousin germans to the King, James the second. And pairtlie for that cause the said Earle followet[11] him aganes[12] the Earle of Douglas; pairtlie also[13] counting it right[14] to follow him as[15] his King[16]; and pairtlie perswadit[17] by his brother to take that course, as fittist[18] for him, wha needit[19] not (said he) luike[20] for anie advancement, during the standing of the Earldome of Douglas;[21] that the decay of it wald[22] be his preferment. There was also Johne, or rather James Lord of Dalkeith, wha[23] had maried the Kings sister, as Holinsyde wryteth in the lyfe of Makbeth, where he deducis the genealogie of the Stewarts from Fleanchus, sone to Banquho; as also the Manuscript on this same place; and the contract whilk[24] the Earle of Morton zit hes[25], testifeeing the samein; also the Manuscript in the lyfe of Gros James (this mans father) sayth that the Lord of Dalkeith, **[479]** or rather Henrie his sone maried the said Gros James Douglas eldest daughter, this Earls sister, callit[26] Margaret. Wheather therfore having maried the Kings sister, and sa[27] frack on that syde; or having maried the said Earles sister, and being of the Name, the Earle of Douglas was sa meikle[28] the more incensit aganes[29] him[30] that without regarde theirof he ioynit to their Enemies[31], and therfore[32]

[1]to the fore [2]wold [3]^the^ [4]who stuck to the King [5]next [6]witt [7][vterine] [8]the [9]by which [10]were [11]followed [12]aganst [13]But cheeflie [14]his duetie [15]followe [him as] [16]Soverane [17]as also he was perswaded [18]^the^ fittest [19]himself, who needed [20]^to^ looke [21]^and^ [22]wold [23]who [24]which [25]yett hath [26]called [27]^being^ so [28]so much [29]incensed aganst [30]^in^ [31]ioyned with the other partye [32]^he^

Earle Douglas seigeth Dalkeith in vaine

laid seige to the Castle of Dalkeith, binding him selfe with ane oath not to depairt therefrom, til[1] he had gotten it. bot[2] it was valiantlie defendit be[3] Patrik Cokburne of Ormistoun[4] (or rather Clerkingtoun) in sik[5] sorte, that he was constrainit[6] efter great travel[7], and trouble of his men with watching, and manie woundes to lift the seige[8], and departe. The King had in the meane tyme conveinit ane[9] companie of men to have releivit[10] the seige; bot[11] finding that his power was not[12] sufficient to that effect, he determinit[13] to attend the coming of Alexander Gordoun Earle of Huntlie, his brother in law (or sister sone) whom he made Lieutenant, wha[14] was said to be[15] coming, with ane[16] great armie collectit[17] out of the farrest[18] pairts of the Northe; bot as he was marching throgh Angus the 28 of May he was rencountered[19] **[480]** at Breichen, by the Earle of Crafurde, intending to have stayet[20] his passage; where was foughen[21] a great battle betwixt them; in sik[22] sorte, that the Earle of Huntlies mid[23] battle was almost defate, and readie to give bake, not susteining the impression of the Earle of Crafurds men; whilk[24] was so vehement, that they had almost overthrowen the Kings standart[25] brought there, and displayed be[26] the Earle of Hunlie[27]; had not bene the cowardlie and treacherous flight of Johne Collesse of Bonnimoone, to whom the left winge of the Earle of Crafurds battle was committit; wha[28] in the mids of the conflict (offendit[29] with the said Earle) for that he refusit[30] him that same morning a pairt of the Baronie of Ferme (nixt[31] adiacent to his house) fled of purpose out of the battle; and so left the middle ward[32] naiked on the one syde of the special[33] force, that the said Earle had; whilk[34] was the battle[35] axes,

Earle of Huntlie vanquishit the Earle of Crafurde

[1]till [2]taken it in. but [3]defended by [4]Ormestoun [5]such [6]constrained [7]travell [8]seege [9]conveined a [10]releived [11]but [12]^yett^ [13]determined [14]who [15]^in^ [16]a [17]collected [18]furthest [19]encountered [20]stayed [21]fought [22]such [23]midd [24]armye; which [25]standard [26]by [27]Huntlie [28]committed; who [29]offended [30]refused [31]next [32]warde [33]speciall [34]which [35]^of^

(or bil men as they cal[1] them in England) be[2] whose flight, they wha war[3] almost victors, being terified; turnit[4] bakes, and left the victorie to the Earle of Hunlies[5] syde, fare bezond[6] his awen[7] expectation; bot[8] not without great slaughter of his freinds, and[9] servands[10] followers, and[11] of his[12] Name. Among whom war[13] also twa[14] of his brethrene. **[481]** He had before the battle that same day geven lands to the principal[15] men of these[16] surnames, that war[17] with him; as Forbesis, Leslies, Vruins, Ogilvies, Grants, and dyvers vthers; whilk[18] made them[19] fight[20] more valiantlie. The Earle of Crafurde lost also manie of his with his brother Johne Lindsay; sa[21] that the slaughter on both sydes was counted almost equal. Whilk[22] was the cause that the Earle of Huntlie thogh he had the name of victorie, zit[23] could not marche foreward to the King, as he intendit; bot[24] pairtlie for the great slaughter committit[25] on his syde also, pairtlie because he was advertisit[26] that Archbald Douglas Earle of Murray had invadit[27] his lands, and brunt the Peil[28] of Streabogie; he returnit[29] speidelie to his awen[30] countrie, whilk[31] gave the Earle of Crafurde occasion and leasour to powre out his wraith aganis[32] them that had so traiterouslie desertit[33] him; whose lands he waistit[34] with fyre and sworde, and demolishit[35] their Castles; Bot[36] the Earle of Huntlie being returnit[37] to the North, not onlie recompensit[38] the domages done[39] him by the Earle of Murray; bot[40] also expellet[41] him out of the hail[42] bounds of Murray; Thus sayes our histories summerlie; bot[43] it was not done with **[482]** out conflict, and mutual harme: for the Earle of Huntlie coming to Elgen in Murray, fand[44] it devydit[45], the one halfe standing

Hol.

Hol.

Huntlie expelleth the Earle of Murray.

---

[1]call [2]by [3]who were [4]terrifyed, turned [5]Huntlies [6]farr beyond [7]owen [8]but [9][and] [10]^and^ [11]^those specially^ [12]^owne^ [13]were [14]two [15]principall [16]those [17]were [18]others; which [19]^to^ [20]^the^ [21]so [22]equall. Which [23]yett [24]intended; but [25]committed [26]advertised [27]invaded [28]Peill [29]returned [30]owen [31]which [32]aganist [33]deserted [34]waisted [35]demolished [36]But [37]returned [38]recompensed [39]^to^ [40]but [41]expelled [42]wholle [43]But [44]found [45]devyded

for him, the vther[1] halfe (and almost the vther syde of the streit[2]) standing for the Earle of Murray: „ therefor he brunt the vther[3] halfe, whereof raise a „ proverbe to this day: halfe done as Elgen was „ brunt. Whils he is there, the Earle of Murray conveinit[4] his power; and[5] standing most be[6] footemen, set him selfe downe on a hil some twa[7] or thrie myles callit[8] the Drum of Pluskardein; inaccessible to horsmen. The Earle of Huntlie furrowit[9] his lands to wite[10],... . Bot[11] the Earle of Murray finding them so skatterit, invadit[12] them, coming from his strenth, and falling vpon 400 or 500 horsmen, dryves them to a boge[13] callit[14] the Boge[15] of Dunkintie in the boundes of Pittindriche ful[16] of Quavis[17] or Marashis so deipe, that a speire may be put in[18] them, nather[19] find the ground[20]. In this Boge[21] manie war[22] drowned, the rest slane, few or nane[23] of that companie escaping. It is zit[24] to be seine[25] some swordes, some steil bonnets[26], and sik[27] thinges[28] to be found in it now and then. Also they made of it[29] in their rude [**483**] forme, thus[30]:

> Quhere left thow thy men, thow Gordoun the gay?
> In the Boge[31] of Dunkintie mawing[32] the hay.

Alwyse these victories in the north pairts together with the repulse of the Douglas[33] (at leist[34] his retreit[35] from the seige of Dalkeith, in vaine asseigit) encouragit[36] the King so that he begoude to conceave a better hope of his affairs[37]; and by the Counsel of Bishope James Kennedie convocats[38] a Parlament in[39] Edinburgh, and summonds the Earle of Douglas and his adherents to compeire at it; whilk[40] he was sa fare fra[41] obeying, that he causit[42]

---

[1]other [2]street [3]other [4]conveined *changed to* assembled [5]which [6]by [7]twoe [8]^of^ called [9]forrowed [10]witt [11]But [12]skattered, invaded [13]bogge [14]called [15]Bogge [16]full [17]Quagmyres [18]into [19]and not [20]bottome [21]Bogge [22]were [23]none [24]yett [25]^that^ [26]cappes [27]such [28]^are^ [29]^this rhyme^ [30][thus] [31]Bogge [32]mowing [33](^and^ [34]least [35]retreet [36]asseiged) encouraged [37]effairs [38]calles [39]to [40]which [41]farr from [42]caused

wrytings to be affixit[1] vpon the kirke[2] dore, and vther[3] publike places (sealit[4] with the Douglas[5] seale) conteining in effect, that the Earle from that furth wald[6] nather obey citation, nor vther[7] commandement of the Kings, nor in anie sorte commit his lyfe vnto him; wha[8] having allurit[9] his Cousigns to Edinburgh,[10] his brother to Stirling vnder[11] saife conduct had traiterouslie murderzit them[12] without anie order of lawe. Here vpon war[13] the Earle, and his thrie[14] brethrene, Archbald, George (or rather Hugh) and Johne, with Beatrix their sister in law (wyfe to the defunct Earle) declared rebels and forfaultit[15]; and with them Alexander Earle [**484**] of Crafurde, and James Lord Hamiltoun, and that the number of the Nobilitie sould not seeme to be diminishit be[16] their forfalture, dyvers war[17] made lords, and some of them rewardit[18] with the guds[19] and lands of the forfaultit[20]. Therefter ane armie was gatherit[21] to persue them, their lands waistit[22], their guds[23] driven away, their Cornes destroyet[24]; and then (the winter being comed on) because the armie could not ly in the feilds, they war dimissed[25], and appoyntit[26] to meite agane in the spring tyme. But the Earle of Douglas seemit[27] to panse[28] lytle by[29] these thinges, or the Kings malice[30]. And the Earle him selfe that the grandour of his house (whilk[31] was growen to that great height be[32] that great mariage) sould not be imparit[33], and transferit[34] to strangers, takes to wyfe the foresaid Beatrix relict of his vmquhil[35] brother, and deales with the Pope to gette the mariage confirmit: bot[36] that sute was impedit[37] by the Kings letters. I find it in ane ancient buike[38] of the Douglases written in meitter, that she her selfe

Douglas forfaultit Buch. Hol.

Hol.

[1]affixed [2]Church [3]other [4]sealed [5]his [6]wold [7]other [8]who [9]allured [10]^and^ [11]wnder? [12][traiterouslie... murderzit *changed to* murderd them] putt them to death contrary to his promise and [13]were [14]three [15]forfaulted [16]diminished by [17]were [18]rewarded [19]goods [20]forfaulted [21]gathered [22]waisted [23]goods [24]destroyed [25]were dismissed [26]appoynted [27]seemed [28]count [29]^all^ [30][or... malice] [31]which [32]by [33]impared [34]transfered [35]defunct [36]confirmed *changed to* dispensde ^withall^; but [37]impeded *changed to* Crosd [38]booke

alleadgit[1] hir first husband had never carnal copulation with her, and that she gave her oath ther vpon, whilk[2] geveth some colour to this fact (vther[3] ways so enorme[4]) and not apparand[5] he could have bene sa[6] shameles, as to have interprysit[7] **[485]** without some sik[8] reasone, or pretext. Whilk[9] therfore I wald[10] not omit[11] to admonish[12], thogh the buike be not ancient; and I remember not to have red[13] els where. How ever it be, he keipit[14] her stil[15] in place of his wyfe, and continued the warres that zeir[16], and the nixt twa zeirs; harrying[17] and spoyling the Kings possessions; and the King on the vther[18] syde waisting[19] his; cheiflie Annandail, Galloway, and the Forrest, whereon folowit[20] famine, and on[21] famine pest[22]; Townes and Castles ware destroyet[23] on both sydes, and no kynd of hostilitie pretermittit[24]. The King not the lesse causit[25] indirectlie the essaye, if the Earle could be perswadit[26] to zeild[27] him selfe to[28] him. And the wysest of his freinds counsellit[29] him so to do; alledging his forebeares had often tymes done sa[30], cheiflie since he had a King gentle of Nature, and

Treatit to zeild to the King

exorable by freinds; that he wald[31] not by his gratiousnes[32] extinguish so noble a familie, and vndoe the Estates of sa[33] manie noble men as folowit[34] him, or redact them to that necessitie, that they sould be forcit[35] to take a Course for them selves: that it wald[36] be easie for him to gete[37] some gud[38] appointment, since affairs war zit in a gud estate: bot[39] if he war[40] once desertit[41] **[486]** be[42] his freinds, there restit[43] no[44] hope of pardone: To

Refuseth

whilk[45] the Earle made this answer: He wald[46] never

---

[1]alleadged [2]which [3]other [4]enormous [5]^that^ [6]so [7]interprysed ^it^ [8]such [9]^at least^; Which [10]wold [11]omitt [12]intimate [13]^it^ [14]keipd [15]still [16]yeir [17]two yeirs; [harrying?] haerying [18]other [19]waesting [20]folowed ^a^ [21]^the^ [22]^a^ peste [23]were destroyed [24]pretermitted [25]caused [26]perswaded [27]yeeld [28]vnto [29]counselled [30]so [31]wold [32]obstinacye [33]so [34]folowed [35]forced [36]wold [37]gett [38]good [39][affairs… zit *changed to* yett… gud *changed to* good estate] matters were not as yet past reconcilment; but [40]were [41]deserted [42]by [43]rested [44]^more^ [45]which [46]wold

commit[1] him selfe to the[2] credit of them[3], wha[4] had nather shame nor honestie, wha war[5] not holden with anie band to God, or man, bot[6] having allurit[7] his Cousins, and brother with faire promises, had so traiterouslie, and cruellie slane them;[8] that he wald[9] rather suffer al extremities, nor[10] come in[11] their credit[12]. This speiche was approvit[13], and reprovit[14] according to everie mans disposition; some[15] praising his magnanimitie and Courage; some disalowing his obstinatnes, and exhorting him not to tyne the gud[16] occasion of making his peace, whilk[17] if his freinds (weirie of troubles) sould abandone him, he wald[18] repent efterward; him selfe persistit[19] in this opinion, and what for detestation of the fact, what for feare, that he sould lyke ways be so vsit[20], if he came in the Kings danger[21] (as it falles out, and most[22] of necessitie, where trust, the ground of al peace, and reconcilment is taine away) not suffering thoughtes of peace to come in his mynd, resolvit[23] him self on[24] warre.

The Earle of Crafurde weirie of so long troubles apprehending the iniquitie[25] of the [**487**] cause he susteinit[26], weying with him selfe the commone changeablenes of humaine affairs[27], and knawing that pardone wald[28] be easie to him, wha[29] sould preoccupy the Princes favour; vneasie to them wha[30] sould continue in armes, being left be[31] a pairt of his freinds,[32] suspecting the fidelitie of the rest, as the King was journeying throgh Angus, he castes him selfe in his waye with ane habit most „ composed to move mercie, bair headet[33], and bair „ footit[34]; plainlie confessing the offence[35] in tyme „

Earle of Crafurde zeilds to the King.

---

[1]committ [2]into [the… slane them] *corrections of scored out pasage will be noted individually* [3][them] his Ennemyes hands [4]who [5]who were [6]but [7]allured [8]^Butt^ [9]wold [10]than [11]into [12]reverence ^who made away so perfidiously his brothers and his cousins^ [13]approved [14]reproved *changed to* desaproved [15]others [16]good [17]which [18]wold [19]persisted [20]vsed [21]reuerence [22]must ^do^ [23]^hee^ resolved [24]vpon [25]danger [26]susteined [27]effairs [28]wold [29]who [30]who [31]by [32]^and^ [33]pittie, baere headed [34]baere footed [35]his offences

„ past, putes[1] himself in the Kings wil[2]; calling to „ mynd the gude[3] offices done be[4] his predecessors, „ that he acknawledgit[5] what ever was[6] happened, „ to have happened be[7] his awen[8] default; what ever „ lyfe or fortune he sould have heirefter, he sould „ awe[9] it to the Kings clemencie. This[10] and sik „ vther[11] speiches to this effect, movit[12] the noble men present, speciallie[13] the gentilmen of Angus, wha[14] thogh they had always followit[15] the King, zit war louth[16] that so ancient and noble a house sould perishe; bot[17] cheiflie, James Kennedie, thogh he had recevit[18] manie iniuries of the Earle **[488]** (or his father) zit[19] considering what importance it was to the King to have his awen[20] forces eiked[21] by the accressing, and his Enemies forces diminishit[22] by the want of so great a man, dealt earnestlie with the King to receive[23] him in favour. Nather[24] was the King difficile[25] to be intreatit bot receivit[26] him to pardone[27], and restorit[28] to his wontit[29] place of guds[30] and honour; onlie admonishing him to do his duetie in tymes to come. It is reportit[31] that the King willing to performe his promise, whilk was[32] to raze the house of Phinevin (that[33] is the special mansion of the Earles of Crafurde) and to make the heigest stone theirof the lowest; that therevpon the Earle tuike[34] the King to the tope[35] of the house, and[36] conforme to his promise,[37] threw downe a lytle stone, (whilk[38] was laid above the built worke) to the ground; and is to this day keepit[39] in ane yron chanzie[40] as ane[41] monument[42]. Some also wryte that the King tuike[43] the lands of Badenoch, and Loquhabre, and gave[44] the Earle of Huntlie, for the lands whilk[45] the Earle of Huntlie had geven away

[1]putts [2]will [3]goode [4]by [5][that he] and acknawledged *changed to* acknawledging [6]whatsoever had [7]^him^ by [8]owen [9]would owe [10]These [11]such other [12]moved [13]especiallie [14]who [15]followed [16]yett were [*illegible*] louth *adopted* [17]but [18]received [19]yett [20]owen [21]augmented [22]diminished [23]receave [24]Neither [25]difficille [26]entreated, but received [27]graciously to favour [28]restored [29]wonted [30]goods [31]reported [32] vowe, [whilk *changed to* which was] [33]which [34]tooke [35]topp [36][and] where [37]^he^ [38]which [39]keeped [40]chaine [41]a [42]^hereof^ [43]tooke ^from him^ [44]^to^ [45]which

at the feild of Brichen; as also the second place in Parlament and honour of bearing the scepter; howbeit it was[1] he livit[2] not[3] six monethes **[489]** dieing of a hote[4] fever in Phinevin. The Earle of Douglas informit[5] heirof, and seing his forces decay daylie and the Kings augmenting, tuik[6] purpos to see what support he might have out of England; and to that effect sent James Hamiltoun of Caidzow[7], to Henrie of England for his helpe in this estate. Whilk[8] the King of England considering, and thinking the occasion fite[9] for him to incrotche vpon Scotland, perswading himselfe that the Douglas his passion of revenging[10] on the ane[11] pairt, and the necessitie of his Estate on the vther[12] pairt (twa powerful[13] perswaders to move men) sould[14] drive him to accept whatsomever[15] condition[16] was content[17] to give him: bot ioynit[18] this condition with it[19], that he sould[20] become his subject, sweir[21] him self ane Englishman, and so[22] continue for ever; and for his better assurance sould[23] render vp to him sik[24] strenthes and Castles as he had in his custodie in Scotland. Wherevnto the vther replyit[25] verie generouslie and honestlie, that he wald[26] never leave sik ane[27] blot on[28] his house, and wald choise rather[29] to die be what ever[30] hand, nor commit sik[31] a cryme agains[32] his Contrie, for ane fault[33] done by his Prince, **[490]** and some particular men onlie; whereof he hopit[34] to be avengit[35] with out that shame. This being so honest a fact,[36] and testifieing so honest a hart, as few hes[37] had; and even[38] of them, wha hes pretendit[39] to be kings themselves, of whom some hes[40] not refusit[41], for obteining theirof, and to be avengit[42] of their Enemies, to rander them selves, and their Kingdomes to the English

Douglas seiking help of England

Is desyrit to sweir himself ane Englishman

Refuseth

---

[1][it was] [2]hee lived [3]^above^ [4]hott *changed to* burning [5]informed [6]took [7]Caidyow [8]Which [9]fitt [10]revenge [11]one [12]other [13]two powerfull [14]^to anything^ would [15]^of^ whatsoever [16]^he^ [17]contented [18][but ioynit *changed to* ioyned] hee therfor added [19]him [20]would [21]sweer [22]^to^ [23]would [24]such [25]other replyed [26]wold [27]such a [28]vpon [29]wold rather choose [30]by whatsoever [31]then committ such [32]against [33]a faulte [34]hoped [35]avenged [36]parte [37]have [38]^some^ [39]who have pretended [40][of... hes] that haue [41]refused [42]avenged

servvitude; is over[1] lightlie past be[2] our wryters without the due testimonie, approbation, and praise that it weil deservis[3]. Besydes that, there can be hardlie a clearer argument of no affectation[4] of the Crowne[5] laid to his[6] predicessors charge by his Enemies, and put in[7] the Kings mynd; whilk[8] if the Douglases had bene set[9] for, and wald[10] have taine halden[11] of England, questionles sould never have bene refusit[12] them by these[13] kings, in that their common practise. Frome whilk[14] how manie wald[15] have absteinit[16] in sik[17] power on sik[18] occasion? For as touching titles (whilk[19] they seime not to have anie sufficient colour of) seildome wantis there pretences to them[20] that[21] affectate them. the more pitie that in[22] so modest exercising so hard warres[23], the event sould have bene so sharpe on the Earls[24] syde. Whilk al[25] kythis zit better[26] in that whilk folowit[27]. So left thus be[28] him self, without anie help, [**491**] be[29] the instigation of his favorers, and namelie the Laird[30] of Cadzow[31], he gatherit[32] his freinds and followers to releive the seige of Abercorne, (whilk[33] the King lay at). When he[34] was comed within fyve myles, or (as vthers[35] say) being comed in[36] sight eich armie of vther[37]; they of his syde luiking surelie[38] that the Earle had resolvit[39] to fight because he pute[40] his armie in order of battle, and[41] being them selves very readie and[42] foreward[43] and making shaw so, Cadzow[44] exhorting him therto[45] that the Earle wald[46] end these[47] warres with a notable victorie to his perpetual[48] praise; or with

Raisis ane armie to relieve Abercorne

[1]too [2]^over^ by [3]weill deserveth [4]affecting ^of^ [5]^in him, which was^ [6]^and his^ [7]putt into [8]which [9]sett [10]wold [11]holden [12]refused [13]those [14]which [15]wold [16]absteined [17]such [18]^and^ vpon such ^an^ [19]which [20]those [21]^do^ [22]affect and haue the power to sease vpon a kingdome. So as the greater was the pittie that in [23]moderate prosecution of such a quarrell [24]Earles [25]all which [26]appeares more clearly yett [27]which folowed [28]by *changed to* to [29]by [30]of Hamilton [31]Cadyow [32]gathered ^togither^ [33]which [34][lay... he] had besett and lay at in his owne persone. And when the Earle with that Cumpanye [35]others [36][being... in] within [37][eich... vther *changed to* other] of the beseegers [38]^of his syde^ looking assuredlie [39]resolved [40]putt [41]^they^ [42][and] [43]^and resolut^ [44][making... ^no^ shaw so] ^And^ Cadyow ^also^ [45][therto] [46]hee wold [47]those [48]perpetuall

a[1] honorable death as became his house[2] vindicat him selfe[3] from these[4] miseries and contumelies[5]; he vtterlie refusit[6] to fight[7], thogh he was moe[8] in number; saying plainlie his hart wald[9] not suffer him, nor serve him[10] to fight against[11] his Soverane. Whereby it may be coniectured (as sayes[12] the Manuscript) his meaning to have bene[13] to have terrifiet[14] the King, and[15] brought him to some real conditions of peace; bot[16] there wanting mides-men[17] to deale therin pairtlie al[18] being affectionit[19] to the one, or to the vther[20] syde;[21] pairtlie beleiving him stil[22] to insist in his former opinion of mistrust[23] and indignation, [**492**] nothing was done be[24] anie. Vthers[25] interprete it to be cowardise[26], and laike[27] of courage (for the worde[28] imports that[29]) a faulte that fel[30] in few of that stoke[31]; and we never find[32] to be imputit[33] to anie of them against England, or against anie their privat Enemies; nather to[34] this[35] man else where, bot[36] at this ane[37] tyme. And we hard[38] vpone the slaughter of his brother, his courage is commendit, joynet[39] with pietie, to wite[40] his anger was then[41] recent and kyndlie aganes[42] the actors; whilk[43] tyme had now mollified[44] towards his King, as being bot[45] a borrowit[46] hand be[47] the Courtiours; and natural[48] affection, and[49] regarde of a subject to his Prince returnit[50] peice and piece to the hart whilk[51] it had long possessit[52], as the awin[53] propertie: And certane these facts hes proceedit of ane[54] and the same hart,[55] the refusal[56] to betraye his contrie to another King; whereof sen[57] the first

Wil not fight against his Prince.

The wryters iudgment of that his fact.

ignauia Buch.

Qui aderant pietatem et animi magnitudinem laudare

[1]an [2]^to^ [3]^and them^ [4]those [5]^which they sustained^ [6]refused [7]give battell [8]more [9]wold [10][nor … him] [11]^the person of^ [12]sayeth [13]^onely^ [14]terrified [15]^by that meanes to have^ [16]but [17]intercessors [18][therein… al] between them; all men partlie [19]^altogither^ affectioned ^either^ [20]other [21]^and^ [22]still [23]distrust [24]^therein^ by [25]Others ^do^ [26]have been his fayntnes [27]lacke [28]^ignavia^ [29]no les [30]fell [31]stocke [32]^it^ [33]imputed [34]nay not vnto [35]^same^ [36]anywhere else, but [37]speciall [38]^have^ heard ^that^ [39]commended, joyned [40][to wite *changed to* witt] whilles [41][then] yett [42]greene aganst [43]the edge whereof [44]^and blunted^ [45]but [46]borrowed [47]by ^his enemies^ [48]^his^ naturall [49]^the^ [50]returned [51]which [52]possessed [53]owne [54]certanely this deed hath proceeded from one [55]^with that of^ [56]refusall [57]sith

sould be heighlie praisit[1], I see not how this hindermost[2] can be condemnit[3] so greatlie, by them[4] that so[5] heighlie respects that heige[6] place. The words wil[7] also import not altogedder cowardise, bot ane lethernes[8], whereof the cause some tymes is the same Cowardise (as thay concure often) whilk[9] **[493]** is a natural slugishnes and want of action; bot[10] there is another affection, that takes[11] men in[12] action, whilk[13] proceidis not of ather[14] of thir[15] nether[16] slugishnes, nether Cowardise, bot[17] of[18] irresolution; when[19] a man swimming betwixt twa[20] judgements, resolves not[21] fullie on ather.[22] this[23] seemeth to have bene his[24] disposition (a great impediment in his actions) and at leist in[25] this last fact[26] of importance (the cause of his wrake) whils[27] nather could his hart suffer him to betake him selfe aganes his[28] Prince, whom naturallie he affectit; nather[29] could digest or forget[30] the fact[31] done, nor efter it commit[32] him selfe to the[33] King, whilk[34] disposition thoght[35] it hathe broght out the lyke effects, as vses to do Cowardise and lithernes[36]; to wit, lingring, and eshewing[37] of the battle, zit was it nather of them; and hes[38] the original fra[39] a verie honest mynd to duetie[40]; his love[41] to his Prince fighting with another duetie, his love of the defunct, and[42] to his awin[43] honour; out of whilk whils[44] he ather[45] can not, or occasion representis not to explicate it[46] self; he sufferit[47] him selfe to be caryit[48]

---

[1]praised [2]hindmest [3]condemned [4]them [5][so... want of action; bot] *corrected items in this scored out passage will be noted separately* do respect as duty and divinity enioynes the high place and person of these Gods vpon earth. But lett vs examine this deed of his a litle better [6]heigh [7]will [8]lasines [9]which [10]But [11][makes] takes *adopted* [12]^there^ [13]actions, which [14]either [15]these former defects [16]^of^ [17]nor want of Courage, but [18]^a meere^ [19]^as^ [20]two [21]^not^ *adopted* [22]vpon eather. ^And^ [23]^is it which^ [24]this mans [25][at leist *changed to* leest] now [is] in *adopted* [26]deed [27]vtter ruyne) whiles [28]aganst the person of his native [29]affected *changed to* respected; neither [30]^he^ disgest nor forgett [31]^which was^ [32]submitt [33]his [34]Which [35]thogh [36]Cowardise and sluggishnes vses to do [37]eschewing [38]yett did it not proceed from either of the two. But hath [39]from [40]^and dutifull^ mynde [to duetie]: ^Even from^ [41]^and respectt^ [42]^the regarde^ [43]owne [44]which whiles [45]either [46][representis... it] is not offered to him to ridde him [47]suffered [48]caryed

to that[1] he was most inclynit to; his love[2] to his Prince; and **[494]** thereby[3] the[4] occasion oft tymes[5] was representit to[6] him, or[7] no lesse (in the judgment of his freinds) then casting the dyce for the Crowne; wherof the lyke faire occasion (sayes[8] the said James Hamiltoun) ze sal[9] never see agane; assuring him withal[10] that his irresolution wald[11] be his wrake and overthrow, as it was indeid. For James Hamiltoun that samein[12] night left him, and went to the King, and was so honourablie[13] and weil receivit, that he gave him his eldest daughter in mariage; and by that is the Marquies so neir to the Crowne[14]. Howsoever vthers[15] wryte[16] he was willed to byde in[17] warde in Rosling for a tyme and efter releivit[18] as he to whose coming[19] the cause of the Kings[20] victorie without bludshed[21] was imputit[22]. Efterwards vthers[23] by his exemple[24] made their peace lykwise; at last be[25] his information to the King of the Estate of the[26] Douglases armie, how foreward they had bene in the fight, how fare[27] they war[28] discouragit be[29] his lingring, and how discontentit[30] therwith, how the greattest cause that held them on that syde was[31] doubt to be forgeven the bygane faults[32]; the King causit[33] make a proclamation, that wha[34] ever wald[35] come to[36] him from the pairt of[37] the Douglas, sould have frie[38] remission for al[39] faults bypast; provyding **[495]** they came[40] within 48 houres. Efter whilk[41] the most pairt of his[42] armie left him and come to the King[43], so that on the[44] morne there restit[45] not with him aboue 2000 men; whereby he was constrainit[46] to leave the feilds, and his freinds and servands in

Hol. 1455

Hol.

General pardon

The rest of his armie leavis him.

[1]^which^ [2]inclyned vnto; the due respect [3]^slipt and lett pass^ [4]^faire^ [5][oft tymes] which [6]presented vnto [7]of [8][faire occasion] sayeth [9]yee sall [10]withall [11]wold [12]same [13]of him graciously [14]weill received [that... Crowne] [15]others [16]^that^ [17]Committed to [18]releived ^at George Douglas then Earle of Angus intreatye^ [19]^in that sorte to the Kings side^ [20][the Kings] that vnexpected [21]bloodshed [22]^truely^ imputed [23]others [24]example [25]by [26]^Earle^ [27]farr [28]were [29]discouraged by [30]discontented [31]^the^ [32][bygane faults] former offences [33]caused [34]who [35]wold [36]into [37][from... of] and forsake [38]free [39]all [40]^vnto him^ [41]which ^publication^ [42]the Earles [43][and... King] [44]^next^ [45]rested [46]constrained

Abercorne to be cruellie slane, and hangit[1]; for the Castle was wonne be[2] force and cassen downe[3], to his[4] reproche in that he did not resolve better[5]; and be[6] some meanes procurit[7] honest composition to himselfe or[8] them, or[9] have venturit[10]: where if he wald[11] not have taine the Kingdome, in caise of victorie; zit[12] might he honorablie geven[13] conditions of peace: or if he had lost the feild,[14] could not have lost more then he did: for be thir[15] meanes abandonit[16] of al[17], he was constranit[18] to retire in[19] England.

He retirith to England

Hol. 1455

The second battle of Sarke

Earle of Murray slane Earle of Ormond taine Prisoner and execute.

In the 1455 zeir[20] having gotten togidder[21] a smal companie of men returnit in[22] Annandail,[w] thinking to have found freinds in those pairts, whilk was[23] his awen[24] lands of before; bot[25] was there rencountred be[26] them that followit[27] the King; speciallie[28] by his awen[29] Cousine, (also[30] the Kings Cousine[31]) the Earle of Angus (as some wryte) **[496]** wha defait[32] him[33]; His brother the Earle of Murray being slane in the feilde;[34] his vther[35] brother the Earle of Ormond hurt and taine prisonner, and efter his wounds war curit[36] brought to the King, and execute[37], with greatter respect[38] to[39] his last facts, nor[40] his former victorie obtinit[41] not far from the same place (at Sark[42]) so greatlie praisit[43] by the King before, and so acceptable to al: Sik[44] is the course[45] of humaine affairs[46]. (We heire[47] of one onlie sone of his callit[48] Hugh Dean of Brichen, of whom[49] some[50] lytle efter in the lyfe of Archbald Earle of Angus[51] great Chanceller.) His takers war[52] the Lord of Carleil[53], and the Laird of Johnstoun, to

---

[1]hangd [2]by [3]demolished [4]^no small^ [5][did... better] was so irresolute [6]^had not^ by [7]^or other^ procured ^at least some^ [8]and [9]^else to^ [10]adventured ^all^ [11]wold [12]yett [13]have sett doun [14]^hee^ [15]by these [16]abandoned [17]all [18]constraned [19]withdrawe into [20]yeir [21]togither [22]^he^ returned into [23]which had been [24]owen [25]but [26]by [27]followed [28]Especiallie [29]owen [30]and [31][Cousine] also [32]whoe defaeted [33]^there^ [34]^and^ [35]other [36]were cured [37]executed [38]regarde [39]^these^ [40]actions, then respett to [41]obtined [42]^Against the English and Magnus their insolent Champion) which was [43]praised [44] all ^both in the Courte and the Countrie^. Such [45]^and^ vicissitudes [46]effairs [47]heare [48]called [49]^we are to speak^ [50]somewhat herefter [51]^the^ [52]were [53][of] Carleill

whom the King gave in recompense the fourtie pound land of Pittinane, everie one twentie pound land theirof. The thrid brother Johne Lord of Balvennie escapit[1] in a wode[2]; and the Earle him selfe be[36] flight gat[4] him to Dumstafage; where finding Donald Earle of Rosse, and Lord of the Isles he procurit[5] him to make warre in his favour aganes[6] the King. And efter he had prescryvit him a work to doe, the Earle of Douglas retirit[7] him selfe to[8] England. This is noted to have bene in the zeir[9] 1455. Efter whilk[10] was there another Parlament about the fyft of June (or of August **[497]** as the Acts say) in the whilk[11] he and his brother Johne,[12] his wyfe Beatrix war[13] agane forfaultit[14], and their lands of Galloway annexit[15] to the crowne.

Buch.

This[16] Beatrix is said be[17] them wha hes[18] seene the Actes, to be callit[19] mother to these[20] (him and his brother) whilk[21] they think not appearand[22]. It is hard indeid if it be Beatrix Douglas; and[23] their mother was also callit[24] Beatrix, bot[25] Sinkler to[26] surname, if she had bene then living and forfaultit[27] with the rest; whilk[28] I refer to them that sal[29] reid the said actes. Alwyse[30] Beatrix Douglas his brothers wyfe (and keipit[31] for his awen[32] wyfe now certaine zeirs[33]) came to the King and excusit[34] her selfe as being a woman, and compellit[35] to what she had done, whom the King receivit[36], and maryit on[37] Johne Stewart his half brother, and gave her the lands of Balvennie (this man was efter made Earle of Athol[38] in King James the Thrids tyme) and had by her twa[39] daughters onlie, of whom the eldest was maryed on[40] the Earle of Errole: this is cassen be vthers in[41] the nixt zeir[42]. The Earle abandonit[43] on

Beatrix cometh to the King. Manusc.

House of Athol

Buch. Hol.

[1]escaped [2]woode [3]by [4]gott [5]procured [6]aganst [7][prescryvit *changed to* prescryved... doe] ingaged him therein, hee retired [8]into [9]yeir [10]which [11]which [12]^and^ [13]were [14]forfaulted [15]annexed [16][This... said actes. Alwyse] *corrections of individual items in this scored out passage will be noted separately* [17]by [18]who have [19]called [20](^to^ [21]which [22]to be probable [23]for [24]called [25]but [26]^her^ [27]forfaulted [28]which [29]sall [30]Howsoever this [31]keipt [32]owen [33]yeirs [34]excused [35]compelled [36]receaved [37]maryed ^her to^ [38]Atholl [39]two [40]to [41]casten by others on [42]next yeir [43]abandoned

Donald of the Isls.

al[1] hands, he travellit[2] with Donald of the Isles, Earle of Rosse, conforme to their old[3] band made with his wmquhil[4] brother Earle William, to assist him, and to renew[5] his old title to the Isles, wha waistit[6] Argyle, **[498]** Arran, Loquhabre, and Murray; tuik[7] the Castle of Innernes, brunt the towne, and proclamit[8] him selfe King of the Isles.

His wyfe leaveth him

Bot[9] his wyfe also (wha[10] was daughter to James Livingstoun, geven him at the Kings desyre to reteine him in freindshipe[11] by that band) when she sawe she could not effectuat anie gud[12] that way, bot[13] also was contemnit[14] by him, and his peoples barbaritie,[15] withdrew her selfe[16] and was gladlie acceptit[17] by the King.

Patrik Thorntoun slayes Johne Sandilands

About this same tyme Patrik Thorntoun a quyet favourer of the Douglas faction, bot wha[18] had followit[19] the Court a long tyme, slew Johne Sandelands of Calder, the Kings Cousine, and Allane Stewart favourer[20] of the King,[21] having found the occasion[22] at Dunbarton; bot[23] efter[24] was taken by the Kings men[25] and execute. These things zit vnquyetit[26] the King greatlie, perplexit[27] betwixt domestike and forrane Enemies; til[28] efterwards in the zeir[29] 1457 that the Earle of Douglas came in with Henrie Percie of Northumberland to the Mers, whilk[30] as they waistit[31] and furrowit[32], they were

Earle Douglas defait in the Mers be the Earle of Angus. Hol. 1455

rencounterit[33] be the Earle of Angus, and put bake to their Campe, with whilk[34] indignation being irritate, before their furrowers[35] were comed in, they come to battle, **[499]** The noyse whereof coming to the furrowers[36] eares, they for greidines of the great praye whilk[37] they had before them, that[38] they sould not[39] tyne it, past[40] to England; at the narest, wherbe[41] the battle whilk[42] was vtherways[43] almost

---

[1]all [2]travelled [3]the former [4]late [5]reviue [6]wherevpon he waested [7]took [8]proclamed [9]But [10]who [11]the better in dutye [12]good [13]but [14]contemned [15]^she^ [16]^from him^ [17]accepted ^of^ [18]but wha [19]followed [20]^a^ favourite [21]Kings, ^hee^ [22]^so to do^ [23]but [24]efterwards ^the said Thorneton^ [25]officers [26]yett desquyeted [27]perplexed [28]till [29]yeir [30]which [31]waisted [31]forrowed [33]rencountered by [34]which [35]forrowers [36]forrowers [37]which [38]least [39][not] [40]^directly bake again^ [41][at... narest] wherby [42]which [43]otherways

equal, was lost be[1] the Englishmen[2] not without slaughter of almost alyke on both sydes. This victorie[3] greatlie recreat[4] the King, and so effrayit[5] the Lord of the Isls[6], that he sent, and submittit[7] him selfe to the King, and so[8] was receivit[9] by him. Nather was there anie further insurrection within the Countrie; Nather without the Countrie[10] did the Earle[11] Douglas interpryse anie thing be[12] the ayde of England, they being distractit among[13] them selves be[14] the dissention of the house[15] of Zork[16], during this King James the seconds dayes, whilk always was[17] not long,[18] about two or thrie zeirs[19] efter this: for in the 1460 zeirs he[20] was slane with the wadge[21] of a great piece of artillirie[22] of his awen, his alone[23], and with him was hurt George Earle of Angus among 30000 of his armie, at the seige of the Castle of Roxburgh in the zeir[24] of his age <u>29</u>,[25] September, some eight zeirs[26] efter the slaughter of William Earle **[500]** of Douglas, whom he slew[27] in the Castle of Stirling, being then bot 21 or 22 zeirs old at that tyme[28]. Nather[29] in the nixt Kings tyme, during his minoritie, thogh[30] he was but sevin zeirs[31] old at his coronation: Nather in his maioritie; Nather in the dissention betwixt the Kennedies and the Boyds; Nather[32] betwixt the King and his Nobilitie heir[33] we anie mention in Chronicles of the Earle[34] Douglas his stirringe[35] at anie tyme or[36] anie occasion; whether by slooth[37] of wryters that hes[38] not written sik[39] things as was[40]; or by his want of power, he not being able to interpryse anie thing (his freinds, dependars and wassals[41] having taken another course, and his lands disponit[42] for the most pairt amongs them, with

The King slane

[1]by [2]English ^but^ [3]^did^ [4]recreate [5]effrayed [6]Isles [7]submitted [8][so] [9]received [10]same [11]^of^ [12]by [13]distracted amongs [14]by [15]houses [16]^Lancaster and^ York [17]which were [18][about] ^as being not above^ [19]yeirs [20]yeire the King ^allone^ [21]wedge [22]artillerie [23]owen [his alone] [24]yeir [25]^in^ [26]yeirs [27]slane by him [28][being… tyme] [29]^ceasd the foresaid dissention in England^ [30]for [31]yeirs [32]^in that^ [33]heare [34]^of^ [35]sturring [36]^vpon^ [37][sl??th] slooth *adopted* [38]have [39]such [40][was] ^then fell out^ [41]vassals [42]disponed

Earle Douglas made Knight of the Noble Order of the Garter by King Edward the fourt of England.

sindrie vthers[1]) for the space of twentie thrie ziers, to wit, til[2] the 1483 zeirs[3]. Alwyse we find that[4] he was made Knight of the Noble Order of the Garter be[5] King Edward the fourt of England; and is placit[6] in order first of al[7] the Earles, and nixt to him the Earle of Arrandail (who is the first Earle in England) in the buike intitulit[8], *Nobilitas Politica*; and the English Heraulds say of him[9] he was a[10] verie valiant[11] **[501]** gentilman, weilbelovit[12] of the King and Nobilitie, and verie steadable to King Edward in al[13] his troubles. Which troubles perhaps has[14] bene the cause they could interpryse nothing in Scotland til[15] the said zeir. However it be, he hes[16] the honour to be the first of the Scots nation, admittit[17] to that Order. At whilk[18] tyme (and not til[19] then)[20] seimes a verie strange thing that he sould have bene so lang tyme[21], and so troublesome[22] tyme, so ydle in England; that[23] Alexander Duk[24] of Albanie, and brother to King James the thrid, being banishit[25] also in Richart the thrids tyme (vsurper of[26] England) they twa[27] (the said Duk[28] and Earle)[29] desyrous to knawe[30] what was the affection of the Countrie[31] people towards them, wowed[32] that they sould offer their offrings upon the Magdalene day on the heigh altar of Louchmaben[33], and to that effect conveinit[34] not above the number of 500 horse, what Scots, what English, and ane[35] number of English footemen, that remaynit[36] with the Musegrave at Burnishwarke to assist them in case they neidit; raid[37] towards Louchmaben.[38] at their incominge the fraye was raisit[39] through Niddisdail, Annandail and Galloway, wha convenit[40] to the **[502]** Laird of Moussil[41] (then Warden) and rencounterit[42] them with great courage. The

---

[1][with] and sundrie others [2]till [3]yeire 1483 [4]^in this time^ [5]by [6]placed [7]all [8]booke intituled [9]^that^ [10]^a^ *adopted* [11]^noble^ [12]weilbeluved [13]all [14]have [15]till [16]hath [17]admitted [18]which [19]till [20]^it^ [21]long [tyme] [22]^a^ [23]when [24]Duke [25]banished [26]^the Crowne of^ [27]two [28]Duke [29]^being^ [30]knowe [31]their Countries [32]vowed [33]Loughmaben [34]conveined *changed to* raised [35]a [36]remayned [37]needed ^they^ raed [38]^and^ [39]raised [40]who conveined *changed to* assembling [41]Moussell [42] [and] rencountered

Englishmen wha war[1] on the[2] Burnishwarke at the first sight of the Enemie fled, so that the rest behovit[3] to doe or die. It was faughten[4] betwixt twelf hours[5] and the Glomming[6] with skirmishis in the border fashone; some tymes the one syde, some tymes the vther[7] having the advantage; at last the victorie inclynit[8] to the Scots men, though with meikle bludshed[9]. The Duke of Albanie escapit[10] by flight; bot[11] the Earle[12] Douglas being ane aged man, was striken from his horse, and tane prisoner with his awen[13] consent, be ane[14] brother of the Laird of Closburns[15] in this maner;

Earle Douglas at Louchmaben

King James the thrid had causit[16] make a proclamation, that wha ever wald[17] take the Earle of Douglas sould have a hundreth pound land; the Earle being on foote thus in the feilde, wearied of so long[18] exile, and thinking he[19] perhaps[20] might be knawen[21] of some vther[22], seeing in the feilde ane[23] Alexander Kirkpatrik a second sone of the Laird of Closburns, wha[24] had bene his awen[25] servand of before[26], calleth on[27] him by his name; who coming vnto him, the **[503]** Earle sayes: I have faughten[28] long aneugh[29] against my fortune, and since I must die I wil[30] rather that ze (wha hes[31] bene my awen[32] servand of before[33], and whom[34] I knaw to have[35] bene faithful to me as long as I did anie liklie thing for my selfe) have the benefite therby, then ane other: Wherefor take me, and delyver me to the King according to his proclamation, and[36] see ze[37] be sure he keipe his word before ze[38] delyver me. The zoung[39] man wha lovit[40] the Earle inteirlie in his hart, weipit[41] (as is reportit[42]) for sorowe to see him thus aged and altered in disgysit apparel, offerit[43] to passe in[44] England with him: bot[45] he allvterlie

The maner of his taking

---

[1]who were [2]^hill^ [3]behoved [4]foughten [5]the noone tyde [6]twyelight [7]other [8]inclyned [9]much bloodshed [10]escaped [11]but [12]^of^ [13]owen [14]by a [15]Cloesburns [16]caused [17]whosoever did [18]^an^ [19]that [20]^he^ [21]knowen [22]other [23]one [24]Cloesburns, who [25]owen [26][of before] [27]vpon [28]foughten [29]eneugh [30]will [31]yow (who hath [32]owen [33][of before] [34]who [35]know hath [36]but [37]yow [38]yow [39]young [40]who loved [41]weiped [42]reported [43]disgysed apparell, offerd [44]into [45]but

Hol.

Put in Lendors

refusit[1] it being yrkit[2], onlie he desyrit him[3] (if he could obteine it) to gette his lyfe saife; if not; to be sure of his[4] rewarde vpon the water of Eie.[5] Alexander Kirkpatrik quyetlie convoyit[6] him out of the feilde and keipit[7] him secreit in a Sheil[8] some few dayes vntil[9] he had spoken the King, wha grantit his[10] lyfe, and gave the vther[11] the fiftie pound land of Kirkmichel[12]; whose airs dois[13] possesse the sameine to[14] this day. Some give the honour of this victorie to the Lairds of Cokpule and Johnstoun; and makes[15] the armie of the Englishmen[16] greatter, **[504]** and say the King of England blamit[17] the Duk of Albanie, for the lose theirof; and he mislyking to be blamit[18], withdrew him selfe quyetlie into France. The Earle[19] Douglas being brought to the King, he ordeynit[20] him to be put in the Abbacie of Lendors; whereof advertised he said no vther thing, bot[21], He that may no better be, most be a Monke. Whilk[22] is past in proverbe to this day. He remaynit[23] there to[24] the day of his deathe; efter the death of King James the thrid, whilk[25] was in the zeir 1488;[26] being of a gude[27] age[28] having bene a man in action from the beginning of his brother Earle William, now 44 zeirs, to wit, fra the 1444, or before[29]. Some wryte, that whils he was in Lendors, the faction of the nobilitie, that had taken order with Couchrine and vther[30] Courteours, and war contraire to the King,[31] especiallie the Earle of Angus, requyrit[32] him to come furth[33], and[34] be head of their faction; promising he sould be restorit[35] to his haile[36] lands (whilk[37] seemes not verie probable). Vthers (whilk hes[38] more

---

[1]vtterlie refused [2]yrked *changed to* weryd ^of that endles trouble^ [3]desyred the young gentleman [4]^owne^ [5]^Herevpon^ [6]convoyed [7]keiped [8]Sheile *changed to* Shede or Cottage [9]vntill [10]who granted him the Earles [11][the other] vnto himself [12]Kirkmighel [13]do [14]same till [15]make [16]^to be^ [17]blamed [18]^that^ hee [mislyking… blamit *changed to* blamed] displeased thereat [19]^of^ [20]ordeyned [21]nothing else, But [22]Which [23]remayned [24]till [25]which [26]^hee^ [27]gude [28]^and^ [29]yeirs [to… before] [30]^some^ other [31][and war… King] supported by the Kings favour, Most [32]requyred [33]foorth [34]^to^ [35]restored [36]holle [37]which [38]Others (which hath

apparance)[1] that the King desyrit[2] him to be Lieutenant against[3] his Enemies, against the Lords, bot[4] he heavie with age, and wearie of troubles refusit[5], saying The King had keipit[6] him, and his[7] blake Coffer in Stirling over long, **[505]** wherof nather wald[8] do him gud[9]; he[10], because his freinds and followers war[11] fallen from him, and[12] gotten vther[13] Maisters, and moyen[14]; his Coffer, because his Enemies was[15] betwix him and it, or (as vthers[16] say) because there was in it a sorte of blake Coyne, that the King had causit[17] Coyne be[18] his Courteours counsel, whilk[19] money (sayes he) Sir if ze[20] had put[21] out at the first, the people wald[22] have taken it: and I if ze[23] had imployit[24] me in my[25] tyme[26] might have done zow[27] service; bot[28] now there is none wil ken[29] me, nor tak zour[30] money. So he remaynit stil[31] in the Abbay[32], where he died the 1488 zeir[33], and was buried in Lendors.

Hol.

His death and burial. Anno 1488

Thus begoud[34] and grew; thus stude,[35] thus decayit[36], and endit[37] the Earles[38] of Douglas; beginning[39] at Lord William father to Lord Hugh and maker of the Endenture, who we have be[40] a continuit[41] lyne… (who was in the dayes of King William, anno <u>1200</u>)… for the[42] love of his Countrie, fidelitie to his King, and disdane of[43] English tyrannie; whilk[44] honest, noble, and praise-worthe[45] disposition[46] of mynd was so natural[47], and of sik[48] force and vigor[49], that it had[50] power to continue and propagat[51] the selfe from, **[506]** age to age[52] now the space of <u>288</u> zeirs, from[53] his death;

[1]^write^ [2]desyred [3][against] [4]but [5]refused [6]keiped [7][his *changed to* the] [8]neither could [9]good [10]hee [11]were [12]^had^ [13]other [14]meanes, the house of Anguss [15]were [16]others [17]caused [18]by [19]counsell, which [20]yee [21]putt [22]wold [23]yee [24]imployed [25]due [26]^I^ [27]yow [28]but [29]will take note of [30]take *changed to* medle with your. *See note for insert* [31]remayned still [32]Abbaye [33]^in^ the <u>1488</u> yeir [34]began [35]stoode ^and floorished^ [36]decayed [37]ended [38]renouned house [39][beginning… love]*see endnote for insert and corrected continuation of this muddled passage. Ellipses indicate grammatical hiatuses; corrections of items in this scored out passage are noted individually.* [40]by [41]continued [42]^rare^ [43]^the^ [44]servitude; which [45]praise-worthy [46]^and composition^ [47]naturall [48]such [49]efficacy in him [50]^had^ *adopted* [51]propagate [52]^in his noble line and successors^ [53]yeirs, efter

from branche to branche[1], not in the stoke onlie bot[2] in the by[3] branches, and lateral[4] also, so manie as hes[5] bene here spoken of: that they[6] have continuallie reteinit[7] that natural juis[8], and sape[9] that amang[10] them al[11] it is vncertaine, whilk[12] of them hes[13] bene[14] most that way affectit[15]. This vertue joynit[16] with valour no lesse natural[17] and hereditaire[18] from man to man, wroght their increase; their Princes favoring them,[19] they serving their Princes in defence of their Countrie; their affection therto pressing them[20]; their worth and valour suffising them; the harts of the people favoring them[21] and folowing them; their Enemies regarding them; al[22] men admiring them; that in effect the weight of warlike[23] affairs was hailelie[24] laid vpon them, that the kings neidit[25] not bot[26] gyve them selves to administrate iustice,[27] consult and direct; living at peace, at ease, quyetnes, and honest recreations from the last dayes of King Robert Bruce; with a plaisant harmonie, and happie concurrance; the Kings (as the great wheil[28], and first mover) carying their first place in honour, in motion and commanding;[29] they in the nixt rowme serving **[507]** them as vnderservands[30] couragiouslie, faithfullie, honorablie and happelie[31]: to the great honour of their Prince and Countrie[32]. This behovit[33] to have[34] greatnes: for nather could service (to anie purpose) be without respect and greatnes; nather[35] had greatnes bene worthie without service. Their power is said by some to have bene such that if they had not revoltit[36] amongs them selves, be[37] the Kings assistance[38] no

[1] [from branche to branche] the father to the father, the brother to the brother, Or to the vncle And that [2]^and direct offspring^ but [3][by] [4]collateralls [5]have [6]and who [7]reteined [8]juss [9]sappe ^in such sorte^ [10]amongs [11]all [12]which [13]^all^ hath [14]^the^ [15]affected [16]joyned [17]naturall [18]hereditarye [19]^and^ [20]pressing them therto [21][favoring them] affecting [22]all [23]the martiall [24]wholly [25]needed [26]but ^to^ [27]^to^ [28]wheile [29]^and^ [30]vnderwheeles ^turned about by the greaters motion^ [31]happilie [32]Countree [33]behoved [34][have] be accompanyed and vpheld with [35]nor [36]revolted *changed to* been at variance and divided [37][be *changed to* by] and continued in [38] favour

subject in this Isle might compaire[1] with them in puissance. Bot[2] the diminishing of this their power, and the ruining of the Earle of Douglas, was the revolt whilk[3] the houses of Angus and Morton made Hol. 1455 against them be the Kings instigation[4]: for the last battle the Earle of Douglas was at, the Earle of Angus disconfite him; so that it became a proverbe[5] Maior. in to[6] Scotland this day;[7] The Rid Douglas put[8] downe the Blake[9]. Lykwise they might have raisit[10] Hol. 1451 30000 or 40000 men of[11] their awen commanding[12], of their awen[13] onlie servands[14]; and[15] most valiant men: for their commanding[16] was ever the most expert, and most exercit[17] with warres, by their vicinitie to their Enemie[18] England, their[19] onlie matter[20] and whetstone[21] of valiantise. They who geves **[508]** them leist[22] geves them <u>15000</u> men vnder their commanding, of their awen onlie servands, wassals and dependars;[23] to have riden within[24] England vpon their privat quarels, stayit[25] there twentie dayes,[26] brunt and laid waist from Durhame north; whilk[27] no vther[28] privat subiect could ever do vpon their[29] particular, without the Kings armie, whilk[30] power (as hes[31] bene said) they vsit[32] ever weil[33], without geving offence to their Prince in anie sorte, that we can reide[34] notoriouslie set downe. Zit[35] (sayes[36] our wryters) it was over[37] great for Scotland. bot how ever[38] great, that[39] was thus[40] to the weil[41] of it; to the service of the Kings; to their honour; to their ease; making no rebellion[42], no resistance, no contradiction; whilk[43] we see they come never to, til[44] Earle Williams slaughter in Sterling[45]. In effect (if we wil[46] speik without

---

[1]^have^ compaired [2]But [3]falling of from them of [4][made… be *changed to* by… instigation] [5]^and continues^ [6][to] [7]^That^ [8]putt [9]Blacke. (Those of the howse of Angus being of the fayrer complexion) [10]raised [11]under [12]owen command [13]owen [14]dependars [15]^that^ [16]command [17]exerced [18][their Enemie] [19]the [20]subiect [21]^there^ [22]least [23][vnder… awen *changed to* owen wassals *changed to* vassals… dependars;] ^And with that number^ [24]into [25]stayed [26]^and^ [27]which [28]other [29]^owne^ [30]which [31]hath [32]vsed [33]weill [34]reade [35]Yett [36]saye [37]too [38]but howsoever [39]it [40]still [41]well [42]insurrection [43]which [44]till [45]Stirling [46]will

Boet. lib.14 Cap. 8

partialitie) their greatnes was to the weil[1] of the countrie[2], ease and honour of their King[3], in sik[4] sorte, that Hector Boetius doubtes not to say; The Douglases were ever the siker tairge, and warre wal[5] of Scotland; and wanne manie lands be[6] their singular manhead[7] and wassaledgis[8]: for they decorit[9] this Realme with manie noble acts, and be[10] glorie of[11] martial deids: **[509]** And thoght[12] their puissance hes[13] bene suspect to[14] their Kings, and was the cause of their declyning; zit[15] since that house was put downe, Scotland hes[16] don[17] few valiant deids[18]. Lib. 14. Cap. 8. of the English translation. And we can not say[19] they gave anie cause of Jalousie[20]; Princes conceivit[21] it without fault made be[22] them (except it war[23] a fault to be great.) Whether[24] by their awin natural (as jalousie is countit naturallie to folow the heighest Estate[25]) or be[26] the suggestion[27] of the meane men[28] invyous of the great[29]; the one inclyning to jalousie[30] the vther[31] working on that inclination. Zit[32] it seemes their Princes[33] rather tuik[34] that jalousie nor[35] that there was anie great occasion geven them. They not the lesse stil behavit[36] themselves towards their Princes modestlie[37], obeying them to warding; to[38] releiving, and[39] warding agane, at their Kings pleasour without anie resisting[40]; as may be seine in the Earle of Wigtoun: That being weil considerit[41], the cause of their stirage[42] or commotion against their Prince (whilk[43] was never til[44] this last man) wil[45] appeir[46] to have bene in them not through[47] their greatnes, interprysing aganes[48] their Prince, or

[1]well [2]^and the^ [3]Kings [4]such [5]wall [6]by [7]manhood [8]vassaledgis [9]decored [10]by ^the^ [11]^their^ [12]thogh [13]hath [14]^some of^ [15]yett [16]hath [17]^but^ [18]memorable deeds ^of battle *changed to* armes^ [19]^iustly^ saie ^that^ [20]Jealousie [21]^might be moued to^ conceive [22][fault made] just occasion given; by [23]were [24]^they conceaued so^ [25]owne naturall ^disposition^ [as... countit *changed to* counted... Estate] [26]by [27]suggestions [28]meaner sorte [29]ther greatnes [30]jealousie ^and^ [31]others [32]Yet [33]^war stird vp^ [34]^to^ taek [35]^causeles^ jealousie then [36]still behaved [37]moderately [38]Efter [39]to [40]resistance [41]well *changed to* duely considered [42]sturring [43]which [44]till [45]will [46]^not^ [47][bene... through] proceeded from [48]against

aspyring to the Throne thoght[1] **[510]** the meane[2] men (to make their advantage) persuadit[3] the King to think sa[4]; but[5] the aspyring of[6] meane men to climb vp in their rowmes be[7] their decay; Nather aspyring so by vertue, but[8] calomnies,[9] and flatteries; fostering[10] the foresaid jalousie[11]. I knaw[12] it is a Maxime in policie, and plausible to manie; That Princes sould not suffer over great subjects in their Dominions, thogh it be[13] sure[14] without great subjects, never great services[15]. Parbroulzie[16] things they may at home, bot never[17] do meikle fra hame. Zit[18] being great, whether[19] it be best thus[20] to vndoe them, and mak vp new men be[21] their vndoing, or not[22], it is worthie to be considerit[23]: or if there be a possibilitie to vse the great[24] to goode vses; and (if possible) whether better sa[25], then to cast[26] to vndoe them; if also there be in vndoing them great hazard, as we see there is; and (though it succeidit[27] here at last) if it be wyslie done to adventure it in sik[28] a sorte. Certainlie that whilk[29] made it here succeid[30], was the verie honest hart of the man himselfe; wha[31] if he wald ather[32] have bene ane[33] Englishman, and cassen[34] af the[35] respect of his[36] Prince, or enterit in battle[37]; it had proven an vnwyse course so to have affectit[38] the advancement of the meaner[39] and not rather vsit[40] them weil[41] that war[42] become great[43]. **[511]** And therefor the[44] wryters finds[45] no vther[46] cause bot[47] the[48] providence[49], whilk[50] had determinit[51] not to give the Crowne to the Douglas, but to continue it in the right lyne. Whilk the Hol. an. 1455

[1]thogh [2]^and newe^ [3]^thereby^) persuaded [4]^it^ so [5]^it was^ [6]^those^ [7]^and to rise^ by [8][Nather… but] which they did not also go about by any vertuous meanes; But by [9]^but by lies^ [10]^still^ [11]jealousies [12]know [13]^most^ [14]^that^ [15]^can be don^ [16]Parbroullie [17]^be able to^ [18]^great matters abroad^. Yett [19]^or not^ [20]^waye^ [21]by [22][vndoing… not] fall [23]considered [24]^ones^ [25]so [26]about [27]succeeded [28]such [29]which [30]succeide [31]who [32]wold either [33][have bene] ^tourned^ [34]cast [35]^due^ [36]^native^ [37][or enterit *changed to* entered… battle] Or had not forborne to prosecute the battell against his sacred persone [38]affected [39]^sorte^ [40]^to have^ vsed [41]well [42]were [43]^already^ [44]^best^ [45]find [46]other [47]^of this success^ but [48]^onely^ [49]^of God^ [50][whilk… … indeid] *see note for replacement; corrections of the scored out passage are noted individually.* [51]determined

Douglas (thogh he never so intendit[1]) driven to this necessitie to tyne his awen[2] or to take the Crowne in case of a victorie could hardlie have refusit. Zit[3] venterd he rather to tyne his awen, and tint it indeid with a rare[4] modestie even disallowit[5] by wryters; interpreting it[6] fearfulness, or lithernes[7]. So hard[8] is it to knaw the[9] right, and not to incure sour[10] censure[11]. However it be, this appearis for[12] most sure,[13] their meaning to their Prince and Countrie hes[14] bene ay gude[15], and even in[16] this man. Their evils whatever they were, their[17] errours and faults what ever[18] they fel in[19] they war[20] driven to[21] them by the importunitie[22] of their particular Enemies and their Princes assisting, fostering, and mainteining of it, therbe[23] to vndoe that Earldome, Emulous of their Crowne and reigne (perhaps) with greatter libertie and more absolutnes in commanding.[24] Bot whether[25] it comes aye[26] to passe sa or not[27]; and if it came[28] to passe sa here[29] not in this Kings tyme, (for his days war[30] short) bot[31] in his sones tyme, wil[32] be seene[33] efter. And if out of these meane men[34] **[512]** (at leist[35], not so puissant[36] men[37]) there rose[38] vp restrainers of that libertie[39], no lesse, zea perhaps[40] more[41] then ever we reade of the Earls of Douglas. That[42] if that be the end of cutting af[43] great men we see it workes not aye, zea it workes almost never, or[44] verie short whyle[45], that[46] effect.[47] Worthie therfore to be considerit whether it be to be sought, or to be bought with sike hazarde. Bot[48] this is the

---

[1]intended [2]owen [3]refused; Yett [4]^example of^ [5]moderation ^of mynd^ though disallowed [6][writers… it] thayme; Imputing it to [7]want of resolution [8]difisle [9]do what is [10]incurr the hard [11]^of some men^ [12]appeareth to be [13]^that^ [14]hath [15]ever goode [16][in] [17]mans want of dutie, not to haue risen to the hiest Degree. The [18]whatsoever [19]fell into [20]were [21]vnto [22]craft and calumnyes [23][and their Princes… it] at Courte Goeing about, thereby [24][Earldome… commanding] *see endnote for correction* ; But [25]^or not^ [26]alwayes so [27][sa or not] [28]^ever so^ [29][sa here] in this case, though [30]were [31]but [32]^it^ will [33]^here^ [34][men] [35]least [36]powerfull [37]^by fare^ [38]^not^ [39]authoritie [40][zea *changed to* yea perhaps] Nay much [41]^dangerous^ [42]So as [43]aff [44][aye… or] ever, Nay rather never, Or, but for a [45]space [46]^alleadged^ [47]^A thing most^ [48][considerit *changed to* considered… hazarde] deeply and most seriously thought vpon by Princes; But

1 vicissitude of this rolling warld[1]: Let men considder[2] it, and reverence the Reuler[3].

[1][of… warld *changed to* world] of these worldly things [2]^duely of^ [3]^who disposes of all these revolutions ever for the best.^

The Author to the Reader

I know (Reader) that he who undertakes to write, makes himself a mark of censure for men to level at. For to please all men, shall then only be possible, when all men shal be of one minde; til then, we may look for as many dislikings, as there is diversities of opinions, each man condemning what is not according to his own humour and palate. Some will storm or scorn (perhaps) our writing as un-necessary scribling, and paper blurring: others will quarrell at the subject, that we should write a History; others that such, so composed, and formal of a private family, with such commendation. Again, some will accuse us of partiality; and some will even question the truth of it. Neither will there bee wanting such as will blame the forme and fashion of the work, as too short, or too long; and many (I doubt not) will carp at the Stile, the Phrase, the Periods, the Diction and Language. In all these particulars, to satisfie all men, is more then we can hope for: yet thus much shortly of each of them, to such as will give eare to reason: That I write, and of this subject, I am constrained to do it; not by any violence or compulsion, but by force of duty as I take it: for being desired to do it by those I would not refuse, I thought myself bound to honour that name, and in, and by it, our King & Countrey. And so I have done what I can, & should have been glad to have done more, if it had lyen in my power. As for the writing of a History I could never have dreamed I should have needed to make Apologie for it: neither did I ever hear it accounted prophane, till I had done. Then by chance I lighted on a certain Authour who excuseth himself for so doing, and promiseth to doe so no more. It may be neither shall I. Yet dare I not promise so much: neither see I any reason why I should: for if by prophane, they mean that History maketh men prophane, and leadeth to prophanitie and atheisme; then certainly we may justly say, that it is nothing lesse. For in it we see and behold, as in a Glasse, Gods Providence guiding and ruling the World, and mens actions, which arrive often to unexpected events, and sometimes even to such ends as are quite contrary to the Actors intentions. In History also we see men, and ourselves in them, our vertues or vices, which is the second point of wisdom: this leads us also to God. But if (by prophane) they mean whatsoever is not Scripture, and would have men to read and write nothing but what belongs unto it; then we must condemne all humane learning & knowledge, all Arts and Sciences, which are the blessings of God, and in which *Moses* and *Paul* were trained up, and well seen. It is true, there is no knowledge comparable to that of holy Scripture, and we cannot be too conversant about it; yet there is no kind of knowledge but is usefull, & may and ought to be esteemed and embraced. Our last end should ever be to God and Christ: but to speak alwayes of him directly, is neither required nor possible. As he is the end, so the way to this end is by speaking of him, or of things which may lead us to him: yet it is not necessary at all times to speak of such things professedly as lead us that way. He is our end in himself, and for himself, and happy were we if in him we could terminate all our desires. Vertue leads to him, and is to be embraced as such: but to obtrude it at first for that consideration, and on that respect, it may be doubted whether or not that be alwayes the right Method and best way of proceeding. The other may happen to prove more available with some, which is, to learne first to be enamoured & to love honour; then vertue for honour; then vertue for it self; then to account nothing vertue without God, who not being found but in Christ, must needs be sought for above all things. Now History is, as it were, the A B C. of this Method, and the beautifull Picture; by looking on which, our desire of honour is kindled, and so of vertue, which onely brings true honour with it. Neither is it needfull to proclaim this intention to the world: yea, I know not whether to say thus much, be not even too much. It is enough to set the object before them, and to furnish them matter for their thoughts to work upon: as for the measure of praise wee give them, if after thou hast read and weighed, thou shalt think it too much, all I can say, is, that I think it but their due, and speak as I think, & according to the scantling of my own judgment. Touching partiality, I deny it not, but am content to acknowledge my interest. Neither do I think that ever any man did set pen to paper without some particular relation of Kindred, Countrey, or suchlike. The Romanes in writing their Romane, the Greeks in writing their Greek Histories; friends writing to, of, or for friends, may be thought partiall as Countrey-men and friends. The vertuous may deemed to be partiall toward the vertuous, and the godly toward the godly and religious: All writers have some such respect, which is a kinde of partiality. I do not refuse to be thought to have some, or all of these respects, and I hope none wil think I do amisse in having them. Pleasing of men, I am so farre from shunning of it, that it is my chief end and scope: But let it please them to be pleased with vertue, otherwise they shal find nothing here to please them. If thou findest anything here besides, blame me boldly. And why should any be displeased that wil be pleased with it? would to God I could so please the world, I should never displease any. But if either of these (partialitie or desire to please) carry me besides the truth; then shall I confesse myself guilty, and esteem these as great faults, as it is faultie and blame-worthy to forsake the truth. But otherwise so the truth be stuck unto, there is no hurt in partialitie and labouring to please. And as for truth, clip not, nor champ not my words (as some have done elsewhere) and I beleeve the worst affected will not charge mee with lying. I have ever sought the truth in all things carefully, and even here also, and that painfully in every point: where I find it assured, I set it down confidently; where I thought there was some reason to doubt, I tell my Author: So that if I deceive, it is myself I deceive, and not thee; for I hide nothing from thee, that I myself know, and as I know it; leaving place to thee, if thou knowest more or better. Which if thou doest, impart and communicate it; for so thou shouldest do, and so is truth brought to light, which else would lye hid and buried. My paines and travel in it have been greater then everyone would think, in correcting my errours; thine will not be so much. And both of us may furnish matter for a third man to finde out the truth more exactly, than either of us hath yet done. Help therefore, but carp not. Concerning the manner & form, this is partly the cause why I have used this, which I do here follow, that all things being laid open, & exposed to thy view, thou mayest have to choose on, or to finde somewhat of thine owne; & where I could not resolve a doubt, thou mayest see it, and have some mean (perhaps) to solve it better. I have also in many places interposed my judgement of mens actions: I think it the life of History, & without which it were little better, than an old wifes tale. It is true, it were not so needfull if all men were alike judicious: but seeing they are not so, it is absolutely necessary; that so those who read carelessly and sleepingly may bee awaked; who minde onely pleasure, may have profit thrust upon them; that the dull may be quickned, and the judicious have his judgement sharpened, and a finer edge put upon it, by this whet-stone. I know there are that think otherwise, and that all should be left to the collection and discretion of the Reader: But this is my opinion, and I know no Writer of note, or account, but interposeth his censure of things. What name you give this piece, I am very indifferent; Call it History, Chronicle, Commentarie. Annals, Journal lives, or (if you please) discourses or exercitations, it matters not much. Let who will, for me, define, divide, and dispute of the nature, of the bounds and Marches of Airts, and writings, and of their Lawes, this kinde is my lot or choice at this time. For the same cause or reason (that men may not take anything on meer trust), I sift the judgment of others, and am content that thou likewise canvase mine. I do it without partiality, or respecting any mans person: though otherwise, and in other things I reverence them never so much, yet I cannot but respect reason more: where they bring not that strong enough to satisfie, I do not conceal or dissemble it, I do not refuse the same measure from others: if thou doest not like my reason, reject it, but let reason be thy rule, for it is mine according to my capacity. For the language, it is my Mother-tongue, that is, Scottish: and why not, to Scottish-men? Why should I contemne it? I never thought the difference so great, as that by seeking to speak English, I would hazard the imputation of affectation. Every tongue hath the owne vertue and grace. Some are more substantiall, others more ornate and succinct. They also have their own defects and faultinesse, some are harsh, some are effeminate, some are rude, some are affectate and swelling. The Romanes spake from their heart, The Grecians with their lips only, and their ordinary speech was complements; especially the Asiatick Greeks did use a loose and blown kinde of phrase. And who is there that keeps that golden mean? For my own part, I like our own, & he that writes well in it, writes well enough to me. Yet I have yeelded somewhat to the tyrannie of custome, and the times, not seeking curiously for words, but taking them as they came to hand. I acknowledge also my fault (if it be a fault) that I ever accounted it a mean study, and of no great commendation to learn to write, or to speak English, and have loved better to bestow my pains and time on forreigne Languages, esteeming it but a Dialect of our own, and that (perhaps) more corrupt. I say the same of the Stile: I follow no rules, but according to my disposition for the time, so it is high or low, long or short, sweet or sharp, as was my humour for that houre. As in Poesie, so in Prose; who can choose? or how many are there that care for these things, or can discern? The Age is too secure for Writers to be too curious. And thus much shall suffice to have spoken of these things, and to satisfie (I hope) the candide Reader. As for those who delight to carp, we say no more to them, but onely this, That as they take a libertie to themselves to judge others, so there will bee found some that will pay them home in their own coyne. Farewell.

THE HOUSE OF DOUGLAS ACCORDING TO HUME

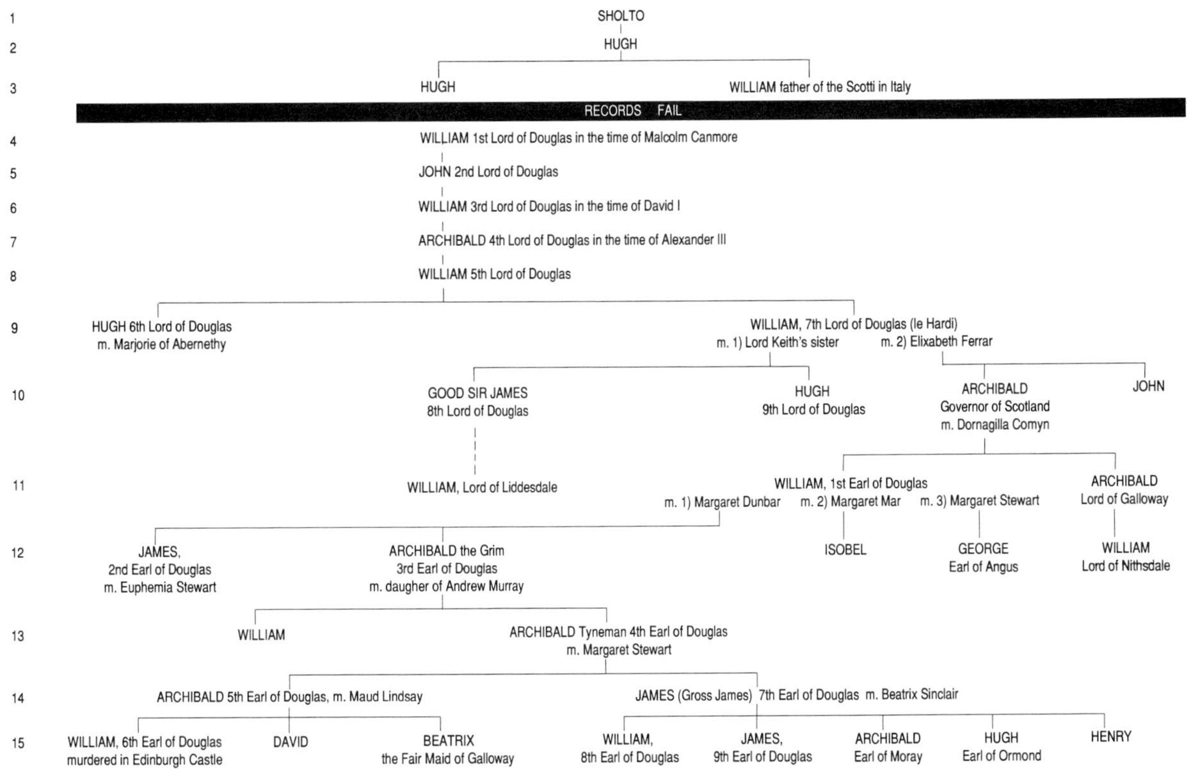

THE HOUSE OF DOUGLAS ACCORDING TO SIR WILLIAM FRASER (abridged)

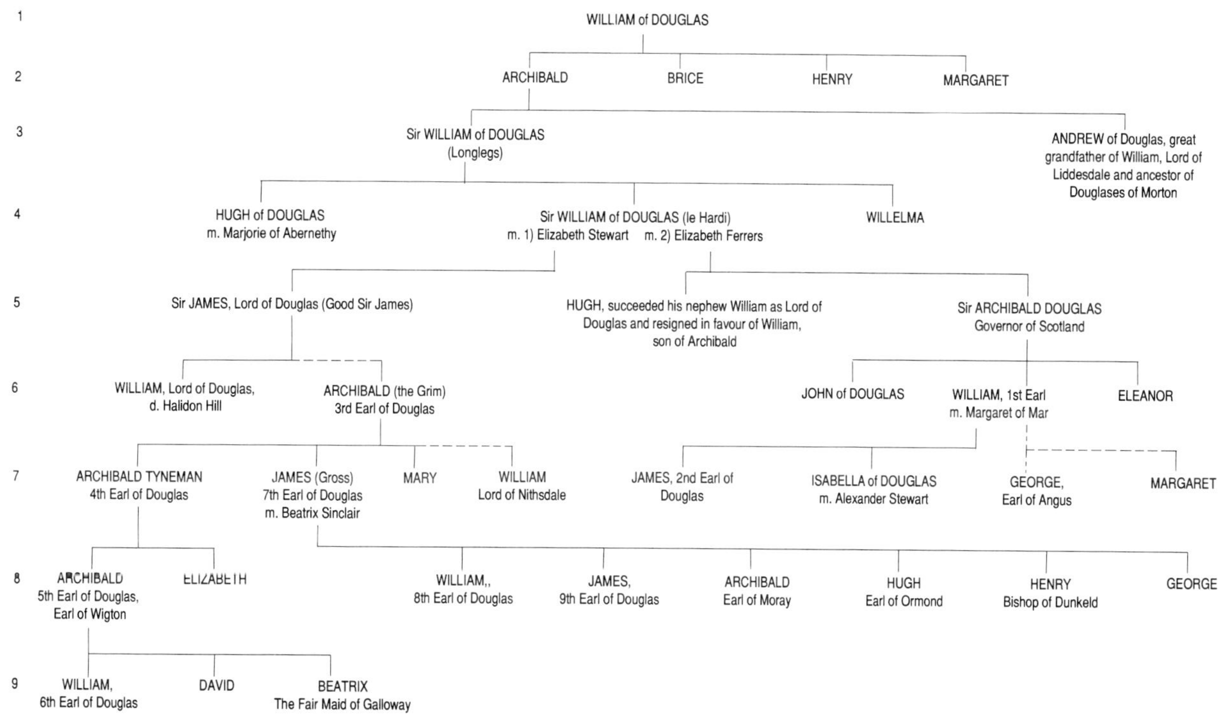

NOTES

The manuscript is not paginated before the Life of Sholto, and so I have supplied pages with Roman numerals. Page numbers after '<u>A</u>' in titles of sections or lives refer to the pages of the manuscript; page and line numbers in brackets after '<u>A</u>' in the notes refer to the text of this edition. The dates supplied from Fraser beneath the titles of the lives are the dates during which the lordship or earldom of Douglas was held. See also the List of Sigla and Abbreviations, ppv-vii, and the statement of editorial policy with respect to the Notes on plxxii-iv.

Angus's dedicatory letter to Charles I (<u>A</u>, pi).

This must have been written before 17 June, 1633 when the 11th Earl of Angus was made Marquis of Douglas and would have signed himself Douglas. In substance, though not in expression, it corresponds to Sir George Douglas of Mordington's letter to Charles in <u>HP</u>, p8, except that Sir George writes as an old friend of Hume's, the Earl as a patron, and it is Sir George's letter that has the verses to James (the translation is the same as in <u>A</u>, Letter to Angus).

The letter is written in the same hand as the insertion about French help to Scotland on p115, l.33 (see note) and the one on p174, l.8 (see note) about the death of the Lord of Liddesdale are, as well as many of the shorter revisions.

The letter is missing from the two extant copies of <u>1633</u>, if it ever prefaced them, and has no place in <u>1644</u>.

Hume's dedicatory letter to Angus (<u>A</u>, ppii-iv).

This letter is addressed to the Earl of Angus. Since he became the Marquis of Douglas on 17 June 1633, the copy must have been made before that date. It is missing from both surviving copies of <u>1633</u>. The version in <u>HP</u>, pp10-11, is dedicated to the Marquis. It follows <u>A2</u> closely, but omits the passage on the contribution of the 11th Earl and 1st Marquis ('and therefter... industrie') and the congratulatory verses to James VI (instead these are appended to Sir George Douglas of Mordington's dedication to Charles) and the comments on them ('which I was bold... desadvowe the same'). <u>1644</u> omits Hume's letter, but its

Preface ends with the verses to James, though with a different English translation. Anna Hume wrote a dedicatory letter to the Marquis of Douglas's son, the lord of Angus, dated December 11, 1643, for 1644. This, however, was cancelled for reasons summarized in the Introduction, ppxxi-xxiii (see Johnston, p152, for a printing of the one surviving copy and for an account of the circumstances bearing on the cancellation).

The dedicatory letter to Angus introduces two important themes of the history, the Douglases as patterns of virtue and the Douglases as loyal and exemplary subjects of their king, the second theme to be maintained in the face of the Stewarts' trouble with both the house of Douglas and the house of Angus and a well-established view that the Douglases, whether Red or Black, grew to be arch examples of the overmighty subject.

4, ll.23-24. *the absolute command of honoured Soveraine*: The insertion of 'his and our much' by a reviser need not have been undertaken before James's death in 1625. The reviser would simply be trying to improve Hume's sense and would not feel he should adjust the compliment to the reign of a new king. As I have argued in the Introduction, the MS would have been revised after Hume's death and James's, but the revisers, if they were different from the one at work here, still left this and the other (by then) anachronistic reference to James (Preface, p24, l.2).

4-5, ll.32 -1. *their names in order, their deids in particular, were hitherto remarked by few; and sett downe by none*: Maitland sets down the lives of the Black Douglases from William the Hardy to James, the 9th Earl, chronologically and recounts at least some of their deeds, as Hume well knew.

5, ll.14-15. *James... his joyful return*: in 1617.

5, l.17. ^These verses togither with the English are to be the last words of th'Epistle to the King And to be insert in that place^ has been inserted in the margin.

6, l.8. The inserted translation of Hume's verses is as follows:

^In English thus.

But Sir, Desdaine not if there added be
To your high styles, and nombrous pedegree
A private house; But sproung of Royall race,
Allyed with Kings, and beareing oft there place
in peace and warr. And yett a rarer thing,
Whose gen'rous seede brought foorth a mighty king
A king than whome none greater hath bin knowne
that weelds three Brittain scepters all in one.
The noble stock, and house whereof I speeke
Is that of Douglas, and of Angus eeke.
A race whose worth in vertues did not ceede
To such as Greece, or ancyent Rome did breede:

A nombrous race, that as much matchles proue
in myndes and armes, and in there Countrees love
That though you sould adde thousand scepters more
to these you haue, and breede of kings great store
Lett this not be the least of y*ou*r renoune
that from these worthies you descended doune.^

In 1644, sig.B^2, the Latin verses, with a different translation, conclude the Preface.

6, l.27-28. *Qui genus iactat suum, aliena laudat*: 'The man who praises his own race, praises what belongs to strangers' (Seneca, *Hercules furens*, 340).

To the Reader (A, ppv-vii)

To the Reader in its altered form corresponds almost exactly with 'To the Reader' in HP, pp12-13. It is missing from both copies of 1633. 1644's version may be found in Appendix I; it differs markedly in expression, though it elaborates the same points.

8, ll.13-15. *The cheif poynts may incure here to a carping humor, or the weaknes of the wryter*: A2 gives the sense ('The cheif poynts then that may here incure the censure of a carping humour, 1. are the weaknes of the wryter; 2....'). 'or' introduces a series of points for carping at.
8. l.21. ^1.^ is inserted in the margin.
8, l.28. ^2^ is inserted in the margin.
9, l.4. ^3^ is inserted in the margin.
9, l.9. ^4^ is inserted in the margin.
9, l.16. ^5^ is inserted in the margin.
9, l.22. ^6^ is inserted in the margin.
9, l.29. ^7^ is inserted in the margin.
10, ll.2-4. *if not, thow must by reason expect of vthers, a meeting in the lyke action conforme to thy merites*: i.e. 'if this is not good enough for you, the sensible thing would be for you to go to others for a performance that comes up to your standard'.

The Preface (A, ppviii-xxxiii)

The preface is missing from both copies of 1633. It remarks on the heads on which evidence for the pre-eminence of the Douglases may be drawn from the succeeding lives. As with 'To the Reader', 1644 A-B[2], is superior in eloquence, vigour and succinctness. But A, HP (pp16-23) and 1644 elaborate the same topics in the same order and differ little in matters of fact. HP is close to A, a shortened version with alterations in phrasing.

11, ll.7-8. The couplet, present in all three versions, was inscribed with three others on the sword of state, said to have been presented by Robert the Bruce to the Good Sir James, once to be found in Douglas Castle (Fraser, I, 184, and illustration on facing page); the castle was demolished in the Thirties and the sword disappeared in a sale of its treasures. The couplet is quoted in Boece (1536) Bk.XIV, ch.8.
11, l.31-12, l.2. ^*though... nations*^ is pasted in so that the marginal note is hidden.
12, ll. 21-24. HP, p16, omits the branches enumerated in A and 1644, sig.A[b]. *Liddisdail*: see William Lord of Liddesdale, the Flower of Chivalry (pp145-75); *Nethsdail*: William Lord of Nithsdale (pp254 ff); *Galloway*: Archbald, Lord of Galloway (pp251 ff); *Ormond, Murray, Balvennie*: the three brothers of William the 8th Earl, slain at Stirling Castle. *Ormond*: Hugh, Earl of Ormond, won the Battle of Sark (below, p384, ff.). *Murray*: Archbald, Earl of Moray, fought against the Earl of Huntly (below, pp423-24). *Balvennie*: John, Lord of Balvennie (below, p435), was defeated with his brothers at Arkinholme but escaped. *Dalkeith*: A James Douglas, heir to the Lord of Dalkeith was captured at Homildon, according to p263, l.32, but see note.
12, ll. 29-31. The four heads under which the preeminence of the Douglases will be adduced are enumerated in all three versions (1644, sig.A[b], HP, p17) and elaborated at length. ^1.^, ^2.^, ^3.^, ^4.^ are inserted in the margin against the various heads.
13, l.26-14, l.6. A returns to Edward's destruction of historical records on p45, ll.25-35, a theme taken from Boece, Bk.XIV, ch.7 and Buchanan, Bk.VIII, fol.78v. 1644's abbreviated account of the Antiquity of the house defers mention of Edward's destroying records to the life of Sholto, pp2-3, and passes immediately to Sholto Douglas (sig.A[b]).
14, l.8. *William the Hardy*: William, 7th Lord of Douglas (pp59-67). Not mentioned at this point in HP, p17, or 1644.
14, l.20-15, l.5. The story of Sholto Douglas is repeated in the life, pp31-34. Neither HP nor 1644 mention the Tillisaule MS, but both mention it in the life of Sholto, 1644, p4, HP, p29.
15, l.14. *William the thrid*: In 1593, William, 10th Earl of Angus, escaped from Edinburgh Castle and joined the other rebellious Catholic earls, Huntly and Errol in the North East; 'banishment' is a bland gloss on this further trouble between the house of Angus and the Crown. In 1609, he went into voluntary exile in France,

his second banishment. *William the fourt*: William, 11th Earl of Angus and 1st Marquis of Douglas.
15, l.19-20. *Sir Alexander Hay, Clerk of Register*: Lord Newton, Clerk Register, d. 1616.
15, ll.30-31. *Vmbertus Locatius and Franciscus Sansovinus*: see Notes to life of William Douglas, p42, ll.5-13.
15, l.31-17, l.10. See life of William Douglas, A (pp38-44). HP (p18) omits the Scoti in Italy, passing immediately from Sholto to the Parliament of Forfar. 1644 does not argue here, as A does, from the Italian record that Sholto Douglas must have received the name of Douglas before Achaius (in the reign of Solvathius) and consequently have defeated a Donaldbane 330 years before the one rebelling against King Edgar; it does so in the life of Sholto, p4.
15, l.33. *819*: See p42, ll.26-27, where suggested dates are as in 1644, sig.A[b], '800 or 801'.
16, l.1. *Plaisance*: Piacenza.
16, l.36-17, l.1. *Donald Bane... King Edgar*: See Boece, Bk.XII, ch.13; see also note to p32, l.5.
17, l.20. *Parlament holden at Forfare*: See p46, l.18.
17, l.21-21, l.2. HP, p18, omits other records of antiquity, leaving the burden of refuting those who think that the rise of the house of Douglas took place in the time of William the 7th Earl and the Good Sir James to the evidence adduced in the lives.
17, l.24. *William Douglas*: William, 1st Lord of Douglas.
17, l.32. The foundation of Lesmahagow is not again referred to. A charter was witnessed in 1240 in the time of Alexander II by William, 5th Lord of Douglas, which granted Little Kype to the monks of Lesmahagow (Fraser, I, 56).
18, l.9. *a certaine chartour granted to the towne of Aire*: A (p22) mentions William, 3rd Lord as witness. 1644, sig.A[2], omits the evidence of the 1st Charter of Ayr.
18, l.13. *William de Douglas*: William, 3rd Lord Douglas.
18, ll.21-22. *Bishope of Murray*: Fraser, p10, notes a Bishop of Murray, Brice, younger son of William of Douglas (fl.1174-1199), possibly the bishop in question. *Alexander and William Douglases*: See pp20, l.1, and 49, l.10.
18, l.31. *Archbald de Douglas*: Archibald, later 4th Lord of Douglas (p51). 1644, sig.A[2], says that William and Alexander were probably witnesses.
18, l.32. *ane Endenture*: See p53, ll.17-35.
19, l.2. *William Lord Douglas*: William, 5th Lord of Douglas.
19, ll.4-5. *Hew Lord Abernathie*: Sir Hugh of Abernethy, see Life of William, 5th Lord of Douglas, p53, ll.22-23.
19-20, ll.31-1. *Androwe Douglas of Creswal... Sir William Douglas of Glendening... Alexander and William Douglases*: See p49, l.10. *Lord Wintoun*: Roger Quincy, Earl of Wintoun and

Winchester and Constable of Scotland did not suffer forfeiture. His lands in Galloway passed through marriage into various hands including the Balliols', whose lands were of course forfeited (Archibald A. M. Duncan, *Scotland: the Making of a Kingdom* [Edinburgh: Oliver and Boyd, 1975], p532). *William Douglas of Mordringtoun*: William, second son of Sir James Douglas of Dalkeith (fl. 1372-1406) 'is said to have received Mordingtoun from his father' (*SP*, VI, 348).

21, ll.3-8. 1644, sig.A[2b], expands the general topic of virtue in Hume's best sententious manner as A and HP, p18, do not.

21, ll.16-17. Archibald the Grim, 3rd Earl of Douglas scorned a Dukedom, pp249-50.

21, l.28. *their lands in Regalitie*: If this refers to the Emerald Charter (see pp104-105), the grant of jurisdiction to the Good Sir James on which Hume bases his defence of the resistance of William, 8th Earl of Douglas, to the King's officers, Livingstone and Crichton, the Douglases did not properly hold their land in regality, where the King delegates all powers of the crown, but on more limited terms (Barrow, p398). But the Life of William, 1st Earl of Douglas, p177-78, speaks of a later charter of 1354 (see note to p179, l.8) that united the Douglas possessions in one Regality (Fraser, III, 361).

21, l.33-24, l.6. HP, p19, merely states the fact of royal alliances and passes on without enumeration to the next head, the greatness of the Douglases.

22, l.9. *Galloway... Cummeins, Baliols*: See pp129-30, ll.19-5, 195, ll.27-35; *Carrick*: See pp52-53, ll.8-17; *Abernathie*: See pp53, ll.19-23.

22, l.15-24, l.6. The sequence of royal alliances in A and 1644, sig.A[3], differs.

22, ll.15-17. For the supposed relation of Robert Bruce and the Good Sir James, see pp52-53, ll.8-10.

22, l.14. *Marginal note*: 'fourtein' is scored out and ^15^ inserted.

22, l.19. *Margaret Stewart*: See pp178-79, ll.34-21 197, l.19.

22, l.24. *Eupham*: See p209, ll.14-15.

22, l.29. *Egidia*: See p242, l.11.

22, l.35. *Isabell Douglas*: See p179, l.23.

23, l.2. *Marjorie*: See 178-79, ll.8-6.

23, l.7. *Margaret Stewart*: See p257, ll.11-12. 'Archbald the second of that name' is in fact the third Archibald who was Lord of Douglas according to Hume's reckoning, as 1644 correctly has it. 1644, sig.A[3], adds evidence for this marriage.

23, l.9. *Elizabeth*: See p275.

23, ll.14-15. *Marie Stewart*: See p197, l.23.

23, l.20. *James Douglas Lord of Dalkeith*: See p421, ll.17-22. 1644, sig.A3, wrongly says that James Douglas's wife was daughter to James II.
23, l.19. *Henrie Douglas*: See p344, ll.30-31, note. Omitted in 1644.
23, ll.23-33. Items '12' to '14' have been renumbered '13' to '15' to accommodate the inserted '12'.
23, l.28. *Archbald Douglas*: See pp344, ll.15-20.
23, l.29. *Margaret Tueder*: See 1644, p238. See Fraser, II, 287.
23. l.33. *Lady Margaret Douglas*: See 1644, p238. She became Countess of Lennox (Fraser, II, 289-92).
24, ll.2-4. *our most gratious Soveraine... eternal felicitie*: Like the revision of the similar reference to James as still living in the epistle to the Earl of Angus (p4, ll.23-24), the insertion that James 'now lives' need not mean that this revision was undertaken before James died. The reviser wished to improve what Hume had wanted to say not to impose the temporal perspective of the new reign.
24, l.6. *Lady Arabella Stewart*: She was the innocent victim of James VI's suspicions, exacerbated by Cobham's plot of 1603 (G. M. Trevelyan, *England under the Stuarts* (London, 1947), p91.
24, ll.13-14. *Syria and the Holy Land*: For the Good Sir James's crusade with Bruce's heart, see pp124-25.
24, ll.25-28. *to stay by times*: See accounts of the Good Sir James's expeditions of 1321 (p101) and 1321/22 (pp102-103) and later to Stanhope-park (p109-13) and of James, the 2nd Earl of Douglas's expedition to England (pp216-17, ll.32-3) and to Otterburn (pp220, l.6ff).
24, l.28-26, l.27. HP, p20, passes from a general remark about the Douglases' dependants to William the 1st Earl in France, then adds, after the honours to William '6th' (i.e. 8th) Earl of Douglas and George, 4th Earl of Angus, some general remarks about dependant houses. 1644, sig.A3b, has more to say than A (p24, ll.31-32) about the Humes.
24, ll.29-30. *Flemings and Hamiltons*: See the part played by Sir James Hamilton of Cadzow in the Life of James, 9th Earl of Douglas, pp419, 429, 430, 433; as for the Flemings, Hume, p324, l.28 (cf. Holinshed, *SC*, p386) says that Lord Fleming of Cumbernauld was sent by William, 6th Earl of Douglas, to Charles VII of France to negotiate his investiture as Duke of Touraine.
24, l.31. *Humes*: 'This is verified by a bond of a thousand nobles... made by Archbald Earle of Wigtoun, and Long Willie [Longueville]... to Alexander Hume of Hume, dated at Bothwell 1423. The same Earl also... gave the lands of Wedderburne to David Hume brother to the said Alexander... for his many good services' (1644, Preface, sig.A3b). See also below, p288, l.4, and note.

24, l.33. *Logans*: Robert and Walter Logan of Restalrig accompanied the Good Sir James to Spain (p124, l..23).
24, l.33-25, l.3 *Lauders,... Setoun, Saltoun, Gray, and Oliphant*: See p390, ll.31-33, and note.
25, l.4. *Marginal note*: Boece (1574), Bk.XVI, fol.345, does list the men of Scottish families in the army of Archibald Tyneman at Verneuil in 1424, but not Bellenden's translations (Bk.XVI, ch20), nor, following them, Holinshed, *SC*, 376. See p279, ll.11-13, below.
25, ll.7-8. *Murdok Stewart*: Earl of Fife, fought under Archibald, 4th Earl of Douglas at Homildon (p262, ll.16-17).
25, ll.12-16. The martial exploits of William, 1st Earl of Douglas in France, are not recorded in the life, p183, ll.29-31.
25, l.16. *Marginal note*: William, the 1st Earl was at Poitiers in 1356, according to Boece (1531), Bk.XV, ch.15 (correctly), but 1355 according to Holinshed, *SC*, pp353-54.
25, l.16 *Archbald the thrid*: Archibald, 4th Earl of Douglas took the title of Duke of Touraine (p285, ll.1-3), earned by his son the Earl of Wigton at the Battle of Baugé (p308). HP (p20) is more circumstantial about this than either A or 1644.
25, l.24. *Marginal note*: I cannot find Holinshed refer to a compact with either; on this subject see, however, Fraser, I xxxvii, and II, 59-60, 92-93.
25, l.31. *William the fourt*: Hume supposes that William, 8th Earl of Douglas (p397, ll.17-26), was offered a duchy on the same terms as George, 4th Earl of Angus (p448; see 1644, p216). This material is rehearsed in 1633, pp236-237, as part of a summary of the grandeur of the house of Douglas (see note to p441, ll.21-26). HP (p20) says that Henry IV made a contract with William 4th of that name (i.e. the 8th Earl of Douglas, which is not possible), and Henry VI only (as in 1644) with the Earl of Angus.
25, l.34. *James last Earle of Douglas*: James, 9th Earl of Douglas, was made knight of the Garter by Edward IV (p438, below).
26, ll.2-3. *Archbald the second, Earle of Angus*: Archibald, 7th Earl of Angus (see 1644, p270).
26, ll.6-7. On *William the thrid, sixt Earle of Douglas*, and his keeping of state, see pp324-25, ll.17-6. *Marginal note*: Holinshed, *SC*, p386; Boece (1574), Bk.XVIII, fol.359v.
26, ll.11-20. On the journey to Rome of William, 8th Earl of Douglas, see p440. *Pape (Nicholas the fyft)*: Nicholas V, pope from 1447 to 1455. *Marginal note*: the journey took place, not in 1456, but in 1450-51, as Holinshed, *SC*, p391 has it. See also Boece (1574), Bk.XVIII, fol.371.
26, l.28-27, l.4. A and HP, p21, refer valour, the fourth topic under which the greatness of the Douglases is considered, to the lives. 1644, sig.A^4, elaborates the topic, grants a possible preeminence to Wallace, only to snatch further cause for congratulating the Douglases from the comparison, quotes a

stanza from Daniel's *Ciuile Wares betweene the houses of Lancaster and Yorke* (1609), Bk.4, sts.50-51, about Archibald, 4th Earl of Douglas, (below, pp273-74) at Shrewsbury and gives other instances of the family valour.

27, l.12-30, l.36. Comparison with other families: HP, p21, says comparisons are odious, but still brings in comparisons with the Cummings and the Percies (pp22). 1644, sig.A^{4b}-B, treats the same families as A, but in a different order. Needless to say most of the material on other families drawn from Boece is legendary and is not taken seriously in *SP*.

27, ll.14-26. *Murrays and Grahames*: Murrays and Grahams are attached to the succeding phrases chiastically so that it is the Murrays who, according to Boece, Bk. IV, ch.5 (1531), ch.8 (1536), took their rise in the reign of Corbredus and the Grahams who, according to Boece, Bk VII, ch.4 (1531), ch.6 (1536), took their rise in the reign of Fergus.

27, ll.27-33. *Hays*: For their legendary founder in the days of Kenneth III, see Boece, Bk.XI, ch.7 (1531), ch.8 (1536).

27, l.34-28, l.17. *Cumings*: See Boece, Bk.XII, ch.16. For the Battle of Roslin, see Boece, Bk. XIV, ch.6.

28, ll.20-27. *Cambels*: According to clan tradition, the heiress of Clan Duibhne married a Norman named Campbell (*SP*, I, 318); *Gordons*: *SP*, IV, 507 sees no reason to think that the Scottish family came from England; *Hamiltons*: According to Barrow, p273, Walter, son of Gilbert, commanding Bothwell Castle for Edward II, surrendered on the morrow of Bannockburn to Edward Bruce, and as a result of this belated patriotism or timely treachery, 'survived to become the ancestor of the powerful Hamilton family'. But see Boece, Bk.XIV, ch.15.

29, l.5-30, l.11. 1644, sig.B, gives an account of the Percies and the Romans, much longer and more particular than the accounts in A and HP, p22.

29, l.27. *Fabii, Cornelii, Marcelli, Scipions*: The most famous soldier of the Fabii was Maximus Verracosus; why the Cornelii should be mentioned here is not clear since none of that name were celebrated soldiers; Marcus Claudius Marcellus was a statesman and soldier during the Punic Wars (others of the same name were more celebrated as patrons than as soldiers); among the Scipios, famous for their part in the Punic Wars were Africanus major and Aemilianus Africanus Numantius.

30, l.11. 1644, sig.B^{b}, returns to the opening couplet about the exceptional goodness of the Douglas line, restates Hume's belief in its preeminence and ends with the Latin verses he wrote to King James that in A (with a different translation inserted) are included in his dedicatory letter to the Earl of Angus. A and HP reiterate some of the earlier subjects of congratulation.

30, ll.25-26 The passing references to The Marquisat of Salluce and Antwerpe are taken up in 1633 (p10) and HP (pp40--41).

The Life of Sholto Douglas (A, pp1-4)

Even when corrected, A only approximates to 1633 (pp1-3) in phrasing, though it corresponds in sense closely, sentence by sentence, except in these two places: (1) between ll.2 and 3, p32, i.e. between first and second paragraph, on the difficulty of ascertaining the origins of a family and, citing Livy on the need to embrace 'whatsoever the common and constant fame of many former ages, haue with confidence delyvered to us', it settles for the evidence of traditions (1633, p2); (2) after 'Douglasdaile' (p33, l.33), 1633, p3, has a passage citing the Tillysaule MS (cf. Preface, p15, ll.9-13, above).

HP, pp26-29, corresponds in both these additions (pp26-27 and 28-29) to 1633, and throughout corresponds to 1633, except for minor details in phrasing.

1644, pp1-4, omits the opening passage on mutability, a persistent, and even unifying, theme of A (and 1633). Instead 1644, pp1-3, opens with an account of the difficulties in ascertaining the origins of families, particularly of the Douglases. This is a lively version of points made in attenuated form in 1633 and HP in the first addition to A noted above. On the subject of defective records of antiquity 1644, pp1-3, has, besides, a dig at Camden and the monks of the dark ages, and brings up Edward I's destruction of the records of Scottish families, conceding, however that the destruction may not have been intentional (in this, contrast the malice stated as fact in A, p14, ll.3-6). 1644's account of Sholto's distinguishing himself (pp3-4) is much shorter and less detailed than the one in A, 1633 and HP. Like 1633 and HP, after noting the reward of lands to Sholto, 1644 adds an argument (p4) for the authenticity of this tradition by citing the MS of 'Alexander Mackduffe of Tillysaul, who dwelt at Moore alehouse near Straboguie' and how the 10th Earl of Angus, confined to that region in 1595 for his Catholicism, examined it. At this point 1644 brings in the Scoti in Italy (as A did in the Preface, pp16-17, ll.22-9) to show how traditions harmonize to evidence the antiquity of the Douglases.

The story of Sholto and his sons closely resembles the founding legend of the Hay family (Boece, Bk.XI, ch.7 [1531], ch.8 [1536]). At the Battle of Luncarty against the Danes, a country man, named Hay, with his two sones, restored the fight by a timely intervention and was ennobled. Hume wants to make out that the Douglases were an older family, hence the pains he is at to establish their famous ancestor in the reign of Solvathius in the

Eighth Century (the Battle of Luncarty took place in the Tenth). He also insists on Sholto's being already a noble man (though a stranger to the King), so to make a claim for the indeterminate antiquity of the Douglases' aristocracy and to outbid the Hays. Neither Boece, Bk.IX, ch.29, nor Buchanan, BkV, fol.57, nor Holinshed, *SC*, p158, mention Sholto Douglas at the defeat of Donald Bane. Major, despite the marginal note does not mention either Solvathius or a Donald Bane at that time.

32, ll.4-5: Fraser remarks (1, 20) that Solvathius 'is unknown to accurate history'. The tissue of argument adduced in the Preface (pp14-17) to prove the antiquity of the Douglases is not soundly based. Fraser proposes rather that Sholto lived in the days of William the Lion and fought against the Donald Bane who was defeated in the battle of 31 July 1187.

The Life of Hugo Douglas I (A, pp5-6)

A, corrected, corresponds almost verbatim to 1633 (p4) and HP (pp29-30). 1644 (p4) in three lines says only that we know nothing of Hugo except that he helped his father to overthrow Donald Bane. On this datum A, 1633 and HP expand with such topics as family piety and a wish to improve will suggest.

The Life of Hugo 2 (A, pp6-7)

1633 (pp4-5), and HP (p30) correspond almost verbatim to A2.

As with the Life of the 1st Hugo, so here 1644 (pp4-5) does not embroider on what Hume thought were facts, namely that Hugo succeeded to the title, while his younger brother William went abroad.

The Life of William Douglas (A, pp7-16)

1633 (pp5-10) corresponds to A2 except for three additions: (1) at p41, l.3 (' ...1622;'), 1633 (p6) inserts a note on the family tree the 11th Earl of Angus sent to the Conte d'Agazzano in return, which acknowledges the strange gap between William, the grandson of Sholto, and William the 1st Lord of Douglas, created such at the Parliament of Forfar in Malcolm Canmore's time, but argues that the Italian line shows that the Scottish line must have continued unrecorded; (2) between paragraphs p42, ll.1-2 ('... descryvit. [new paragraph] Besyds...'), 1633, (pp7-8), inserts the letter of the Conte d'Agazzano in Italian without translation; (3) at p44, l.25 (' ...the lyke'), 1633 (p10) inserts a note on the spread of the Scoti outside in other parts of Europe such as France and Flanders, giving the recent case in which Cornelius and Petrus Scoti, merchants in Antwerp had to apply to the 11th Earl of Angus for permission to use the Douglas arms (cf A, Preface, p30, ll.26-27, for abbreviated allusion).

HP has the same insertions: (1) p34; (2) pp37-38 (including a translation of the letter into English different from the one in 1644); (3) pp40-41. In addition it inserts a digression (pp31-33) on the Scottish Order of the Thistle with a founding legend set in the days of Achaius and Hungus taken from Boece, Bk.10, ch.5, and 'the worthie French Author, in his great booke of Estates and Empires'.

1644, pp5-10, as usual is more concise, avoiding eulogistic padding, and yet in places more specific. It is organized more as a defence of the antiquity of the house of Douglas than as a narrative and rearranges the material accordingly. 1644's treatment of the arms of the Scoti on pp8-10 (see pp41-42, ll.19-22) explains the absence of the crowned heart present on the Douglas arms as a consequence of the Scoti's having branched off from the Scottish Douglases before the Good Sir James took the Bruce's heart on crusade. The reason why the Scoti have only two stars, whereas the Douglases have three, is left to be explained by the letter from the Conte d'Agazzano, given in Italian and translated (the translation differing from the one in HP). 1644, p7, is more circumstantial than the other versions of the family tree of the Italian Scoti.

Neither Boece, Bk.X, chs.2-4, nor Buchanan, Bk.V, fol.57, nor Holinshed, *SC*, pp159-60, mention William Douglas's part in the Scottish expedition. Holinshed, *SC*, p284, copying from Lesley, Bk.VIII, p323, mentions the descendants of the Douglases in Northern Italy, adducing the arms of the Scoti as evidence, but this is in a context of fifteenth century Scots settlement on the Continent.

Fraser, p21, scotches the notion of a league between Achaius and Charlemagne and the founding by William Douglas of the Scoti.

38, l.18. *Desiderius*: Desiderius, king of the Lombards was captured by Charlemagne in 774, see *Cambridge History of Medieval Europe*, vol. 2 (Cambridge, 1913), pp219-20.
38, l.30. *Pope Leo the thrid*: It was Pope Adrian I who called in Charlemagne against the Lombards.

39, ll.14-17. The rhyming couplet substituted for the original prose version in A2 is adopted by 1633, HP, p33, and 1644, p5.
39, l.29. *Scots Gilmor*: According to Major, Bk II, ch.13, Prince William was accounted 'one of his twelve famous soldiers who was commonly known among our own people as Scotisgilmor'.
Marginal note: Boece, Bk.X, ch.4, fol.185, not 195, in 1536. *Scottish Chronicle Anno 787*: Holinshed, pp162-63.
39, l.33. ^15 Abacies erected^ inserted in margin.
40, l.6. *Plaisance*: Piacenza.
40, ll.10-17. Instead of having the Spittinis seek out an honourable connection with William, 1644, p6, has him, weary of travel, seek a good alliance in Piacenza.
41, l.35. *St Jenes Church*: 1633 p7, HP, p35, have St Laurence Church, and the letter from the Conte d'Agazzano seems to imply that the Scoti's burial place is there.
42, ll.l6-7. *Umbertus Locatus*: *De Placentinae urbis origine, successu, et laudibus* (Cremona, 1563), pp32-33, tells of Gulielmus Scotus, Anno 805. The book is introduced by a letter to the Christoforo Scoto mentioned in Leslie's history.
42, ll.7-13. *Franciscus Sansovinus*: Francesco Sansovino, *Della origine et de fatti delle famiglie illustri d'Italia (*Venice, 1540), Bk.1, fol.111v. HP, p38, translates Sansovino's Italian.
42, ll.13-22. *John Leslie*: *De origine, moribus, et rebus gestis Scotorum* (Rome, 1578), pp324-325. HP, p39 translates Leslie's Latin account of Scots settlement on the Continent in the Fifteenth Century.
13, l.6. Preface, p15, l.33, dates William's expedition as 819. 1644, p6, notes the discrepancy between Sansovino's date (779- omitted in A's quotation) and the one given by 'our writers' (800 or 801).
42, l.38. *Donatus Scoti*: A St Donatus, bishop of Fiesole (died c. 876), was an Irish churchman with ties to Iona, who would have been known as Scotus, and may have been associated with Bobbio in Piedmont at one time (see John J. Delaney and James E. Tobin, *Dictionary of Catholic Biography* [London, 1962]). Hume's source is Sansovino.
43, l.15. *Albertus Scoti*: Fraser, p21, dismissively notes how in 1279 Edward I granted protection to the passage of the merchandise of Albert Scot, merchant of Piacenza, through his dominions.
44, ll.2-3. *Charles the fourt, and Sigismond Empereurs*: The Emperor Charles IV, reigned from 1346 to 1378, Sigismond from 1410 to 1438.
44, l.11. *Johne*: 1644, p7, has it that Petrus, not John, died without issue. 1644 also traces the descent from William to Albert the Great.
44, l.25. 1644, p7, adds further distinctions and services of the family in Pavia and Cyprus.

The Life of William, 1st Lord of Douglas (A, pp17-20)

1633, pp11-12, corresponds to A2 almost exactly.

HP, pp42-44, corresponds almost exactly to A2, except that on p42 it adds wordily at A, p45, l.25 ('... truethe') some material about how the Scoti supply evidence for the Douglas line in the absence of Scottish records, and on p44 (A, p47, l.18) notes that, according to Buchanan and Holinshed, Patrick Dumbar was created Earl of March four years after the Parliament of Forfar for his services in quieting the eastern march.

1644, pp10-11 (mispag. 15), covers the same material in the same order more concisely, but omits the by now repetitious material about Edward's having destroyed the Scottish records (A, p17).

45, ll.25-26. Note how the correction suppresses the tyrannophobe and immoderate expression 'tyrannical oppression' with the more neutral 'vsurpation'.
45, ll.33-35. *as shal be declared more at lenth herefter in the Life of Lord William the Hardy*: see p45, ll.33-35.
46, l.16-48, l.5. According to Fraser (pp21-22), the Parliament of Forfar is an invention of Boece's, so William Douglas cannot have been created Lord of Douglas there, this in spite of the Hume's Iona MS. Boece, Bk.XII, ch.9, does not mention Douglas among the many promotions at the Parliament of Forfar. Buchanan, Bk.VII, fol.74v., mentioning promotions at Forfar, singles out only Macduffus for mention. I cannot find any reference to a Parliament of Forfar in Major.
46, l.25. Colmkille: Iona.
47, l.29. John Reid: HP, p44, has a marginal note in a hand other than the scribes' saying that John Reid sent the Marquis of Douglas the MS in 1613. The note must have been added after the Earl of Angus was created Marquis of Douglas in 1633.

The Life of John, 2nd Lord of Douglas (A, pp21)

1633, p13, corresponds to A2 almost exactly.

HP, p45, has, pasted over the original, a life writtten by a different hand at the behest of a marginal note, possibly in the Marquis of Douglas's hand (cf. his letter to the Laird of Guthrie of 23 February, 1644, SRO 90188/25/4, though of course this letter may have been written for him as may the marginal note). This differs in phrasing and in some matters from A and 1633: after the first mention of John (A [see p49, l.7] '... Peebles') it notes that from John's son, William, descend the houses of Douglas, Angus and Morton; a marginal note in another hand after the line descending from William's son, William, says, 'the descent of this to be remitt to the tree of Douglas'.

1644, pp11-12, while giving the brothers excellent characters, avoids the formula of A and 1644 that they maintained the glory of their ancestors. It wonders whether the two brothers may have had an elder brother.

49, l.9. *Tiuidail*: Teviotdale; *Eusdail*: Ewesdale.
49, l.11. *Androwe Douglas of Creswal*: see Preface, p19.

The Life of 2 William, 3rd Lord of Douglas (A, pp21-22)

c.1174-c.1214

1633, p13, departs in places from the phrasing and details of A2. It dates the first Charter of Ayr in the 25th year of the reign of David (said to be David I), instead of the 27th (A, p50, l.6).

HP, pp45-46, also departs in places from the phrasing and details of A2, without corresponding more closely to 1633, except that it dates the first Charter of Ayr in the 25th year of David's reign 'about... 1148'. It adds the information after dating the charter (A, [p50, l.10]) that he was known as St David for his piety, died at Carlisle in 1152 and was buried in Dunfermline.

1644, p12, says that the Charter was given in the 25th or 27th year of David (first son to Malcolm, not third as A [p50, l.7], 1633 and HP have it), who died in 1153.

According to Fraser, I, 37, this William of Douglas is the first owner of Douglas or Douglasdale known to authentic history.

50, ll.8-10. Fraser, I, 38-39, dismisses the existence of a charter given to Ayr in 1151 (no such charters were granted before William the Lion), but says that William of Douglas witnessed a charter given to Ayr by David II. Cf. Preface, p18, ll.8-13.

The Life of Archibald, 4th Lord of Douglas (A, p22)

c.1213-1240

1633, pp13-14, corresponds to A2 almost exactly.

HP, p46, corresponds to A2 almost exactly, except that William is said to grant the Charter to Ayr in 1234.

1644, p12, says what A says in 4 lines without attempt at eulogy.

51, ll.6-7. *the Chartour granted to the Towne of Aire*: Cf. Preface, p18, ll.27-32. See Fraser, I, 39.

The Life of William, 5th Lord of Douglas (A, pp23-29)

c.1240-1276

1633, pp14-16, corresponds to A2 almost exactly, except that on p14 (A [p52, l.8]) and p16 (A [p55, l.24]) 1633 names Alexander of Carrick's sister 'Martha' not 'Isabelle', followed in this by 1644, p14, but not HP, p49. For both A and HP, Martha is Alexander of Carrick's daughter.

HP pp46-50, departs considerably from A2, both in phrasing and matter, though not in order of topics. The first section (p46) is pasted over the original. Citing Maitland's MS history [p1], which had come into the hands of the Regent Morton, it transfers to William, 5th Lord of Douglas (correctly-see Fraser, I, p56) from William the Hardy 7th Lord, the nickname Longlegs and the reason given in A p31 that he was tall. The account of the struggle between Gilbert and Ethred (A [pp52-53, ll.14-9]; HP, pp47-48) is considerably, if not pertinently, more detailed. The Endenture (A [pp53, ll.13-32]; HP, p48) is said to have been entered into on Palm Sunday, 1259, in the 'place of' the Castle of Edinburgh. The long passage in A [pp53-55, ll.36-15], dealing with the confusion of William, 5th Lord of Douglas, with William, the 7th Lord, is omitted. HP, p50, supplies an account (no authority cited) of the actions omitted in all the other versions that would justify the claims made in A [p56, ll.25-30], and 1633, p16 for his noble parts: he assisted Alexander III in driving out King Hakon, first from Western Scotland, then from the Isle of Man, of which he was made governor.

1644, pp12-15, rearranges the material of A and 1633, beginning (p12) with the Endenture (dated on Palm Sunday, 1259) and ending (pp14-15) with William's marriage (to Martha) and its lineal connections and consequences. Where A (p53, ll.23-26) declines to specify the conditions of marriage to Marjorie, 1644, pp12-13, enters into them at length and puzzles over their oddities, including a discrepancy between the Endenture in the Douglas charter chest and the account of an Endenture given in Maitland. It also tries to make out the seal on the Endenture as stamped with the Douglas arms. On p14, it adds to the other reasons for thinking that the Good Sir James, not Hugh, was the heir of William the Hardy, 7th Lord of Douglas (A [pp54-55, ll.30-15]), the fact that Bishop Lamberton asked Edward I to restore him to the lands confiscated from his father.

According to Fraser, 1, p58, William was a supporter of the English party under Alexander III since he had estates in Northumberland.

52, ll.8-9. According to Fraser, I, 67, there was no Earl of Carrick at that date and so no sister and no argument for an alliance with the house of Carrick. William's only known wife was Constance.
52, ll.9-11. HP, p46, says that Isabelle bore William a daughter, Isabelle, as well as two sons (according to Fraser, I, 67, William's daughter was called Willelma).
52, l.14-53, l.9. The story of the sons of Fergus may be found in Buchanan, VII, fols.73v.-74.
52, l.16. *Ethred*: Uchtred (*SP*, II, 421) was the elder brother, and joint lordship between brothers was not unusual at the time.
52, l.23. *Alexander*: According to *SP*, II, 422, Gilbert's son was Duncan and came to terms with Roland in 1186. He was created Earl of Carrick between 1225 and 1230 (*SP*, II, 423). According to Boece (1536), Bk.XIII, ch.20, the Earl of Carrick who went on Crusade was called Thomas. 1531 and 1574, fol.290, say the earl went with the Earl of Athol, and 1574 lists other companions.
53, ll.5-10. This account of Robert I's ancestry leaves out, as Boece, Bk.XIII, ch.20, and Bk.XIV, ch.I, and Buchanan, Bk.VIII, fol.74, do, Robert Bruce, the Competitor, who married Isabel de Clare. Duncan's son, Neil, 2nd Earl of Carrick, was father to Marjorie, who married Robert Bruce, Lord of Annandale and Cleveland (*SP*, II, 426). This Robert Bruce's son, Robert 'the noble', great grandfather to Robert I, married Isabel, 2nd daughter of David of Scotland, Earl of Huntingdon (*SP*, II, 430). *Allane*: son of Roland, Lord of Galloway, maried Margaret, eldest daughter of David of Scotland, Earl of Huntingdon, in 1209 (*SP*, IV, 139-40)
53, ll.13-16. See p194-96, ll.21-31, as an added marginal note (^fol. 199^) indicates.
53, ll.19-32. *The Endenture*: See Preface, pp18-19, ll.32-9. It is printed in Fraser, III, 1, and dated [6th April] 1259.
53, ll.27-28. *Reginald Cumein*: Reginaldo Cauers (Fraser, III, 2), presumably conflated with Alexander Comyn, Earl of Buchan (*SP*, II, 254-55), who precedes him in the list of witnesses to the endenture; *Johne of Dondie Muir*: 'or rather Dundas mure' (HP, p48). Johanne de Dundemor (Fraser, III, 2). *one Douglas*: Andrea de Douglas in the Endenture printed in Fraser, III, 2.
53, ll.36-38. *Some doe esteime... Doughtie Sir James*: e.g. Maitland, p1.

54, l.24. *without partialitie*: i.e. 'without anything to make one take its part (?).' Hume usually uses 'without apparence' for this sense, but partialitie can hardly be a scribal misreading for that.
54, l.34-55, l.4. *ane Chartour*: the charter of 1320 (see pp101-102, ll.36-16).
55, ll.5-6. *ane Chartour of the same dait*: printed Fraser, III, 357-59 (see also below, pp176-77, ll.21-8).
55, l.32-56, l.1. Cf. Preface, p22, ll.15-17.
56, ll.5-25. Cf. Preface, p19, ll.2-25.

The Life of Sir Hugh, 6th Lord of Douglas (A, pp29-31).

Married 1239

1633, pp17-18, corresponds closely to A2.

HP, pp50-52, corresponds closely to A2 and 1633 (with differences from both in phrasing), except for two additions: (1) at A (p57, ll.13-17), HP, p51, adds the Comyns' reasons for taking Alexander III and imprisoning him at Stirling; (2) at A (p58, l.19) HP, p52, adds a tradition surviving in Douglasdale about Patton Purdie of 'Wndrawod', who set upon Hugh Douglas with his sons and was killed. One cross marks where Purdie, and another where one of his sons, died. The fray is commemorated in verse:

Pattane purdie brack a chaise
  wpon the Lord douglas
Hugh Lord Douglas turned agane
  and there was Patton purdie slane.

HP explains the report of his prudence and activity (A [p58, ll.21-22]) by saying that he shared in his father's expedition to the Isle of Man.

1644, pp15-16, is closer than usual to A and 1633, yet differently, though not more concisely, phrased.

57, ll.1-2. The heading to A, p30, has an insertion: '3. S*i*r Hugh ^(that sleyed neuer)^ Sext Lord of Douglas'; this cannot be reconciled with the story in HP, p52, about Patton Purdie noted above.
57, l.8. *doughter to Alexander*: Marjorie was in fact daughter to Laurence de Abernethy (*SP*, VII, 399).
57, ll.20-24. *Lord William Abernathie... Church of Abernathie*: Orm de Abernethy, grandfather of Hugh de Abernethy, was granted a charter of the Abbacy of Abernethy in 1172.

57, l.27. *Leurii*: 1633, p17, Leurie; HP, p51, Leuris: 1644, p16, Lenrie. A charter of 1264 by Alexander III gives the lands of 'Lure' to Hugh of Abernethy (Fraser, III, 3). *Halkstone and Lylstone* are not mentioned in it; they will be Oxton and Lylstone in Lauderdale (see *SP*, VII, 399).
57, l.34. *Patrik styled Earle of Dumbar*: Patrick, 7th Earl of Dunbar (*SP*, III, 157-59).
57, ll.36. *Isabelle Countesse of Stratherne*: Isabella, Countess of Menteith, was probably a daughter of Maurice, Earl of Menteith, and married Walter Comyn, whom she is reputed to have poisoned before marrying Sir John Russell (*SP*, VI, 127-29).
58, ll.3-4. *the Earle of Fife*: On 25 September, 1288, Sir Partick de Abernethy (son of Hugh) and Sir Walter de Percy, probably instigated by Sir Hugh, murdered Duncan, Earl of Fife, one of the guardians appointed on the death of Alexander III in 1285 (*SP*, VII, 11, VII, 400). I have found no mention of the involvement of Balliol in the murder. *ovirseen*: 1644, p16, 'winked at'.
58, ll.27-28. *St Brids Kirk of Douglas*: in Douglas, Douglasdale.

The Life of William, 7th Lord of Douglas (A, pp31-42)

1288-1302

1633, pp18-22, corresponds almost exactly to A2.

HP, pp53-63, corresponds closely to A2, except for the following additions: (1) at A, p60, l.9, HP, p54 says that William the Hardy retired with his wife to Douglasdale; (2) at A (p60, l.16) HP, p54, notes the taking of the castles of Lochmaben and Crawford by Wallace and Sir John the Graham; (3) at A (p60, l.29) HP, p55, adds that first Dickson cut the 'rigvodie' (rigwiddy) so that the load fell in the middle of the gateway and that he killed the porter with a poleaxe supplied by Anderson; (4) at A (p61, ll.2-), HP, p34, gives the names of the nearby Castles (Tibersmoor, Durisdeer, Enoch); (5) at A (p61, l.30) HP, p56, digresses on Sir William Oliphant, (married to Isobel Douglas, William's sister) who held Stirling Castle against Edward I, citing Samuel Daniel; (6) at A, p63, l.10, after the verses on the Chair of Scone, HP, p57, inserts information about the bestowal of other items of the Scottish regalia at Canterbury, with information drawn from Drummond about Alexander III and St Thomas of Canterbury; (7) at A (p65, l.16) HP, pp59-62, sets down at length the victories of the Scots over the Romans; (8) at A (p66, l.20) HP, p62, fills out some details of the Percy conspiracy; at A (p66) l.34, HP, p62, records another story that William was taken to Newcastle, then York, where he died.

1644, pp16-20, more or less follows A and 1633 in its own words, without being conspicuously less prolix. The sentences are shorter.

The picture of William as patriot and martyr needs to checked against Fraser's account (I, 72 ff.) of this violent, but by no means unshakeable man (he acceded to the Treaty of Irvine). Cf Barbour, I, 282-284.

59, 9. *called Longleg*: It was his father William the 5th Lord, who was known as Longleg (Fraser, I, 56; HP, p46). *As testifies the Manuscript*: Maitland (p1) confuses William the 5th Lord and William the 7th and calls them both 'Longleg'.
59, ll.16-17. *maryed, first with the Lord Keyths sister*: According to Fraser, I, 73, William married Elizabeth Stewart, daughter of Alexander, High Steward (not Keith's sister), who bore the Good Sir James to him, but not, according to Fraser, I, 104, Hugh. *Wallace*, Bk.X, l.865, however, says that Robert Keith was uncle of the Good Sir James (see below, p68, l.13).
59, ll.22-23. *ane English Lady called Ferrair or Ferrais,... the Earle of Darbie was of that name*: The name of the earls of Derby from 1138 to 1266 was Ferriers according to *CP*, IV, 191, 203; see Holinshed, *EC*, 197, at the beginning of the reign of Henry III. William abducted as second wife the widow, Eleanor de Ferrers, a liege of Edward's, from Tranent (Fraser, pp75-76). To him she bore Hugh and Archibald, according to Fraser, I, 104.
59, l.30. *Marginal note*: ^Note that this assertion better be examined^. Yes, indeed. Archibald Douglas, whom Hume calls Lord of Galloway, married Beatrice Lindsay; Dornagilla Comyn is a mythical personage (Fraser, I, 212).
59, l.29. *Johne*: Fraser, I, 104, makes no mention of a son of William called John. He thinks that the house of Dalkeith was descended from Andrew, son of Archibald the 6th Lord of Douglas.
59, l.32. *Marginal note*: Holinshed, *EC*, pa. 298.a .
59, l.35. *1295*: From Fraser, I, 92, it appears that Berwick was captured in June 1296.
60, l.16. *Disdeir*: Durisdeer.
60, l.34. *Beaufoord*: Cf. *Wallace*, X, 885. In his note McDiarmid, says that there is no record of a Beaufort in Scotland at this time. Hume's account of this incident is drawn from Hary's.
61, l.18. A heart in the margin marks the place for the following insertion, adopted by 1633, p19, and abridged at the end of 1644's life, p20, (HP, puts this material in the Life of William the 5th Lord, p50): ^It is also recorded that this Lord did posess the Yle of Man, whether as Inheritor or Gouernor therof it is uncertain. But that the same belonged of olde unto the Croune of Scotland, And that the Douglasses had a more than ordinary

interest therin. It is not to be douted of: Seeing there is in it such manifest monuments therof to this daye, As a castle, a port, a hauen bearing the name of the Douglas, though posesd these many yeares by the English^.

61, ll.25-27. Boece, Bk.XIV, chs.4-5, certainly makes no mention of William the Hardy, but he has a generous notice of Wallace. Like Barbour, Holinshed, *EC,* p298, mentions Douglas's imprisonment after the siege of Berwick. Later, Holinshed, p303, says that he joined Wallace, but for Buchanan, Douglas dies imprisoned after Berwick, Bk.VIII, fol.76.

61, l.31. *the house of Simontoun*: Fraser, I, 114, says that the barony of Symington was conferred by Robert I on Thomas Dickson and that the family took the name of the estate See p78, ll.20-31, and the Life of William, 8th Earl of Douglas, p392, l.7, where the Laird of Symingtoun is the Earl's baillie in Douglasdale.

61, l.29. *the booke of Wallace*: *Wallace* mentions William's deeds in Bk. VII, ll.771, ff., Bk.VIII, ll.337, ff., Bk.X, ll857, ff., Bk.X, ll.1138, ff., Bk.XI, l.806.

61, l.37. *Hissilsyde*: now Hazelside in Douglasdale.

61, l.38. *holden to this day of the Lords of Douglas*: 1633, p20, and 1644, p18, mention the Lords both of Douglas and of Angus; HP, p56, has simply 'the Marquis of Douglas'. The lord of Douglas was, at the time I suppose A to have been written, the Earl of Angus.

62, l.1-63, l.21. The description of Edward as tyrant is much toned down in A2 and in 1633 (p20), HP (p56) and 1644.

63, l.1. *Marginal note*: Holinshed, *SC*, p309.

63, ll.14-15. *Clifforde Earle of Cumberland*: Robert de Clifford, 1st Lord Clifford (*CP*, III, 290-91).

63, ll.16-21. Cf Preface, p14, ll.3-11. HP, p57, refers back to the Scoti in Italy for corroboration concerning the antiquity of the house.

66, l.7. *Marginal note*: Buchanan, Bk.VII, fol.76.

66, l.18. *the Bischop of Glascow*: Robert Wishart (Barrow, p84). This makes out that Douglas and Wishart behaved honourably after the Treaty of Irvine (when Wallace was deserted), a possible interpretation of Holinshed, *EC*, p304, but equally erases Holinshed's story that Douglas and Wishart hurried to Edward to betray the plot before they could be accused of joining it.

66, ll.32-34. According to Fraser, I, 100-102, on Wallace's incursion into the North of England, Edward had William taken from prison in Berwick to the Tower of London, where he died. So also *Wallace*, Bk.XI, l.806.

The Life of Good Sir James, 8th Lord of Douglas (A, pp42-118).

1298-1330

1633, pp23-59, follows A2 closely, apart from a few insertions which will be marked in notes to pages that follow.

HP, pp64-156, as usual, has a great deal of material, not bearing strictly on the Douglas life in hand but sometimes supplying historical information that explains events more fully, sometimes giving correct versions of what is erroneous in A. Like the other versions, it relies heavily on Barbour for its stories, but cannot resist bringing in more of them. The writing is much blander, more prolix, more cushioning in every point to Douglas *amour propre*. It is tempting to think that this widely differing version may have been drawn up in response to the complaint in the papers, bound up with HP, p7, but referring to A, that from the life of the Good Sir James on the style is less sweet than it was, and to think in consequence that HP is not an anglicized fair copy of a compilation from which A and the published versions were redacted, but an expansion and rewriting, supervised closely by the Marquis of Douglas, if not actually executed by him. It is not, however, quite certain that HP is not largely Godscroft's work. Some of the extra examples brought in suggest considerable classical learning. He would not be incapable of the extra moralisings, though repetitious and commonplace, on the subject of the vanity of earthly glory. Even what seems like an increased distance between the classes, between noble and common, may be more an effect of anglicizing than of a new Caroline caste consciousness; it is not indeed as if A shows much feeling for commoners. And still the emphasis on how Sir James's men put on 'clownish' garments (HP, p87), only to throw them off and show the soldier in disguise, is a characteristic note of HP, and one that suggests a romantic and snobbish concern with one's image not to be found in A.

1644, pp20-53, perhaps deciding that this splendid life could not be much improved on, follows A and 1633 closely even in phrasing, apart from a few salient departures, which will be marked in the page notes. In places it prefers the phrasing of 1633 where that differs from A, an argument for 1644's having had an eye on the printed version when its manuscript was revised for publication (see Introduction, ppxxxii-xxxiv).

68, l.5. *Marginal note*: For Holinshed, *SC*, p313, as for Boece, Bk.XIV, ch.8, the Good Sir James is the one from whom the family takes its rise, though *EC*, p298, mentions William the Hardy. *Boeti 9*: perhaps Bk.XIV, ch.8. He makes no mention of William.

68, l.13. For his mother, see note to p59, ll.6-17, in the Life of William the Hardy. Robert Keith was Marischal of Scotland (*SP*, VI, 32-33).
68, l.18. *Philip le bel*: Philip IV, the Fair.
68, l.21. *Marginal note*: Buchanan, Bk.VII, fol.80, from whom the account of Douglas's rejection by Edward comes. It is not likely that such a humanist education, suitable for a Renaissance gentleman, could have been had at that time at some school in Glasgow or at the University of Paris. Barbour, I, 330-35, says he led a scapegrace existence in Paris.
68, l.22-23. HP, p64, expands on Douglas's beautiful behaviour in willingly returning to a land struck by disaster.
68, ll.28-29. *William Lambert*: William Lamberton, bishop of St Andrews, like other prominent Scottish churchmen, was a persistent opponent of English rule, in spite of occasional submission to Edward I.
69, ll.11-13. The theme of service runs throughout the life. James, and, by extension, the Douglases, though preeminent in their achievements, keep their ambitions within the scope of subjects and serve their kings. With grinding irony, the Life misses no opportunity to call attention to the services Douglas did Edward II and Edward III.
69, ll.30-31. For Edward's escape from Dunbar, see pp93, ll.18-29.
70, ll.5-17. HP, pp65-66, smooths out this agitated series of questions and then supplies the bishop with a speech assuaging Douglas's anger, matters being worked up as an example of counsel moderating passion. *in his roofe*: i.e. 'in his pride, his exaltation'. Priscilla Bawcutt points out out that while 'in his ruffe', as A2 has it, was a current English phrase (see *OED* ruff , sb.[6]), 'roofe' appears to be a different word, 'roof' in the figurative sense of highest point. This may be a case of Hume's adapting an unfamiliar English phrase to words and ideas with which he was familiar (see Introduction, pl).
70, l.25-71, l.3. It was Bruce's father that Edward derided in this way (Bower, Bk.XI, ch.25; Buchanan, Bk.VII, fol.76; Barrow, pp73-74). Buchanan, rather than Boece (despite the marginal note), is the source of this passage.
71, ll.3-7. A2's 'Nather could modestie by the same vnbridlednes of the tougne (set louse by successe) containe itself from expressing the pryd of the hairt, by eluding what he had promised in a mocking sorte' makes easier sense, though it is not modesty that cannot contain itself. A may perhaps be expanded as 'Neither could modestie [bind ambition] by [=because of] the same vnbridlednes of the tougne (set louse be successe) to expresse the pryd of the hairt, be eluding etc'. 1633, p24, has 'Neither could modestie tye... to containe it selfe'.

71, l.3. *Marginal note: Boeti 9* is perhaps Bk.XIV, ch.9, where Edward is described as a tyrant, by Bellenden, though not by Boece, fol.300.
71, l.22. HP, p68, has an extended passage of Biblical, Egyptian and Roman examples to show power is not above the law.
71, ll.30-31. *Johne Cumein*: John Comyn, Lord of Badenoch, the 'Red Comyn' (Barrow, p139-40). HP, pp68-67, has a story of Comyn's luring Bruce into a plot against Edward, then betraying the plot, and of Bruce's escape from Edward's court, all this to explain and palliate the murder.
71, l.31. 1644, pp22-23, adds a paragraph on how God's providence stirred up Wallace, followed by a celebratory Latin verse prefixed to *Wallace,* with a translation added, presumably by Hume.
72, ll.10-11. *vnder the tyranes feit*: 'under the beastes feet' (1644, p23).
72, l.31. *Atrikstone*: Erickstane, by the Devil's Beef Tub near Moffat (Fraser, I, 109).
73, ll.6-26. *Johne Leslie*: Bk.VII, p242.
74, l.12. *omnis terra*: Moot Hill, now in the grounds of Scone Palace. The ceremony described here seems to be a re-enacting in reverse of the original form of sasine, in which those who held lands from the king were given earth and stone from the lands. No record of this ceremony is noticed in Professor Cooper, 'Four Scottish Coronations', *Transactions of the Aberdeen Ecclesiological Society and of the Glasgow Ecclesiological Society*, Special issue (Aberdeen, 1902), or Roderick J. Lyall, 'The Medieval Scottish Coronation Service', *Innes Review*, 28 (1977), 12-17.
74, ll.15-16. *a battle in Meffen*: the battle of Methven. *Odomare de Valence*: later called Aymore de Valence. in this A is followed by 1633, p26, 1644, pp24-25, and HP, p74, i.e. Aymer de Valence, Earl of Pembroke, Edward I's lieutenant in Scotland.
74, l.24. *Thomas Randulfe*: Sir Thomas Randolph, son of Bruce's half sister, later Earl of Moray (see Barrow, Table 2).
74, l.25. *Sir Alexander Fraseir*: Sir Alexander Fraser of Touch Fraser (*SP*, IV, 107).
74, l.25. Sir Dauid Barclaye: Sir David Barclay, later present at the signing of the Treaty of Edinburgh (Barrow, p258).
74, ll.26-27. Inchmartin: David of Inchmartin, son of John of Inchmartin (Barrow, p358, n.89; *CSD*, II, no.1811). *Hugh de la Hay*: a brother of Gilbert de la Hay (*SP*, III, 559), whose land of Errol was forfeited for his support of Bruce at this time. *Somervail*: possibly Sir Thomas de Somerville, an adherent of the English party and subscriber of the Ragman Roll (*SP*, VIII, 3-4).
74, l.35-75, l.2. HP, pp74-75, describes how, Bruce was driven from Kildrummy by the Earl of Pembroke, and how his Queen

and daughter were handed over to Edward by William Comyn, Earl of Ross.

74, l.36. *Kildrimmie*: Kildrummy Castle on Donside.

75, l.6-7. *Earle of Athole Dauid Cumein*: John of Strathbogie, Earl of Athol, had married a daughter of the Earl of Mar (Barrow, p156) and was in consequence a brother in law of Bruce; so far from joining John of Lorne, he had fought on Bruce's side at the disastrous Battle of Methven. Nor was John of Lorne his sister's son (*SP*, I, 425-27). For his son David, who did fight against Bruce, see note to p149, ll.1-2, below. Neither were Comyns. *the Lord of Lorne*: John Macdougal of Lorne (Barrow, p160), not at this point the lord of Lorne and Argyll. His father, Alexander MacDougal, Lord of Lorne and Argyll, was brother in law of John Comyn (Barbour, I, 72). This lies behind Hume's confused account.

75, l.9. *Dalrie*: Dalry (or Dalrigh), near Tyndrum (Barrow, p227). *Marginal note*: Holinshed, *SC*, p311, drawing from Buchanan, Bk.VIII, fol. 79-79v. Boece, Bk.XIV, ch.8 does not give 1306 as a date.

75, l.26. *expert*: A2's 'vnexpert' makes easier sense, but A also makes sense: 'however versed in managing a boat (probably not much)'. 1633, p27, 'vnexpert'; 1644, p25, 'expert'.

75, l.30. *this sayeth the manuscript*: Maitland's manuscript says nothing of this or other adventures of Sir James, referring the reader to the 'Bruces buke' (i.e. Barbour). HP, p75, follows Barbour's account (III, 405-466) in which a band of men crosses Loch Lomond, ferried over two at a time in the course of a day and a half, though some swim with packs on their backs. A, 1633, and 1644, come round to this only in the end as a second opinion, so eager are they to make it look as if Douglas was Bruce's almost sole companion and servant, and chief actor in the business. Boece, Bk.XIV, ch.8, has Bruce accompanied by the Earl of Lennox and Gilbert Hay, not Douglas, though the germ of Hume's account of the heroes in adversity is drawn from him.

76, l.30. *heir we note that*: The A reading means, 'we do not hear that', the A2 one, 'here we do not note that'.

76, l.12-77, l.9. HP, p76, describes at length the joy of Lennox at finding the king's party alive, omits the moving passage on fortitude at the low point of their fortunes and tells how they stayed at Dunaverty on the Mull of Kintyre before passing to Rathlin.

77, ll.10-26. HP, pp76-77, following Barbour, III, 680-762, has boisterous seas and no King of Rathlin on arrival. On the contrary the islanders pay homage to Bruce as their overlord. To Douglas is given the story of the persistent spider.

77, l.25. *Masinissa*: King of Numidia, who, defeated by Syphax, was forced to hide in a cave, and then take refuge on the

Mediterranean coast, until the coming of Scipio restored his fortunes (Livy, XXIX, 31-33).

78, l.10. *Malcome Earle of Lennox*: Malcolm, 5th Earl of Lennox (*SP*, V, 334-35).

78, l.12. HP, p77, says that some call the castle, Turnberry, and on p78, for further details of the King's adventures, refers the reader to Barbour. *Marginal note*: Boece, Bk.XIV, ch.8. These events took place in January to February 1306/7.

78, ll.25-28. It sounds as if Dickson were rewarded for his part in the capture of the Castle, but that does not square with his being killed in the fight in the church. 1644, p28, however, says the gift of Hissilside was given to Dickson before he was killed in the ensuing fight as reward and encouragement for his services so far. HP, p81, has another solution to what looks like a confusion in A and 1633, p28: the gift was given to Thomas Dickson's heirs. See also p61, ll.30-38. Fraser, I, 114, says that the barony of Symington was given to Thomas Dickson by Robert I, after the capture of the Castle of Douglas, so that in fact he cannot have been killed in the fight. See also p392, l.7, and note.

78, ll.28-29. *ane monument to the receaver, and encouragement to vther*: 'vther' means 'others', so that A2's 'a hon*our*able monument to the giver, and encouragement to the other' is not necessary to secure an antithesis; A2 makes the munificence of the Douglases half the point of the gift, absurdly if not unrealistically.

78, ll.35-36. HP, p79, works this up as a pathetic recognition scene.

79, l.16: ^The word of the house of Douglas^ has been inserted in the margin.

81, ll.10-11. *in the revenge of his trustie and valiant servand Thomas Diksone*: HP, p80, adds that Douglas was also moved by the memory of English cruelties. Dickson is not killed in Barbour, V, ll.346-353. It sounds as if Hume felt some excuse was needed for the savage prank of the Douglas Larder.

81, l.16: HP, p81, says Douglas threw in for good measure dead cats and dogs.

81, l.20. Above 'Douglas', 'English', has been written, as an alternative name for the Larder. 1633, p30, has 'the Douglas, or the English Laidnery', in this followed by HP, p81, but not 1644.

81, l.31. *Clifforde*: Robert Clifford, had been given the Douglas lands forfeited by William the Hardy (Barrow, p157).

82, l.2. *Harries Tower*: a ruined tower, left standing in the eighteenth century rebuilding, is all that remains now of the Castle of Douglas and is called 'Castle Dangerous' after Scott's novel. But it is doubtful if that tower dates from the early fourteenth century. Hume's statement that Harrie's Tower was still standing in his day does not seem to accord with Douglas Castle's being razed by Sir James on its third capture (p85, ll.32-33, below) or by James II in 1450 (p395, ll.4-5). But the demolition on either occasion need not have been total. The Clifford who built the tower and after whom it should have been named was Robert Clifford, confused perhaps with the Henry Clifford of Edward III's reign (Fraser, II, 595).

82, l.3. *Thriswale*: presumably Thirlwall from Thirlwall Castle, Northumberland; not in Barbour, but Fraser, I, 115, accepts the story.

82, l.4. HP, p81, says some write that Douglas lurked in Douglasdale, but thinks it more probable that he joined Bruce.

82, l.5. HP, p83, places the joining up with Bruce at Cumnock and the Battle of Loudoun Hill after the killing of Thirlwall at the Castle of Douglas, and also places various adventures of Bruce from Barbour first. It mentions that the Lord of Lorne, used Bruce's bloodhound to track him down and (p85) gives details of how Bruce prepared the battlefield with ditches so that a mere 500 (A, 800; 1633, p31, and 1644, p29, 500) might defeat 3000.

82, l.23. *a pairt*: i.e. 'apart'.

82, ll.30-31. *Machanakis Way*: 'The name Makyrnok... , shown in the maps of Timothy Pont and later cartographers is lost today. It described a stream flowing from Fenwick parish into the marshes of "the Moor of Maucharnock" in the barony of Rowallan, which lay a few miles north of Kilmarnock' (Barbour, I, 80, note to VIII, l.28).

82, l.32. *Edderfurde*: 'has not been identified, but the marshes about it fix it in the Rowallan or Polkelly area' (Barbour, I, 80, note to l.34.

83, ll.13-14. *Marginal note*: in Holinshed, *EC,* p318.

83, l.14. *Johne de Brittone*: John of Brittany took over from Aymer de Valence in September 1307 (Barrow, p173).

83, ll.15-16. 'Thir' particulars are not omitted by Barbour, surely one of 'our wrytters' (see Bk.VIII).

84, l.18. ^The Aduenterous Castle^ has been inserted in the margin.

84, l.19. *Sir John Waltone*: Sir John Webton in Barbour 'is unidentified, but there was a castle Webton on the east side of the river Dore in Herefordshire' (note to Bk.VIII, l.453).

84, l.32. *Lenrik*: Lanark.

85, l.21. *this letter*: It sounds as if Hume meant to quote it. It is at any rate quoted in HP, p88, in a verse expansion of Barbour, VIII, 493-99:

> If you would gaine of me some grace,
> See that for one years time and space,
> you stoutlie keepe th'adventurous Towre
> of Douglas, as if it were my owne bower;
> When you haue done this valiant deed,
> you may presume to come some speed.
> Assure yourself, I will not marie

A coward, though I should longer tarie.
God haue yow in his owne protection,
Keepe this my letter in your direction.
In all your dangers still thinke on me,
If you proue stoute, I true shall be.

This romantic tale is the basis of Scott's *Castle Dangerous*, a recasting of traditions with less respect for its sources than Hume's history.

85, 27-28. *whilk is not to be thought he wold have done, if he had taken it at outrance*: Cf. Barbour, VIII, ll.505-511. HP, p88, says that Douglas threatened to kill the prisoners if the castle did not surrender.

86, l.2-4. *Thomas Randulphe*: Thomas Randolph, captured by Aymer de Valence at Methven, had been put under the charge of *Adam, lord of Gordon*, though at the time of this incident the Earl of Lincoln was responsible for him. (*SP*, VI, 291). *Alexander Stewart* of Bunkle was son of Sir John Stewart, who was a brother of Douglas's mother (see p32, ll.15-16, below; *SP*, I, 13). That would make him son to Douglas's uncle. This, Hume queries (p86, ll.13-15), though it has Barbour's authority (IX, l.733), for Hume believes Robert Keith was Douglas's mother's brother.

86, l.7. *ane house vpon the water of Lyne*: McDiarmid's note to Barbour, IX, 688, suggests the house may have been 'the Lyne castle marked on Gordon of Straloch's map'. The Lyne flows from the Pentlands to the Tweed at Peebles.

86, ll.27-33. Cf. Barbour, IX, ll.744-762.

87, ll.2-4. ^The author of the Bruces booke^ has been inserted in the margin.

87, ll.5-8. The amount of the pension of forty shillings is omitted in 1633, p33 1644, p31, and HP, p90. McDiarmid, Barbour, I, 8, says sceptically that Robert II's gift of a perpetual annuity of twenty shillings came to be thought a reward for Barbour's poem. And on pp10-11, he records that the annuity was willed, not to the Hospital at Aberdeen, but to the chapter of the cathedral there, who 'were enjoined to celebrate the poet's anniversary... on the Wednesday following the first Sunday after Easter'.

87, l.9. HP, p90, has an account of Edward I's approach to the Scottish border and his falling ill there, followed by reflections on death as the universal fate and by a notice of Edward II's policy. *Marginal note*: Boece, Bk.XIV, ch.9.

87, l.14. The defeat of John Comyn, Earl of Buchan, was followed by his flight to England and subsequent death and by the harrying of Buchan, a grim episode passed over by Hume. *ascention day*: in 1308 Ascension Day fell on May 23 (Bower, XII, ch17, and note). Barrow, pp176-79, correcting the view of his first edition that the battle fell on 24 December, 1307, declares that the exact date is uncertain.

87, l.16. *conquesing of Argyle*: HP, pp91-92, expands this notice of Bruce's campaign against Alexander Macdougall, lord of Argyle and Lorne and his son John of Lorne, which culminated in Bruce's victory at the Pass of Brander. It notes also (p92) a defeat of the Donald of the Isles at the hands of Edward Bruce at the 'water of Dyre' (i.e. Dee) (Cf. Boece, Bk.XIV, ch.9).
87, l.22. HP, pp92-93, has an acount of Edward II's invasion of Scotland foiled by Bruce's scorched earth policy and Bruce's siege of Perth.
87, l.30-89, l.18. The account of the taking of Roxburgh Castle follows Barbour, X, 357-496, closely.
87, l.33. *Marginal note*: Boece, Bk.XIV, ch.10.
89, l.8. *Giliaum de Firmes*: 'Guillemin de Fenes from Bouglon in Gascony' (Barrow, p195).
89, l.24-96, l.24. The account of the battle in A, 1633, pp35--38, and 1644, pp32-36, does not attempt consecutive narrative, is indeed more in the way of a patriotic reflection, with a Douglas slant, on the narrative to be found in Barbour. 1633, p38, like A2, at A (p96, l.24) disclaims any intention of comprehensive treatment since the story has been told in Buchanan, Froisart and Boece (Barbour is not mentioned). HP does attempt a fairly consecutive nararative of the battle, though on p100, and again on p102, it disclaims comprehensiveness, only both times to lapse into detailed accounts of the fighting. On p98 the digging of ditches is described (a mere allusion in A, 1633, p38, and 1644, p35); on p99 there is a much more circumstantial account of Randolph's interception of Clifford on the way to Stirling Castle, together with a softened account of Douglas's disobedience and a considerably elaborated justification of it. On p100 the piety of the Scots on the morning of the second day, led by Maurice of Inchaffray, the King's chaplain, is detailed and on p101 Bruce delivers a speech to Douglas and Randolph, which bears little relation to the speech Bruce addressed to his army according to Abbot Bernard of Linton (Barrow, p225). On this second day hostilities begin with Bruce's meeting the charge of Henry de Bohun, with a lethal stroke of his battle axe, a surprising displacement of what is usually put on the the evening of the first day.
89, ll.24-29. HP, p95, having noted the capture of Edinburgh Castle and of the Isle of Man, gives a circumstantial account of the pact Edward Bruce made with the commander of Stirling Castle, Philip Moubray, and Bruce's anger at what must draw Edward II to Scotland to the castle's rescue.
89, l.29. ^to be further extended or referred to the larger histories^ inserted in the margin, but not done in 1633.
90, l.1. *Marginal note*: Maior, Bk.V, chs. 1-2; Boece, Bk.XIV, ch.10; Holinshed, *SC*, p315. The list is from Holinshed rather

than Boece (1574), fol.101v., who has '*Aquitania*' (not in 1531 or 1536) but not Guienne.

90, l.3. *Guian*: Guienne; *Burdelois*: Bordeaux region; HP, p96, has it that Edward was backed by hosts of men eager to settle a dispossessed and probably depopulated Scotland.

90, ll.7-8. *whilk some cal so many footmen and als many horsemen 300000 in al*: i.e. 'some say that Edward brought 150000 foot and 150000 horse'. Barrow's estimate (p207) of Edward's 'monstrous army' is 2,000 or 2,500 horse and 15,000 foot; Bruce's army he puts at 500 horse and 'say 5,000-6,000 men', sufficient odds to gratify the sturdiest patriotism.

90, l.12. HP, p97, develops the theme of how Edward's vainglory had been encouraged by flattering courtiers.

90, l.16. *21 day of June 1314*: Barrow, pp216, 223, dates the battle on the 23rd and 24th June.

90, l.25. *Marginal note*: Holinshed, *SC*, p316; Boece (1574), '*aemulus*', Bk.XIV, fol.302. 1536, Bk.XIV, ch.10, fol 212v., not 313, simply speaks of the Good Sir James's 'dred' for the sake of Randolph.

90, ll.29-31. Barrow, p219, puts the number of Clifford's horse nearer to 300 than Barbour's 800. Randolph met them, not with cavalry, but with a schiltrom of spearmen. According to Barrow, p298, it is unlikely that foot could overcome horse except in a proportion of 2:1. So Hume's victorious 500 must be an underestimate.

91, l.20. *Malignet*: probably a slip for 'malignant'.

91, l.26. *Marginal note*: Major, Bk.V, ch.3; Holinshed, *SC*, p318.

91, ll.26-29. Barrow, p225, says Edward Bruce led the vanguard. To his left Randolph led his brigade, and to his left, nominally under Walter Stewart, younger son of James the Stewart, the third brigade was in fact commanded by Douglas (Barrow, p210).

92, l.5. *Marginal note*: ^knighthood most hon*oura*ble of olde^ inserted in margin.

92, ll.5-36. 1644, p33, picks out for emphasis how knighthood has become a matter of wealth. HP, p105, gives French examples of the honour of knighthood in addtion to English ones and on p106 adds that in any case, since Douglas's father, William the Hardy, had forfeited his lands to Edward I, Douglas was known only as James Douglas till he was knighted.

92, l.14. *Marginal note*: Holinshed, *EC*, p314, refers to the knighting of Prince Edward; Boece, Bk.XII, not '7', ch.17, does not speak of the knighting of Henry II by David I, but Holinshed, *EC,* p59, not '259', does, . A marginal insertion has it that ^He was sonne of the Empresse^ (i.e. Maud).

92, ll.24-25. *Holinshed*: *EC*, p259, not p58; *Boetius fol. 107*: Bk.XII, fol.267 (1574), ch.17, fol.107 (1536).

92, l.27. ^of Late^ inserted in the margin. *the Earle of Clanrikert*: Richard Burke, Earl of Clanricarde was knighted at the Battle of

Kinsale (1601) for his conspicuous part against the 'rebel' forces of the Earl of Tyrone (*CP*, III, 230).

93, ll.3-4. *Marginal note*: ^*Vincere scis Hannibal. Etc*^ (Livy, XXI, 51).

93, ll.26-27. *Earle of Merch*: Patrick Dunbar, 9 Earl of Dunbar, 2 or 4 Earl of March (*SP*, III, 264).

93, l.28. HP, p103, adds the biblical example of Sennacherib to the classical one of Xerxes and tells how Sir James laid an ambush for Edward at Berwick, which he escaped by arriving by boat instead of overland. The parallel with Xerxes is drawn by Boece. *Marginal note*: Holinshed, *SC,* pp318-19.

93, l.34-94, l.1. *a weil quyte commone*: i.e. 'a well paid debt' (Cf. 'Quit him a common' [Carmichaell, 1303]); 1644, p34, 'A Christenmasse feast may be quit at Easter, sayes our Proverb' (cf. 'A Zule feast may be quat at Pasche' [Fergusson, 126]).

94, l.7. *Marginal note*: For Stanhope park see Boece Bk.XIV, ch.16, (1536, fol.217; 1574, fol.308) and Holinshed, *SC*, pp326-27.

94, ll.14-15. *if not report their pride and crueltie intendit:* i.e. 'if they did not get what their pride and cruelty intended'.

94, ll.17-18. *the Earle of Glocester*: Gilbert de Clare, 2nd Earl of Gloucester (Bower, VI, Bk.XII, ch.20, note, p453). *Sir Gyels of Argentie*: Sir Giles d'Argentan; 'He was ye thrid best kny*cht* perfay/ Y*at* men wyst lywand in his day' (Barrow, p207; Barbour, XIII, 321-322).

94, l.21. *Nortfoorde*: Hartford, in 1633, p37, 1644, p34, HP, p104; in fact Humphrey de Bohun, Earl of Hereford (McKissack, pp35, 40).

94, l.22. *Sir Gilbert Gilbeston*: Sir Walter Gilbertson according to Barbour, XIII, 406; Walter son of Gilbert, till that time Edward II's man, imprisoned the fugitives and handed over them and the castle to Edward Bruce (Barrow, p231).

94, ll.23-26. *Sir John Sagrave*: John lord of Segrave, Edward I's lieutenant in Lothian (Barrow, p231). *Johne Clatengrave*: ^Cottegrave^ inserted in the margin. A Thomas de Cotegrave, who, if not the man Hume means, may at least be related to him, was made Chamberlain of the Exchequer in Dublin in 1313 (*Calendar of Patent Rolls, Edward II, 1307-1313*, p590. Robert de Cotegrave, perhaps his son, was appointed to the same post in 1322 (*Calendar of Patent Rolls, Edward II, 1321-1324*, p113. *William Latimer*: would be a veteran from the time of the wars with Wallace (Barrow, pp127, 142). *Sir Robert Northbrook*: Roger Northburgh, keeper of the Privy Seal (McKissack, p.40). *Sir Ralph Mortimer*: Joan, eldest child of Edward I married Ralph de Monthermer; Lord Monthermer (see the table of the House of Plantagenet, McKissack, p599; *CP*, IX, 141 *Marginal note*: Major says nothing of Monthermer.

94, l.35-95, l.37. *two Holland knights*: Not mentioned in HP. *Marginal note*: Holinshed, *SC*, p319.
95, l.13. *Marginal note*: Boece, Bk.XIV, ch.11.
95, ll.27-28. The translation of the verse in HP, p104, is in pentameter instead of tetrameter.
96, l.24. The following passage has been inserted: ^This memorable battell with all the particulars in the occasion and other circumstances therof is so well and so at large sett doun by Buchanan, Froissard, Boethius and others in their severall histories As I have of purpose to avoyde impertinencie been sparing to extend the same further than doth directly concern the essentiall points of this present story; referring the Reader in the reste vnto the more ample discours of the most famos Authors and historians of that tyme^. Froissart, vol.1, ch.2, p.3, contains only the briefest notice of the battle.
97, l.2-5. HP, pp106-107, says that Edward Bruce was invited by the Irish to deliver Ireland from the English. *Marginal note*: Holinshed, *SC,* p320.
97, l.6. *tooke that occasion by the haire*: i.e. 'seized time by the forelock'. Tilley, T311, gives examples where 'hair' rather than 'forelock' is used.
97, l.18. *Marginal note: Blake booke of Scone, 1318*: Bower, Bk.XII, ch.24 says nothing about the Good Sir James as regent, though it quotes the document appointing Thomas Randolph.
97, l.21. *Marginal note*: Major, Bk.V, ch.4; Boece, Bk.XIV, ch.13.
97, ll.24-25. *played quytte (for he thought himself sure eneugh of double)*: i.e. 'when the stake already due is to become doubled, or to be cancelled, according to the issue of another chance' one speaks of 'double or quit' (*OED*). So Edward by invading tried to pay off the score, but, losing, only increased it.
97, l.31-98, l.15. HP, pp107-112, treats each of the following three victories at length.
97, ll.32-33. *Sir Edward Lyllowe à Gascogne... whom others cal Callok:* At Skaithmuir by Coldstream, Sir James defeated a party from Berwick and killed Raymond de Calhau (see Barrow, p238; Barbour, XV, ll.320-417).
98, l.4. *Sir Robert Nevil*: HP, pp108-109, gives Sir Robert or Ralph Neville a speech; 'Sir Robert Neville of Raby, the "Peacock of the North"' (Barrow, p238).
98, l.7. *Johne of Richmond*: HP, p110, and Barbour speak of a Sir Thomas of Richmond (Barbour, XVI, 335-492). McDiarmid's note says that Barbour (and so Hume) has confused Thomas Richmond, Lord of Burton Constable in Yorkshire with John of Brittany, Earl of Richmond, Edward II's former commander in chief in Scotland (see p83, l.14, and p103, ll.15-16; CP, X, 814-18). The party was at any rate sent by the Earl of Arundel and defeated at Lintalee (Barrow, p238). A side note in HP, p108,

refers to 'Richmonds oke... not 2. or 3. bowdrauche from the lintallie'.

98, l.15. *Marginal note*: Holinshed, *SC*, p320, relates the first two encounters, but not the one with Richmond, but says that he killed three champions with his own hands in separate encounters. Boece, Bk.XIV, ch.13, merely records that the Good Sir James killed three valiant champions of England with his own hands in a battle with Edward II. Buchanan, Bk.VIII, fol.82v., says no more. Maitland (pp10-11), in a condensed and uncircumstantial way, mentions all three. These writers are the 'vthers' and the 'some also' Hume speaks of in his text as if somehow they were different. Hume himself has folowed Barbour. I have not been able to find who they are who think that it was from the third engagement that the Douglases have 'the staiks and rice about their Armes'.

98, ll.15-17. *From this it is... that the Earles of Douglas hes the staiks and ryce about their armes*: See Fraser, I, xxv, and illustrations of seals of the Earls of Douglas in that volume.

98, l.32. *on the Kings return*: HP, p112, notes defeat in Ireland.

99, ll.14-15. In May 1318 a raid burnt Northallerton and Boroughbridge (Barrow, p239).

99, l.18. *Skairbrugh*: 1633, p40, 1644, p37, Scarborough; HP, p113 Knaresborough; Barrow, p239, Knaresborough, Yorkshire; *Marginal note*: Holinshed, *SC*, p321.

99, l.21. *Skipton in Cravan*: in upper Airedale in Craven.

99, ll.29-31. *Mittone*: Myton-on-Swale; *William Milton*: not mentioned in any of the other texts; William Melton, Archbishop of York (Barrow, p239); *Bishope of Ely Chancelor*: John de Hothum, Chancellor of England (*Fasti Ecclesiae Anglicanae*, ed. John le New and 1644. Duffus Hardy, 3 vols. [Oxford, 1854], I, 334)

100, l.5. *Holinsyde in his Chronicles of England*: *EC*, p324.

100, l.14. *Marginal note*: Buchanan, Bk.VIII, fols.82v-83.

100, l.20. [85]: mispaginated '54'.

100, l.24. *Gilsland*: a district in East Cumberland and West Northumberland.

100, l.29. *Burgh under Stan-mure*: Brough in Westmoreland.

101, l.2. The fourth expedition (January 1321/ 22) is placed in HP, p120, after the the charter of Douglasdale and the Black Parliament of Perth.

101, l.4. *vpon ane complainte made to the Pope*: Edward II to Pope John XXII. Excommunication followed in 1318 and the Scots were cursed in England (Nicholson, p99). The Scottish diplomatic response culminated in the Declaration of Arbroath of 1320 (Nicholson, pp99-100).

101, ll.12-14. *(as some say) the king himself also by himself also or be the Earle of Murray*: It looks as if there were a slip here, but the uncorrected phrasing might possibly just be a clumsy way of saying that the king was there as well, either commanding in his own person or through Randolph. Boece, Bk.XIV, ch.15, says that Robert led this expedition; Holinshed, *SC*, 323, at first concurs, then gives Southwel's view that Randolph was in charge.

101, ll.18-22. *Recrosse*: 1633, p41, Reecrosse; 1644, p38, Redcrosse; Holinshed, *SC*, p323, Ree Cross by Stainmore, i.e. Rey Cross, near Bowes, Yorkshire. *Darntoun*: so also 1633, p41; Darlington (1644, p38; Barrow, p242). *Careland*: Cleveland (Caveland in the other texts).

101, ll.18-19. *the feast of the Epiphanie*: the 6th of January [1322] (Barrow, p242).

101, l.31. *Duke of Lancaster*: Thomas, Earl of Lancaster (*CP*, VII, 394-96); *Pomfrit*: Pontefract.

101, l.35. 1633, pp41-42, and HP, pp115-118, but not 1644, have a section dealing with the Black Parliament of Perth, which provoked a conspiracy of nobles against Bruce. Among the executions that followed, that of David, Lord Abernethie, meant that his estate passed to the Earl of Angus, a matter to be discussed at large in the history of the house of Angus.

102, l.4. *1320 or 1321*: So 1633, p42, and HP, p118, but 1644, p38 has either 1320 or 1322; 1321 in HP could be read as 1322, a possible indicsation that HP was consulted in editing 1644. 1st April, 1320, according to Fraser, I, 147. The Charter is printed in Fraser, III, 354-55.

102, 12-16. HP, p118, is careful to point out that this merely restores what Edward I had confiscated from William the Hardy.

102, l.18. *theirwith*: As 1633, pp42-43, and 1644, p39, make clear, this means that Edward II was grieved at the raid of 1321/22. Perhaps there was clumsy pasting here before A was written out. HP, p119-122, putting here the papal remonstrance (A [p101, ll.3-9]) against war on fellow Christians that would be better waged on the Turks [sic], inserts an account of the antiquity of the Scottish Church, expanding the brief remark it makes on that topic as it tells of Bruce's reply to the papal legate. HP, p122 then turns to the fourth raid (A [p101, l.2]).

102, l.24. *the Monasterie of Holme*: in Southern Cumberland.

102, ll.27-29. The Scottish incursion of July 1322, burnt Lancaster and Preston (Barrow, p243) while the English army was repelled from the Lothians by Bruce's scorched earth policy. HP, p124, details Edward's depredations.

103, l.2. *St James evineing*: According to Barrow, p243, the Scots would have returned across the Border about the 25 of July, the Feast of St James the Great.

103, l.14. *the Abbey of Beiland*: the Abbey of Byland, between Thirsk and Malton. John of Brittany, Earl of Richmond, was not ransomed for two years (Barrow, p244). HP, p124, adds that Sir Henrie Souelie was taken (cf. Holinshed, *SC,* p324). The battle took place c. October 12, 1322 (Barrow, p244).

103, ll.20-21. *Androw Barclay, Earle of Carleil*: Sir Andrew Harcla, Earl of Carlisle, realising after the defeat of Byland that peace would have to be made with the Scots if the north of England were to be free from Scottish raiding, entered into negotiations with Bruce in January 1323, while Edward still refused to come to terms with the Scots. It was for this reason he was executed for treason (Barrow, p248).
103, ll.24-25. *Maister Johne Major*: Bk.V, ch.6.
103, ll.29-30. *by any man*: i.e. 'of any man'
103, ll.34-35. Barrow, p243-44, implies that Bruce conducted the battle himself. *Marginal note*: Holinshed, *EC*, pp332-33, but also *SC*, p324.
104, l.4. *tuke four prisonners*: Hume names only three; the valets would make it more than four; 'four' is the best, but by no means certain reading of the scored out word. The other texts all have 'three'.
104, ll.5-6. *Robert Bartrom, William Bartarhame*: Robert and William Bertram (Fraser, I, 154); *Elye Anyallage*: Elias Anillage (Fraser, I, 154). According to Barrow, p244, Bruce returned the French captives free of ransom.
104, l.11. *next zeir*: This should be 1323, since the Battle of Byland was fought in 1322, but the Emerald Charter is dated *'Nouembris... 1325'* on p105, ll.17-18; according to Fraser, I, 155, it was dated 8th November, 1324, at Berwick, 'a gift, not of lands, but of the criminal jurisdiction of all the extensive baronies which Douglas held of the crown at that time'. *Marginal note*: Neither Holinshed's *EC* nor his *SC* mention the Emerald Charter.
104, l.16. *officiarius*: A, *officiarum,* A2, *officiarus*, 1633, p44, and 1644, p40, *officiarius* (the correct form).
104, ll.16-20. *Laudre*: Lauder. *Bathreule*: Bedrule, Teviotdale. *Stabilgorthane*: Staplegorton, Eskdale. *Romanok*: Romanno, Peebleshire.
104, ll.32-34. *eorundem*: A, *earundem*, HP, p125-126, 1633, p44, 1644, p40, *eorundem* (the correct form).
105, l.7. *curiagiis*: A, *curagiis*; HP, p126, 1633, p44, and 1644, p40, *curiagiis* (the correct form, adopted). It is unlikely that Hume, an accomplished Latin poet, would have let these errors through (even if the Latin is not humanistically acceptable) if he had any part in the revising of A.
105, l.20. *Bernard Abbot of Arbrothok*: Bernard of Linton, Abbot of Arbroath, chancellor of Scotland, in charge of the Great Seal (Barrow, p178).
105, l.31. *takinge of seasinge*: 'the act of giving possession of feudal property by the delivery of symbols [such as earth and stone, a standard symbol, or an emerald ring, a special one]; infeftment' (*OED*).
106, ll.6-20. See Preface, p21, l.28, and note, and the Lives of Archbald, 5th Earl, and of William, 8th Earl of Douglas, esp.

pp402-403, ll.26-8, 405, ll.30-33. The quarrel between the Douglases and the Livingstons and Crichtons was, according to Hume, most bitter in the times of William, 6th Earl and Willliam 8th Earl.
106, l.6. *the former Chartour*: See pp101-102, ll.36-16.
106, ll.25-28. For the the overtures made by Andrew Harcla, Earl of Carlisle, see note to p103, ll.20-21.
106, l.29. *a truce*: presumably 'the thirteen-year truce... concluded at Bishopthorpe, near York, on May 30th, 1323, and confirmed by Bruce at Berwick on June 7th' (Barrow, p353).
107, l.2-108, l.24. Probably the embassy to Balliol was a fiction invented to make the claim of the Bruces, and following them, the Stewarts, look more solid. It is at any rate recounted in Boece, Bk.XIV, ch.16, Holinshed, *SC*, 325, Maitland, p11, Buchanan, VIII, fol.84, but not in Barbour.
107, l.2. In HP, pp129-30, Sir James's employments are an embassy to Pope John XXII (p128) (according to Barrow, p250, Randolph, went to the Curia in 1323), an embassy to Philip the Fair to renew the Auld Alliance (pp128-129) and the embassy to Balliol, who delivers a speech resigning, not only the crown of Scotland, but all worldly ambition.
107, ll.5-33. The pasage, 'whilk the king thought fit... the principal charge', is placed after '... vnto that present day' (p108, l.22) in 1644, p41.
107, l.25. *Marginal note*: The trimmed margin leaves only the 'h' of 'his'. For references see note to pp107-108, ll.2-24, above.
107, ll.28-29. *he was a kin to the Baliol be his grandmother (as hes bene said)*: On pp52-53 and 55-56 the relation of the Douglases to the Bruces through Isabel sister to Alexander of Carrick has been traced. Through that a further connection to the Balliols might be traced, though even for Hume's exceptional nose for these matters to claim kinship would be tenuous. Fraser, I, 67, says that his grandfather's only known wife was called Constance and that there were no earls of Carrick at his time.
108, ll.25-26. *a Parlament at Cambus-Kinnethe*: took place on July 15th, 1326 (Barrow, p294).
108, ll.30-31. *or 26 zeir, as other writters*: e.g. Holinshed, *SC*, p326.
109, ll.7-8. Edward III was crowned on 1st February, 1327.
109, ll.9-11. Barrow, p252, suggests the overtures of the English may have been genuine.
109, l.16. The Scots entered England on 15 June, 1327.
109, l.24. *Lord Boumond*: Lord Bea(u)mont, HP, p132, 1633, p46, 1644, p42. Henry Beaumont probably the cousin of Edward II, married the heiress of the earldom of Buchan, but forfeited the estate under Robert I (Barrow, p259; see also Life of William, Lord of Liddisdail, p149, l.12).

109, l.21. *Marginal note*: Major, Bk.V, ch.7, makes no mention of Wardelperk but cites William Caxton, *Chronicles of England* (1480), ch.214, and draws on Froissart, vol.I, chs.18-19, as does Hume. Wardelperk, I take it, is Weardale Park and an alternative name for Stanhope Park, which lies in and to the north of Weardale.
109, l.28. *Marginal note*: Boece, Bk.XIV, ch.16, tells of Edward's invasion but not of the derisive rhyme.
109, ll.30-31. *St Peter towards Chanigate*: i.e 'towards the Canongate'; HP, p133, says it was 'Now adayes the Abbey Church'. See Holinshed, *EC*, p347 for verses. At the Reformation the Abbey Church was used as the church of the parish of Canongate, but there is no record of its being called St Peter's (John Mackay, *The History of the Burgh of the Cannongate* [Edinburgh and London, 1900], p7). No account of the churches of Edinburgh that I have consulted speaks of a St Peter's before the 19th Century.
110, ll.22-34. HP, p134, 1633, p47, and 1644, p43, say the young man, Thomas Rokeby (according to Barrow, p253), was rewarded with lands as had been promised.
111, ll.1-2. *Holinshed in his English Chronicles calleth it the Water of Weir*: p347.
111, l.16. *in baird*: i.e. 'defiantly, in the face of the enemy'.
111, l.26. *Marginal note*: Boece, Bk.XIV, ch.16; Holinshed, *SC*, 327; *EC*, 347.
112, l.14. ^The parable of the Foxe and the Salmon^ has been inserted as a marginal note.
112, ll.23-24. *escaped the fishers great greif*: 1633, p48 and 1644, p44, have 'escaped to the fishers great grief'. But 'to' is not necessary if we understand 'grief' as 'passion, fury'.
112, ll.25-30. Sir James's application of the fable (ll.25-30) is rather loose. But the night attack would keep the English on guard against further attacks instead of against the Scots' escaping, just as the fisherman's fear for his cloak drives out his fear for the salmon, which would represent the plunder the Scots took with them. The fable may be found in Barbour, Bk.XIX, ll.654-87, but no exact analogue elsewhere.
113, l.11. *flaikes of wandes*: perhaps hurdles of woven willow wands.
113, l.30. *or 28 (as others write)*: Holinshed, *SC*, p327; *EC*, p346.
113, l.31. *Caxton*: ch.214, cited by Major, Bk.V, ch.7.
113, l.33. *Marginal note*: *Maior lib.5 cap*; the chapter number has been clipped; it should be 7.
113, l.34. *Roger Mortimer, Earl of March*: lover of Edward II's queen, Isabella.
113, l.36. *Earle of Lancastre*: Henry, succeeded to the earldom of Lancaster on the execution of his brother, Thomas, for his rising

against Edward II with the support of the Scots (Barrow, pp247-48, 252).
114, l.2. *Marginal note*: Holinshed, *EC*, p347.
115, l.29. HP, p142, 1633, p50, and 1644, p46, have the saying '*Qui veut la France gagner, à l'Ecosse faut commencer*'. HP's defence of the Scotland's being worth the trouble of conquering differs on a number of points from the other texts: p139, on poverty, the Scots have more mines of silver and gold than England, and, p140, the courts of Scottish nobles surpass those of the English in pomp; p140, on fertility, Scottish soil may not overall be so fertile as the English, but much of it is quite as good, and besides the country supports so much cattle and game that everyone lives well (having made these claims for Scotland, HP, cannot say that spareness makes Scots hardy); p140, on mountains, the Highlands are regretably mountainous, but the main part of Scotland is plain; p140, on France, discussion is deferred to the accounts of the help furnished France by William, 1st Earl of Douglas, and Archibald, 4th Earl; p142, on English embroilment with France, England actually had recruits from its French dominions to aid its invasions; pp141-142, on English sour grapes, cites the tale of the fox who affected to despise the bacon he could not reach; p143, 'the walls of Paris are in Scotland'.
115, l.30. ^*Vide fol. 227.*^ has been inserted in the margin (i.e. A, p227; pp216-17, below).
115, l.33. 1644, p46: 'for since the league with Charlemaigne, it may be said without any poeticall hyperbole, *nulla unquam Francis fulsit victoria castris, sine milite Scoto*'.
115, l.33. The following passage is inserted in A, and adopted by 1633, pp50-52 but not by HP or 1644: ^For the cleere verifieing of which truth; As also for expressing of the manifold domage and skarse recoverable losses, which the State of Scotland hath susteined from time to time for there fidelitie and constancye, by inviolable keeping of the league with France/ The indifferent and ingenuous Reader (as I hoipe) will not think it impertinent, to pervse these short Collections, particularly recorded in the histories of both Nations/ Which league was first contracted in the yeare of our Redemption 789 between Charle-le-maigne and Achaius kings of France and Scotland, and hath continued now without breache on either side these 830 yeares, and vpwards/ dureing the raignes of 47 kings of Scotland, and 41 of the Frenche./
1. For at the first, the said King Achaius in the said yeare 789 Sent 4000 of his subiects vnto Charl-le-maigne, conducted by his brother germain Williame/ who served in those warres against Desiderius king of the Lombards, with no small comendation./ [The marginal note says, 'Vide fol. 8 [A]': see The Lyfe of William, p38]

2. Malcom the third, Sent to Hugh (broth*er* to Phillip the 1) 2000. of the Scottes nation, To accumpany him in the voyages of Jerusalem, which he made with Godfrey de Bouillon An*no* 1096. Or therebye./ [Malcolm III, or Canmore died in 1087]. 3. Alex*ande*r the second, sent 3000. to St Lewis, Conducted by Patrik Dumbarre, Earle of Marche,/ for his first voyeage to the Leuant, An*no* 1246. [Boece, Bk.XIII, ch.15].
4. Alex*ande*r the third sent to the same St Lewis 2000. S[c]ottesmen vnder the conduct of the Earle of Carrict *and* Athole, for his second voieage to Afrike, An. 1269. [See above, p53, l.23, note].
5. In the time that King Dauid Bruce was kept prisoner in England/ W*illia*me Earle of Douglass brought to king John of France, an Armye of 3000. To the battell of Poictiers/ where the king was taken prisoner, An. 1356. To the great slaughter of the /Scottes./ [See the Life of William, 1st Earl of Douglas, pp189-90, ll.23-3]
6. In the time of Robert Stuarts governement, dureing the detention of James the 1. into England/ There went an ayde of 7000 Scottes to Charles the dawphin of France, (conducted by the **[115b]** Earle of Buchan (second son to the Gouernor, and by Archibald Earle of Wigton/ son to the E*arl*. of Douglas. Who wan the battel of Baugye/ against the English, and slew the Duke of Clarence, their Generall. An. 1422./ [See Life of Archibald, 4th Earl of Douglas, pp279-83]
7. Charles the 7 sent his Chancellor Ronald de Chartres, and the Archbishop of Reims into Scotland, for succours to whome was decreed an armye of 10000. men/ vnder the conduct of the E*arl* of Douglas and his son in law the E*arl* of Buchan (being then Constable of France) [retourned] with ^which they accompanied^ the said Embassador back into France/ And were both slaine, at the battell of Vernoille, with the most part of their Armye An*no* 1424. And for there memorable seruice, king Charles erected of the rest of them that escapte vnslayne a companie of 100. Gens D'armes, and of 200. Archers/ honouring them with the formost place and precedency to all the Gens D'armes of France; And giving the first charge tharof vnto the Seigneur D'Aubigny (a branche of the noble howse of Lenox in Scotland. And the last Captane therof was Charles, then Duke of Yorke etc. [The marginal note says 'See fol. 313': see pp285-87; Charles, Duke of York, became Prince of Wales, then Charles I].
8. John Stewart Constable of Scotland brought 4000. to the ayde of the said Charles the 7. in the yeare followeing/ 1425. Besides some other Companyes and bands, led by Dauid called the Pitulett./ [This was in 1426/1427 according to Francisque-Michel, *Les Ecossais en France: les Français en Ecosse*, I, 154; *Dauid called Pitulet*: Robert Pittilloch of Dundee, 'Petit roi de

Gascoigne' (see Boece, Bk.XVI, ch.21 [1531], ch.20 [1536], and Francisque-Michel, I, 165-166)].
9. And lastly Robert and John Stuarts, And Robert and Bernard Stewarts, Lord of Aubigny. Alex*ande*r Duke of Albanie, *and* John his son, Earle of Bulloigne (All being of the Scottes race or nation) did notable services in that kingdome/ during the raignes of Lewis the 11./ Charles the 8., Lewis the 12., Francis the 1., and Henry the 2.// [See p279, l.11, below for the first Robert Stewart and 278, ll.7-8, for John Stewart; Francisque-Michel, I, ch.ix].
1. As concerning the domages reseaued for France, It is manifest that the State of Scotland hath not onely been contented to assist and succour the French in their own countree of France/ But hath divers tymes diverted the warre out of France, and drawne it vpon them-selves./ For vpon such an occasion did King Dauid Bruce mak an incursion into England/ in the which himself was hurt/ and tane prisoner, with the Earle of Dowglass, and many others defeated at the battell of Durhame, in the year <u>1446</u>./ [i.e. 1346; see Life of William, 1st Earl of Douglas, p183-84, below]
2. Likewayes, King James the 4. made warre against his own brother in lawe King Henry the 8. of England/ and was him self slayne at the battell of Flowdane/ with the best parts of the nobilitye/ and <u>14000</u> of his subiects besides./ [Flodden, 1513] **[115c]**
3. King James the 5. made warre also to his vncle the said Henry the 8 for the pleasure of his father in lawe Francis the 1. King of France). And he tooke such hie despleasure for the evill success of that interpryse, and the loss of his armye, which was commanded by his favorite Oliuer Sinclare, at the Solem-moss/ with affront to all the nobless which were there (as they did interpret it)/ In such sorte that his Ma*jes*ties self died, vpon the eight daye tharefter/ and that in the flower of his age/ without any other knowen Siknes at all./ [Oliver Sinclair of Pitcairns; the Battle of Solway-Moss, 1542].
4. And lastly, the said kings only daughter and heyre/ Marie Stewart the late Queene of Scotland, being first promised in marriage to Edward the prince of Walles/ and she being notwithstanding sent to tharefter into France, to be maryed vnto the Dauphin thare; The said Edward comming to be king of England tooke such miscontment thareat/ That (though Minor) he sent his vncle the Duke of Somersett, in reuenge tharof with an huge armye into Scotland, who defeated and slew <u>15000</u>. of the Scottish nation/ at the feeld of Mussell-brough, or Pinkye'. [The Battle of Pinkie, 1547].

115, l.33. <u>1633</u>, p52, has a paragraph protesting that the passage on Scots aid to France is a defence against English malice, not a complaint about French ingratitude, a charge that the numerous Scots estates in France and companies of Scottish soldiers sufficiently rebut.

118, l.5. *fremde*: 1633, p53, and 1644, p47, have 'freinds', but 'fremde' looks the more plausible reading of A, and is not illogical.
118, l.9. 1644, p47, omits reference to the the two knights from Brabant.
118, ll.26-27. The Treaty of Edinburgh was ratified by the English Parliament of Northampton, 4th May, 1328 (Barrow, p260-61).
118, l.31. *Marginal note*: Holinshed, *SC*, 328.
118, l.31. If Sir James did confer with Mortimer, ruler of England with Isabella in Edward III's minority, it was not to change the terms already agreed on at York and Edinburgh, where the real negotiating had gone on.
119, ll.1-21. For the terms of the treaty, see Barrow, pp258-60, where a number of different points are brought out.
119, ll.18-21. 'King Robert bound himself to pay to King Edward £20,000 "for the sake of peace"' (Barrow, p259). If this is the payment for the damage done by Douglas and Randolph, then Hume's 3000 merks at 13 shillings and four pence a merk, is a considerable underestimate of what the Scots agreed on as the price of peace.
119, ll.25-28. This suggests that the Black Rood of St Margaret and other jewels were handed back in fulfilment of the Treaty of Edinburgh. According to Barrow p260), the English Government offered later to restore the Black Rood and the Stone of Destiny after the treaty in the course of negotiating the return of estates owned by Englishmen north of the border. Neither were returned.
119, l.30. *Marginal note*: 'Major, 'cap.8' should be 'cap.9'.
120, ll.5-9. Barrow also remarks on the generosity of the Scottish terms, p255.
120, l.25. HP, p146, says that before he died, Bruce gave a hospital he founded in Kyle, called Kincaice (from King's case) into the keeping of Craggie Wallace (i.e. Wallace of Craigie).
120, l.32-121, l.25. 1644, p49, omits this dying speech; HP, p147, omits the counsel that there should be no Lord of the Isles (A [p111, ll.1-2]).
121, l.22. *Marginal note*: Boece, Bk.XIV, ch.17, (1531, 1536), fol.218 (1536), fol.309v (1574).
121, 30-122, l.7. Major Bk.V, ch.9, suggests that perhaps Robert sent Sir James abroad to avoid dissension.
122, l.5. *Marginal note*: Boece, Bk.XIV, ch.17, (1531, 1536), fol.309v. (1574) say nothing about rivalry between Douglas and Randolph; Holinshed, *SC,* 329.
122, l.15. HP, pp148-149, inserts a eulogy of Bruce, supported with a tale from Boece, Bk.XIV, ch.17, and Holinshed, *SC*, 328-9, about his praise at the court of Edward III.
122, l.26. *Laurence Twine*: Twyname Lowrysown (Fraser, I, 177).

122, l.33. *the Official*: the presiding oficer or judge of the bishop of Glasgow's court; HP, p150, 'the officiall of Glasgow, named Herfoord'; Willelmus Hekfurd, according to Goodall, XIII, ch.20 (II, 300).
123, ll.16-18. HP, p151, omits the account of poisoning and defers the discussion of the chivalrous rivalry between Douglas and Randolph to the final eulogy of Sir James on p154.
123, l.28. *not the les of*: in spite of.
123, l.29-124, l.17. emulation: See note to p71, l.10.
124, l.19. *Marginal note: Manuscript*: Maitland, p14; *Boece, lib.14, fo 21...* : Bk.XV, not 'lib.14', ch.2 (1531, 1536) fols.218v.-219 (1536), 311v-312 (1574). The last digit has been clipped at the margin. *Hol. pa 319* should read [*SC*], p329.
124, ll.22-23. *Sir William Sincler*: Sir William Sinclair of Roslin (Barbour, XX, 481; Barrow, p324). See also p343, ll.25-27, below, where he is said to be the son of Henry Sinclair. *Sir Robert Logane*: Robert and Walter Logan (Barbour, XX, 483-4). Fraser, I, 180, says they were of Restalrig (now part of Edinburgh), but Barrow, p324 and index, makes 'Sir Walter Logan' Sir Walter Logan of Hurlside, sheriff of Lanark. *Sir William Keith*: of Galston (see Barbour, XX, ll.601-5; Barrow, p324).
124, l.24. HP, p151, 1633, p57, and 1644, p50, have a brief note from Froissart concerning Sir James's landing in Sluys and his subsequent journey to the Holy Land.
124, ll.25-26. HP, p152, says that Sir James buried Bruce's heart in the church on Calvary. The legend of the burial of Bruce's heart in Jerusalem goes back to Holland's *Buik of the Howlat,* st.35, though Hume would probably have taken it from Boece, Bk.XV, ch.1 (1536), ch.2 (1531) and Maitland, p14. Barbour, XX, 332-480, says that Sir James landed in Spain on the way to the Holy Land and was killed there.
124, ll.26-27. *the cause why the Douglas beares the bludie hart... in their armories*: For examples of seals bearing this device, see Fraser, II, 549; the earliest, he supposes to have belonged to Sir James's son, William.
125, l.5. HP, p152, says Sir James landed at Valencia.
125, l.18. *St Brigides Kirk*: St Bride's in Douglas, Lanarkshire.
125, l.22. HP, p154, has a long eulogistic reprise of acts that have already been eulogized in narration.
126, l.8. *Marginal note: Ballandin in Polychronicon*: A puzzling reference; Richard Higden's *Polychronicon* has nothing to the point and Boece, in Bellenden's translation, Bk.XV, ch.1 (1536), ch.2 (1531), has no formal eulogy, though it speaks in the highest terms of Sir James's valour.
126, l.10. *Marginal note*: Holinshed, *SC*, p330, not 230.
126, l.33. HP, p156, expands on the subject of his not having married. Fraser, I, 184, contends that Sir James was married and

that his son, William, succeeded him as Lord of Douglas, 1330-1333; he was killed at Halidon Hill.
127, ll.1-7. According to Fraser, I, 186, William of Liddesdale, 'The Flower of Chivalry' was the legitimate son of Sir James Douglas of Lothian, but Archibald, later known as Archibald the Grim, was Sir James's illegitimate son. It was, however, a William Douglas, not Archibald the Grim, that the lord of Liddesdale put in charge of Edinburgh Castle (see p163, ll.3-5, and note).
127, l.19. Cf. Barbour, II, 491-92: 'James alsua of Dowglas/ Yat wycht wys an awerty was'.
127, l.25. 1633, p59, unlike the other texts, runs the life of Hugh, 9th Lord of Douglas, into the life of Sir James as a final paragraph. 1644, pp52-53, ends with a Latin eulogy from Johnston's *Heroes*, pp12-13 (unattributed) and an English translation, both in verse.

The Life of Hugh, 9th Lord of Douglas (A, p119)

1333-1342

HP, p157, has scored out the life of Hugh. It adds the information in both a note to the title and a marginal addition that he was called the Dull Douglas. It opens with an account of Scotland mourning the death of the Good Sir James. In other respects it adds nothing to the other texts, though it is differently expressed.
1633, p59, and 1644, p53, follow A2 closely.

According to Fraser, I, 191-7, Hugh was a churchman, Canon of Glasgow. He resigned the Douglas estates in 1342 (not 1343) in favour of William, son of Archibald.

128, l.3. *Marginal note*: I cannot find any reference in Buchanan or Holinshed to Hugh, despite the marginal note.
128, ll.10-12. *in favours of his brother Archbald slane at Halydon-hil, his sone William*: i.e. 'in favour of William, son of his brother Archibald slain at Halidon Hill'. See pp176-77 and, for a printing of the document, Fraser, III, 357-59.
128, l.14. *Marginal note*: Boece, Bk.XV, ch.3 (1531,1536), fol.221 (1536). Holinshed, *SC*, p336, not 335, presumably.
128, l.19. *witnes*: 'witnesses'. In some Middle English texts forms of this type may be inflected forms of WITNE (*OED*).

The Life of Archibald Douglas, Lord of Galloway (A, pp119-138)

b.1296, d.1333

1633, pp61-70, generally follows A2 as usual, except for a long genealogical addition and a different account of the Douglas inheritance of Galloway through John Comyn's daughter.

HP, pp158-170, returns to following 1633 fairly closely in matter and phrasing, with additions that will be noted as they crop up. This is not a life sufficiently brilliant to engage the ambition of a reviser. At two points there are signs of careless joining of parts.

1644, pp53-62, generally is closer to 1633 than to A, in a number of places preferring 1633's phrasing where it differs from A's. Nevertheless it preserves certain features of A (and A2) following, for example, its account, not 1633's, of the Douglas inheritance of Galloway through John Comyn's sister, and even keeps some of A's phrasing where it has been altered in A2 and 1633.

Goodall, Bk.XIII, ch.27 (II, 310) and Maitland, p15, call this Archibald Douglas, not the 4th Earl of Douglas, 'Tyneman'.

129, ll.9-10. *Marginal note*: Boece, Bk.XV, ch.5 (1531, 1536), fol.221 (1536); Holinshed, as in the marginal note above, should presumably be *SC*, p336; Maitland, p15. *Boetius in his Latin booke*: Bk, XV, fol.313v (1574).
129, l.13. *Archbald did not outlive good Sir James thrie zeirs*: Sir James died in August, 1330 (Fraser, I, 181), Archibald, according to Hume, on July 22, 1333, but according to Fraser, I, 210, on the 18th of July .
129, l.19-30, l.5. 1644's account (p54) of the inheritance of Galloway is more or less A's. It explains, however, that there are two Dornagillas, the eldest daughter of Allane, Lord of Galloway, whom John Balliol (father of King John) married, and the daughter of John Comyn and Mary (second daughter of Allane), whom Archibald married. 1633, p61, and HP, pp158-159, have it that John Comyn married a daughter of John Balliol called Adama, and Archibald married their daughter Dornagilla. 1644 noting this version (unlike A) asks how John Comyn could style himself Lord of Galloway by right of his wife when Balliol had at least one son (the king) to inherit the title. It is indeed also surprising that Comyn, who married the younger sister of the Lord of Galloway, rather than Balliol, who married the elder, should get the lordship, According to Fraser, I, 212-13, Dornagilla, daughter of Comyn, is 'wholly mythical'. He has it (I, 200-201) that Archibald was not Lord of Galloway and that he

married Beatrice Lindsay; Hume has confused Sir Archibald of Douglas with Archibald the Grim, on whom David II conferred Galloway in 1369.

129, l.27. *Earle of Alremarbre*: ^Albermale^ in margin. William de Forz titular Count of Aumale, married Christian 2nd daughter of Alan Lord of Galloway (*Complete Peerage*, I, 355).

129, l.37-30, l.1. *deduced... in... Lord William his life*: See Lyfe of William, 5th Lord of Douglas, p53, ll.10-17.

130, l.5. At this point 1633, p61-63, and HP, pp158-59, have a long divagation beginning with the mariages of the three daughters of David, Earl of Huntingdon, and recounting how John Comyn betrayed Bruce to Edward (HP, pp68-67, has already told this story).

130, ll.5-11. Archibald's children by Beatrice Lindsay, according to Fraser, I, 213-14, were John, who died in France; William, to whom Hugh resigned the Douglas lands in 1342; Eleanor, who married 5 times (but never Donald Earl of Mar).

131, l.15. *Marginal note*: Buchanan, Bk.IX, fol.88.

131, ll.17-29. HP, pp161-162, expands this very abridged account of Edward Balliol's invasion. 1644, p55, omits almost all detail of the invasion in A (pp122-123, ll.18-8). The death of Randolph and the absence of the Good Sir James encouraged Edward III to try again. Alexander Seton, the son of the Governor of Berwick (see p136, l.2), below) not *Alexander Stewart*, was killed at Kinghorn meeting Balliol's forces (Nicholson, *Ed III*, p83). 'Alexander Stewart' has been underlined and 'Seton' written in the margin. Dupplin Moor was in fact two battles (Nicholson *Ed III,* pp85-89), though Buchanan, Bk.IX, fols.88v.-89, and Boece, Bk. XV, ch.2, make it one. *the Governour Donald (or as vthers cal him Duncane) Earle of Mar*: Donald, 2nd Earl of Mar was nephew to Robert I (*SP*, V, 581-3). Not Duncan in Goodall, Major, Boece (who calls him David [1536]), Holinshed or Maitland.

131, l.26. ^Dupplin feeld^ has been inserted in the margin.

131, ll.33-34. *Robert Keith*: according to Boece died at Dupplin Moor, but he probably survived to die at Durham in 1346 (*SP*, VI, 32-33). *Alexander Lindsay*: possibly the 2nd son of Alexander de Lindsay (*SP*, III, 9).

132, l.1. *William the principal of the house*: *SP*, III, 560, is noncommittal about whether Nicholas Hay, who died heir apparent to Sir Gilbert Hay probably before April 1333, might be the William Hay mentioned by Boece as dying at Dupplin.

132, ll.5-11. *Robert Bruce*: a bastard son of Robert I (Goodall, Bk.III, ch.23 [II, 305]; *SP*, I, 8), not to be confused with *Alexander Bruce* (l.11), Earl of Carrick, a bastard nephew of Robert I, who made peace with Edward Balliol (Goodall, Bk.XIII, ch.25 [II, 308]) and was killed at Halidon Hill (*SP*, II, 436-7). Who they are who call Alexander 'Robert', I cannot discover.

Mordake Earle of Strathairne: HP, pp162, 163, has Mordake Earl of Menteith. *SP*, VIII, 252, gives Malise as Earl of Strathearn contemporary with Dupplin, though not killed there, but Murdach, Earl of Menteith was killed at Dupplin (*SP*, VI, 137). *William Sinclar Bishope of Dunkelden*: William Sinclair, Bishop of Dunkeld, a staunch supporter of Robert I, who called him 'my bishop' (Barrow, p266). *Duncan Makduffe Earle of Fyffe*: according to HP, p164, he later held Perth for Balliol and was imprisoned in Kildrummy when the town was recaptured by the Bruce party. He was not a Macduff, a supposed descendant of a legendary forebear from Fordun (*SP*, IV, 1).

132, l.8. HP, p163, salutes the staunchness of the Douglases, when others had yielded or changed sides, and says Edward Baliol was crowned September 22, 1332.

132, l.20. *Androw Murray Earle of Bothuel*: Andrew Murray of Petty and Bothwell, made Guardian of Scotland after Dupplin Moor, son of Wallace's colleague (Barrow, p258, 309).

132, l.27. *Marginal note*: Buchanan, Bk.IX, fol.89v; Maior, Bk.V, ch.11; Maitland, pp15-17.

132, l.29. *Johne Randulph*: Earl of Moray, second son of Thomas Randolph, regent of Scotland on Bruce's death (Nicholson, *Ed III* p104). *Simon Fraser*: See Nicholson, *Ed III,* p104; Goodall, Bk.XIII, ch.25 (II, 307). See also below p139, l.21, below.

132, l.36. *Marginal note*: Boece, Bk. XV, ch.3; Holinshed, *SC,* p335.

132, l.36. *a barme horse*: a pack horse; so also 1644, p55; HP, p164, and 1633, p64, like A2, have 'a barebacked horse'.

132, l.37. *Vthers write*: Boece and Holinshed say nothing about secrecy, but do say that the approach of the patriots was well advertised and the battle long fought.

133, l.37. *Henrie Baliol*: Sir Henry Balliol had submitted to Bruce and been granted Branxholm when others of his family, notably John and Edward, forfeited their lands (Barrow, p279-80).

133, l.10. *Johne Moubray*: The Mowbrays had been disinherited for their support of Edward by Robert I. See also p149, ll.2-12 (Barrow, p281).

133, l.10. *Walter Cuming*: one of the two Walter Comyns (Nicholson, *Ed III,* p104), probably another beneficiary of Bruce's clemency towards families who had fought against him (Barrow, p279-80).

133, l.10. *Richart Kirchy*: 1633, p65, and HP, p164, have Kirky/ Kirkie, while 1644, p55, has Kirbie: Goodall, Bk.XIII, ch.25 (II, 308), has Kirby, Holinshed, *SC*, p336, has 'Kyrkby' and Boece (1574), Bk.XV, fol.314, 'Kyrkbi'. *Marginal note*: Holinshed, *EC*, p350; Boece, Bk.XV, ch.3.

133, l.18. *to the Galloway men*: so also 1633, p65, meaning 'by' (HP, p164) or 'because of the Galloway men' (1644, p56).

133, l.20. *Eustache Maxvel*: Sir Eustace Maxwell of Caerlaverock (Fraser, *The Book of Caerlaverock*, [Edinburgh, 1873], I, 105).
133, l.31. *St Johnstoun*: Perth.
133, ll.32-33. *apparentlie, to wit that they lay neirest to it their freinds that war slane at Duplin*: A2 makes easier sense of this passage, which, unemended, bears the same sense with strain: 'probably the besiegers were those that lay nearest to Perth, who were the friends of those slane at Duplin'.
134, l.14. *honest hart*: a key term of approbation with Hume.
134, l.22-33. *Clifforde*: Robert de Clifford, 3rd Lord Clifford (see note to p81, l.31; CP, III, 291). How else could Balliol have acted?
135, ll.6-7. *on both the borders*: i.e. 'on both west and middle marches'.
135, ll.13-18. Edward III's invasion took place in 1333.
135, ll.24-25. *Sir Alexander Setoun*: Lord of Seton, Warden of Berwick (Nicholson, *Ed III*, pp125-26).
135, l.30. *Marginal note: Boece fol.222,* in (1536) Bk.XV, chs.3, and fol.314v. (1574).
136, l.2. *Alexander Setoun another sone of the Governours*: According to Nicholson, *Edward III*, pp85-89, he had already been killed at Kinghorn. See above, p131, ll.17-29, note. Nicholson, p126, says that the Warden's sons Thomas and William were hanged at Berwick.
136, l.26. The Buchananite and Knoxian terms 'tyrannical' and 'monstrous' have been suppressed in A2, 1633, p66, and HP, p166 but are kept in 1644, p57.
136, ll.28-29. *past with silence by the same writers*: Holinshed, *EC*, p350.
136, ll.30-33. 1644, p57, expands Hume's ideas of the task of the historian: he should, like a witness under oath, tell the whole truth and nothing but the truth.
136, l.33-137, l.7. *But as they... tyme*: This violent expression of tyrannophobia is kept in 1644, p57, though omitted in A2, HP, p166, and 1633, p66.
138, l.14. HP, p167, at this point close to A, scores out the information from Major, Bk.V, ch.12.
138, l.23. *Marginal note*: Holinshed, *SC*, 338; Boece, Bk. XV, ch.5.
138, l.34. *Marginal note*: Holinshed, *EC*, p350. He says that 32,000 Scots were killed to only 15 English.
P138, l.35. *vthers say 14000*: Boece, Bk.XV, ch.5; Goodall, Bk.XIII, ch.28 (II, 311) has 10,000 and more.
139, l.16. *Johne, James and Alane Stewarts*: sons of Walter, Steward of Scotland. Of these, only John is noted in *SP*, 1, 14, though Goodall, as above,, names them. The list of the fallen may also be found in Boece, Bk.XV, ch.5.
139, ll.18-21. *the Earle of Ross*: Hugh, Earl of Ross (Goodall, Bk.XIII, ch.28 [II, 311]; *SP*, VII, 235). *Kennethe Earle of*

Sutherland: the 4th Earl of Sutherland (Goodall; *SP*, VIII, 324). *Alexander Bruce Earl of Carrik*: see p123, ll.3-5. *Androw, James and Simon Fraseirs*: So Goodall. According to the not very authoritative Alexander Mackenzie, *A History of the Frasers of Lovat* (Inverness, 1896), p33, Simon Fraser of Lovat was killed with his brothers, Andrew and James at Halidon; see also note to p132, ll.5-11, above. HP, p168, adds 'David Lord Lindsay cheefe of his name', who would have succeeded to Alexander, the chief of the family, killed at Dupplin Moor with 80 men (see above, p131, l.34).

139, l.30. *the 22 day of July callet Magdalens day*: The battle was fought on 19 July, 1333, according to Nicholson, p128.

140, l.4. *Marginal note: Whether it proceidit... or*: The alternative is completed in the next marginal note.

140, l.29. *Fabius*: Maximus Verracosus, Cunctator, the delayer, who overcame by avoiding pitched battle. The story of his command being divided with the rash Minucius, Master of the Horse, is told by Livy, XXII, 14-29.

141, ll.14-18. *Scipio*: P. Cornelius Scipio Africanus Major. '*Imperatorem mater me peperit non bellatorem*', quoted in Preface, 1644, A[3]. The saying may be found in Ps. Frontinus, *Strategematica*, 4, 7, 4.

141, ll.21-31. For Sir James's flyting at Stanhope Park, see pp111, ll.7-16.

142, l.17. *Patrik Dumbar*: 9th Earl of Dunbar, 4th Earl of March (*SP*, III, 264).

142, l.29. *Robert Talbot*: Richard Talbot, titled Lord of Mar in Balliol's last Parliament in Edinburgh (Nicholson, *Ed III*, p158; *CP*, XII, 612-14). In spite of having introduced him on p161, HP here (p170) following the phrasing more or less of A, speaks of him as if for the first time, another example of careless putting together of parts.

142, l.33. *confirmet be a Parlament*: the Parliament of 13 February 1334 at Holyrood (*APS*, I, 539).

143, ll.1-2. For the castles untaken, listed in Major, Bk.V, ch.13, and Buchanan, Bk.IX, fol.90v., see Nicholson, *Ed III,* p149. *Vrquhart*: Castle Urquhart on Loch Ness; *Lowdin-peile*: the castle on Loch Doon (Major has Lauder).

143, ll.4-5. *except the bairnes playing*: omitted in HP, p170, and 1633, p70; retained 1644, p61, 'except young children in their playes'. This touching phrase comes from Wyntoun, Bk.VIII, ch.29, probably through Major, Bk.V, ch.13.

143, l.7. *Marginal note*: Assuming that this note refers back to the Battle of Annan, Major, Bk.5, ch.12, and Buchanan, Bk.IX, fol.89v.

143, l.33-44, l.1. *ten or twelf zeirs, or perhappes twentie zeirs*: On p183, ll.35-36, Hume says that the first action of William, 10th Lord and 1st Earl of Douglas, after his return from France was at

the Battle of Durham in 1346, 13 years after the Battle of Halidon; Fraser, I, 216-17, denies that he was there.
144, l.4. 1644, pp61-62, concludes with Latin lines from Johnston's *Heroes,* pp16-17 (unattributed), and a translation into English verse.

The Life of William, Lord of Liddisdail (A, pp138-175)

b. c.1300, d. 1353

William Drummond of Hawthornden in a letter to the Marquis of Douglas picks on this life for particular condemnation: 'His life of the Lord of Liddesdale is like a Romanze. This is rather commentaryes and discourses vpon the Lyues of the Noblemen of the Name of Duglas, than a Historie' (Second draft of a letter of 1644 to the Marquis of Douglas, among the Hawthornden MSS in the National Library of Scotland [2061, 81-82], printed, Johnston, p157). The casting of historical narrative in romance epic forms is certainly one way in which Hume makes his Douglases inspiring examples and also a way of offering incense to his patron. The romance element may have been to the Marquis's taste and he may not have been altogether pleased at Drummond's sour comment. At any rate HP, where his revising is usually most evident, is content to follow A2, and adopts its romantic palliation of the Lord of Liddisdail's conduct in the final eulogistic summary.

1633, pp70-87, corresponds closely to A2.

HP, pp171-192, follows 1633 closely, even in phrasing, apart from a few corrections and a digression on the subject of the Carmichaels.

1644, pp62-78, corresponds to 1633 approximately, sometimes in details of phrasing, but also in places to A. It has a way of smoothing some of A's elliptical or abrupt effects.

In this life Hume plays down the famous exploits of Alexander Ramsay, '*omnium ea aetate belli artibus princeps*' (Boece, Bk.XV, fol.318), '*qui omnes illius aetatis Scotos rei militaris anteibat*' (Buchanan, Bk.IX, fol.94), so that the splendour of the Douglas may not be eclipsed. He probably did not know that the 'Flower of Chivalry' secured his liberty from captivity in England on his undertaking in 1352 to further the designs of Edward III and allow his armies free passage through his lands (Fraser, I, 220). The Lord of Liddesdale had been rewarded for his earlier services against Edward III with the Earldom of Athol. This, he exchanged with Robert Stewart in 1342 at the Parliament of

Aberdeen for the Lordship of Liddesdale, which rightly belonged to the inheritance of his godson and probably ward, William, later first Earl of Douglas (Nicholson, p144).

145, l.4. HP, p171, begins with a short pompous farewell to Archibald, Lord of Galloway.
145, l.14. *the space of 13 zeirs or thereby*: the Battle of Halidon was in 1633 and of Durham in 1346.
145, l.16. HP, p171, 1633, p71, and 1644, p62, omit 'Tyrannes' with A2. *marginal note*: Bellenden's Boece, 1536, Bk.XV, ch.14, says he was 'son', but 1531 says he was 'nepott to Schir James Douglas that was slayn in Spanze'; Boece, Bk.XV, fol.325 (1574), says he was '*filius Archembaldi germani Wilhelmi Douglas qui in Hispanis adversus Saracenos pugnans occubuit'*. Maitland, however, says he was Sir James's illegitimate son (p18). He was a descendant of Sir James's great grandfather.
145, ll.17-18. For his parentage, see note to p127, ll.1-7.
145, l.19-21. *they cal Johne Lord of Dalkeith... sould they say*: The Good Sir James had no brother John to be the Lord of Liddesdale's uncle by Hume's reckoning, The Lord of Liddesdale had a brother John, who was killed by Sir David Barclay (see p171, ll.11-12 below).
145, ll.23-26. Major, Bk.V, ch.15, calls 'the Knight of Liddesdale' 'the Knight of Nithsdale' when he wants to distinguish him from William, Lord (later Earl) of Douglas, which is rarely (see the confusion in ch.16). I cannot find where he confuses William with David or calls him Sir James's bastard (I am not sure how the genitive forms come in). He does, however, call him James in Bk.V, ch.14. Holinshed *SC*, p335 does call the Captain of Edinburgh Castle, William, but Boece does not mention any Captain (1531, 1536, Bk.XV, ch.11; 1574, fol.322-322v). *Archbald, that was made Captane of the Castle of Edinburgh*: in 1341, the Lord of Liddesdale put his illegitimate brother, Sir William Douglas, the elder in charge of Edinburgh Castle (Goodall, Bk.XIII, ch.47 [II, 332]; *SP*, VI, 344). See also p165, ll.29-31.
145, ll.31-32. *Sir Johne Grahame, Lord Abercorne*: Sir John Graham of Dalkeith, Abercorn and Eskdale. *SP*, VI, 196, 343, 345, says that the Lord of Liddesdale is said to have married Graham's daughter, though his only known wife was called Elizabeth. Graham's daughter, Mary, married Sir William More of Abercorn and Thomas Erskine. HP, p171, inserts that Graham married Margaret Lockhart.
145, l.30-146, l.18. 1644, p62, abridges this genealogical information drastically.
145, l.33. *the lands of Dalkeith, Newlands, Drochols and Kilbugho*: For the resignation of Newlands and Kilbucho (these two in Peebleshire) and Dalkeith by John Graham, Lord of

Abercorn and Dalkeith, see *SP*, VI, 339-40. HP, p171, scores out Drochols. Drochil Castle on the Tweed is not named in *SP* as among the lands of the Lord of Liddesdale.

145, 35-146, l.2. *ane doughter callit Marie, wha was mariet to Sir James Douglas of Lowdon*: for the descent of Sir James Douglas of Lothian, the first lord of Dalkeith, the Lord of Liddesdale's nephew, from Archibald, 4th Lord of Douglas, through Sir John Douglas, the Lord of Liddesdale's brother, see *SP*, VI, 337-44. The Lord of Liddesdale's daughter was married first to Peter Tempest, a courtier of Edward III's, second, to Reginald More, heir of Sir William More of Abercorn, and third, to Sir Thomas Erskine, son and heir of Sir Robert Erskine (*SP*, VI, 342; Fraser, I, 253), but never to Sir James Douglas of Lothian and Dalkeith. He succeeded to her lands, but had to compensate her widower, Erskine.

146, l.10-11. *Earls of Morton, Whittinghame, Langnidderie, and Maynes*: For the succession to Morton (in Midlothian, near East Calder) and Whittinghame (in East Lothian) see *SP*, VI, 350, 354. Sir James Douglas received the lands of Mordington, Whittinghame and others in free regality from Robert II, 1381-82 (*SP*, p350). For the inserted ^Tilliewhillie^, see *SP*, VI, 353-54, on Douglas of Tillywhilly.

146, l.11. HP, p171, inserts a passage on the Dalkeith branch of the Douglases.

146, l.11. ^The Originall of the house of Morton etc^ inserted in the margin.

146, ll.13-16. *James who suceidit to the Lordshipe of Dalkeith,... right of the Isle of Man*: It was James, 1st Lord of Dalkeith, his father, who married Agnes of Dunbar; her brother, George Earl of March granted the first Lord of Dalkeith £100 of land in the Isle of Man (*SP*, VI, 346).

146, l.19. *the battle of Annand*: see p132-33, ll.33-14.

146, l.24. *Marginal note*: Holinshed, *SC*, p336 (not 337), mentions Liddesdale's prowess but not that he was Warden of the West March. But Goodall, XIII, ch.48 (II, 333) says that William Douglas was warden of the Middle March when John Randolph was Warden of the West and Alexander Ramsay Warden of the East.

146, l.28. *was taken at Roxburgh*: See Life of Archbald, Lord of Galloway, p135, ll.7-13.

147, ll.9-12. *a worke to doe*: The work, as A2 adds, is a work of God, the deliverance of Scotland from tyranny. Compare this passage on human instrumentality in divine work and the wrongness of despair with the passages in the life of the Good Sir James, pp76-77, ll.12-9, and Life of Archbald, Lord of Galloway, p143, ll.20-29.

147, ll.14-18. On the importance of circumstances in historical narration, see Life of Archbald, Lord of Galloway, p136, ll.30-33.

147, ll.22-23. *except the bairns in their play*: Cf. the Life of Archbald, Earl of Galloway, p143, ll.4-5. (A2, 'except it was little children in their play'); in the Life of Archbald, 1644, p61, has 'except young children in their playes' and here (p63) repeats, 'but the little children in their play'; HP, p172, and 1633, p72, having omitted the phrase in the Life of Archbald, use it here to better effect, 'except (by) the little children in their play'.
147, ll.29-31. *Wise men were putt to silence, but stones behovit to cry, and fulish bairnes bear witnes, that the Bruce was stil King*: When Christ entered Jerusalem on Palm Sunday, he answered the Pharisees who complained about the crowds cheering a Messiah, 'If these should hold their peace, the stones would immediately cry out' according to Luke, 19, 40, or, according to Matthew, 21, 16, quoting Psalm 8, 2, 'the mouths of babes and sucklings' would bear witness.
148, l.8. *(able) so fairis it heere*: i.e. 'perhaps this is how it will turn out now'.
148, l.13. *ane blenk from Rome*: See Nicholson, p142, on the general for the role of the Scottish Church in the Second War of Independence. Papal arbitration was offered after the Pacification of Perth in 1335 and rejected by Edward.
148, l.25. HP, p173, 1633, p72, and 1644, p64, all incorporate A2's Latin tag: '*stat pro ratione voluntas*'; c.f.'*sit pro ratione voluntas*' in Juvenal, VI, 233, a witty twisting of a stoic maxim to describe women's will.
148, l.29. *a midges wing*: C.f.'The mother of mischief is na mair nor a midge wing', Fergusson, 840; Carmichael, 1468. ^A gnatt. a mole hill^ is inserted in the margin.
148, l.32. *Talbot*: Richard Talbot, Lord Talbot (Nicholson, 129-30). See Life of Archbald Douglas, Governor of Scotland, p142, l.29. He was captured in 1334 (Nicholson, *Ed III*, p169). When John Mowbray, one of Balliol's suporters died, Alexander Mowbray claimed his estates. This claim was opposed by others of Balliol's supporters, Henry Beaumont, Richard Talbot and David of Strathbogie, and Mowbray defected to the side of Sir Andrew Murray (Nicholson, *Ed III*, p168.
149, ll.1-2. *David Cuming, Earle of Athol*: Robert I had given the Earldom of Athol to Sir Neil Campbell after David of Strathbogie (not a Comyn as Hume, following Boece and Holinshed, thinks) had forfeited his lands for treason. Thereafter David of Strathbogie was one of those '"pretender" earls of Atholl, recognized only in England' (Barrow, p387). Balliol appointed him Steward of Scotland (Nicholson, *Ed III*, p148). *Henrie Beaumont*: had organized Edward Balliol's invasion on behalf of the dispossessed Earls (see also Life of the Good Sir James, p109, l.24). *Johne Moubray*: a veteran of the English party in Scotland (see Life of Archibald Douglas, Governor of Scotland, p133, ll.9-10).

149, l.26. *without lofe or liefe*: i.e. 'without praise or leave granted'. For this saying *DOST* quotes William Stewart, *Buik of the Cronikilis of Scotland* (London, 1858), 3, 464, l.58028.
149, l.27. *takis that whilk he had judgit for him*: i.e. 'Beaumont takes what he (not his King) judged to be his by right'; but it is most likely that the correction 'from' for 'for' is correct since below ll.34-35 Edward Balliol 'grantis Beaumont the Lands he had judgit fra him'.
149, l.28. *Dungard*: HP, p174, scores out and writes in Dunidure. Dundarg on the Aberdeenshire coast (Nicholson, p131).
150, ll.16-17. *50000 men*: Edward III invaded Scotland with over 13,000 troops, an English army 'unsurpassed in Edward's reign until the Crécy-Calais campaign' (Nicholson, p131).
151, l.5. *Marginal note*: Buchanan, Bk.IX, fol.91v.
150, l.18. *Marginal note*: Holinshed, *SC*, p340.
151, l.13. *Malcolme Fleming*: Warden of Dumbarton, Earl of Wigtown in 1341 (Nicholson, *Ed III*, p149).
151, ll.16-17. *Colan or Duncane Chambel*: According to Boece, Bk.XV, ch.7, Dougall Campbell of Lochowe, who according to Nicholson, *Ed III*, p164, captured Dunoon in 1334.
151, l.19. *Dunholme in Kyle*: HP, p175, has Dundonnell. In fact Dunoon in Bute.
151, l.22. *Alan Lyl*: Alan de l'Isle, made sheriff of Cowal in 1333 (Nicholson, *Ed III*, p148).
151, ll.24-25. *Thomas Bruce Earle of Carrik*: While M. E. Cumming Bruce, *Family Records of the Bruces and the Cumyns* (Edinburgh and London, 1870), p165, speaks of this Thomas Bruce as after 9th Earl of Carrick, *SP*, II, 437, recognises no Bruce Earl of Carrick after the death of Alexander, who died at Halidon in 1333.
151, ll.26-27. *William Carruders*: HP, p175, has William Karudise of Howmaines; Karrudise in 1633, p74, and 1644, p65. See Goodall, Bk.XIII, ch.32 (II, 316); *The Book of Pluscarden*, vol.2, Bk.IX, ch.31, p208.
151, ll.31-33. *Godfred Ross*: Sir Godfrey Ross changed to the side of the patriots (Nicholson, *Ed III*, p166). 1644, p65, confuses matters, 'and with hopes of forreign help of Jeffrey or Godfrey Rosse'.
152, ll.4-5. *Dauid Cuminge*: David of Strathbogie (who was not a Comyn) was forced to David II's side 27 September, 1334 (Nicholson, *Ed III*, p172).
152, l.9. *Marginal note*: Boece, Bk.15, ch.7.
152, l.11. *Marginal note*: Buchanan, Bk.IX, f.92.
152, l.17. *sayes our writers*: e.g. Buchanan, as above.
152, ll.21-22. *he lay in waite in Paintland-hils*: Goodall, Bk.XIII, ch.35 (II, 319).
152, l.24. *Marginal note*: Buchanan, Bk.IX, fol.92.
152, ll.26-27. *Perth, til a Convention*: probably the Convention

held at Dairsie; 1644, p66, says that it was held on the 2nd of April, 1335 (Nicholson, *Ed III*, p203, agrees with month and year). The story that the Earl of Athol prolonged the Lord of Liddesdale's imprisonment is in Buchanan, Bk.IX, fol.92.
152, l.35. *Marginal note*: Holinshed, *SC*, p341-2.
153, l.18. *Marginal note*: Maior, Bk.V, ch14; Holinshed, *SC*, p342; Buchanan, Bk. IX, fol.92; Maitland, pp18-19.
153, ll.22-23. *Alexander Ramsay of Dalhousie*: See Goodall, Bk.XIII, chs.48, 50 (II, 333-34, 335-36).
153, ll.25-26. *the Duke of Gelders*: in fact Guy, Count of Namur, the Queen of England's cousin (Nicholson, p131). The ensuing battle took place on 30 July, 1335. Boece, Bk.XV, ch.8, attributes the leadership to the Duke of Gelders, Holinshed, *SC*, pp341-342, to the Earl of Namur.
153, l.27. *Burrow-mure*: a large area stretching from south of the Meadows to the Pow Burn.
153, l.34. *Vthers write*: Buchanan talks of a ruined castle ('*semiruta arx*'); others (Boece, Holinshed) talk of Edinburgh Castle.
153, l.36-154, l.2. HP, p176, 1633, p75 and 1644, p66, omit the Black Friars' Wynd (now Black Friars' Street, running down from the High Street to the Cannongate, east of the South Bridge). 1644 adds that they fought valiantly up the High Street. Since St Mary's Wynd (now St Mary's Street) and Blackfriars Wynd run parallel from the Cowgate up to the High Street, we must suppose that the Count of Namur's troops split in two.
154, l.13. It is not clear from A, HP, p176, 1633, p75, who 'he' is, both Holinshed and Major being cited, but 1644, p67, shows that Holinshed (*SC*, pp341-342) is meant: 'They ascribe also the winning of the field, to the Lord of Liddesdale, who was not (as Holinshed sayes) present at their first joyning battell'.
154, l.18. *Marginal notes*: Maior, Bk.V, ch.14; Holinshed, *SC*, pp341-42. See also Goodall, Bk.XIII, ch.35 (II, 319).
154, ll.18-19. *Vthers make no mention of Randulph*: I cannot find any of Hume's authorities who does not mention Randulph, though Boece, Bk.XIV, ch.8, is so abbreviated that he might possibly be interpreted so.
154, l.22. *Sir Dauid Annand*: The writers who mention him will include Holinshed (see marginal note). David de Annan 'presumably the man captured at Neville's Cross' (D. E. R. Watt; see *CDS*, III, item 1504, where in August 1347 he is said to be a prisoner in the Tower of London with William Lord of Liddesdale).
154, l.31. *Robert Shawe*: 'Richart' a correction that seems to be written in hand different from the other revisers' and perhaps later, is adopted by none of the other texts. Goodall, Bk.XIII, ch.35 (II, 319), Boece (1574), Bk.XV, fol.319 and (1531, not 1536), ch.8, and Holinshed, *SC*, pp341-42, have 'Richard'.

155, l.7. The identity of 'He' is again unclear, in A, 1633, p76, 1644, p67 ('This same writer'); HP, p177, talks of 'Some'. Holinshed, *SC*, p341, is probably meant.
155, ll.14-15. *sure... vnsure*: The wordplay is avoided in HP, p177, 1633, p76, and 1644, p67.
155, l.18. *the Governour*: Sir John Randolph, Earl of Moray.
155, l.22. The other texts omit the dismantling of the castle.
155, ll.25-26. *to clame to the stranger*: i.e. 'to cleave to the stronger'. But there is no form, *claiue*, 'cleave', in *DOST*, though it is a possible if strained reading. '*Clame*' is perhaps a form of '*clam*', 'grip, clutch' (*SND*). '*Clame to*' meaning 'make claims upon' is not a sense given in *DOST* and does not fit easily here.
155, ll.28-29. Robert Stewart had shewn favour to David 'Cuming' (i.e. David of Strathbogie) at the Convention of Dairsie (see p152-53, ll.26-9).
156, l.25. *Marginal note*: Buchanan, Bk.IX, fol.92v.
156, l.35. *Marginal note*: Holinshed, *EC,* p352.
156, l.35-157, l.1. *to whome some joyne the Earle of Rosse, and William Lord Keyth*: William Earl of Ross (Nicholson, *Ed III,* p232) and William Keith of Galston, who defected from Balliol (Nicholson, *Ed III,* pp169, 227). HP, p178, adds 'the Lord Hay' to the three worthies. See also Wyntoun, Bk.VIII, ch.33, ll.4907-4916.
157, l.9. *the forrest of Kilblaine*: Culblean. The battle took place on 30 November, 1335. David of Strathbogie died with his back to an oak tree (Nicholson, p132).
157, l.12. *Johne Craig*: John of the Craig of Auchindoir, probably Captain of the Castle of Kildrummy (Nicholson, *Ed III*, p233.
157, ll.17-19. *Sir Robert Meinzeis*: or Sir Thomas (ll.22-23), in fact Sir Robert Menzies (Nicholson, *Ed III*, p235); *the Castle of Kenmure*: HP, p178, adds 'in Marre'. The castle on Loch Kinnord (Nicholson, *Ed III*, p235). *sayes Boetius*: Bk.XV, ch.8.
157, l.20. *Alexander Gordoun*: according to Boece, Bk.XV, ch.8, he killed David of Strathbogie (or Comyn as he has it). Possibly Adam Gordon (*SP*, IV, 513-14) (D. E. R. Watt). Who the others are who say that the Lord of Liddesdale killed David is not clear but they are not, at any rate, Goodall, Wyntoun, the Book of Pluscarden, Maitland, Buchanan, or Holinshed.
157, l.24. *Louchindurt*: Lochindorb, Moray (Nicholson, *Ed III,* p168). Lochindors in HP, p179, 1633, p77, 1644, p68.
157, l.25. 1644, p69, mispaginated '59'.
157, l.26. A marginal note has been added, ^Lord of Liddisdale made Earle of Athole^
157, ll.26-31. See headnote for this exchange. *the Evident is zit extant in Register*: See *RMS,* I, Appendix, no.1124.
157, ll.30-31. *Walter Braid*: Robert Brade (Goodall, Bk.XIII, ch.36 [II, 321], Wyntoun, Bk.VIII, ch.31, l.4691, Nicholson, *Ed*

III, p235). *Robert Cuminge*: perhaps Walter Comyn (Wyntoun, 6, 68). *Sir Thomas Cuminge*: according to Goodall, Bk.XIII, ch.36 (II, 321) and *The Book of Pluscarden*, vol.2, Bk.IX, ch.34, he was a brother of Sir Walter Comyn, but Wyntoun, 6, 68, speaks of 'Schyre Thomas Brown'. *Marginal note*: Holinshed, *SC,* p342. *Jourdan*: perhaps a mistaking of Fordun; Holinshed, *SC*, p342, refers to him in the margin at this point (see Goodall).

157, l.36-158, l.1. *the battle was foughten the last day of December*: So Holinshed, *SC,* p342, but according to Nicholson (p133) it was fought on the 30 November, 1335.

158, ll.17-20. *This Maior refereth... the Cuminge*: In Bk.V, ch.14, Major mentions a James Douglas helping Murray, but may mean the Lord of Liddesdale. Goodall, Bk.XIII, ch.39 (II, 324) mentions William Douglas, Lord of Liddesdale, in this connection.

158, l.28. *Robert Pranderghest*: Goodall, Bk.XIII, ch.42 (II, 327-28), tells this story at length.

158, l.34. *Thomas Knawetoun*: Knenton (HP, p179); Knatoun (Goodall and Holinshed, *SC*, p346). John Stirling seems to have been the captain of the Castle at this time (Nicholson, *Ed III*, p223).

159, l.2. *Marginal note*: Holinshed, *SC,* pp345-46.

159, ll.11-12. *About this tym died Androw Murray*: according to Nicholson (p137), he died in spring 1338.

159, l.15. *Marginal note*: Boece, Bk.XV, ch.10; Buchanan, Bk.IX, f.93; Maitland, p21.

159, ll.26-28. *Marginal note*: Buchanan, Bk.IX, fol.93; Maior, Bk.V, ch.15.

159, l.32. *Marginal note*: Boece, Bk.XV, ch.14, does not say that the Lord of Liddesdale was made joint Governor; Holinshed, *SC*, pp346-47; Maitland, p21.

160, ll.2-3. *Henrie of Lancastre Earle of Darbie*: Henry, Earl of Lancaster arranged this tournament in 1341, i.e. after David II's return (Nicholson *Ed III*, p143); Hume's chronology is most unreliable (*CP*, VIII, 401-10). Wyntoun, Bk.VIII, ch.xxxi, pp101-103, on whom Major draws, also places the tourney before the return of David but makes Ramsay, not Douglas, the centre of the affair.

160, l.10. *Maior mentioneth this justinge*: Bk.V, ch.15. Cf Goodall, Bk.XIII, ch.43 (II, 329).

160, l.12. *Patrick Grahame*: mentioned in Wyntoun, 6, 110, Major, Bk.V, ch.15. Patrick de Graham was heir to David de Graham (*SP*, VI, 213).

160, l.17. [157] mispaged '167'.

160, l.21. *heigh displeasour at these doings... Blaikburne*: Holinshed, *SC*, p346.

160, l.22. *Sir Thomas Barclay*: A Thomas Berkeley is listed among the bannerets of Edward III's 1335 campaign (Nicholson, *Ed III*, p248). *CP*, II, records two Scottish appointments of Lord

Thomas De Berkeley, neither at this time.
160, l.25. *Blaikburne*: See Goodall, Bk.XIII, ch.44 (II, 329). 'Since Lord Berkeley was... escorting a convoy from Edinburgh to Bothwell in Lanarkshire,... Blackburn, south of Bathgate in West Lothian, is meant' (D. E. R. Watt).
160, l.31. *Johne Stirling*: Sir John Stirling, captain of Edinburgh Castle (Nicholson, *Ed III,* p223).
161, l.4. *Cragins*: specified also in Wyntoun, 6, 116, as 'Cragis by Cragy'. *Marginal note*: Holinshed, *SC,* p346; Boece, Bk.XV, ch.10.
161, l.5. *Chrigton*: Crichton, in Midlothian. This indecisive engagement took place in 1337. See Goodall, Bk.XIII, ch.44 (II, 329); Wyntoun, 6, 116.
161, l.11. *Blak-shawe*: So Maitland, p22, but 'Blak Sollyng' in Wyntoun, 6, 116, and 'Blak-sawing' in Goodall, as above, which suggests that these engagements took place in 1338 or 1339; Maitland, p23, dates the battle in 1338, Holinshed, *SC*, 1339.
161, l.15. *as vthers*: not Goodall, Boece, Major Maitland, Holinshed or Buchanan.
161, l.20. *Marginal note*: Buchanan, Bk.IX, fol.93.
161, ll.22-23. *Laurence Vauch*: alias Rolland Vauch, according to, HP, p181, 1633, p79, 1644, p71. 'Rolandus de Waus' in Goodall, Bk.XIII, ch.44 (II, 330); 'Rollance Wass' in Maitland, p23. *CDS*, III, item 1357, says that in 1357 Roland de Vaus was exempted from taking knighthood in view of the losses his lands on the Scottish march had suffered (D. E. R. Watt).
161, l.25. *Laurence Abernathie*: See Goodall, as above. Maitland, p23, has 'Lowrence alias William Abirnethie'. Laurence de Abernethie was the younger son of William of Abernethy; the father turned to Bruce, but the son followed the English party and was forfeited (*SP*, VII, 403). But *The Lanercost Chronicle*, Maitland Club (Edinburgh, 1839), p278, says that he allied himself with William Douglas against Macdowell in 1334 (D. E. R. Watt). *Marginal note*: Boece, Bk.XV, ch.10; Buchanan, Bk.IX, f.93; Holinshed, *SC,* p346,; Maitland, p23.
161, ll.26-28. *having gote the worse four tymes... wanquishit him*: 1633, p79, 1644, p71, cite Boece (1536, Bk.XV, ch.10) for his having lost five times and won the sixth and Holinshed, for his having lost four times and won the fifth. Perhaps this is what A means to say here. Boece, Bk.XV, fol.321v. (1574), and ch.10 (1531), say he suffered only four defeats before victory in the fifth fight, in which Holinshed concurs. HP, p181, perhaps wants to say this, but the punctuation does not make the sense clear or how we are to take the other view that he lost 5 battles and won the sixth. Wyntoun, 6, 122, says he lost 5 but won the 6th.
161, l.34-162, l.4. *sent ambassador to France... whilk vthers signifie rather*: the embassy took place in 1338. Buchanan, Maitland and Holinshed say he went alone.

162, l.2. *Marginal note*: Holinshed, *SC*, p346; Buchanan, Bk.IX, fol.93; Maitland, p23.
162, l.6. *Hugh Hambels*: Hampill, p161, l.22; Haudpyle in Goodall, Bk.XIII, ch.45 (II, 330); Haupile (*Fordun*, CLIX); Hew Pyle (Wyntoun, 6, 126); Handpile in Holinshed. *Marginal note*: Buchanan, Bk.IX, fol.93v.; Holinshed, *SC,* p347.
162, ll.11-12. *Mans Mowbray*: Magnus Mowbray according to HP, p181, 1633, p80, and 1644, p71. Mauritius de Moravia, Lord of Clydesdale in Goodall, Bk.XIII, ch.45 (II, 330) and Major, Bk.V, ch.16. A Mauritius de Moravia forfeited Balnacrefe, by Linlithgow, in 1337 under Edward III (*CDS*, III, 386).
162, ll.22-24. *Knights of the familie of Castle-Galliard*: Phillip II had given David Bruce Château Gaillard as residence in France (Nicholson, p130). *Gilis de la Hoise*: according to HP, p181, 1633, p80, 1644, p71, Giles de la Hayes, and according to Holinshed, *SC*, p347 (mispag. p335), Giles de la Hois; Giles de le Huse (Goodall, Bk.XIII, ch.45 (II, 330); Egidium de Hay (*Book of Pluscarden*, Bk.IX, ch.37. *Johne de Breise*: Johannnes de Braysi (Goodall); Johannes Broys (*Book of Pluscarden*, Bk.IX, ch.37); de Bruyss (Wyntoun, 6, 124). Francisque-Michel, I, 63, identifies these men as Galios de la Huse and Jhon the Brws.
162, ll.30-31. *William Bullok*: among other things was a priest and had been Balliol's chamberlain (Nicholson, *Ed III*, p149).
163, l.12. *Thomas Othred*: Sir Thomas Ughtred (Nicholson, *Ed III*, p167; *CP*, XII, Pt.2, 158-61). *Marginal note*: Maior, Bk.V, ch.16. Maitland, pp23-24.
163, l.14. *so being going on dry land*: Compare with this odd redundant use of 'being' 'the Bishope of Durhame being approching to invade them the nixt day' (p243).
163, l.16. *Marginal note*: Holinshed, *SC,* p347.
163, l.19. *with in few dayes*: HP, p182, 1633, p80, 1644, p72, say in four days.
164, ll.14-15. *(a great thorne in his foote, whilk must be plukit out)*: omitted in the other texts. Edinburgh Castle was captured on 16 April, 1341 (Nicholson, p139).
164, ll.18-19. *Walter Tours*: Walter Towers; HP, p183, adds 'chief of his name and one of the auncient barons of Louthiane'. *Marginal note*: Buchanan, Bk.IX, fol.93v, following Maior, calls him 'Currius'. See also Goodall, Bk.XIII, ch.47 (II, 332); Wyntoun, 6, 138, calls him 'Towrys', but on p139 the Cotton MS version has 'Wat... of Curry'. *CDS*, III, 345, speaks of a Walter Curry as a burgess of Edinburgh, Wyntoun that he purveyed a ship from Dundee (D. E. R. Watt).
165, l.10. *Simon Fraseir*: According to Mackenzie (pp36-8), he was the son of the Simon Fraser killed at Halidon Hill (see p132, ll.2-3). But Goodall, Bk.XIII, ch.47 (II, 332), says it was William Fraser who was involved in the capture of Edinburgh Castle; see also *ER,* I, clvi. *William Bulloke (sayes our wryters)*: e.g. Goodall,

Bk.XIII, ch.47 (II, 332), Major, Bk.V, ch.16. William Bullock, according to Nicholson, *Ed III*, p149.
165, ll.28-29. *Marginal note*: Maior, Bk.V, ch.16; Holinshed, *SC*, p347.
165, ll.29-30. *his brother William Douglas*: His elder brother, William Douglas, the elder bastard son of Sir James Douglas of Lothian, was put in charge of the Castle by the Lord of Liddesdale in 1341(Goodall, Bk.XIII, ch.47 [II, 333]; *SP*, VI, 344).
165, ll.34-35. *Johne Montigue*: John Montague, Earl of Salisbury, had been exchanged for Randolph in Autumn 1640 before the capture of Edinburgh Castle (Nicholson, p139).
165, l.35-166, l.1. *sayes Maior*: Bk.V, ch.16, who calls Montague, William.
166, l.9-167, l.12. An important statement of Hume's idea of aristocratic service freely rendered to a king, who rewards his peers by enhancing their authority.
167, ll.17-18. *that samein zeir the second of June*: 1341.
168, l.13. *Marginal note*: Boece, Bk.XV, ch.11.
168, l.23. *Our wryters sayes*: e.g. Major, Bk.V, ch. 18.
169, l.1. *Marginal note*: Boece, Bk. XV, ch.11; Buchanan, Bk.. IX, f.94v; Maior, Bk.V, ch.18.
169, l.4. *Marginal note*: Maitland, p25.
169, ll.7-8. *Armitage*: the Castle of the Hermitage. *Marginal note: Blak buik of Scone*: Goodall, Bk.XIII ch.50 (II, 335), says the incident took place in 1341.
169, ll.9-13. HP, p186, and 1633, p83, but not 1644, p75, cut this passage from the Black Book of Scone.
169, ll.28-29. *Robert Stewart the Kings sister sone*: i.e. the son of Walter Stewart and Marjorie Bruce.
170, l.10. *at the head Court*: According to Nicholson, p144, Ramsay was holding a court 'in the parish kirk of Hawick on 20 June 1342' a year after David's return. See also Goodall, Bk.XIII, ch.50 (II, 335).
170, ll.18-19. *the Earle of Rosse had slane the Lord of the Iles*: Earl William of Ross had had Ranald MacRuaridh, 'leader of the people of the Outer Isles', murdered at Perth, where the army was mustering in October 1346. John, Lord of the Isles was not present (Nicholson, p146).
170, l.25. *Marginal note*: Buchanan, Bk.IX, fol.95.
171, l.6. 1644, p76, repeats the date of the Battle of Durham, 1346, previously given in A (p170, l.12).
170, l.33-171, l.1. *freindshipe towards France... (sayes our wryters;)*: Goodall, Bk.XIV, ch.1 and 2 (II, 340-41) tells of counsel of the lord of Liddesdale and of how David listened to others, but censures him for youthful rashness rather than Francophilia; Boece, Bk.XV, ch.13, remarks on the French interest in the campaign without censure.
171, ll.10-11. *Sir Dauid Barklay*: Sir David Barclay of Brechin,

killed at Aberdeen, 25 January, 1350 (*SP*, II, 223), by John of St Michael (Goodall, Bk.XIV, ch.7 [II, 348]). *Johne Douglas*: see p32, ll.26-27. John Douglas, brother of the Lord of Liddesdale, father of James Douglas, Lord of Dalkeith, was killed by Barclay between 1346 and 1350 (*SP*, VI, 342-43). *Marginal note*: Boece, Bk.XV, ch.14; Holinshed, *SC*, p352; Blak buik of Scone: Goodall, Bk.XIV, ch.7 (II, 348).

171, l.13. *sayes our wryters*: Goodall, Bk.XIV, ch.7 (II, 348). *Horswude*: Forgy-wod, according to Goodall, Bk.XIV, ch.7 (II, 348); probably Forgewood near Motherwell (D. E. R. Watt).

171, l.14. *father-brother*: 1644, p76, has 'they should say rather, brother', clearly a slip and noted in the errata (see also A, p146, ll2-3). John Douglas would have been an uncle if Hume's story of the Flower of Chivalry's being the Good Sir James's bastard were true. Fraser, I, 497, does not mention John as one James's half-brothers and traces the descent of the Lord of Liddesdale from Andrew, brother of William, the fifth Lord of Douglas (not illegitimately from the Good Sir James).

171, l.21. *Lendors*: Lindores, Fife, but Goodall, Bk.XIII, ch.50 (II, 336) says that Bullock was left to die in Lochindorb in Moray.

171, ll.23-24. *the writers layeth the blame of it on the nobilitie*: Goodall Bk.XIII, ch.50 (II, 336)

171, l.27. *Captane*: A2, HP, p187, 1633, p84, 1644, p76, have 'Chaplain', which seems more probable, though on p162, l.32, he is said in A2 as well as A to be Captain of the Castle of Cupar.

171, l.33. *Chussay*: Hushai, a friend of David, whose wiles helped to defeat Absalom and Achitophel (see 2 Samuel, 15-17). The comparison ('*alter Chusi*') is made in Goodall, Bk.XIII, ch.50 (II, 336).

172, l.13. *he casteth*: it is not clear what authority is being cited here from marginal captions; the other texts cite no one. Boece, Bk.XV, ch.11, would seem to date the taking of Edinburgh Castle about 1341.

172, ll.14-15. *the wryters*: Goodall, Bk.XIII, ch.47 (II, 332): '*de consilio et praevisione domini Willelmi Bullok*'; cf. Maitland, p23.

172, l.17. *Marginal note*: Holinshed, *SC*, p352; Boece, Bk.XV, ch.14.

172, l.19. *Johne St Michel*: John Carmichael (See *SP*, IV, 563). HP, p188, adds 'a progenitor of the lairds of Carmichels in Douglasdale', for whom 'was set upp a crosse called to this day Williams crosse', and then adds a long digression in another hand on the descendants of Johne St Michel down to those who accompanied Archibald, 4th Earl into France, see p287, footnote 2.

172, ll.27. *he had before (we hard) slane*: 'he' is the Lord of Liddesdale, not God, obviously.

172, l.34. *sone in Christianitie and baptisme*: i.e. his godson. *the blak buike of Scone*: Goodall, Bk.XIV, ch.8 (II, 348): '*per*

consanguineum suum et filium spiritualem'.
173, l.1. *Marginal note*: Boece, Bk.XV, fol.325v (1574), Bk.XV, ch.14 (1331, 1536).
173, ll.5-23. Fraser, I, 223, dismisses this story of jealousy. William did not become Earl of Douglas until January 1357/58 so there would be no 'countess' to weep for the Flower of Chivalry. Probably the Lord of Douglas (as he would have been at the time of the murder), was not yet married.
173, ll.6, 20. *Galswood, Galla-rods*: A2 transposes these names, though presumably they refer to the same place; the other texts, HP, p188, 1633, p85, 1644, p77, have Galswood in each case; HP adds that it was in Minchmoore. Goodall, as above, has 'Galvord'. The murder took place at what is now called Williamhope, according to Fraser, I, 222.
173, ll.11-15. The lines are quoted in Francis James Child's *English and Scottish Popular Ballads*, III (Boston, 1890), p288, from 1644, p77.
173, l.21. *Lindine Kirk*: 'a myle from Selkirk' (HP, p188, 1633, p85, 1644, p77). Lindean Kirk.
173, l.26. *sayes our writers*: Goodall, Bk.XIV, ch.8 (II, 348).
173, ll.27-28. *and so it was on gods pairt, but wha does beleive him, for his pairt?*: i.e. 'who believes the Earl of Douglas that he took the part of divine justice for his own part in revenging Ramsay and Barclay?' 'Him', and 'his' are pronouns with uncertain antecedents, but probably both, with a turn on 'on his pairt', refer to the Earl of Douglas. 1644, p77, confusingly says not only that 'our Writers' alledge that revenge was the cause but that 'no Writers... beleeve it, not untill this day', a nonsensical interpretation of what is relayed in A rather than of 1633, p85, which has it that 'our Wryters' say that the Earl made this excuse but no writer believes it.
174, l.8-175, l.2. In A2, HP, p191, and 1633, p86, but not 1644, pp77-78, the following passage, written in the same hand as the prefatory letter to King Charles and the digression on Scots aid to France, replaces the one scored out [Ambition it is... ill exemples]; it tries to overwhelm the regretful censure of A with the romantic excuse of sexual jealousy: 'Neither do I, when I consider of the oth*er* actions of his life, easely and without douting concurre in opinion with the foresaid writers. As esteeming it skarce probable, that anie of those base and vniudicious thoughts formerly mentioned by them, could haue overruled so heroicall a hart, so farr as to haue driven him to cutt off in that sorte so noble *and* worthie a member of his owne bodie; whose matchles actions of honour did still reflect vpon him self, and of whome he might ever haue disposed, vpon all his occasions, as the Cheef and head of the familye. For brave Myndes love vertue *and* honour it even in strangers, even in Enemies, much more in their owne. Generous harts strive to do better, not to detract what is well don by others.

It is a strange Maxime of an ill ground; A wicked wisdome, *and* perverse pollicye to hold back ones friends in whome any eminent vertue appeeres. I think it of follyes the greatest that can be to hinder their grouth, for feare that they should overgrowe the others greatnes; w*hi*ch when they hapne vnhappily to do It iustly comes to pass that themselves they are overgrowne by thare Enemyes: Yea vndermyned oftentimes, whiles friends holden at vnder, are vnable to vnderproppe them, as they both should and would do, if they were not curbed by the others envyous greatnes. A most iust rewarde, of so vniust a pollicye! But yett them selfs to putt hand in them for their worth, I can not find the least shadow of reason for it. And therefore to vindicat this worthie Earle from so vile an aspersion/ I do esteeme farre rather that to be most probable w*hi*ch was the comonly receaued opinion of all in that age, Even (as was some what glaunced at before) The deepe iealousye that he had conceyued of his ladyes vnchaste love, to this Lord. The iust desdaine whareof was so much the more vnsuffarable (as thought) Becaus proceeding from so neer and so much respected a kinsman. W*hi*ch taking root in so great *and* generous a mynde, brought foorth this so vnkyndlie Tragedie. The like wharof, vpon the like suspicions/ hath no few examples in all Ages. Yett is not this to be allowed, but lamented rath*er*/ And to be avoyded rather than excused, Sith we are still to readie to Imitate such badd examples'.

Compare the reflection on not envying one's friends in the life of William, 8th Earl of Douglas, pp372-74, ll.28-11.

175, l.5. *and cited by the manuscript*: Maitland, p27. The eulogy echoes Boece on the Douglases (Bk.XIV, ch.8).

175, l.6. *Marginal note*: Buchanan, Bk.IX, fol.94v.

175, ll.14-15. *with 50 men to ovircome 500*: A (p157, ll.6-7) says that the Lord of Liddisdail defeated John Stirling's 500 with 40 men, in this followed by HP, p180, 1633, p79, 1644, p70; only HP, p192, sticks to the original number in this reprise of the exploit (1633, p87; 1644, p78).

175, l.16. *Marginal note*: Boece, Bk.XV, ch.10; Holinshed, *SC*, p346, in 1338. See note to p161, ll.26-28.

175, l.18. *Marcellus*: Marcus Claudius Marcellus, see Livy, xxi, 35, 57, xxiii, 14-17, 19; Plutarch, 'Marcellus', *Lives*, V, 9-11.

175, ll.18-19. *nather overcum or overcumed*: 'comed' or 'cumed' is the normal past participle of 'come' in A. Even so, it is hard to make sense of this passage and there is much to be said for A2's emendation, 'nather overcuming nor overcomed'.

175, l.28. 1644, p78, concludes with Latin verses attributed to 'Johns Heroes' (Johnston's, *Heroes* p19), and an English verse translation.

The Life of William, 1st Earl of Douglas (A, pp176-216)

1342-84

1633, pp87-106, apart from some digressions on genealogy and French rewards to Scottish soldiers (A [p189, l.35]) and a reflection on the importance of the King's rewarding great men (A [p197, l.25]), follows A2 closely.

HP, pp192-20, is close to 1633 and A2, as usual adding information, which is sometimes pertinent, genealogical by-ways especially unresisted.

1644, pp79-92, in parts condenses, but in the moral reflections follows A closely, even in phrasing. For the first time since the life of the Good Sir James, there are no celebratory verses, though the concluding eulogy is in the highest vein.

The life does not sufficiently bring out William's important diplomatic activities, for which see Fraser, I, ch.6.

176, l.10. In the margin ^Originall of the house of Anguss^ has been inserted.
176, 15-17. 1644, p79, omits the addition of the two Earldoms.
176, l.21-177, l.14. See p128. ll.10-13.
176, l.28. The date of this Confirmation in the transcript in Fraser III, 360-361, is 12 February, 1354, which may support Hume's guess that there was another charter of resignation.
176, l.37-177, l.8. 1644, p79, omits the translation and the following account of the Douglas lands set down in a Confirmation.
177, l.21. *4. et Twidde*: omitted 1633, p88, and HP, p193.
177, l.24. *Bathrewl*: Bedrule, Roxburghshire.
177, l.24. *Rammanok*: Romano, Peebleshire.
177, l.25. *Bottil*: Buittle in Galloway.
177, l.26. *Rotherylen*: 1633, p88, and HP, p193, have 'Rugline', i.e. Ferme of Rutherglen.
177, l.27. *Hughstoun*: 1633, p88, and HP, p193, have 'Howstoun/ Houston', i.e. Hughston in Strabrock, W. Lothian (Fraser, II, 586)
177, ll.28-29. *Familtoun et Bondingtoun*: Badingtoun (1633, p88, and HP, p193); Bondingtoune or Bonyngtoune in Fraser, IV, 490. MS has a blank after '*Baronia*', as if a barony should be specified. But 1633, p88, and HP, p193, put a full stop after it and pass on to Northberwick, correctly. Familton and Bondington are in the barony of Northberwick.
177, l.30. *Skaitraw... Glenrosse*: Glencros (1633, p88, HP, p193); *Scotteraw et Aynestoun infra baroniam de Glencrosk*

(Fraser, III, 360).
177, l.31. *Tolbothie*: Polbothy, Moffat (Fraser, III, 360).
177, ll.33-36. *Terras*: this and the three succeeding incidences of the word should read '*terris*', and are so written in 1633, p88, and HP, p193.
177, l.34-78, l.7. *Kirkanders*: Kirkandrews, Dumfriesshire (Fraser, I, 200) *Rethrie*: Rattray, in Buchan (Fraser, I, 201). *baroniam de Neill, et de Cowll*: O'Neil and Coule, Aberdeenshire (Fraser, II, 586). *Logyochry*: Logyathry, Perthshire (Fraser, III, 360). *Trauariglis*: Terregles, Dumfriesshire. *Greydon*: Graydon, Berwickshire (Fraser, II, 586).
178, l.1. *mediatata*: *medietate* (1633, p88, and HP, p193, correctly).
178, l.2. *Baroniam*: Baronia (1633, p88, and HP, p193), Baronie (Fraser, II, 586)
178, l.8. *Regalitie*: regalitie, or countie Palatine (HP, p193); Fraser, III, 361 ('*in regalitate*'); see Preface, note to p21, l.28, and Fraser, I, 226-28 (for a discussion of the date). Despite the claims on pp106, ll.6-20, above, it must have been on this Confirmation, not on the Emerald Charter granted to the Good Sir James, that William 8th Earl, based his resistance to the king's officers. A regality meant that the earl exercised all the powers of the crown and was answerable only to the king (Barrow, p398).
178, l.15-183, l.13. Fraser, I, 287-90, dismisses Hume's account of William, 1st Earl of Douglas's three marriages. Margaret (or Agnes HP, p194) of Dunbar married James Douglas, Lord of Dalkeith and seems to have been daughter of Sir Patrick Dunbar who died on Crusade, not of the Earl of Dunbar and March (*SP*, III, 260). Margaret of Mar survived William and was his only wife, who bore James, 2nd Earl of Douglas, killed at Otterburn. Margaret Stewart, Countess of Angus was the sister-in-law of William's wife, Margaret of Mar; she bore him adulterously and incestuously George, who became first Earl of Angus.
178, l.20. 1633, p88, HP, p194, and 1644, p79, add that by this marriage he had a daughter married to the Lord Montgomerie. His daughter, Margaret, according to Fraser, I, 499, married Thomas Johnson, and giving birth to John of Douglas, was ancestress of the Douglases of Bonjedward.
178, l.23-179, l.21. 1644, p79, omits the introductory sentences and condenses the portion of the following account of the earldom of Mar relevant to the Douglases.
178, l.32-179, l.6. *Thomas was twise mariet*: Thomas, son of Duncan, was married twice, once to Margaret Stewart, but had no children and hence his sister took the title, Countess of Mar (*SP*, V, 583-85)
179, ll.19-21. 1633, p89, HP, p194, and 1644, p79, omit mention of the Douglas lands Isabell succeeded to.
179, l.24. 1633, p89, HP, p194 and 1644, p79, omit 'and

Liddisdail'. That possession had, after all, been returned to William of Douglas (see note to p185, ll.3-6, below).
179, l.27-180, l.1. The account of Isabell's resignation of the earldom of Mar to her husband Alexander Stewart (for which see Fraser, I, 289) contradicts what seems to be an account on pp181-182, ll.29-2, of her disposing of it to her brother, also with royal approval. But it is the Douglas lands she inherited from her father (not the Mar ones) that she made over to George, her illegitimate half-brother.
179, l.28. *Alexander Stewart*: the bastard son of 'the Wolf of Badenoch', Alexander Stewart, Earl of Buchan and Lord of Badenoch (*DNB*). None of the other texts has this reference to fraud and force.
179, ll.33-34. *ane new chartour geven therevpon by King Robert the Thrid 1414 zeirs*: none of the other texts mentions the date or the lands expressly mentioned in the charter. Fraser, I, 288-290, gives the date as 1404/1405. See also *SP*, V, 587.
179, l.37. ^The lands of Kildrimy and Gariogh etc. prouided to Isobelle D*ouglas and* her aires^ inserted in margin.
180, ll.3-13. All the other texts omit the passage, 'whereby the Lords Eskin... doughter Helene'.
180, l.14. *Gratnay*: or Gartnet, Earl of Mar (*SP*, V, 578-81).
180, l.32-181, l.8. 1644, p79, omits the claim of the Erskines to the earldom of Mar; 1633, p89, and HP, p195, abridge drastically the descent of the Erskines, but add an account of the Bruce connection from Isabell, a sister of Helen and Duncan or Donald, not mentioned in A. According to *SP*, V, 579-81 and 597-98, Hume's version of the Erskine claim is correct.
181, ll.13-16. See note to pp178-83, ll.15-13, on this third marriage. William could not have married Margaret Stewart, Countess of Angus, since Margaret of Mar survived him (Fraser, I, 290).
181, l.17-20. *killit in the battle of Falkirk*: omitted in the other texts. For Sir John Stewart, see also, p86, ll.2-4.
181, l.24. *Cadyowe*: HP, p195, has 'Innerwick', correctly. Alexander Hamilton married Elizabeth, 2nd daughter of Thomas Stewart, Earl of Angus (Fraser, II, 12), and was, granted lands of Innerwick in 1389 (*SP*, IV, 304).
181, l.30-183, l.7. See note to pp179-80, ll.27-1. A note has been inserted in the margin: ^Geo*rge* the 1. Douglas that was Ea*rl* of Ang*us*.^
182, l.2-185, l.13. 1644, p80, omits this recapitulation.
183, l.19. *Eleonora de Bruce*: 1633, p91, and HP, p197, insert information about the Bruce connection through her. She was the daughter of Archibald Douglas, Regent of Scotland, and married Alexander Bruce, Earl of Carrick.
183, l.22. *Sir James Sandilands*: 1633, p91, and HP, p197, add here that the Sandilands crest bears the Douglas arms. For Sir

James Sandilands of Sandilands, see Fraser, I, 214.
183, ll.22-23. *the transumpt of the Charter*: For the original charter, see Fraser, III, 15-16; for the transumpt, see Fraser, III, 54.
183, l.29. At this point 1644, p80, explains how Eleonora de Bruce came to be William's half sister and adds the information about the Douglas arms on the Sandilands crest.
183, l.30. *as the Manuscript*: Maitland, p28, says that William spent his youth in the wars in France.
183, ll.35-36. Fraser, I, 216-217, says that William was not present at the Battle of Neville's Cross.
183, l.36. HP, p198, gives an account of the Battle of Durham, or Neville's Cross, which explains why on p190, ll.18-19, David on his release from captivity wished to punish those who had deserted him in the battle, and says that John Copeland took him captive, later (A [p186, l.31]) to be taken captive himself by William.
184, l.6. *Marginal note*: Boece, Bk.XV, ch.13; Holinshed, *SC*, p350.
184, ll.17-18. *Coburnspeth*: Cockburnspath, Berwickshire. *Sowtray*: Soutra, a summit in the Lammermuirs. *Carnilops*: Carlops. Corscaue: 'Cors cryne which is the march betwixt Cliddesdale and Tueddale' (HP, p197). This account of the marches may be found in Goodall, Bk.XIV, ch.5 (II, 346).
184, l.33. HP, p199 has an insertion saying that the Earls of Douglas and Liddesdale were so ill treated in captivity that the Earl of Douglas vowed to found a chapel to St William, who had been martyred in England, if he were released .
185, ll.3-9. At least the Liddesdale lands returned to their rightful owner, William of Douglas. The Flower of Chivalry had acquired them by a shady transaction with Robert the Steward while William was a minor and probably his ward (see Fraser, I, 226-228).
185, ll.3-4. *the Earle of Douglas actor*: The sense is made clear by A2,s 'the Earle of Douglas (the actor)'.
185, l.17. *sayis our wryters*: Goodall, Bk.XIV, ch.8 (II, 348).
185, l.26. *Marginal note*: Holinshed, *SC*, p352; Boece, Bk.XV, ch.14.
185, ll.27-28. *Our histories testifies*: See Boece, as above.
185, l.33-186, l.15. *Lowdon, Kincavil and Caldercleir*: HP, p201, omits Kincavil (in West Lothian) and Caldercleere (in West Lothian), scores out Lowdon and substitutes Dalkeith. It is not clear what difference 'that of' in A2 and 1633, p92, makes. 1644, p81, follows A. 'Lowdon' is a misleading version of what is usually rendered 'Lothian' (Latin, 'Laudonia'). Whatever his lands before William resigned the lands of Dalkeith, James Douglas was a cousin of Mary, daughter of the Lord of Liddesdale. She married Thomas Erskine but James Douglas succeeded to the Lord of Liddesdale's estate (see Fraser, I, 252-254, and note to pp145-46, ll.33-2, above, on this exchange).

186, l.2. *them of Strabroke*: Strabrock, now Uphall (Fraser, IV, 521) belonged to the Earls of Douglas in the 8th Earl's time when Crighton harried it in 1443 (see p362, l.33, below; Fraser, I, 458).
186, l.8-11. *Dalkeith, Newlands, Kilbugho*: see p145, l.33. *Marginal note*: ^Kilbugho^ inserted in the margin. The Lord of Dalkeith was in fact in dispute with Thomas Erskine, who had married the Lord of Liddesdale's daughter, Mary, over the inheritance of her father's lands (*SP*, VI, 345). According to *SP*, VI, 342, the Lord of Liddesdale conveyed Dalkeith, Newlands and Kilbucho to James, later Lord of Dalkeith, his nephew, at Peebles in 1351. What is now *extant in our publike Registers* is a confirmation of Dalkeith (not Newlands or Kilbucho) to Marie de Douglas in 1370 (*RMS,* I, no.340).
186, ll.12-14. The insertion in HP, p202, gives as an example of the reconciliation effected by this resignation of lands to the heiress of the Lord of Liddesdale the presence of his brother (imaginary), Archibald Douglas, with William (10th Lord and to be 1st Earl) at Poitiers and details how Liddesdale passed through Isobel, Countess of Mar to her half brother, George, Earl of Angus.
186, ll.16-20. *James Douglas... Robert the first of the Stewarts*: See *RMS,* I, no. 646.
186, l.31. *Johne Copland*: see p183, l.36, note. See Wyntoun, 6, 194, 200. John de Coupelande is mentioned in a letter of 1340 as being with his company at Wark (*CDS, 6*, V [Supplementary], 809).
187, l.11. *Norram*: Norham Castle in Northumberland.
187, l.14. *William Ramsay*: *DNB* says he was a kinsman of Alexander Ramsay (murdered by the Lord of Liddesdale) and succeeded him; *SP*, III, 89, though allowing that a William Ramsay might have been a brother of Alexander, says that Sir Patrick Ramsay, a nephew, succeeded Alexander. See also Goodall, Bk.XIV, ch.9 (II, 350).
187, l.19. *Marginal note*: Boece, Bk. XV, ch.14; Holinshed, *SC*, p353.
187, l.22. *Thomas Gray*: according to Major, Bk.V, ch.20, there were two Thomas Grays, father and son, one of which was lieutenant of the English (cf. Fordun, CLXXII); according to Holinshed, *SC*, p253, Thomas Gray was the son of Edward Gray, see below, p192, ll.6-8, but according to Clay, p88, both father and son must have been named Thomas Grey of Heton (they were Constables of Norham).
187, l.23. *John Darrese*: Darcy or Darcie in the other texts, Darras in Holinshed, *SC*, p353, and Boece, Bk.XV, ch.14 (1531, 1536); d'Arras in Boece, Bk.XV, fol.325v. (1574); Darres (Goodall, Bk.XIV, ch.9 [II, 351]). James Darres 'a brave and famous squire' (Fordun, CLXXII). John Lord Darcy of Knaith, if he is meant, is not reported in *CP* or the *CDS* to have been taken

at Nisbet Muir.
187, l.29. *Eugene de Garenters*: Eugenie de Garrantiers in the other texts, improbably; i.e. Eugene, Sire de Garancières (Nicholson, p160).
187, l.31. *four thousand crownes*: 'some say 20,000' (HP, p203). According to Nicholson, p160, 50 men at arms and 40,000 *deniers d'or à l'escu* or 10,000 marks as *Scalacronica* has it.
188, l.7. *Marginal note*: Maior, Bk.V, ch.20; Buchanan, Bk.IX, fol.95v.
188, l.12. *Vthers make no mention of him*: see marginal note for those who do. Goodall, Bk.XIV, ch.10 (II, 351) does not mention Douglas.
188, l.14. *Marginal note*: Boece, Bk.XV, ch.14, and Holinshed, *SC,* p353, mention Douglas; Maitland, does not mention the taking of Berwick.
188, ll.14-16. The following are among those named in Boece, Bk.XV, ch.14. *Alexander Ogil*: killed at Berwick (*CP*, X, 26); *Thomas Percie*: there was no Thomas Percy, brother of the Earl of Northumberland to be killed at Berwick according to Clay, p161, and *CP*, X, 463. *Edward Gray*: probably Thomas Grey (see note to p187, l.22).
188, l.21. Citing Maitland and Holinshed, HP, p203, offers more details of the Earl of Angus's reported part in the capture of Berwick, which took place in 1355.
189, l.9. *Donald Makdowel*: HP, p204, 1633, p94, and 1644, p83, have 'Donald Mackdougall'; Sir Duncan or Dougal MacDowell, forced to change sides in the Kirk of Cumnock, was carried off by the English in 1345 to the Tower (Nicholson, p145).
189, l.12. *William Lord of Nethsdail his brother sone*: in fact his cousin's illegitimate son; see note to p240, ll.6-7. William, 1st Earl of Douglas, was the son of Archibald, Governor of Scotland, killed at Halidon Hill and brother of the Good Sir James, while William Lord of Nithsdale was illegitimate son of Archibad the Grim, himself an illegitimate son of the 1st Earl's uncle, the Good Sir James. *Marginal note*: Maitland, p29; Holinshed, neither in *EC* nor in *SC*, says anything about MacDowell; *SC*, 353, however, mentions the Lord of Nithsdale's capture of Dalswinton.
189, l.15. *razed on condition*: razed on composition (1644, p83). Goodall, Bk.XIV, ch.18 (II, 359), says that David razed the castles of Dalswinton, Dumfries, Morton and Durrisdeer in fulfilment of a promise made on his release from captivity in England.
189, l.17. *Johne Stewart (sone to the Governour)*: eventually Robert III, the son of Robert Stewart, later Robert II.
189, l.19. *Roger Kirkpatrick*: Major, Bk.V, ch.20, names him alone. Goodall, says, Bk.XIV, ch.15 (II, 356) that he took and razed Dalswinton and Caerlaverock (nothing about surrender on terms), and Bk.XIV, ch.15 (II, 356) that he was murdered by James Lindsay in 1357. See also Hoge Kyrkpatryke in Wyntoun,

6, 222-24).

189, ll.30-31. *knight of that order*: 1633, p94, says that it was the 'chiefest order' of France, and HP, p205, specifies the order of the Cockle.

189, l.30. *Marginal note*: *Blak buike of Scone*: Goodall, Bk.XIV, ch.16 (II, 357).

189, l.32. HP, p205, gives the date of the battle of Poitiers as 1355 (actually 1356 as in marginal note); both HP and 1633, pp94-95, insert a digression on the services of Scots soldiers to France and the honours won there by the Douglases, Stewarts and Hamiltons.

189, l.35-90, l.1. *vnslane or taine*: i.e. 'neither killed nor taken'.

190, ll.2-4. The following are listed in Holinshed, SC, p354 and in Boece (1574), Bk.XV, fol.326 and 1536, not 1531, ch.15: *Androw Stewart*: a son of Walter, the 6th High Steward is mentioned in *SP*, I, 15, without any reference to Poitiers, but if he had been the Andrew Stewart Hume meant, he would most likely be distinguished in some way. *Robert Gordoun*: See Francisque-Michel, I, 68. *Androw Halyburtoun*: perhaps a brother of Sir Walter Haliburton, but *SP*, IV, 332-33 lists no Andrew. *Androw Vase:* perhaps of the family of Vaus of Dirleton. *Archibald Douglas*: in reality Archibald the Grim (see headnote to the life of Archibald the Grim). Boece (1574) calls him the son of William but clearly means of Sir James. William *Ramsay of Colluthie*: later Earl of Fife by right of his wife (*SP*, IV, 13). On William's escape, see Francisque-Michel, I, 68, and *Book of Pluscarden,* Bk.IX, ch.43.

190, l.8. *duging*: 'base, drudging'? Cf. *DOST*, 'dogon', and as Priscilla Bawcutt points out *SND*,'dugone', *a worthless person* .

190, l.11. HP, p206, and 1633, p96, digress on the Houglas family of Bordeaux, supposedly descended from Archibald Douglas, the Good Sir James's illegitimate son (actually Archibald the Grim). In A2, this information is placed in the Life of Archbald, Lord of Galloway, p239, note 12.

191, l.4. *Marginal note*: Manusc.: Maitland, p30; Maior, Bk.V, ch.23.

191, ll.11-12. *Patrik Earle of Merche, George Earle of Murray his brother*: Patrick Dunbar, 9 Earl of Dunbar, 2 or 4, Earl of March, claimed the earldom of Moray through his wife, Agnes Randolph. He had no brother George, Earl of Moray (*SP*, III, 266-67).

191, ll.25-26. *The English writers*: Holinshed, *EC*, 391.

191, l.30. *Marginal note*: Boece, Bk.XV, ch.16.

191, l.30-192, l.10. This incident recorded, without mention of the Douglas, by Boece, Bk.XV, ch.16. Goodall, Bk.XIV, ch.25 (II, 367), is the point of departure for the reflections scattered throughout the rest of the life on the subject of trust between subject and prince. In fact the rebellion preceded David's proposal in the Parliament of 1364. According to Fraser (I, 240-241) it was a protest against David's extravagant misgovernment; according to Nicholson (pp168-169) it was a self-interested revolt against a king who made use of counsellors drawn from the knights and burgesses instead of magnates such as Douglas and the Stewarts themselves.

192, l.24. *Marginal note*: Buchanan, Bk.IX, fol.96.

192, l.25. *he thus wryteth*: he will be 'the most judicious of our writers', meaning presumably Buchanan, who is cited in the margin of A, and 1633, p97, but not 1644, p85. The difficulty does not arise in HP.

192, l.29. *Marginal note: Boe. fol.339*: Boece, Bk.XV. fol.327 (1574), and ch.16 (1531, 1536), fol.231 (1536).

193, ll.11-17. See the Life of Archibald, Governor of Scotland, for Edward III's supposed attempt at poisoning Thomas Randolph, Earl of Moray, p131, ll.14-17.

193, ll.19-22. Another incidence of the theme of tyranny's being will as law.

194, ll.1-8. In fact there was considerable friction between David and William, according to Fraser (I, 246-250), over the King's extravagance and distribution of offices. But see Nicholson for a critical account of what had been the traditional view of David's reign. *worse than any warre*: 1644, p85-86, adds 'and nothing else but a snare to entrap men'.

194, l.10. *Dauid's Towre*: this was built 1368-77; the Half Moon Battery was later built round its lower floors (John Gifford et al., *Buildings of Scotland: Edinburgh, 2nd ed.* [Edinburgh, 1988], pp85, 89-90).

194, l.11. HP, p209, has '39 of his raigne' and written above '41', correctly.

194, ll.13-14. Fraser (I, 257) dismisses the idea that there was such a convention of the Estates to settle the succession.

194, l.18. *Marginal note*: Buchanan, Bk.IX, fol.96; Maior, Bk.V, ch.24; Holinshed, *SC*, p356.

194, ll.25-26. *Dauid Earle of Huntingtoun*: David of Scotland, Earl of Huntingdon, brother of William I, who was the grandfather of Alexander III (Barrow, p455).

194, ll.31-33. *the thrid Alda, or Ada to ane Englishman callit Henrie Hastings*: Ada married Henry de Hastings (Bower, Bk.IX, ch 27). The Hastings became earls of Huntingdon in 1529.

194, l.35-195, l.27. *This Alane... which is cairfullie to be considderit*: Cf. the Life of William, 5th Lord of Douglas, p24, and the Life of Archbald Governor of Scotland, p129, ll.19-30. According to *SP*, IV, 142, Elena married Roger Quincy Earl of Winchester and Constable of Scotland and Dornagilla married John Balliol. The second daughter of Elena married Alexander Comyn, Earl of Buchan. *some write*: Bower, Bk.IX, ch.48; Watt's note says that the 2nd daughter (the 3rd according to Bower),

Christina, married William de Forz count of Aumale.
195, l.7. *and he be her lord of Galloway*: i.e. 'by her John Comyn became Lord of Galloway'.
195, ll.10-11. *Roger Earle of Wintoun*: Roger Quincie (see note to p19, l.31-34).
195, l.14. *Buchanan*: Bk.VII, fol.83. He mentions three daughters but not their names or whom they married.
195, l.16. *Boetius*: Bk.XIII, ch.15.
195, l.22. *Hay Earle of Arrol*: Robert I made Gilbert de la Hay of Errol Constable (Barrow, p338).
195, ll.27-28. *Holinshed Scottish Chronicle*: p285.
195, l.25. *ane onlie doughter*: According to 1644, p86, the daughter was called Dornagilla. Fraser, I, 257, says that William's mother was Beatrice Lindsay and that Dornagilla Comyn and the Douglas connection with the Comyns is a legend. Cf. *SP*, III, 141.
195, l.35-196, l.9. HP, p210, 1633, p99, and 1644, p86, like A2, number the degrees of relation in such a way that William Douglas is fourth person and Robert Stewart, fifth. HP and 1633, do not recapitulate Douglas's claim, but 1644 does.
196, l.20-197, l.10. This bland account of how the Earl of Douglas was brought round is based on Buchanan, Bk.IX, fol.96-96v. Wyntoun, 6, 264, speaks of armed confrontation and Boece says William Earl of Douglas was 'repressit' (Bk.XVI, ch.1). See also Goodall, Bk.XIV, ch.36 (II, 382). Fraser, (I, 256-60) dismisses both the Douglas claim and the attempt, but Nicholson (p185) accepts both.
196, l.32-197, l.1. *George and Johne Dumbars Earls of Merche and Murray*: George, 10 Earl of Dunbar and 3 or 5 Earl of March and John Dunbar, Earl of Moray (*SP*, III, 270, VI, 298-301). For William's supposed marriage to Margaret Dunbar, see pp178-83, ll.15-13, and note. If he had maried an Agnes Dunbar, daughter to Sir Patrick Dunbar, who died on crusade, he would have been brother in law to these earls (*SP*, III, 260).
197, l.1. *Robert Eskin*: Robert Erskine married Beatrix Lindsay, William's mother (though not according to Hume) after the death of his father Archibald at Halidon Hill; he was a distinguished office holder under David II and Robert II (*SP*, V, 592-96).
197, l.15. *Euphame*: James Douglas was married to Robert I's daughter Isabel (Fraser, I, 293).
197, l.17. HP, p211-212, inserts a digression on Robert's issue and their descendants.
197, l.19. *Margaret Stewart, Countess of Mar and Angus*: See note to pp178-83, ll.15-13. The King gave William Margaret, Countess of Mar, to wife. Margaret, Countess of Angus, was his mistress and bore him George, later Earl of Angus. Whenever William was married to Margaret, Countess of Mar, it must have been before she bore him James, to whom Robert II gave his daughter in marriage. As widow of Thomas, Earl of Mar,

Margaret Stewart, Countess of Angus, styled herself Countess of Angus and Mar, though her brother in law and lover, William, styled himself by an arrangement traced in Fraser, I, 274, Earl of Douglas and Mar and his widow, Margaret of Mar, styled herself Countess of Douglas and Mar.

197, l.22. this note is inserted in the margin: ^Earls of Angus becom Douglass^

197, l.25. HP, pp212-213, and 1633, p100, have a reflection on how those with truly great minds may be engaged by benefits, perhaps a nudge to Charles I to do something for the Earl of Angus. It laments that such a policy was not pursued by James I and James II, who let suspicion grow until the house was extirpated. A final addition is that Douglas was won round, not just by honours, but by the convincing arguments of his friends that the Stewarts had a better claim. *Marginal note*: Holinshed, *SC*, folio (or rather page) should be 356.

198, l.1. *honest harts*: another instance of this key term, here brought into a life that illustrates the importance of cordial affection between subject and prince.

198, l.19. *Marginal note*: Holinshed, *SC*, p356; Boece, Bk.XVI, ch.1, speaks of the various creations at the beginning of the reign of Robert II (in 1371, not 1377).

198, ll.21-22. *James Lindsay of Glenask Earle of Crafurde*: in fact the grand nephew of William's mother, Beatrix Lindsay, though not according to Hume's genealogy. Sir James de Lindsay, Lord of Crawford, was not Lord of Glenesk (*SP*, III, 12), though Holinshed, *SC*, 356, and Boece, Bk.XVI, ch.1, say so. Sir David Lindsay of Glenesk was created Earl of Crawford in 1398.

198, l.24. *Marginal note*: Buchanan, Bk.IX, fol.96v; Boece, Bk.XVI, ch.2.

198, ll.24-25. *thrie or four*: 'foure or five' (1644, p88). The 14 year truce was made in 1369, so c. 9 years had elapsed (Nicholson, p194).

198, ll.26-27. *14 or 1*: HP, p213, and 1633, p101, say 'first' only, 1644, p88, gives no date. For this expedition, see Holinshed, *SC*, p357. The Fair of Roxburgh of 1378 (Nicholson, p194) was held on the Feast of St Lawrence (Goodall, Bk.XIV, ch.37 [II, 384]). Several St Lawrence's have their feast on 10 August, none on 1 or 14.

199, ll.7-25. See Fraser's caveats on this story (I, 276-278). 1644, p88, does not give Douglas's numbers, and both HP, p214, and 1633, p102, omit the yeomen's being armed 'with Glaiffis and vther weapons'. But they say that the English Earls sent out Sir Thomas Musgrave with 300 spears and 300 archers, and it was with him that Douglas encountered, having a superiority of numbers not elsewhere confessed to in Hume's history. In this account they follow Holinshed's *English Chronicle*: p418; *Holinshed Scottish [Chronicle]*: does not mention Douglas, p357.

Earles of Northumberland and Nottinghame: Henry de Percy was created Earl of Northumberland and John de Mowbray, Earl of Nottingham, both in July 1377 (CP, IX, 710, 780-81) presumably in time to encounter the Earl of Douglas under these titles.
199, l.22. *Sir Thomas Mousgrave*: Sir Thomas Musgrave, Warden (HP, p214, says 'Captane') of Berwick (Holinshed, *SC*, p357; *CP*, IX, 436; *SP*, IV, 515).
199, ll.18-28. 1644, p88, omits this passage. *Sir Johne Gordoun*: of Strathbogie, according to *SP*, IV, 514-15, which, however, speaks of a battle of Melrose under the leadership of Archibald Douglas.
199, l.30. *Penuire*: Penrith (HP, p214). See Goodall, Bk.XIV, ch.43 (II, 391).
199, l.31. *Holinshed English Chronicle*: p419.
200, l.1. *a Scotis shipe*: John Mercer's ship was wrecked on the coast of Northumberland, his goods impounded and himself imprisoned by the English in 1376 (Nicholson, p194). *Marginal note*: Buchanan, Bk.IX, fol.97; Maior, Bk.VI, ch.1.
200, ll.4-13. 1644, p88, omits this passage; HP, p214, and 1633, p102, omit 'who defait... Salloway'. According to Major, as above, the Scots caught plague from the booty they took. *Lord Talbot*: At this time Lord Talbot was Gilbert Talbot though *CP*, XII, 614-16, says nothing specifically about this exploit.
200, l.15-202, l.10. The story of John Lyon follows Boece (1574), Bk.XVI, fols.329v.-330, closely except for the omission of the seduction of Lyon by the King's daughter (a Boecean touch) and of the Earl of March as sharing with the Earl of Douglas in the intercession for the Earl of Crawford (for Boece (1531) see Introduction, ppl-li; 1536 is much abridged). *SP*, VIII, 267, suggests that the facts were much embroidered by poets. John Lyon had been made Chamberlain by David II in 1369, Keeper of the Privy Seal by Robert II in 1371 and Chamberlain in 1377 (*SP*, VIII, 263). There is no suggestion in *SP* that he was Lindsay's man.
200, l.32. *the kingis doughter by Elizabeth Mure*: Joanna. HP, p214, has written in 'Euphame' above 'the kings daughter by Elizabeth Mure', which contradicts A (p197, l.15) where Robert is said to have given his daughter Euphame in marriage to James Douglas (but according to Fraser gave his daughter Isabel).
201, ll.12-13. *ane whyt sheild with a blew lyon*: Boece says the field was black. According to Mrs C. G. W, Roads, Lyon Clerk and Keeper of the Records, the colours in the Lyon shield, as far as is known, have always been blue and white, though evidence for this early period is mostly by way of seals, which do not show tincture. There is no reference in *RMS* to the granting of the Lyon arms at the same time as the lands.
201, l.13. *treasor*: tressure, a heraldic term meaning 'a diminutive of the orle... consisting of a narrow band of one quarter the width

of the bordure; usually borne counterfleury, or double and fleury, as in the arms of Scotland', *OED*.

201, ll.14-17. HP, p215, says the occasion of hatred was that when the Earl of Crawford asked Lyon to secure the barony of ... ? [illegible] for him from the King, Lyon instead secured it for himself. He was killed in 1382 according to Goodall, Bk.XIV, ch.45 (II, 395).

202, ll.1-3. This observation on how great men are quick to resent what they take to be ingratitude rather undercuts Hume's ideal theme of openness and freedom between king and subjects.

202, l.11. *In the nixt zeir*: 1381 (1644, p89). John of Gaunt came for the March Day of 18 June 1381, but no peace was concluded (Nicholson, p195).

202, ll.14-16. *who was then king... before him*: omitted by the other texts; 'his gudshire being thrie or four zeirs before, (and his father the blak Prince before him)' has presumably omitted 'dead' after 'being', perhaps deliberately for elliptical effect. Richard's grandfather was Edward III.

202, l.23. *Straa*: not entirely legible; Boece (1536) has 'Stro' (Bk. XVI, ch.4).

202, l.25. *Marginal note*: Buchanan, Bk. IX, fol.97v.

203, l.4. *Marginal note*: Holinshed, *EC*, p439. In Holinshed there is no speech, only narration of facts.

203, l.13. *Captane Johne Ridman*: Sir Matthew Redman (Holinshed, *EC*, p439). 'Mauritius Redman' was at the Battle of Otterburn according to Goodall, Bk.XIV, ch.53, (II, 405). Buchanan, Bk.IX, fol.101, retailing a story out of Froissart, says that a Matthew Redman was captured by James Lindsay. He was probably the same as the Matthew Redman found in *CDS*, IV, in 1381-82 as Warden of Roxburgh (nos., 302, 306, 309) (D. E. R. Watt).

203, ll.18-21. 1644, p90, omits the details of the Duke of Lancaster's being turned away from Berwick.

203, l.22. *the Captane*: Jack Straw, as HP, p216, makes clear.

203, ll.28-30. This is apparently not said with irony. Buchanan Bk.X, fol.104v, remarks on his clemency in 1384.

203, l.26. *Marginal note*: Boece, Bk.XVI, ch.4.

203, ll.31. *Archbald Douglas*: the uncle of William, the first Earl, Archibald the Grim, not his brother.

204, l.8. *Roxburgh exceptit*: and Jedward Castle, according to Fraser, I, 285.

204, l.11. HP, p217, has an insertion in the same hand as wrote the earlier insertion on p199 (above, p184, l.33, note), to the effect that William did indeed build the chapel he had vowed in captivity to St William at the West end of Douglasdale.

204, ll.15-16. *1384 as they count it*: 'they' would be, for example, Wyntoun, vol.3, Bk.IX, ch.5, l.440; the date is accepted by Fraser, I, 286.

204, l.16-212, l.23. HP, p218, and 1633, p104, like A2 omit 'For his sone.. Durhame'.
205, l.4. *I might say not els where*: i.e. 'I might add it was different when he was not in command (e.g. at Poitiers or the Battle of Durham)' as 1644, p90, makes clear.
205, l.29. *doubteslie*: either 'in doubt and anxiety (but none the less courageously)', from 'doutous' meaning 'dubious, uncertain', or a slip for 'doubtleslie', meaning either 'no doubt', or 'without hesitation'.
206, l.23. *Catastrophe*: 'The change or revolution which produces the conclusion... of a dramatic piece' (*OED*).
206, l.24-208, l.12. This interesting special pleading on ambition, almost seems to undercut much of what Hume has tried to establish about the Douglas's ideals of aristocratic service to their prince. But perhaps the ironies against Stoic renunciation are not to be understood as directed against an unworldliness guided by true divinity. Meanwhile one may praise Douglas as a man of action for not allowing his ambition to run to the lengths of the Balliols', who were willing to destroy the country. Given the case Hume has already made for Douglas's claiming the crown and his story that he easily yielded to the reasoning of his friends, this defence of him may seem beside the point, unless, of course, Hume was remembering accounts such as Boece's that say that the Douglas claim to the crown had to be met with force.
207, ll.13-16. *and what they like to be for fault of power, or dexteritie to obtain, not of judgement to contemne or neglect*: HP, p219, and 1633, p105, have 'like not', which would mean that stoics say they have no desire for things that they reject only because they do not have the power to compass them. 1644, p92, has 'and what they lack', which would mean that, what stoics do without, they simply cannot get. Either version makes good sense where A does not, and both are good examples of one sort of humanist critique of the stoics.
207, ll.23-26. HP, p220, 1633, p108, but not 1644, p92, omit the portion on pedants and theologians.

The Life of James, 2nd Earl of Douglas (A, pp217-250)

1384-88

1633, pp106-120, follows A2 closely.

HP, pp221-240, follows 1633 and A2 closely apart from some more defintite information on a number of points and a digression on the Auld Alliance. The rephrasing occurs chiefly at the beginning of the life.

1644, pp92-106, follows 1633, but in places keeps words or sections from A, frequently condensing and usually rephrasing.

The narrative of events throughout, and especially of the Battle of Otterburn, follows Buchanan to the extent that it is more a translation than a paraphrase for the most part, but Buchanan himself has followed Froissart very closely.

209, ll.6-8. He was also Earl of Mar, but the title ceased with him as far as the House of Douglas was concerned and was transmitted through his mother, Margaret of Mar, to her daughter, Isabelle (Fraser, I, 298). *Marginal note*: Buchanan, Bk.IX, fol.98; Boece, Bk.XVI, ch.4.
209, ll.14-15. *Euphame Stewart*: see p197, ll.14-16, and note.
209, l.23. *Drumlanrige*: in Dumfriesshire; ^Drumlanrige^ is inserted in margin. For William Douglas, see *SP*, III, 157; III, 112
209, ll.25-26. *Archbald Douglas of Kavers*: Cavers, in Roxburghshire; HP, p221, 1633, p106, and 1644, p93, add that he was sheriff of Teviotdale. ^Kauers^ is inserted in margin. See *SP*, II, 587; Fraser, I, 320. Cavers had originally been the posession of Archibald, Governor of Scotland, brother of the Good Sir James (*SP*, III, 141).
210, l.7. HP, p222, 1633, p107, and 1644, p93, insert the descent from William Douglas of Drumlanrig. Fraser, I, 305, adds that James probably had an illegitimate daughter, Elinor, who married Sir William Fraser of Philorth.
210, l.7. *81 zeir*: 1381 (1633, p107, 1644, p93); 1379 or 1380 (HP, p222). HP adds a brief account of the Auld Alliance down to 1523. According to Fraser, I, 294, there was no embassy in 1381; in 1371 James Douglas, Lord of Dalkeith, acompanied Archibald Douglas, Lord of Galloway, and Bishop Wardlaw, envoys to France.
210, l.19. *Marginal note*: the treaty in question is clearly the truce of 1384, for which see Holinshed, *EC*, p446 (*SC*, pp359-60, says nothing of the truce but mentions the invasion of the Lothians and Fife); Buchanan, Bk.IX, f.98; Maior, Bk.6, ch2.
210, ll.22-23. *this treatise was at Boloigne, or at Lillegham*: Lelighem, 1384 (McKissack, p434). For this and succeeding events, see Buchanan, Bk.IX, fol.98, also Holinshed, *EC*, 445. *as vthers write*: Maitland, p33-34, mentions an embassy but no treaty between France, England and Scotland.
210, ll.27-28. *the Earle of Northumberland, and Nottinghame*: Two expeditions of 1384 are recounted in Holinshed, *EC*, p446. Thomas de Mowbray, Earl of Nottingham and later Earl Marshall and Duke of Norfolk (*CP*, IX, 601), and Henry Percy, Earl of Northumberland (*CP*, IX, 710) invaded with an army of 2,000 spears and 6,000 archers and burnt the country to Edinburgh, and then in reprisal for the Scots having taken Berwick John of Gaunt, Earl of Lancaster invaded (for Lancaster's expedition, see Nicholson, p196; see also p203, ll.24-30, above). Hume seems to have confused the sequence of the two invasions.

210, ll.33-34. *as vthers write*: Holinshed, *EC*, says the Earl of Nottingham had only 500 spears. But see note above.
211, ll.27-8. *The Earles of... Dumbar and Crafurde*: George, 10 Earl of Dunbar, 3 or 5 Earl of March (*SP*, III, 270); Sir James de Lindsay, Lord of Crawford (*SP*, III, 12).
212, l.19. *Jehan de Vien a Burgounge*: Jean de Vienne, a Burgundian.
212, ll.23-23. *2000 armit men arbeletriers*: Confusing or confused; Buchanan says that there were 200 crossbowmen, and Holinshed agrees. Boece, though cited, does not particularize the 2,000 as crossbowmen. Fraser, I, 298-99, says there were 2,000 men and 1400 suits of armour and 50,000 francs, of which a fifth was paid to the King, the rest to the nobles (see Nicholson, p221, drawing on Fordun, for another account). The following account of the Franco-Scottish war with England is almost a translation of Buchanan, Bk.IX, fols.98-99, though he does not give the numbers of the English army that Douglas takes the French Admiral to view.
212, l.32-33. *Wark, Furde and Cornwal*: Ford and Cornhill. According to Fraser, I, 301, Wark was taken with the aid of French expertise.
213, l.31. *Marginal note*: Holinshed, *EC*, p447.
214, l.11. *waist Cumberland*: probably an error for 'waistit', the usual form with Hume, rather than a strong past form.
214, ll.14-16. For the tactics of the Good Sir James at Stanhope Park, see pp109-113.
214, 28-215, l.1. 1644, p95, omits the French reasons for demanding Roxburgh and the Scots reasons for refusing (from Buchanan, Bk.IX, fols.98v.-99). It condenses the following account of hostility between the French soldiers and the Scots.
216, l.20. *Marginal note*: Boece, Bk.XVI, ch.5 (1531), says nothing about a Scottish demand for reparation but 1536, ch.4, and 1574, fol.331, do.
217, l.4. ^Scotland never or seldome leaneing to the ayde of France. Vide supra fol.105.^ is inserted in the margin (see p115, l.33. note, where the issue of French aid to Scottish independence is already discussed at length).
217, l.17. *furnishit*: probably an error for 'surmisit', as the reviser thinks, but possibly on the analogy of 'furnished evidence' here 'testified'.
217, l.30. *Cokit mouth*: Cockermouth (HP, p228). *Marginal note*: Boece, Bk.XVI, ch.5: Holinshed, *SC*, p361. The expedition took place in the summer of 1388.
218, l.12. ^King Robert^ inserted in the margin.
218, ll.21-22. *the Kings nixt sone the Earle of Fyfe*: Robert, the King's second son.
218, l.26. *iii day of August*: all other texts and A2 leave out the date. *or (as vthers say) of July*: i.e. 'or (as others say) the third

day of July'. I cannot find who these others are.
218, l. 34. *the Noble men*: i.e. the English noble men.
219, l.5. *in Tiwidaile*: HP, p229, adds 'at Suddan-church, appertaining to the Lord of Douglas'. Fraser, I, 307, argues for this being the Kirk of Southdean.
220, l.2. *harder punishment*: 'with the rack', (1644, p97).
220, l.9. *Stratharne*: David Stewart, Earl of Strathearn, Robert II's eldest son by Euphemia Ross (*SP*, VIII, 259-60).
220, ll.13-14. *George and Johne Dumbars Earls of Merch and Murray*: See note to pp196-97, ll.32-1. For William's supposed marriage to Margaret Dunbar, see pp178-83, ll.15-13, and note. *William or James Lindsay Earle of Crafurde*: after this called James Lindsay consistently, and correctly (*SP*, III, 12). *Hay Constable Earle of Arrol*: Sir Thomas Hay (*SP*, III, 561-2, where he is not said to have taken part on the Otterburn expedition). *the Lord of Montgomerie*: John Montgomerie of Eaglesham (*SP*, III, 427-28). *Patrik Hepburne of Hails and his sone*: The son was named Patrick too (*SP*, II, 137).
220, l.19. *Marginal note*: Boece, Bk.XVI, ch.6; Holinshed, *SC*, p362; Buchanan, Bk.IX, f.100; Maior (citing Froissart), Bk.VI, ch.3. Froissart, vol.III, ch.124.
220, ll.30-32. *The Earle of Northumberland... his two sonnes Henrie, and Ralf*: Henry Percy, Earl of Northumberland and his sons Henry, Lord Percy ('Hotspur') and Ralph (*CP*, IX, 708-13).
221, l.5. *passis Tyne agane*: 'at Newburne' (HP, p230).
221, ll.9-13. The assault on Newcastle is not recorded in Buchanan, but in Boece, Bk.XVI, ch.4, and Holinshed, *SC*, p362, where it is placed after the joust with Hotspur, and said to have cost the Scots great slaughter.
221, l.32. *Holinshed says of Froissart*: A, followed by HP, p231, and 1633, p113, says that Holinshed says that Froissart makes no mention of the joust; 1644, p98, says correctly that Holinshed has the story out of Froissart (vol.III, ch.124).
222, ll.6-11. *and very... Enemie*: 1644, p98, omits; HP, p231, and 1633, p113, omit 'and very... small number'.
222, ll.17-18. *Marginal note*: Froissart, vol.III, ch.125. *Powclane*: Pontellen (HP, p231), Ponteland (Fraser, I, 310); *Sir Haymer of Alphol*: Aymer or Adomar of Athol (Fraser, I, 310).
222, l.22. *12 or 14 myles*: the other texts say '12'; Holinshed, *SC, p362* says 12 or 14 miles, Boece (1531) Bk.XVI, ch.4, (1574) fol.332v., and 5, and Buchanan, 8 (Bk.IX, fol.100v.). It is about 30 English miles from Newcastle.
223, l.8. *ane Castle*: called Combure/ Cambure (HP, p231, 1633, p114, and 1644, p99). Froissart, vol.III, ch.125, p332, has a marginal note saying that earlier editions call it Combure but that this edition follows Boece's 'Otterburn' (Bk.XVI, fol.333, 1574) and calls it the Castle of Octebourg. Given that Froissart is capable of rendering Dalkeith as 'Alquest' (p334), it is quite

possible that Otterburn is meant. HP inserts Douglas's speech to his men before battle, a different one from the one given him by Boece, Bk XVI, ch.7.

223, l.19. *10000 men*: Fraser, I, 311, estimates Percy's army as about twice the size of the Scottish (600 men at arms and 8,000 infantry).

222, ll.19-20. *not expecting*: i.e. 'not staying for' (1644, p99).

224, ll.16-17. *the moneth of July*: Hume has now settled for July (following Buchanan, who has previously said the levy for the expedition into England was planned for the 5th of August), not either July or August, as on p218, l.26 and p236, ll.5-6. Fraser, I, 317-18, note, remarks that if the expedition set off on the 5th of August, 1388, then it must now be the 12th when there would be little moon. He thinks it more probable, however, that the battle took place on the 11th. Nicholson (p199), undaunted by these arguments, sets the date on the 5th of August, in this agreeing with Maitland (p36: St Oswald's Day) and Goodall, Bk.XIV, ch.54 (II, 406).

225, l.9. *Robert Hairt*: Major Bk.VI, ch.3, follows Froissart, vol. III, ch.127, p336, in calling him Douglas's knight (*'armigero'*,*'un sien Chevalier')*. *Simon Glendinning*: is not mentioned in Froissart or Major but in Buchanan, Bk.IX, fol.101. According to the endenture between Henry IV and Tyneman he was the son of Sir Adam Glendinning (1633, p140, 1644, p123, Fraser, III, p46). A Simon Glendinning witnessed charters for Archibald Tyneman c. 1407 (William Fraser, *The Scotts of Buccleuch* [Edinburgh, 1878], no.22) probably while he was in England as hostage for Tyneman (*CDS*, IV, no. 707; see 1633, p140, and 1644, p123). The Glendinnings held land in Eskdale from the Earls of Douglas. Wyntoun, VI, 334-36, makes no mention of Glendinning, but says 'Schir Robert Hert' was killed along with Douglas; a second knight lying alongside, 'Schire Johne of Towris', recovered. I am indebted to Dr Michael Brown for information about Glendinning.

225, ll.14-22. Major's epic comparison and description of Douglas carrying everything before him (Bk.VI, ch.3) owes something to Virgil, if not Homer. I am not sure that Hume is entitled to sniff at other men's exaggerations. At any rate Buchanan, whom he follows, seems to have imagined the fight very much in terms of the prowess of a hero and subsidiary heroes, as in Virgil. *Marginal note*: Maior, Bk.VI, ch.3; Boece, Bk.XVI, ch.7; Holinshed, *SC,* p363.

225, ll.28. *Holinshed confesseth*: *SC*, 363.

225, ll.31-33. *And Boetius... these dayes*: Boece (1574) here uses an epic formula for Douglas's wielding the mace (Bk.XVI, [ch.7], fol.333): '*clava ferrata maiore quam quisquam id temporis ferre poterunt*'.

226, l.6. *Richart Lundy*: Fraser, I, 314, says that Froissart's contention that Lundy was made Archdeacon of Aberdeen the same or the next year is disproved by Barbour's continuing in that office for some years after the battle; this does not disprove Hume's assertion that he was made Archdeacon afterwards, but he is not listed in that office in Donald E. R. Watt, *Fasti Ecclesiae Scoticanae Medii Aevi* (St Andrews, 1959). Boece, Bk.XVI, fol.333 (1574, but not 1531 or 1536 [ch.7]) says he died with the Douglas, to whom he was related. Froissart's Sir William of Norbenich would be the priest of Northberwick, called William, as (probably) relayed through Maior, Bk.6, ch.3 (see Constable's note, p321, to '*sacerdote domino Guillelmo boreali unico*'). Goodall, Bk.XIV, ch.54 (II, 406) says that William of Londy was fatally wounded in the face by an arrow.

226, l.11. *his kinsman James Lindsay*: certainly a kinsman, since Douglas's grandmother was Beatrix Lindsay, though Hume thinks she was the mythical Dornagilla, daughter of John Comyn.

226, ll.11-12. *Johne and Walter Sinclers*: named in Froissart, vol.III, ch.127, p336, but not to be found in *SP*.

226, ll.12-24. not the speech given him in Boece, BkXVI, ch.7, after the battle (see pp249-250, ll.29-8), but as Fraser, I, 314, says, one to be found in later editions of Froissart (vol.III, ch.127, p.336). It may be found, in Buchanan, Bk.IX, fol.101. The prophecy, which is not in Buchanan, was added, according to Fraser, from tradition.

226, l.33. *Johne Earle of Murray*: John Dunbar, Earl of Moray (*SP*, IV, 298-30).

227, l.1. *Sir Johne Makyrel*: so Maior, BkVI, ch.3. John Maxwell, heir apparent to Pollock (William Fraser, *Memoirs of the Maxwells of Pollock* (Edinburgh, 1863), I, 16.

227, ll.5-6. *Froisart*: vol.III, ch.126, p336; Holinshed, *SC*, p363; Boece, Bk.XVI, ch.7. *Keit-marshel*: Robert Keith, grandson of Sir William Keith, hereditary marischal of Scotland (*SP*, VI, 37).

227, ll.13-14. HP, p235, lists the best English prisoners in addition to the Percies out of Boece, Bk.XVI, ch.7.

228, l.19. *Earle of Marshell of England*: Thomas de Mowbray, Earl of Nottingham (*CP*, IX, 601).

228, ll.22-24. *the Castle of Ponune*: 'pertaining to the Lord of Montgomerie now Earl of Eglinton, neere to Glasgow' (HP, p236, agreeing with A2 and the other texts that it was not in Kyle). Polnoon was 'long the chief messuage of the barony of Eagleshame' (William Fraser, *Memorials of the Montgomeries, Earls of Eglington* (Edinburgh, 1859), I, 14. Eaglesham, near East Kilbryde, is certainly not in Kyle. In the margin 'Carrict' has been written, probably in the original hand, as a correction for 'Kyle'.

228, l.31. *the Governour of Scotland*: HP, p236, and 1644, p102, add that he was the Earl of Fife. Robert, 3rd son of Robert II, became Earl of Fife in 1389 (Earl of Menteith at this time) and

was not Governor until 1406 (*SP*, I, 148; IV, 14).
229, l.13. *Froisart*: vol.III, ch.126, p335.
229, l.17. *Marginal note*: Maior, Bk.VI, ch.4.
229, l.22-230, l.26. Buchanan, Bk.IX, fol.101,101v., expatiates on Scottish chivalry to prisoners, but he talks rather of Border traditions of honour (on both sides) than of Scottish humanity.
230, l.15. *the Bishope of Durhame*: John de Fordham (*Fasti Ecclesiae Anglicanae*, III, 290-91).
230, ll.28-29. *thrie straiks*: 'three market strokes' (HP, p237, 1633, p118), 'three marked strokes' (1644, p103). 'Markit strokes' in fencing are those kept tally of by the fencing master (*DOST*). *Marginal note*: Maior, Bk.VI, ch.4.
230, l.34. *sound of their harnes*: perhaps originally a misreading of a MS 'hornes'. 1644, p103, says they blew their horns, following Buchanan. A and the other texts have it that the English army was dismayed by the clashing of the Scots armour, or harness. See Froissart, vol.III, ch.129, p341, for the description of the Scottish army's way of blowing horns to put fear into the enemy.
231, l.11. *Marginal note*: Holinshed, *SC*, p364, tells of the Bishop of Durham, not of Scottish humanity.
232, l.13. *that of the poet*: 'touching Marcellus' (HP, p238, 1633, p118); see Virgil, *Aeneid*, VI, 869-71, 879-81.
232, l.15-233, l.9. A long replacement for the scored cut passage has been interleaved: ^See if it will not be a litle more pertinent to haue all this between the two starres in the bookes Margine ['*Ostendent...* Enemie'] sett downe in these tearmes,

> *Ostendent terris hunc tantum fata, neq ultra*
> *Esse sinent.*

> The fates shall but, mak of this youth a show;
> Such vertues must not tarrie long belowe.

And a litle efter, the better to expres the first degree of excellencye

> *Nimium vobis (Romam propago!)*
> *Visa potens (Superis), propria haec si dona fuissent.*

> The Heauens had made, thee (Roman race!) to be
> Too blest, if this guift had held out with thee.

Change but the Countries name, applyeing it to Scotland, And yow shall accommodat these vertues more fitly to this man. But most of all, if leaving those Poeticall hyperboles, yow will tak that simple sense, with the Poet (yett contining his praises) sayeth-

Non illi quisquam se impune tulisset
Obuius armato; Seu cum pedes iret in hostem,
Seu spumantis equi foderet calcaribus armos.

No man in armes that dares to him mak heed
Shall scape vnfoyld, on foot or foaming Steed.'

HP, p238, and 1633, p118, follow A2. 1644, pp103-104, has the verse translations of the other texts, rather than the prose ones of A, but it follows A in the prose, apart from translation, between the pieces of verse.
232, ll.27-29. HP, p238, misquotes, '*Nuirium(?) vobis, Romana propago,/ Visa potens superis propria si haec dona fuissent*'.
233, ll.9-11. *Whilk he speiking of Marcellus (if he had livit) in witnissing of this Earle of Douglas (even be the adversarie) whils he lyvit*: Tacitean syntax? Perhaps A2's emendation, followed by the other texts, is necessary. The sense at any rate is, 'what Virgil said of Marcellus (if indeed such a man lived) is said, even by his enemies, of the Earl of Douglas while he lived'.
233, ll.12-13. *Sir Philip Sidney in the defence of poesie*: *Miscellaneous Prose of Sir Philip Sidney*, ed. Katherine Duncan-Jones and Jan Van Dorsten (Oxford: Clarendon Press, 1973), p.97: 'Certainly, I must confess my own barbarousness, I never heard the old song of Percy and Douglas that I found not my heart moved more than with a trumpet; and yet it is sung but by some blind crowder, with no rougher voice than rude style; which, being so evil apparelled in the dust and cobwebs of that uncivil age, what would it work trimmed in the gorgeous eloquence of Pindar?'. Note that Hume defends the factuality of history in opposition to Sidney (p88) because it is has more power to inspire than fiction, not because it simply tells the truth. For other references to Sir Philip Sidney, including the one to the first draft of *The Arcadia*, see 1644, pp362 and 398.
233, l.31. *the hunting of the Chiviot*: see Sidney, p97, and Child, *English and Scottish Popular Ballads*, III, 307-14. None of the versions of 'The Battle of Otterburn' (Child, III, 276-301) accords very closely with Hume's (and Froissart's) account, but they are at least closer than 'The Hunting of the Cheviot'.
234, l.33-235, l.23. This version of the events and the dying speech may be found in Boece, Bk.XVI, fol.333-333v. Evidently Hume did not think Bellenden's translation satisfactory and supplied one of his own.
235, l.29. Johne Bikertoun of Lyfnis: 'of Luf(f)enesse' (HP, p240, 1633, p120, 1644, p105). This story is not in Boece, Buchanan or Holinshed, but Maitland, referring to what 'wtheris sayis' tells the story of 'Johne Bickirtoun of Luffnois' (p36). A Sir Walter Bickerton of Luffness, perhaps, John Bickerton's son, was captured at Homildon (Bower, XV, ch.14, p82).

235, l.29. *Marginal note*: Holinshed, *SC*, p364, mentions his burial, but it is hard to know what the citation to Boece could refer to. Neither have other accounts of his death, though Boece, as above, mentions that his helmet had not been well fastened and that the had received a deadly head wound. Maitland, pp36-37.
236, ll.1-6. *He possessit... Buchanan*: omitted by the other texts following A2. *Manuscript*: Maitland, p33, says William, 1st Earl of Douglas, died in 1385. *Holinsyd, SC*, p364; *Buchanan,* Bk.9, f.102 in fact says 21 July ('12 Cal Aug 1388'). On the dating see note to p224, ll.16-17. HP, p240, adds that Douglas's wife Eupheme was buried in Scone the ancient burying place of the Kings of Scotland. 1644, pp106-107, adds a Latin epitaph and and an English translation, both in verse, the Latin attributed to Johnston's *Heroes* (p19), and tacks the life of Archibald, Lord of Galloway, on to the end of James's life without a separate title.

The Life of Archibald, Lord of Galloway (A, pp252-254)

For dates, see the Life of Archibald, the Grim, p86.

1633, pp121-122, follows A2.
HP, pp241-42, follows 1633. One page is written in one hand and one in another, but this change does not signal insertions.
1644, pp106-107, is tacked on to the life of James, 2nd Earl of Douglas, without funerary verses, and follows 1633, except in not referring to the French family of the Houglases.

According to Fraser, I, 321, Archibald, Lord of Galloway, Archibald who was captured at Poitiers (p194) and Archibald the Grim are the same person, the illegitimate son of the Good Sir James.

237, l.4. *Marginal note: Boece, fol 234.* Bk.XVI, ch.8, (1536), fol.234. Boece (1531, Bk.XVI, ch.8) has 'Eftir *th*e deth of Iames, Erle of Douglas, his cousing Archibald, Lord of Galloway, was maid Erle'. 1531, at least, makes Hume's chimerical Archibald, Lord of Galloway, Archibald the Grim, correctly. See note to p247, l.5, and headnote.
237, l.12. *the battle of Penmure*: Penrith was sacked in 1380 (Fraser, I, 279-81).
237, ll.12-24. For the victory over Talbot's invasion, see also Life of William, 1st Earl of Douglas, p200, ll.6-15. Hume follows Buchanan, Bk.IX, fol.97, closely. The remarkable numbers are his. 1644, p106, says that Talbot came with 50,000, but was vanquished by the less incredible number of 5,000 under the Lord of Galloway. *Marginal note*: Buchanan, Bk.IX, fol.97, says

nothing about Archibald Douglas in this context, but says Sir James, 1st Earl of Douglas (meaning William) sacked Penrith; Maior, Bk.VI, ch.1.

238, ll.1-13. For the taking of Lochmaben, cf. p203, ll.31-34. The account is an abridgement of Holinshed, *SC*, p359, in parts almost a transcription.

P238, l.4. *Earle of... Merche*: George Dunbar, 10th Earl of Dunbar and 3rd or 5th Earl of March (*SP*, IV, 270-76).

P238, l.7. *Marginal note*: Boece, Bk. XVI, ch.4.

P238, l.10. *Sir William Edirstone*: or Fetherston (HP, p242), so Holinshed, *SC*, p359. Fethirstane (Goodall, Bk.XIV, ch.47 (II, 397). Alexander de Fetherstanhalgh, Captain of Lochmaben Castle, lost it to the Scots in January 1385/85 (*CDS*, V [Supplementary], 331).

238, l.14. *he went to France*: in 1383 Robert II made a pact for French aid in the event of war with England (Nicholson, p196). See p210, ll.2-26.

238, l.19. *the taking of Wark, Furde, and Cornwal*: Ford and Cornhill. See Life of James, 2nd Earl of Douglas, p212, ll.31-35.

238, ll.21-25. While the English advanced on Edinburgh in 1385, the Scottish army with Jean de Vienne's French contingent, plundered Cumberland (Nicholson, p197).

238, l.33-239, l.24. Fraser, I, 321, says that Hume 'leads the van of confusion' here: the 'three Archibalds are one and the same person, Archibald the Grim, the natural son of the Good Sir James'.

239, l.7. After 'Poictiers','^In France, who is reported there to have marryed and died/, Of whom there are diuers descended in and about Burdeaux to this daye/ Calling them selfs Houglas, in steed of Douglas^ has been inserted; HP, p242, and 1633, p122, follow; this repeats HP, p206, and 1633, p96 (see note to p194, l.3, below); 1644, p107, says only that Archbald married and died in France.

239, l.11-254, l.22. David gave Archibald the Grim eastern Galloway and Thomas Fleming, Earl of Wigtoun, sold him the western part (Nicholson, p203). Hume's reasoning is not soundly based.

The Life of Willliam, Lord of Nethsdail (A, pp254-262).

m.1387, d.1392?

1633, pp123-126, follows A2 with minor alterations.

HP, pp243-250, written in a faint and not very well-formed or legible hand, reorders and fairly generally rephrases the same material, with particular attention to matters of pedigree. It retains some details from A dropped in 1633.

1644, pp108-111, follows 1633 with small variations. P110 is mispaginated '108'.

The material of this life may be found in Goodall, Bk.XIV, chs. 51 and 56, and in Boece, Bk.XVI, chs.5-6.

240, ll.6-7. *sone Natural to Archbald Lord of Galloway*: The Lord of Nithsdale was the illegitimate son of Archibald the Grim. Buchanan, Bk.IX, fol.99, may be the source of this error.
240, l.8. *Marginal note*: Holinshed, *SC*, should be p361.
240, l.11. HP places this eulogistic portrait at the end and proceeds instead (pp243-244) to the Lord of Nithsdale's marriage and issue and to the marriages of Robert II. The portrait comes from Holinshed, *SC,* p361, almost verbatim. *vpright*: 'bentbackit' according to Maitland (p27).
240, l.24. *the iourney made by Robert Earle of Fife*: Robert Stewart, later the 1st Duke of Albany, according to Goodall, Bk. XIV, ch. 52 (II, 404), led an expedition in 1388 earlier in summer than the next one that he led into the North West while James, 2nd Earl of Douglas, invaded the North East and met his end at Otterburn.
240, l.28-241, l.9. Taken from Boece, Bk.XVI, ch.5.
241, l.9. HP, p247, places the Irish expedition (A [p243-44, ll.7-24]) at this point, quoting some of a ballad, not to be found in Child:

> When the doughtie Douglas took the sea
> That worthie Lord he was full Gay,
> Ten hundreth men he might weill bee
> So many men in Guid Array etc.
>
> To Irland Coast their purpose held etc.

The ballad tells how beset by the English he took 'the great Hulk' and so passed to Carlingford.
241, ll.13-14. *Divel nor the blake Douglas overtake them*: omitted by 1633, p123; HP, p250, applies to the Lord of Liddesdale as the Black Douglas lines more or less from Barbour, Bk.XV, ll.559-62, describing the fear aroused by the name of the Good Sir James:

> In England wheer our fathers wan
> The wyues would both Course and ban
> And luik to their Chilldrin with Angry face
> Beteaching them to the Black Douglas.

1644, p108, has 'the blake Douglas comes, the black Douglas will get thee'

241, ll.14-33. Taken from Boece, Bk.XVI, ch.5. *Marginal note: Boece, fol. 234:* Bk.XVI, fol.331v, (1574) and, ch.5, fol.234 (1536); *Blak buik of Scone*: Goodall, Bk.XIV, ch.52 II, 403-4)
241, l.17. *his doughter Giles*: or Egidia..
242, ll.1-2. *the Lordshipe of Nethsdail*: HP, p244, adds the Castle of Tibers.
242, ll.8-9. *a doughter, wha was mariet to Henrie Sinklar*: c. 1407, according to Fraser, I, 358, who thinks he also had a son, William of Douglas of Nithsdale, who died young (pp358-59).
242, ll.11-13. HP, p244, details the marriages and issue of the son and daughter of Henry and Gilles.
242, l.16. *Prince of Danskein, Duk of Sprusland*: Prince of Danzig, Duke of Prussia. Fraser, I, 357, observes that there are no patents for these titles.
242, l.19. *Holdonburgh*: Oldenburg
242, l.21. 1633, p124, and 1644, p109, omit 'the towne of Dumfreis', but HP, p244, retains it.
242, ll.24-25. *Baron of Ekfurde, Cavertoun, Cousland,... Harbartshyre:* Eckford, N. E. of Jedburgh; Caverton, S.S.E. of Kelso in Roxburghshire; Cousland, E. of Dalkeith; Harbertshire in Stirlingshire (Fraser, I, 345).
242, l.25. *20 Sinkler Dysert*: Dysart in Fife; 1633, p124, and 1644, p109, omit 'Sinkler', but not HP, p244.
242, ll.26-29. Hume does not allow himself to be so unimpressed by Douglas titles, but HP, p245, says all these titles in a branch show the supereminency of the main stem and then proceeds to detail the descendants of this grandchild of the Lord of Nithsdale.
242, l.30-34. *Chanceller of Scotland*: William Sinclair became Chancellor to James II in 1454 (see *RMS*, II, 600, where he is called Chancellor, 27 October, 1454). *Buchanan*: Bk.XI, fol.124v. I cannot find Hume's 'Confirmation'.
243, l.6. HP, pp245-246, inserts the future distribution of the lands of Nithsdale and of Galloway under the Stewarts.
243, l.7-244, l.24. The account of the invasion of Ireland follows Holinshed almost verbatim. The material may be found also in Buchanan, Bk.IX, fol.99-99v. *Marginal note*: Holinshed, *SC,* p361; Boece, Bk.XVI, ch.6.
243, l.22. *800 men*: 500 in HP, p247, 1633, p125, 1644, p109, perhaps following Buchanan (500 horse sent from Dundalk) rather than Holinshed.
243, l.17. *Claringfurde*: Carlingford (Louth) in the other texts.
243, ll.25-26. *Robert Stewart of Disdeir*: Robert Stewart of Durisdeer was perhaps a descendant of James Stewart of Durisdeer, fourth son of James 5th High Steward, and killed at the Battle of Dundalk 1318 (*SP*, I, 14; *RMS,* I, 530, no. 311). He is mentioned in the account of the Lord of Nithsdale in Goodall, Bk.XIV, ch.52 (II, 404).
243, l.30. *Marginal note: Manuscript*: Maitland, pp45-6.

244, l.18. *Craigis*: probably an error for 'creeks' (A2 and other texts).
244, l.22. *Lochrye*: Lochryan in Galloway.
244, ll.29-30. *the Turks*: the infidels as in A2 and the other texts. HP, p249, says that he was invited, his fame having spread, in this agreeing with Boece. *Marginal note: Buchanan*, Bk.IX, fol.102v.; *Boece, fol.236*: Bk.XVI, ch.9, fol.236v. (1536); fol.334 (1574).
244, l.34-245, l.8. HP, p250, omits the first version of this story.
244, l.34. *Marginal note*: Manuscr*ipt*: Maitland, p47, says the Duke of Spruse preferred him to all other chiefs, and does not call him Lord of Danskin, nor does Hol*inshed*, *SC,* p365.
245, l.1. *Clifforde*: Thomas de Clifford, 6th Lord Clifford (*CP*, III, 292).
245, l.9. *the manuscript seemith to say*: Maitland, 47-9.
245, l.21. *Marginal note: Boece, Bk.XVI, fol.236*: 1536, ch.9, fol.236v. or 1574, fol.334v. are Hume's source; 1531, ch.9, says only that Clifford killed him treacherously.
245, l.34-246, l.2 *sure it is... monument foresaid*: an account of the Scots colony in Danzig from the 15th Century may be found in Th. A. Fischer, *The Scots in Eastern and Western Prussia* (Edinburgh, 1903), but there is no mention there of the Douglas arms or of 'little Scotland'.
246, ll.13-14. *how fare even til he conquisit the verie style of a Prince and Duke*: A2 ('even so farre till he purchas...') makes the sense clear.
246, l.16. *about the zeirs 1389 or 1390*: according to Fraser, I, 358, Nithsdale drew rents from Dumfries for 1392 and probably died in 1392.

The Life of Archibald, the Grim, 3rd Earl (A, pp262-273)

1388-1400

1633, pp126-132, follows A2 closely apart from the praise of the Earl's loyalty to his friends and the illustration of his quarrel with the Earl of March on behalf of the laird of Redpath.

HP, pp252-266, reorders the material of 1633, while preserving much of its phrasing, and adds a great deal of extraneous material, not only matters of pedigree. It has pp255-257 twice over, with p257 as an insertion.

1644, pp111-114, abridges 1633, with some vigorous phrasing of its own.

247, l.5. *Archbald his brother*: He was in fact illegitimately his father's cousin. For Fraser's correction of Hume's muddle over

the three Archibalds, see headnote to Archibald Lord of Galloway.
247, ll.7-8. *Holinsyde wrangouslie calleth him his Cousine*: Holinshed says that Archibald, Lord of Galloway, was cousin of James, the 2nd Earl of Douglas (*SC*, p304).
247, ll.8-9. *Androw Murray Governour of Scotland*: 'sisters son to King Robert Bruce' (1633. p126, 1644, p111); HP, p252, gives his daughter's name, Anna, and her maternal descent. Andrew Murray, Lord of Bothwell, had married Christian Bruce, Robert I's sister (Nicholson, *Ed III*, p92, n.6). Against Hume and Fraser, I, 352, *SP*, III, 161-63, maintains that Archibald the Grim married Joanna, the widow of Thomas Moray Lord of Bothwell, and got possession of all the lands of which she was liferentrix.
247, l.12. *twa sonnes*: HP, p252, gives details of William's lands and Archibald's marriage. In fact Archibald had two legitimate sons, Archibald Tyneman and Gross James. Wiliam was an illegitimate son and became known as the Lord of Nithsdale. Fraser, I, 355 See also p257, ll.6-7.
247, l.14. *Marjorie*: 'married to David Prince of Scotland' (1633, p126, and 1644, p111), the Duke of Rothesay. HP, p253 places at this point the story, not to be found in A but in 1633, p131, as part of the concluding eulogy, of Douglas's quarrel with George Dunbar, Earl of March. See note to p255, l.9.
247, l.30. ^The state of the Countree^ has been inserted in the margin
247, l.35-248, l.1. *died... the 10 of April*: 1633, p127, HP, p253, and 1644, p111, give '19 April'; so also *SP*, I, 15, and Nicholson, p202. 13 May, according to Goodall, Bk.XIV, ch.56 (II, 415) and *DNB*.
248, ll.2-3. *a truce taine in hope of peace*: See Holinshed, *EC*, p466, for three year truce between England, France and Scotland.
248, l.7-249, l.29. *The King his alone... Duk of Albanie*: 1644, p111, omits this passage, apart from the information about the accession of Robert III, and (pp111-12) vigorously abridges the account on pp248-250, ll.30.-8 of the rejection of the title of Duke.
248, ll.21-25. *Robert Earle of Fyfe*: Robert III's younger brother, had been made guardian by Robert II in 1388.
249, ll.1-3. *the battle of the Thirties*: the famous staged battle on the North Inch at Perth between 30 of the Clan Chattan and 30 of the Clan Kay, 28 September, 1396 (Bower, Bk.XV, ch3; Nicholson, p208).
249, l.3. HP, p254-256, inserts the chivalric story (in Boece, Bk.XVI, ch.10, and Holinshed, *SC*, 366) of the jousting of the Earl of Crawford and the English Lord Welles on London Bridge, with the excuse that Crawford was the particular friend of William, Archibald the Grim's father. See Bower, Bk.XV, chs. 4 and 5.
249, l.4. *Marginal note, Blak Buik of Scone 1398*: Bower, Bk.XV,

ch.4.
249, ll.6-9. *Lord Houstoun*: Sir James Douglas of Strabroke was laird of Hughston in Strabrock (*SP*, VI, 343). *Sir Robert Morlay*: See Bower, vol.8, Bk.XV, ch.4, note, p153, 'perhaps... the son and heir of Thomas, Lord Morley, 1379-1416'; Watt adds that the joust had not taken place by 25 April,1398, in the spite of Bower's dating. Boece, Bk.XVI, ch.11, and Holinshed, *SC*, p366, tell of the coming of Sir Robert but not of his jousting with Douglas of Strabroke.
249, ll.11-12 *Pomferston, Pittindrich, Earls-milne... Caldercleare*: Pomferston, near Mid Calder, Midlothian; Pittindreich, near Elgin; Calderclear or West Calder in West Lothian. I cannot place Earls-milne. HP, p256-257, is even more circumstantial concerning this branch of the Douglas connection.
249, l.29-251, l.7. This passage continues the scorn for titles expressed in the life of William, Lord of Nithsdale. The creation of titles imitated the chivalric fashions of the court of Richard II (Nicholson, p214). Archibald the Grim's rejection of a dukedom is recorded by Buchanan, Bk.X, fol.103v. *Marginal note*: I cannot find a reference in Boece to Archibald's refusing a Dukedom.
249, l.32. *eivine him thereto*: i.e. probably as Priscilla Bawcutt suggests, 'think him entitled to it'. Cf. *DOST,* 'evin' appraise, compare.
250, ll.12-13. *bot also do*: The reading is uncertain; the unusual uninflected third person plural could refer back to 'names of dignitie'.
250, l.13. *And we shall see*: this certainly suggests that it was planned to follow the publication of the volume on the house of Douglas with one on the house of Angus. The story may be found in the Life of Archibald, 7th Earl of Angus, 1644, pp274-275; also in *The Book of Pluscarden*, ed. Felix J. M. Skene (Edinburgh, 1880), II, 254. The Queen Regent is Mary of Guise, James V's wife.
251, l.8. *the nixt zeir*: 1398 (as Holinshed, marginal note).
251, l.8. *Marginal note*: Holinshed, *SC,* p366.
251, l.23. *Maijorie (or Marie) Douglas*: Marjorie, married in 1400 (Fraser, I, 347).
251, ll.26-27. *gaite infeftement of the hail annuels besouth the Forth*: 'all the rents and revenues which belonged to the King on the South side of the Forth' (1644, p112), a detail not recorded in Fraser.
251, l.29-30. *new made Duk of Albanie*: on 28 April, 1398 (Nicholson, p214).
252, l.8. *Marginal note*: Holinshed,*SC*, p366; Boece, Bk.XVI, ch.12; Buchanan, Bk.X, fol.104.
252, ll.13-14. *in suspense*: 'to be judged of others' (1644, p112); HP, p260, omits this mild doubt of a Douglas's motives.

252, ll.24-27. HP, p260, omits this expression of surprise at the Governor's allowing the marriage.
252, l.8. *Marginal note*: Boece, Bk.XVI, ch.12; Buchanan and Holinshed as above; Maior, Bk.VI, ch.7.
253, l.8. *contempt*: 'rufle and disgrace' (1644, p113).
253, ll.12. *Robert Metlane*: Robert Maitland of Thirlestane was the son of John Maitland of Thirlestane and Agnes, daughter of Patrick Dunbar and sister of George Dunbar (see *SP*, III, 261, V, 284-5). On Hume's erroneous reckoning, William, 1st Earl of Douglas, married Margaret of Dunbar, which, if she was a sister of George Dunbar, would make Robert Maitland a cousin of Archibald the Grim (see note to pp178-83, ll.15-13). But there seems to have been no such Margaret (*SP*, III, 260-62)
253, ll.22-23. *having receivit his Wife and Childrein with the most inward of his freinds*: i.e. he left his wife and children with his most trusted kinsmen. 1644, p113, however says that he went to England accompanied with his wife, children and kinsmen. 1644 agrees with Buchanan, of whose account of the quarrel with the Earl of March Hume's is almost a translation.
253, l.26. *Marginal note*: Holinshed, *SC*, p366; Boece, Bk.XVI, ch.12; Buchanan, Bk.X, fol.104.
254, ll.4-8. The reflection on private and public agreements is from Buchanan, Bk.X, fol.104.
254, l.16. *going to Pople*: Papple. This expedition took place in 1400, before Henry IV's invasion pp258-61.
254, l.17. *Markit*: 'Markil(l)' (1633, p130, 1644, p113); 'Martell' (HP, p262). Markle, like Traprain, Hailes, East Linton and Papple, is between Haddington and Dunbar (see Bower, vol.8, Bk.XV, ch.10, notes, p163).
254, l.21. *Pencraik*: Pencraig hill (Bower, XV, ch.10), near East Linton, East Lothian.
254, ll.25-26. *the Manuscript and Blak Buike of Scone*: Maitland, p42; Bower, Bk.15, ch.10.
254, l.30. *Sir Thomas Coulbooth*: Sir Thomas Talbot, according to Bower, Bk.XV, ch.10 (see note to l.67, p163).
254, l.32. *Boetius*: Bk.XVI, ch.12.
255, ll.2, 10. *Marginal note*: Buchanan, Bk.X, fol.105: '*Nam ut per Duglassium rei militaris splendor, per Tralium ecclesiastica auctoritas, et veteris disciplinae qualiscunque imago stetit, ita ab Regina incolumni aulae dignitas est sustentata*'. Cf. Bower, Bk.XV, ch12. Queen Annabel died in 1401.
255, l.4. *1400*: '1401 or thereby' (HP, p262). Archibald the Grim died on Christmas Eve, 1400 (Nicholson, p220).
255, l.4-5. *to the great losse thereof*: 1644, p114, says the country was destitute of commanders. *he is buried in Bothuel with his wife*: 'which they founded as in the Queir thairof thair armes doe testifie' (HP, p262). HP, pp262-263, gives an account of the murder of David, the heir apparent, by the Duke of Albany and

Robert III's consequent sending of James, his other son, to France for protection, only to have him captured by the English on the way, material dealt with in the other texts (and by HP again) in the life of Archibald, 4th Earl of Douglas.

255, l.10. *Marginal note*: Maior, Bk.VI, ch.7; Holinshed, *SC*, p367.

255, l.12. 1633, p131, adds to his other virtues 'francknesse and reall kindnesse to his friends and dependars' and illustrates with the story (an example of the way manrent might work to the benefit of the dependant) of how Douglas protected the Laird of Ridpath from the oppression of the Earl of March and supplies a letter, supposedly in Douglas's hand. HP, p253, telling the story at the outset of the life, adds to 1633's assertion that the family still enjoy the estate, the information that the estate has only recently passed out of the family through marriage. 1644, p114, tells the story in an abridged form without the letter.

255, l.21. *Marginal note*: Buchanan, Bk.X, fol.104: '*vir nulli maiorum in quovis genere laudis inferior*'; Boece, Bk. XVI, ch.12. Maior, as above.

255, ll.33-34. *he foundit the College of Bothuel*: HP, p265, gives details of the foundation in a letter to the 'richt noble and potent Marquese... of Dowglas, inserted to replace the scored out pp264-66.

256, l.1. *changit it in a College of Clerks*: Boece, Bk.XVI, ch.12, (1531, 1536) says that it was changed, not that Archibald the Grim changed it; but Boece, Bk.XVI, fol.337v. (1574), and Bower, Bk.XV, ch.11, say he did. HP, p265, says that his son Archibald Tyneman turned it into a college of priests. See also HP, Life of Archibald, 4th Earl, p301 (below, p294, l.28, note).

The Life of Archibald Tyneman, 4th Earl of Douglas (A, pp274-323)

1400-24

A more or less translates Buchanan's account of the Battle of Baugé (as Holinshed had done) with additions from other sources. The rest, though frequently indebted to Buchanan, as to others, is digested and recast.

1633, pp132-55, apart from a digression on the French king's Scots Guard, follows A2 closely.

HP, pp267-302, accords with 1633, with digressions and insertions and some more definite information and differences in dating. Where different material is being worked in, the page is frequently written in another hand or a piece in another hand is pasted in or simply interleaved. HP is, I believe, based on 1633 (see Introduction, ppxxx-xxxiii), though with variations in phrasing and some differences of factual detail, and into it later hands worked additions. Some of these anyway must have been written after 1633 was published (see note to p270, l.3, on Archibald Tyneman's portrait). None give evidence of having been written after the 11th Earl and 1st Marquis's time.

1644, pp114-33, follows 1633, abridging in places and rephrasing, sometimes with advantage, but not always quite accurately.

257, ll.7-8. *his second sone*: Archibald Tyneman was Archibald the Grim's first son. See note to p247, l.12, for the sons of Archibald the Grim. *Marginal note: Boe. lib. 16, cap.14*, should be Boece, Bk.XVI, ch. 12, who says that an elder brother, William, had died.
257, l.12. ^George Earle of Angus his uncle having marryed Maria the eldest, as is testifyed at more lenth in his owne life^ has been inserted in the margin.
257, l.13. *the kirk of Lincloudin*: Lincluden College or Abbey by Dumfries.
257, ll.16-18. 1644, p114, has a translation.
257, ll.20-21. *Archbald, to whom Thomas Fleming Earle of Wigtoun*: Archibald the Grim purchased the Earldom from him in 1372 (Nicholson, p.203).
257, ll.23-24. *James... callit Gros James*: was in fact the second son of Archibald the Grim and brother of Archibald Tyneman.
257, l.25. *twa doughters*: Fraser, I, 398-400, thinks he had only one, Elizabeth, who married (1) John Stewart, Earl of Buchan, killed at Verneuil, (2) Thomas Stewart, illegitimate son of Alexander, Earl of Mar, and (3) William Sinclair, 3rd Earl of Orkney.
257, ll.29-32. *this same Duk... Nethsdail*: 1644, p115, omits. As Archibald, Lord of Galloway, was in fact Archibald the Grim, the Lord of Nithsdale was Archibald Tyneman's illegitimate brother and so William Sinclair would have married a cousin of his mother, if Hume's report of the marriage had been true.
257, l.32-258, l.1. *Earle of Buchan*: John Stewart,'second sonne to Robert the Governour, after Constable of France' A2, HP, p267, 1633, p133, 1644, p115.
258, ll.2-3. *Stewartoun, Ormishugh and Dunlope*: Stewarton, Ormsheuch and Dunlop are in Cunningham (Fraser, I, 380-1); *Trabayage*: Trabuyage, according to the other texts, is in Carrick (Fraser, I, 380).
258, l.4. *Marginal note*: Boece does not call him Tyneman.
258, ll.6-7. *the auld manuscript of the Laird of Leidingtonne*: Sir Richard Maitland's MS history of the house of Douglas, usually referred to as 'the manuscript', p15.
258, ll.10-11. *ane battle aganes the Percie*: Homildon.

258, ll.20-21. *in the moneth of August... in the 1400 zeir*: According to tradition, Archibald the Grim did not die until 24 December (but see Bower, vol.8, 163, note 1).
258, l.22-261, l.11. Henry IV's invasion of Scotland of 1400.
258, l.24. **[276]** is mispaginated **[278]** and the rest of the pagination follows in sequence.
258, l.24-59, l.10. At this time David, Duke of Rothesay, was royal lieutenant and more in charge of affairs than Robert, Duke of Albany, 'the Governour' (Nicholson p220-222). Tyneman was in command of Edinburgh Castle. Buchanan, Bk.X, fol.104v, tells the reason for the Governor's dilatoriness, but not the tale of the rewarding of the herald. *Caldermure*: Calder Moor in West Lothian. *Marginal note*: Maior, Bk. VI, ch.7; Maitland, p50.
259, ll.14-15. *Johne Remorgeny*: the Duke of Rothesay's chamberlain; Robert III wished to have his son restrained (Nicholson, pp.216-21).
259, l.20. *William Lindsay*: of Rossie (Nicholson, p221).
259, ll.24-29. Note that Hume would have liked to find the interest of Remorgeny's plot, not just in the light it shed on the workings of past political actions, but in the way it furnished a prudential moral example of political scheming. It is in the implicit moral that Hume finds the life of history. 1644, p116, does not make a connection between the causes of actions and their moral exemplariness.
260, ll.7-11. *the Blak buik of Scone*: *semi-scotus de sanguine Cuminensi*: Bower, Bk.XV, ch.11 ('<Cwminiem>'); Brechin MS, 'Cumynensium'). 'Henry's mother Blanche was a daughter of Henry earl and duke of Lancaster by Isabel, a daughter of Henry de Beaumont and by Alicia Comyn, heiress of the Comyn earls of Buchan' (Bower, vol.8, 164, note 40-41). 1633, p134, HP, p269 and 1644, p116, have '*Cumini*'; Brechin MS, has 'Cuminiensium'.
P260, l.13-14. *some of their great men*: Nicholson thinks 'they' was probably the duke of Rothesay (p219).
260, l.19. *sayes the manuscript*: Maitland, pp49-50.
260, l.25-261, l.6. On Henry IV's mildness, see Buchanan, Bk.X, fol.104v. *the second humanitie... that ever king of that nation kythit towards Scotismen*: possibly the first was Edward the Confessor's sheltering Malcolm Canmore, who according to Boece, *'ab eo regio honore acceptus est'* (BkXII, fol.250). HP, pp269-270, 1633, p134, and 1644, p116, omit this sour observation. *vsing the prisonners not... cruellie*: A2 omits 'not'; this may have been a slip, for 1633 retains it, while following A2 in omitting 'the... Scotismen'
261, ll.2-3. *as a token of being in wil*: i.e. 'as a token of being in Henry IV's power'.
261, ll.6-11. Though Maitland, author of the Manuscript is a Scots historian, he is an exception to the extent that (pp49-50) he

says Henry's plan was to subdue all Scotland (not that he wasted the land) and in this in agreement with the English historians, but he adds that in this intention 'he was not onlie frustratit, bot also returnit hame agane with grit lose of his Men and armye to his grit dishonour and shame'. 1644, p116, says that it will follow Maitland's account of Henry's intentions.

261, l.15. *Marginal note*: should read Boece, Bk.XVI, ch.13.

261, l.31. *Marginal note*: Maior, Bk.VI, ch.7; Boece, Bk.XVI, ch.14.

261, l.34-62, l.6. *1401*: The Battle of Nesbit Muir was fought on 22 June 1402 (Nicholson, p223).

262, ll.1-2. *George Dunbar eldest sone to the Earle of Marche*: later 11 Earl of Dunbar (*SP*, III, 276-77).

262, l.4. *Marginal note*: Maitland. p50, says that Tyneman 'luiffit [Hepburn] ewin as his awin persoun'.

262, l.7-264, l.9. The account of Homildon follows Boece fairly closely.

262, ll.17. *Murdok Stewart:* succeeded his father as 2nd Duke of Albany and was Governor of Scotland from 1420 to 1424.

262, ll.18-20. *George Earle of Angus*: George, first Douglas Earl of Angus, the son of William, 1st Earl of Douglas, from whom Hume numbers the Earls of Angus (see note to pp178-83, ll.15-13, and 1644, p208). *Thomas Earl of Murray*: Thomas Dunbar, 2nd Earl of Moray (*SP*, VI, 302). *Johne Dumbar, the Earle of Merches owne brother*: John, brother of the exiled George, 10th Earl of Dunbar and 4th or 5th Earl of March, had been Earl of Moray, but in February 1591/92 his son Thomas succeeded him, so that he cannot have been on this campaign (*SP*, III, 260). *Marginal note*: Maior, Bk.VI, ch.7, mentions dead and captured, not the muster.

262, l.27. *Milfeild*: North of Wooler in Northumberland.

262, l.29. *Homildoun*: Humbleton by Wooler.

262, l.32. *Marginal note*: For Blak buik of Scone, see Bower, Bk.XV, ch.14.

262, ll.34-35. *fielding pieces*: an anachronism, if artillery is meant, since field guns were not in use until the 16th Century.

263, l.3. *vnles he war overthrowen with schot of the Enemie*: i.e. 'without being... Enemy'.

263, ll.10-11. *Adam Gordoun, and Johne Swintoun*: For the story of how the deadly enemies, Adam Gordon (*SP*, IV, 516-17) and Sir John Swinton of Swinton (*SP*, I, 149) were reconciled on the field of battle see Bower.

263, ll.18-19. *the Blak buike of Scone*: Bower, Bk.XV, ch.14.

263, l.23-264, l.24. This list can be found in Bower, Bk. XV, ch.14; I am indebted to Watt's notes. *Johne Livingstoun of Callender*: See *SP*, V, 425. *Alexander Ramsay of Dalhousie*: Sir Alexander Ramsay, great grand nephew of the Alexander Ramsay of Dalhousie killed by the Lord of Liddesdale (*SP*, III, 90).

Robert Eskin of Alloway: Robert Erskine, son of Thomas Erskine of Alloa, who married Mary Douglas, daughter of the Lord of Liddesdale, also captured (*SP*, V, 598, 601). *James Douglas maister of Dalkeith*: 1633, p136, and HP, p271, but not 1644, p118, say that he became Earl of Morton, (it was in fact his grandson who was made Earl of Morton). *SP*, VI, 350, says nothing about his capture. *and his twa brethren Johne and William*: in Bower, Bk XV, ch.14, the two brothers who accomapany him are called James and William (see also, *SP*, VI, 348-50). *George Leslie of Rothes*: not recorded as taken at Homildon in *SP*, VII, 271-73. *Patrik Dumbar of Beil*: brother of George, Earl of March (*SP*, III, 260). *George Earl of Angus*: died of the plague according to Bower, or *the Blak booke of Scone*, Bk.XV, ch.14, but not 1644, p208. *Alexander Hume of Dunglas*: died at Verneuil, 1424 (see *SP*, IV, 444-45; below p287, ll.9-24).

264, ll.6-9. *Rude-day or (as vthers wryte) the 5 of May, in the zeir 1401 or 1402* and *Marginal note*: 1403, according to Boece, Bk.XVI, ch.13, and Holinshed, *SC*, p369; 1402, according to Maitland (p52); 7th May 1401 according to Buchanan, Bk.X, fol.104v. 14 September, 1402 (Nicholson, p223). *Rude day*: the Exaltation of the Cross, 14 September.

264, ll.16-26. The Duke of Rothesay had died in March 1402, half a year before Homildon. Tyneman and Albany were examined by a general council, but were exonerated by a letter from Robert III (Nicholson, p222). *The blak buike of Scone*: Bower, Bk. XV, ch.12.

264, l.34. *Marginal note*: Maior, Bk.VI, ch.7, says that Rothesay cast off all prudence and that Tyneman helped to imprison him (Cf. Bower, Bk.XV, ch.12).

265, ll.15-20. Cf. the passage on the life of history, p259, ll.24-28. 1644, p118, omits the reflection on history.

265, ll.24-30. A moral absent from its place in the summary at the end of the life of Archibald the Grim, where it would detract from the tone of panegyric. *any thing never so apparentlie, ever carefully*: the sense seems to be 'though with never so plausible an appearance, and never so carefully undertaken'; 'ever' may be the result of a scribal tinkering with 'over', which makes less sense and less syntactical symmetry.

266, l.25. *Marginal note*: Holinshed, *EC*, p523.

267, ll.1-6. 1644, p119, omits the details of the carving up of England between the three.

267, l.9. *Marginal note*: should be Boece, Bk.XVI, ch.14.

267, l.35-268, l.1. *(who was laitlie retirit to the Kings syde)*: He had left Percy for Henry when Tyneman was taken in by that earl (Nicholson, p224).

268, l.6. *Earle of Staffurde*: Edmund, Earl of Stafford (*CP*, XII, 180-1).

268, l.18. *Sir Thomas Blount*: Sir Walter Blount, according to

Bower, Bk.XV, ch,17, and Holinshed, *EC*, 523. But this Sir Walter did not die at Shrewsbury, according to James Hamilton Wylie, *History of England under Henry the Fourth*, 4 vols. (London, 1884-98), III, 275.

269, l.3. *Marginal note*: Maitland, p53.

269, l.12. *Marginal note*: Holinshed, *EC*, p523.

269, ll.17-24. *They sits ful stil, that hes a reiven breik*: Cf. Fergusson, 44. The proverb is in Boece (1536), Bk.XVI, ch.14, but not in either Holinshed, *EC*, or *SC*; *EC,* p523, says he 'brake one of his cullions' falling from a precipice in hasty retreat. *vsurpit*: cf. '*Metaphora vtitur vulgari, & cui non vsurpata?*' (Hume, *Apologia Basilica* [Paris, 1626], p40).

269, l.26. *Marginal note*: Holinshed, *EC,* p523.

270, l.3. ^His picture^ has been inserted in the margin. HP, p276, has an insertion pasted in saying that the Marquis of Douglas bought the portrait 'at a very hye rate' when, owing to the 'iniquities of the tyme', Charles I's collection of pictures was sold by the Commonwealth between 1649 and 1652/3 (Godfrey Davies, *The Early Stuarts: 1603-1660*, [Oxford, 1959], p377). The picture shows him with a Scots wool cap and written above his head, 'Archbald Earle of Douglas called black'; he is wearing about his neck his father's order of the Cockle won at Poitiers. A (p189, ll.30-31) and HP, p205, say that William, 1st Earl of Douglas won the Order of the Cockle at Poitiers, but Archibald the Grim, Archibald Tyneman's father, was apparently present there (A [p190, ll.4-11]; HP, p206), though Hume thinks he was another Archibald. But in any case, this portrait seems to be the one reproduced by courtesy of the owner as frontispiece to volume 2, said to be of the 3rd Earl of Douglas, Archibald the Grim, but adjudged by the Burlington Fine Art Club in 1909, according to a note on the back of the painting, to be of the 9th and last Earl of Douglas and painted by Bernardino de Conti. 'The subject wears, [not the order of the Cockle, but] the order of St Michael, which order was founded in 1469'. *Marginal note*: Buchanan, Bk.X, fol. 105v.

270, l.7. *Marginal note*: Maitland, p54.

270, l.11. *the Magdalene day*: The Battle of Shrewsbury was fought on the 21 July, 1403.

270, l.12. *the death of King Robert the Thrid*: 1633, p139 gives no date; 1406 (HP, p276); 1408 (1644, p121) 4th April, 1406 (Nicholson, p227).

270, l.22. *Marginal note*: Blak booke of Scone (Bower, Bk. XV, ch.21), makes clear that it is Lochmaben Castle and lands (not Dunbar) that were made over to Tyneman. See also Watt's note to ll.15-21, vol.8, 182. Holinshed, *SC*, p372. Boece, Bk.XVI, ch.16.

271, ll.2-3. *nather obtene anie subsidie of him for the honorable enterteinment of his Estate*: In fact Henry heaped rewards on him (Nicholson, p230).

271, ll.7-9. *the Blake buik of Scone*: Bower Bk. XV, ch.21, ll.18-19, says that *Walter Halyburtoun* of Dirleton was *gener tunc Gubernatoris*, i.e. he had married Isobel, Countess of Ross, daughter of Robert, Duke of Albany.
271, l.13. *Birgem*: 'Bridgem in the Merse' (HP, p276). Birgham, near Kelso (Bower, vol.8, 182).
271, ll.15-17. 1633, p140, and 1644, p121, say that the Earl of March was restored one or two years after the Earl of Douglas was set at liberty and that it is with this that Holinshead is in accord. If Holinshed's 'shortly after' (*SC*, p372) means 'one or two years', 1633 and 1644 are correct about Holinshed (HP, p277, simply says 'after'). In fact Dunbar was restored in 1409, perhaps as a move of Albany's to counteract Douglas power (Nicholson, p231). Tyneman was nominally captive until 1413, but visited Scotland on parole several times (Fraser, I, 372ff.).
271, ll.17-29. Holinshed, *SC*, p370, says only that Henry tenderly cherished Douglas, not that he gave him his liberty; *EC*, p523, says wrongly that he was 'for his valiantnesse, of the King frankelie and freelie deliuered'. The quotation from Holinshed, is from *SC*. p372. *liers had neid of a guid memorie*: cf. *'opportet mendacem esse memorem'*, p323, ll.9-10.
272, l.9. *Marginal note*: Boece (1531, 1536), Bk.XVI, ch.14 speaks only of Douglas's valour not of Henry's blighted generosity, but 1574, fol.339, speaks of Henry's benevolence in saving him..
272, ll.5-10. *bot the rute... true magnificence*: HP, p277 omits this passage. For '*kythit*', A2 and 1633, p140, have 'cho(a)kt(e)', which makes easier sense. The sense of A is perhaps that although Henry showed the fruit of princely magnificence in the bud (sparing Douglas's life and honouring his bravery), he bore him a grudge which prevented the bud coming to the fruit of generosity.
272, l.31-275, l.2. All the verses are from Samuel Daniel's *The Civil Wars* , the first set from *The first foure Bookes of the ciuile wars* (London, 1595), the second from *The Civile Wars* (London, 1609). After the first stanza from Daniel ^Hol. Eng. Chron. pag. 523^ has been insertedin the margin.
275, l.4. 1633, pp140-141, and 1644, p123 (after the stanzas from Samuel Daniel), insert notice of an indenture between Henry and Douglas, in which Douglas in 1407 makes various pledges for friendly behaviour to England on his being allowed to return to Scotland, a sign that Henry honoured him by thinking him a formidable enemy. HP, p277, transcribes the indenture, which it says the Marquis of Douglas 'used moyeon to buy' 'at ane hye rate' from Starky a servant of Sir Robert Cotton the antiquary. A 17th century copy of the Indenture, but not the original, from the Hamilton Palace collection, may be found in the National Register of Archives (Scotland), GD 406/2 (2177) NRA(S) bundle 452. Nicholson, p230, says that Tyneman did not return at Easter 1409

as the Indenture required, perhaps owing to involvement with the negotiations for the Earl of March's return.

275, l.12. *sent him to France*: 20 March, 1404, according to HP, p280, which then gives a circumstantial account of the journey and the capture of James, followed by Robert III's letter to Henry IV out of Boece, Bk.XVI, ch.15. The Duke of Rothesay died in March 1402 (Nicholson, p221). Moves for sending James to France began in 1405, so Hume's account telescopes events. James was captured off Flamborough Head, 14 March, 1406 (Nicholson, p226-227).

275, l.14. *Marginal note*: Robert III died in 1406, as Boece, Bk. XVI, ch.16, has it, though Holinshed, *SC*, p372, says it was in 1408. 'An. 1411' refers to Percy and a new conspiracy.

275, l.16-276, l.12. 1644, p124, omits 'The reset of the Percie... in King James the first his tyme'. After Shrewsbury, Hotspur's son Henry took refuge in Scotland (Nicholson, p226). HP, p282, omits the sentence on the profession of letters at St Andrews. The University of St Andrews was formally founded by Papal bull in 1414; James was released in 1424. The summary of events follows Boece, Bk.XVI, ch.16.

275, ll.18-19. *ane expedition made be the king of England's sone*: In 1405, the Prince of Wales led a raid into Scotland (Wylie, *Henry the Fourth*, II, 275). This expedition is not mentioned in Bower, Holinshed, or Boece, but in Buchanan, Bk.X, fol.106.

275, ll.21. *the taking of the Castle Jedwart*: 7 May 1409 (Nicholson, p231).

275, l.27. *the taking of Fast Castle*: Fast Castle North of St Abb's Head was taken by Patrick Dunbar, 4th son of the Earl of Dunbar (*SP*, III, 274).

275, ll.31-32. *Cashogill, Killivaran, Pingirie, Davine &c in Nethsdail*: Coshogle on the Enterkin Burn, Killiewarren and Pinzarie on the Shimell Water and Dalveen. See Craufurd Tait Ramage, *Drumlanrig Castle and the Douglases* (Dumfries, 1876), p80.

276, ll.3-4. *sone to Alexander (the governours zounger brother)*: the illegitimate son of Alexander Stewart, Earl of Buchan.

276, ll.5-6. *wha had by some subtilitie of law taine the Earldome of Ros*: for the contest between Albany and Donald, Lord of the Isles over the succession to the earldom of Ross, see Nicholson, pp233-35; see also note to p338, ll.12-29, below.

276, ll.8-12. ^The Vniversitie at St Androis first founded^ inserted in margin.

276, l.17. *Marginal note*: Maitland, p54.

276, ll.24-28. *Some write... William Douglas and Gawin Dumbar*: according to Bower, Bk.XV, ch.23, it was Sir William de Douglas of Drumlanrig and Sir Gavin de Dunbar, who burnt Roxburgh in 1411; for the first, see note to p209, l.22; Gavin Dunbar was the second son of the Earl of March. So also Boece,

Bk.XVI, ch.17. Who the 'some' are who attribute the burning to Tyneman and the Earl of March, I cannot discover. They did beseige Roxburgh Castle unsuccessfully in the Foul Raid (see p278, ll.18-19).

277, l.4. *Marginal note*: Buchanan, Bk.X, fol.106v.

277, l.7. *Marginal note*: Maitland, p55.

277, l.10. *Pennor*: Penrith (HP, p282). In 1415, according to Bower, Bk.XV, ch.23.

277, l.20-282 l.25. The account of the Scots expedition to France is more or less a translation of Buchanan, Bk.X, fol.107-107v.

277, l.30. *Bourges on Berry*: Bourges en Berry.

277, l.33. *the Earle of Vendosme*: Louis de Bourbon, Count of Vendome, Great Chamberlain of France, was taken prisoner by the English at Agincourt, 1416 (*Dictionnaire de Biographie Française*, VI, cols. 1404-1405) and was not released until 1424; in consequence he cannot have been sent on this mission to Scotland.

278, ll.4-5. *of voluntary*: i.e. 'voluntarily'; possibly 'of voluntare'.

278, ll.7-8. *Johne Earle of Buchan*: See above, p276, ll.7-8, note.

278, l.13. *as testifies the Blak buik of Scone*: Bower, Bk.XV, ch.24.

278, ll.18-19. *the foule reede*; 1417, see Bower, Bk.XV, ch.24.

278, l.20. *Botlehauche*: probably Battlehaugh (Watt). *Johne Hardy and Thomas Smyth*: See Bower, Bk.XV, ch.23. According to Watt, Bower, vol.8, 187, neither the place nor the persons can be identified.

278, l.24. *Sir William*: Crawford (Bower, Bk.XV, ch. 24; see also note, vol.8, p.190, on this puzzling transaction). The other texts omit this less than glorious beseiging.

278, l.26. *Blak buik of Scone, Caput 32.*: HP, p283, has '23'. See Bower, Bk.XV, ch.32.

278, l.28. *Aevelles*: Alnwick, Bower, Bk.XV, ch.32.

278, ll.30-33. The Earl of Wigtown crossed into France in 1419; the Battle of Baugé took place in 1421 (Nicholson, pp250-51).

279, ll.10-13. *another sone of the Governours, to name Robert*: Robert, son of Robert Duke of Albany, later killed at Verneuil (SP, I, 148; see below, p286, ll.34-35). *Alexander Lyndsay brother to the Earle of Crafurde*: There was no brother of David, 1st Earl of Crawford, called Alexander, and David's son Alexander, later 2nd Earl, could not have been at Verneuil with Archibald Tyneman (see pp286, l.34, and p295, l.11) because he was named as a hostage for James I in December 1423 (Brown, *James I,* p31); nor does *SP*, III, 17, suggest that he was in France at the time of the earlier campaign. Hume might conceivably have confused him with another Alexander Lindsay, son of Sir William Lindsay, Lord of the Byres (*SP*, V, 392). *Thomas (or rather Johne) Swintoun knights*: HP, scores out the parenthesis and in a marginal note on p285 (A [p281, l.25]) says that John Swinton, Thomas's father, had been killed at Homildon. According to Watt's note to Bower, vol.8, 203, n.46, he was John, son of the John Swinton killed at Homildon (see p263, l.25). For this list of those who ccompanied Archibald, Earl of Wigtown, to France see Boece (1574) fols.343v. and 344v.

279, l.11. *Marginal note*: Boece, Bk. XVI, ch.18; Holinshed, *SC*, p374.

279, l.16. *Chastillion in Turain*: Châtillon in Touraine.

279, l.20. *Duk of Clarence*: Thomas of Lancaster, brother of Henry V.

279, ll.22-23. *Country of Angeirs*: Anjou. Buchanan, Bk.X, fol.107, puts the wasting in the imperfect (*'populabatur'),* not the future. Holinshed, *EC, p579,* says the wasting took place before the battle of Baugé.

279, ll.25-26. *Vieille Baugé*: Vieil Baugé, near Angers.

279, ll.30-31. *as vthers say*: Bower, Bk.XV, ch.33, says that a truce had been agreed on.

280, l.1. *Androw Frogosa*: Fragosa (HP, p284, 1633, p145); Fregosa (1644, p126). Holinshed, *EC*, p579, credits 'Forgusa' with the intelligence; Robert Gaguin, *De francorum rebus gestis annales* (Paris, 1528), Bk.IX, fol.CCVI, the Scottish prisoners.

280, l.12. *Sir Thomas Beauforde*: in fact Edmund Beaufort, later Earl of Somerset on his brother John's death (Bower, Bk.XV, ch.33; see note, vol.8, p204). Hume follows Holinshed, *EC*, 579.

280, ll.14-15. *of Fraisnie le Vicomte*: Fresnay-le-Comté, near Alençon; omitted in the other texts. The English had just defeated a Franco-Scottish army attempting to deliver Fresnay-le-Comté from siege (Francisque-Michel, I, 118). The Portuguese captains are presumably members of the English multi-national army, though Hume, following Holinshed, expresses himself confusingly.

280, l.31. *Hugh Kennedie*: 'of Dunure of whom are discended the Lord Kennedie and the Earles of Cassills' (HP, p285). 'Apparently a son of Sir Gilbert Kennedy of Dunnure' (Bower, vol.8, note, p203, n.38).

281, ll.15-18. *(whilk the Frenchmen... Spanziards)*: HP, p285, and 1644, p126, omit. The reflection is taken from Buchanan, Bk.X, 107v.

281, l.35. *Sir Johne Swintoune*: see note to p279, ll.12-13.

281, ll.30-33. *the Earle... to the ground*: HP, pp285-286, crosses out and inserts that either St Michel encountered him with a lance or the Earle of Buchan with a hammer. On p290 another insertion says that St Michel was given the 20 pound land of Carmichael by the Earl of Douglas. *as vthers say*: Bower, Bk.XV, ch.33; Buchanan, Bk.X, fol.107v. *Marginal note*: Boece, Bk. XVI, ch.19.

282, ll.2-3. *Anno 1420 as our writers says; and the English 1421*:

The battle took place in 1420 according to Buchanan, and in 1421 according to Bower, as above, Nicholson, p251, Boece (1531, 1536), Maitland, p58 (though one of 'our writers') and Holinshed, *EC, 580.*

282, ll.3-13. The list of the dead and captured may be found in Holinshed, *EC*, p580, drawn here from Edward Hall's *Chronicle.* I am indebted to Dr Anne Curry for the identifications and information for which I have cited her below. For Clarence, Roos and Umfraville, see Henry IV's order of 3 April, 1421, to take over their possessions in Normandy in Thomas Rymer, *Foedera*, vol.10 (London, 1710), p95. *Earle of Tankirville*: Sir John Grey of Tancarville or Tanquerville (*CP*, VI, 137-38); 1644, p127, omits. *Lord Ros*: John, Lord Roos, or Ros (*CP*, XI, 103-4). *Sir Gilbert Wmfreville*: Lord Kyme, called Earl of Angus by the English as a courtesy title because his ancestor, Robert, an Englishman holding lands in Scotland, was disinherited of the Earldom of Angus by Bruce (Clay, p129). *Johne Dumlie*: Sir John Lumley, of Lumley Castle (Clay, p129); 1633, p146, HP, p285 and 1644, p127, follow A2. *Sir Robert Verend*: Omitted in 1644, p127; Derent in HP, p288, and 1633, p146; Verend in Holinshed, *EC*, p580. But neither Derent nor Verend appear in *CP*. Dr Curry has pointed out to me that the College of Arms MS 9 fols.xxxxi-lxv, verso, says he was Robert de Vere, brother of the Earl of Oxford, but that he would be too young to serve at Baugé; she suggests he might be Sir Robert Brent, appointed Captain of Fresnay-le-Comté, 11 January 1421 (Norman Rolls, calendared in the annual report of the Deputy Keeper of Public Records, vol.42, 387; see also PRO E 101/51/2 for his being in the retinue of Thomas, Earl of Salisbury; he is also named in College of Arms MS 9). *Earle of Somersete and his brother*: 'brothers to Lady Jane that was after married to James I' (Holinshed, *SC*, p375), i.e. John and Edmund Beaufort (see Bower, vol.8, note 204, p121). *Earl of Suffolk*: William de la Pole survived until murdered in 1450 (*CP*, XII [Part 1] 443-7). *Perothe*: according to *CP*, X, 437-77, the knights Perot had died out before 1420. Holinshed, *EC*, has Perch, which is not an English peerage, but is named from Perche, the district of Northern France in which Verneuil is situated. Jean de Waus, *Receuil des Croniques et Anciennes stoires de la Grant Bretagne, à present nommé Angleterre*, ed. William Hardy, *Chronicles and Memorials of Great Britain and Ireland during the Middle Ages* (London, 1868), p359, calls him the Comte du Perche. *Lord Fitz-Walter*: Walter Fitzwalter (*CP*, V, 482-484). *Sir Johne Barklay*: Berkely (Holinshed). Dr Curry suggests he may have been a collateral of the Lords Berkeley, perhaps Sir John Berkeley, d. 1428 (*Calendar of Fine Rolls, 1422-30*, p189). *Sir Ralph Neville*: Ralph Neville, Earl of Westmoreland, is not recorded at Baugé in *CP*, XII (Part 2), 546-7, or Clay, but a 'Sire Raoul de Neville' appears in the list in the

College of Arms MS 9. *Sir Henrie English*: Inglis in Holinshed, *EC*, p580. Sir Henry Inglose of Norfolk, who, as Dr Curry points out, is mentioned in the Paston Letters and William Worcester, *Itineraries*, ed. J. Harvey (Oxford, 1969), pp359-61. *Sir William Bouis*: Bowes (HP, p285, 1633, p147, Holinshed. Omitted 1644, p127). Rather than William Bowes, whether the one serving under the Earl of Northumberland in 1417 (PRO E101/51/2) or the one serving under Henry Bourchier, Count of Eu in 1441 (PRO E101/53/ 33m3), Dr Curry suggests he may have been William Bowet in the retinue of the Duke of Clarence, October 1419 (French Rolls, calendared in Annual Report of the Deputy Keeper of the Public Records, vol.44, 613); *Sir William Lantoun*: Longton (Holinshed). Of the many candidates, Dr Curry suggests Sir William Langford, second son of Sir William Langford of Bradfield, Berks., d. 1411, might be the man meant (see J. R. Roskell et al. *The Commons, 1386-1421*, History of Parliament Trust [Gloucester, 1992], 3, 559). A William Langford indented for war service in 1420 (PRO E101/70/645: E404/35/301) and took protection to cross to France (French Rolls, calendared in the Deputy Keeper's Report, vol.48, 264). There is also a William Longton serving in the garrison of Caen under the Duke of Bedford and Sir John Fastolf in June 1433 (Bibliothèque nationale, Paris, manuscrits français 25771/798) and a William Langton in the retinue of Sir John Cressy in 1441 (PRO E101/53/33m2). *Sir Thomas Boroughe*: Of the many rereferences to Thomas Burgh in France (possibly more than one man), see the Fench Rolls calendared in the Annual Report of the Deputy Keeper of Public Records, 42, 432 and 450 (Again I am indebted to Dr Curry).

1644, p127, omits Verend and Bowes and its punctuation does not make clear which were taken and which killed.

282, l.16. *Marginal note*: Maitland, p58.

282, ll.17-25. *But the buik... report*: omitted in 1633, p147, and abridged in HP, p287. *Alexander Makelselane*: Macklellane (1644, p127); Alexander Mackaustelayne in *Liber Pluscardensis,* ed. Felix J.H. Skene (Edinburgh: Paterson, 1880) Bk.10, ch.26. *1000 Angels*: an angel was a gold coin bearing the device of an angel, first struck by Louis XI, considerably after the Battle of Baugé. *Johne Stewart of Darnley*: 'granted the lordship of Concressault' for his part in the battle (Nicholson, p251).

282, l.26. *Marginal note*: Buchanan, Bk.X, fol.107v.; Maitland, p58.

283, ll.2-3. ^The E*arl* of Douglas Created D*uke* of Turrain etc^ inserted in margin. *Lieutenant of France*: 'an office of indeterminate status', according to Watt's, note 8-10, Bower, vol.8, p207. This might account for the dissension with the Constable at Verneuil. See also Brian G. H. Ditcham, The Employment of Foreign Mercenary Troops in French Royal Armies, 1415-1470,

Edinburgh University PhD Dissertation, 1978, pp45 and 49.
283, ll.10-11. *maid them suspectit him*: This is the best reading of a passage that has been tampered with. It may mean 'made them that they suspected him', or the inserted 'by' may have been meant and omitted.
283, l.16. *Cosne*: Cosme in all other texts. ^See if this toun was Chinon^ inserted in the margin. Cosne-sur-Loire is meant.
283, l.19. *Boidevincence*: Bois de Vincennes.
283, ll.24-25. *Marginal note: Annals of France*: Robert Gaguin, *De francorum rebus gestis annales*, Bk.IX, fol.CCVIIv.
283, l.29. HP, p288, says that Henry V died as a result of incurring the wrath of St Fiacre, a Scot, and on his death bed exclaimed against a hostility to the English that persisted even in heaven; so also Boece.
283, l.31. *about the last of August 1422*: 1421 according to 1633, p147, and 1644, p127. Henry died on 31 August, 1421 (Nicholson, p252).
284, ll.3-11. *It is recordit... and then home*: 1644, p128 omits. *this Archbald*: the Earl of Wigtown. HP, p291, says that while the Earl of Wigtown was in France, Archibald, the 4th Earl, remained at home, where he founded the chapel of Crouk beitt in Douglasdale to St John the Baptist and expelled the nuns of Lincluden, an act of reform wrongly (it says) attributed to Archibald the Grim, his father (see A [p255-56, ll.35-3] note, and a scored out passage in HP, p264). *Henrie Sinkler*: the 2nd Earl of Orkney, died in 1420, according to Bower, Bk.XV, ch.32, before 1422 and the return of the Scots to Scotland. *It is recordit by the blak buik of Scone*: as Bower Bk.XV, ch.23, makes clear, this expedition took place, not at this time, but in 1412. *Aemonia*: Inchcolm in the Forth.
284, ll.11-16. See Buchanan, Bk.X, fol.107v., for the recall of the Scots. *Ronald*: Renald (1633, p148); Reynald (HP, 291); René (1644, p128). Renaud of Chartres, Archbishop of Rheims (Wylie, *Henry the Fifth*, III, 6). 'Ronald' is underlined and ^Alan^ inserted in the margin.
284, l.23. *Marginal note*: Maior, Bk. VI, ch. 9, cites Gaguin, (Bk.IX, fol.CCVI[v]), to the effect that James was in Henry's train in 1419, but the Scots remained loyal to the Dauphin, the future Charles VII.
284, l.28. *sayes Holinsyde*: *SC*, p376. *Marginal note*: Boece, Bk. XVI, ch.20. Maitland, p56, estimates the numbers of Scots at 10,000 when the 3,000 going with Tyneman are added to those already in France.
285, l.19-291, l.4. The account of the Battle of Verneuil is much fuller than the notices in Boece, Buchanan and Holinshed, *EC*, p588. It draws largely on Jean de Serres
285, l.4. *Mareshal of his Campe*: lieutenant general of his forces, according to Fraser, I, 389. See note to p283, ll.2-3.

285, l.5. *at the furthest in the 1423 zeir*: Lent 1424.
285, ll.5-9. *since the Constable... the Dauphin*: HP, p292, omits. The Constable's father, Robert, Duke of Albany, died in 1420 (Nicholson, p252).
285, l.20. *Yverie*: Ivry.
285, l.27. *Vernoille*: Verneuil-sur-Avre, 1424.
285, l.15. *the Earle of Bedfurde*: John of Lancaster, Duke of Bedford, brother of Henry V, and regent in France for Henry VI (*CP*, II, 70-72).
285, ll.23-24. *the Earle of Narbon*: William, viscount of Narbonne (Bower, VII, 207, note 21) .
286, ll.15-24. According to A.H. Burne, *The Agincourt War, a Military History of the latter part of the Hundred Years' War from 1369 to 1453* (London: Eyre and Spottiswoode, 1956), pp199-201, the Duke of Alençon and viscounts of Aumâle and Narbonne were for caution, the Scots and the younger French for impetuous attack. In the battle, Aumâle, not Tyneman, was in command, but probably had no authority over the Scots. Aumâle and William, viscount of Narbonne, were killed and Alençon taken prisoner (p209). It is only fair to add that the original accounts of the battle give vastly different reports. See Ditcham, p49.
286, ll.34-35. *Alexander Lindsay*: See notes to pp279, ll.10-13, and 323, l,9. *Robert Stewart*: See note to p279, ll.10-13. *Sir Thomas (or Johne Swintoun)*: see note to p279, ll.11-13. These dead are listed in Boece (1574), Bk.XVI, fol.345.
287, l.1-6. *And of these wha escapit... in France*: 1633, p149, expands A2's account of Johne Carmichael, saying that he assisted Jeanne d'Arc. Presumably this is not the same man as the St Michel who, according to HP, pp285-286, killed Clarence with a lance and later received the lands of Carmichael from the Earl of Douglas. 1633, cites *Annales Ecclesiae Aurelianensis, auctore Carolo Sansei Aureliano*. For John Carmichael, chaplain to Tyneman and later Bishop of Orleans, see Francisque-Michel, I, 153. 1644, p129 omits at this point but places this and the Carmichael material in a recasting of p291, ll. 5-27 *(and for the pairt... to their places)*, on p131; 1633, pp149-150, and HP pp295-297 have a digression on the King of France's Scots Guard down to its present commander, George Gordon, Earl of Enzie (after Marquis of Huntly, according to HP, p295), a note on Scots trading privileges in France and right to French citizenship and a plea for the reform of the Scots Guard in France; HP places this material after the account of the Hume brothers (A [pp287-89, ll.9-8]).
287, l.3. ^The first institution of the Scots companies of Gens d'Armes. An. 1424 supra fol. 105^ has been inserted in the margin.
287, ll.6-10. Holinshed, *EC*, pp588-89, says the Constable was killed and does not mention Alexander Hume of Dunglas.

287, ll.28-29. *Tinighame... Spotte*: Tynninghame and Spotte in East Lothian.
287, l.30. *is said to have conquesit Wedderburne*: Alexander Hume of Dunglas's brother, Sir David, had a charter of the lands of Wedderburn, part of the forfeited estates of George, Earl of Dunbar, confirmed by James I, 1431 (*SP*, IV, 444-45). The story of the Hume brothers is told in Hume's *De familia Humia Wedderburnensi liber,* ed. John Miller, Abbotsford Club (Edinburgh, 1839), pp7-8.
287, l.31. *Marginal note*: Buchanan, Bk.X, fol.108; Maitland, p56. Maior, Bk.VI, ch.9; Boece, Bk.XVI, ch.20; Holinshed, *SC*, p376. None of these mention the Hume affair, though all treat Verneuil.
288, l.4. *1423*: 1424 according to 1633, p152, and HP, p294, correctly according to the new style. 1644, p129, omits the story of the bond, having already said in the Preface (A[3b]) that Archibald Earl of Wigtown gave the bond. It was Hume who gave Tyneman 1000 nobles, the 'obligation' being perhaps an IOU. In HP, however, an inserted slip, p294, says that Tyneman gave Hume 'ane pension'.
288, l.6. *this present Earle of Hume*: James, 2nd Earl of Home, d. February, 1633 (*SP*, IV, 466).
288, ll.8-17. *the sleuth, and vnattentativenes of our wryters*: e.g. Boece, Bk.16, ch.20. *a sone of the Earle of Douglas*: Gross James, the 7th Earl, at this time Lord Abercorn, was a brother, not a son of Tyneman, who did in fact lose his second son at Verneuil (Nicholson, p288). Major, Bk. VI, ch.9, and Boece (1531), Bk.XIV, ch.20, (1574), fol.345, calls this son correctly James, but 1536, Bk.XIV, ch.20, says that Archibald, Earl of Wigtown was killed.
288, l.24-289, l.1. *Bot manie sik... truthe of histories*: 1644, p130 omits. I cannot find any mention of William Earl of Angus as brother of Tyneman in Boece or Holinshed, *SC,* or *EC*. Tyneman was in fact a grandson of the Good Sir James and George, Earl of Angus, a grandson of Sir James's brother, Archibald. But Hume thinks Archibald the Grim (father of Tyneman) was a half brother of George, Earl of Angus. This would make George uncle to Tyneman and half brother to his father. 'Brother children with this Earle' would then have to mean 'in relation of father's brother to nephew'.
289, l.2. *Jean de Serres*: For his account of the battle, Hume folows De Serres, *Inventoire général de l'histoire de France* (Paris, 1608), pp274-76, in the main, except in his praise of the Lombards. Burne's account is very different.
289, ll.8-9. *Annals of France maks mention*: Gaguin, Bk.X, fols. CCVIIv.-CCIXv. makes little mention of Scottish exploits between Baugé and Verneuil; HP, p298, and 1633, p152, have 'no mention'; 1644, p131, recasts this material.

289, ll.11-13. The other texts follow A2 in toning down this expression of resentment.
289, l.14. *the wryters... of our owne folks*: e.g. Boece, Bk..XIV, ch. 20, and Maitland, noted below, except that both blame Alençon, not Narbonne..
289, ll.18-19. *coming to the choke*: i.e. 'coming to the clash of warring sides', from French '*choquer*'. Cf. Maitland, p53: 'in the choke of Battale'.
289, l.19. *Marginal note*: Maitland, p56.
289, ll.24-25. *Be some also blame is laid on the lombards*: Gaguin, Bk.X, fol.CCIXv. *Marginal note*: Maior, Bk.XVI, ch.9; Boece, Bk.XVI, ch.20; Holinshed, *EC*, pp588-89
290, ll.11-35. *where he debaits... before that time*: 1633, p153, HP, p299, and 1644, p130, recast avoiding the less than reverential comment on the blood royal, drawn from Maior, Bk.VI, ch.9. *sone (or rather brother... to the Governour of Scotland)*: son to Robert, 1st Duke of Albany, and brother to Murdoch, the 2nd Duke, both Governors of Scotland. The following replacement for 'where he debaits... for it was to him' has been written in: ^But it is not likely that these two wold contest at such tyme vpon any occasion/ for although the Earle of Buchan had the honnor to be Constable and was the chefe commander and whiles he had no other Collegue but his brother in lawe, the Earle of Wigtown, yett the Earle of Douglas an old experimented leader being there in person and it being ever his due to leade the vantgards at home/ And being even there for his well knowne worth made Mareshall and Duke vpon his first arrival It carryes no appearance that his son in lawe and the younger soldier wold stand out with him. And that the English did acknolege him for Chiftain it is evident^. See note to p283, ll.2-3.
290, l.23. *Marginal note*: Holinshed, *SC,* p376.
291, ll.1-3. *the Earle of Narbon... was taine and hanged*: He was killed in the battle. Hume follows Holinshed, *EC*, p588, here.
291, ll.9-10. *not at home*: 1633, p154, is mispaginated as '158'.
291, l.14. *Marginal note*: Maitland makes no mention of Scots in France after Verneuil. Buchanan, Bk.X, fol.108.
291, ll.15-16. *thrie zeirs efter this*: 'being 1428 at the battell of the herrings', according to HP, p299, which goes on to explain the name. This was the battle of Rouvray, where John Stewart of Darnley was killed in 1429 according to Burne, pp234-36, and 1428, according to Francisque-Michel, I, 160, with William his brother.
291, ll.17-19. *twa Douglases predecessors of the lairds of Dumlanrige and Louchlevin*: William Douglas, illegitimate son of James, 2nd Earl of Douglas, was first to hold Dumlanrig from between 1384 to 1388; he possibly lost his life in France about the time of the Battle of Baugé (*SP*, VII, 112-114). Sir William Douglas, the second holder of of Loch Leven was 'in all

likelihood' killed at the battle of Baugé or of Fresnay-le-Comté (*SP*, VI, 365).
291, ll.21-23. *who despytit there with, hanged vp of their prisoners to the number of 20*: The English, having James I in their hands, claimed the Scots fighting for Charles VII were traitors (Nicholson, p251).
291, l.26. *Marginal note*: Boece, Bk.XVI, ch.21 (1531), ch.20 (1536); Holinshed, *SC*, p376.
291, ll.27-29. *in the principall Kirk... the Scottis daylie*: See Francisque-Michel, I, 154, on *la messe écossaise*, still being celebrated in the 18th Century.
291, l.30-293, l.5. *And among the rest... geven be al*: 1644, p131 omits. Note the toning down of resentment against the English in A2 followed by 1633, p154, and HP, p300, at A (p292, ll.8-12). The outburst expands on a jibe of Buchanan's and probably it is he who has 'sufficientlie answerit'. *Robert Petillok*: see Francisque-Michel, I, 165-66. *Marginal note*: Buchanan, Bk.10, fol.108, discusses Scots in France, but says nothing of Petillock. But see Boece, Bk.XV, ch.21 (1531), ch.20 (1536).
292, l.12. ^supra fol.105^ has been inserted in the margin, i.e. the insertion given above in the note to p115, l.33.
293, l.9. *28 of August*: 20 August (1633, p155, HP, p300, 1644, p131); 24 August (Fraser, I, 394. HP adds that others say he was buried in the family burial place in Glenclendons, i.e. Lincluden, at least his wife was (cf. p257, ll.12-13, above), who later married Lord Dalkeith (she did not remarry, according to Fraser, I, 394-398). Fraser, I, 394 (agreeing with A, 1633 and 1644, p131), says he was buried in Tours.
293, l.15. *Marginal note*: The citation should read Maior, Bk.VI, ch8.
293, l.20. *succes*: i.e. 'how things turned out for him, luck (here bad)'.
293, ll.23-24. *Careat... putat*: Ovid, *Heroides*, II, 85-6.
293, l.27. *Clerce aux armes*: '*le Clerc aux armes*' (1633, p155, HP, p301, 1644, p131).
293, ll.27-28. *We have to do with a more judicious*: Buchanan, Bk.X, fol.105.
294, l.8. *that mans judgement*: Buchanan's, not Maior's.
294, l.28. HP, p301, concludes by saluting the 4th Earl's piety, and complains about the way writers attribute the reform of Lincludin to Archibald the Grim (see note to p256, l.1). 1644, pp132-133, has two Latin funerary verses, one attributed to John Johnston *Heroes* (p22), both with English verse translations.

The Life of Archbald, 5th Earl of Douglas (A, pp323-449)

1424-1439

1633, pp156-168, follows A2 with additions and omissions.
HP, pp306-321, follows 1633, with a few additions and alterations of detail. In the inserted pages that end Archibald Tyneman's life, the life of Archibald, 5th Earl of Douglas begins on p302, but that page has been glued to the next one, and p305 is blank. A scrap, scored out, but referring to Tyneman's tomb, numbered '303-304' has been placed between pp305 and 306.
1644, pp133-144, generally tightens up, especially at first, but in substance follows 1633, though with occasional adoptions of A. This life has no funerary verses.

Hume uses the theme of mutability as a grand explanation of the hints of decline in the Douglas fortunes. A more obvious cause, Stuart hostility is played down and wicked counsellors are blamed. The history elicits reflections on peers as natural counsellors of the king and, perhaps inconsistently, in view of Hume's anti-stoical comments earlier, approval of Douglas's retirement from a court in which the wicked flourish. In presenting the 5th Earl favourably, Hume has to contend with less favourable accounts, above all Buchanan's. For Buchanan, as for Boece and Holinshed, James I was an excellent monarch, even if his severity may have helped to provoke his assassination. Without actually challenging that view of James, Hume makes out that the King unjustly passed over the claims of his greatest subject, who nevertheless bore these slights patiently. On the King's death, Buchanan pictures Douglas as playing a ruthless factional game against Livingston and Crichton. Hume, in this following Maitland, pp61-63, has it that Douglas, too great for politics, withdrew in disgust from the machinations of new men. Neither story accords with Douglas's leading part in politics and government during these years. Nor was he at odds with the Crichtons or the Livingstons.

In some ways Hume imports the animus Buchanan displays against the courtiers of James III's reign, and attaches to Crichton and Livingston the odium, which in Buchanan's account of the later reign belongs to the creatures of royal favour, Cochrane and Preston. The lives of Archibald, 5th Earl, and of William, 6th Earl of Dougas, show the wrongness of a King's neglecting the natural leaders of the country (such as Hume's patrons, the Earls of Angus).

295, l.8. *2 Duke of Turain*: After a false report of his death, Charles VII gave the Duchy to Louis d'Anjou, and Archibald, though using the title, never receved any revenue from it (Fraser, I, 409-10).
295, ll.9-10. *a daughter of the Earle of Crafurds*: Maud Lindsay, daughter of David, Earl of Crawford, married Douglas at Dundee with great pomp according to 1633, p156, and 1644, p133 (from Boece, Bk.XVIII, fol.359; Pitscottie, I, 24). HP, p306, scores out 'David' and writes her father's name, 'James'. In fact he married Euphemia Graham, countess Palatine of Strathearn, daughter of Sir Patrick Graham of Kincardine and sister of Malise Graham of Strathearn. His son William, 6th Earl of Douglas, was married to a Janet or Margaret Lindsay, probably daughter of Alexander, 2nd Earl of Crawford (Fraser, I, 420, 430) or Jean Lindsay daughter of David, 3rd Earl (*SP*, III, 20; McGladdery, p64).
295, l.11. *the Earle of Crafurds brothers going*: Alexander, according to HP, p306. 1633, p156, and 1644, p134, say it was the Earl himself who went to France. Hume says that Alexander Lindsay went over to France with the Earl of Wigtown (p279, ll.11-13; see note).
295, l.13. *his brother sone*: Hume thinks Archibald, 5th Earl of Douglas, and Gross James, 7th Earl, father of William, 8th Earl, were brothers, whereas Gross James was in fact uncle of the 5th Earl. The 8th Earl was, therefore, a cousin of the 5th Earl, and not a nephew. On this count and the nonexistence of the marriage of the 5th Earl to Maud Lindsay, the further genealogical connections that Hume makes are false.
295, ll.14-15. *for the whilk the said Earle William Douglas was slane in the Castle of Sterling*: William, 8th Earl of Douglas was stabbed by James II when he refused to break his band with the Earls of Crawford and Ross without consultation (Life of William, 8th Earl of Douglas, pp409, ll.9-27).
295, ll.20-21. *freindshipe betwix these houses fra the first Earles tyme*: William 1st Earl of Douglas's mother was Beatrix Lindsay, though Hume does not think so (see note to p129-30, ll.19-5; p200, l.15-202, l.10).
295, l.23. HP, p302, adds that, Maud dying childless, Douglas married Euphame Graham, daughter of Patrick Graham, Earl of Strathearn, by whom he had William, David and Beatrix, the Fair Maid of Galloway. After his death, Euphame married Sir James Hamilton of Cadzow. P306, however, has the version to be found in the other texts.
295, l.35. *the death of King Robert the Thrid in anno 1420*: actually 1406.
296, l.2. *for they are not kings... overthrow*: 1644, p134, omits.
296, ll.8-19. This account of the reasons for recalling of James comes from Boece, Bk.XVI, ch.21 (1531), ch.20 (1536), Bk.XVII, ch.1, followed by Buchanan, Bk.X, fol.108, and Holinshed, *SC*,

pp375-76. *No vther cause*: The government of Murdoch, 2nd Duke of Albany, had been sufficiently corrupt and incompetent to provoke a general demand for the return of James I (Nicholson, pp257-60).

296, l.22. *I can not slipe vnremarking it*: i.e 'I cannot slip by without remarking on it'; 'slippe over the remarking' (1633, p156); 'it deserveth not to bee passed over with a dry foot' (1644, p134).

297, ll.2-3. *no vther apparence but to have bruikit*: 'sawe no(t) other app(e)arance but to have enjoyed it still' (A2, HP, p307, 1633, p157, 1644, p134) gives the sense.

297, ll.25-27. The MS has been so written over that it is not clear what the new reading is supposed to be. But probably it is as I have suggested in the footnotes. *Colein Cambel*: Buchanan, Bk.X, fol.108. Colin Iongantanach of Lochawe; see 'Genealogie of the Campbells', ed. J. R. N. McPhail, *Highland Papers,* II, Scottish History Society, 2nd series, vol.12 (Edinburgh, 1916), p93.

298, ll.7-8. *William Hay*: Sir William Hay of Errol, Constable of Scotland. *Henrie Bishope of Aberdene*: Henry de Lichton (D. E. R. Watt, *Fasti Ecclesiae Scoticanae Medii Aevii,* 2nd Draft, 1969, p3); Boece, Bk.XVII, ch.1 (1531), fol.346 (1574), mentions other Scottish delegates as well.

298, l.16. *a wyfe taucherles*: in fact 10,000 marks of James's 60,000 marks ransom were remitted as dowry for Lady Joan Beaufort (Nicholson, p259).

298, l.17-299, l.20. *never being a lawful prisoner... what ever condition it war*: 1644, p135, omits.

298, l.20. *the English writers*: Holinshed, *EC*, p587.

298, l.24. *Marginal note*: Holinshed, *EC*, p587.

299, l.2. *therefore pairtie therefore suspectit*: i.e. 'therefore partial and therefore to be suspected'. HP, p308, inserts a defence of Scottish independence, denying the pertinence of David I's homage for the lands he got by his wife and citing at length the homage Edward II did Philip of France for lands in France.

299, l.22. *21 May*: All the other texts have 22 May. Bower Bk.XVI, ch.2, and Brown, p48, have 21 May.

299, ll.27-28. *120 zeirs*: HP, p309, 1633, p128, and 1644, p135, prefer the unspecific 'many'.

301, ll.5-7. Neither Fraser, nor McGladdery, nor Brown, record any first warding of the Earl of Douglas. The mistake is there in Boece and, following him, Maitland, p60, and possibly originated with him. See note to p331, ll.24-32, below .

301, l.12. *Marginal note*: Holinshed, *SC,* p378; Boece, Bk.XVII, ch.2

301, ll.13-14. *Walter... Stewart*: warded 13 May, 1424 (Nicholson, p281); *Alexander*, Duke Murdoch's wife and father in law were warded at the parliament of Perth, March, 1425

(Nicholson, p287); *his father Duncane Stewart Earle of Lennox*: Sir Duncan, 8th Earl of Lennox was the father of Murdoch's wife, as A2 and the other texts correctly have it, but not a Stewart (*SP*, V, 339-41).
301, l.19. *William Earl of Angus*: William Douglas, 2nd Earl of Angus (*SP*, I, 174-75), the son of George, who had married Marie Stewart, James's sister (see life of William 3rd Earl of Angus, 1644, p209).
301, ll.26-27. *Johne Earle of Buchan*: see note to p257-8, ll.32-1.
301, l.32-302, l.2. *Earle of Marche... sone from his restoring*: George Dunbar, 10th earl of March, 3rd or 5th Earl of March, had been succeeded by George his son as 11th Earl of Dunbar etc; it was the son not the father who was warded (later) and deprived of his earldom.
302, ll.2-12. This list of the warded corresponds closely to Bower's list (Bk.XVI, ch.10) and Major's (Bk.VI, ch.12) of 26 new knighthoods. The muddle seems to originate in Boece, Bk.XVII, ch.1 (1536) and ch.2 (1531), and is passed on to Holinshed, *SC*, p378, who talk of some of this list as warded. *Robert Stewart of Rothose*: perhaps David Stewart of Rosyth (see Bower, vol.8, 353). *Stewart of Dordonald*: MS has a blank before Stewart, closed up in 1633, p159, and 1644, p136; HP, p310, has N. Stewart of Dundonald. Holinshed, *SC*, p378, calls him John Stewarde, rightly perhaps, if he was the John the Red Stewart of Dundonald, illegitimate son of Robert II (Bower, vol.8, 243) killed in 1425 by the Albany Stewart, James, youngest son of Murdoch (Nicholson, p 287). *Johne Stewart of Carden*: Cardney, 'possibly another illegitimate son of Robert II', or a 'successor in the next generation' (Bower, vol.8, 353). *Hepburne of Hails*: Adam Hepburn of Hails. *Hay of Zeaster*: Thomas Hay of Yester. *Ramsay of Dalhousie*: Alexander Ramsay. *Haliburton of Dirltoun*: Walter, at this date a hostage in England (Bower, vol.8, 352). *Walter Ogilvie*: of Lintrathen. *Alexander Setoun*: Alexander Seton de Gordon, a hostage in England at this time (Bower, vol.8, 353). *Gordoun*: a misunderstanding of the preceding. *Hay of Arrol*: William Hay of Errol, Constable of Scotland, later 1st Earl (*SP*, III, 562). *Scrimger Constable of Dundie*: John Scrymgeour, Constable of Dundee.
302, ll.20-28. *of those whom the King... resoluit to redde him self of sik dangers*: the syntax (followed by HP, pp310-11, and 1633, p159) seems faulty, though the sense is clear enough.
303, ll.8-9. *and put vpon their assize also*: see Bower, XVI, ch.10, for a list. *Marche*: George Dunbar, 11th Earl of Dunbar, 4th or 6th Earl of March.
303, l.9. *Maior*: Bk.VI, ch.12.
P303, l.16. *Marginal note*: Boece, Bk.XVII, ch.3, and Holinshed, *SC*, p.380. This second warding was in 1431, according to Bower,

Bk.XVI, ch.16. Douglas was released later the same year, unlike Kennedy.
303, l.30-304, l.7. *Maior*: 'I marvel that the historians have not told us the reasons for putting those Stewarts to death, and for the imprisonment of those others, for then we might be able to form an opinion whether it were after a full and just consideration of every circumstance that men thus imprisoned were set free, or whether the treatment of men so outstanding in the state had its origin rather in some trifling cause, or in the arbitrary judgements of the king' (Bk.VI, ch.13). With this reflection on the light of history, compare p259, ll.24-29, and p265, ll.16-20.
303, ll.25-28. Boece, Bk.XVII, ch.16 (1531), fol.342v. (1574), says Douglas was warded in 1430; others, like Bower, Bk.XVI, ch.16, say 1431, a date accepted by Brown, p133. *Marginal note*: Boece, ibid; Buchanan, Bk.X, fol.111.
304, l.2. *Johne Lord Kennedie*: Sir John Kennedy of Cassillis (Bower, Bk.XVI, ch.16; Fraser, I, 412).
304, l.8. *mints at*: the sense required is 'hints at, insinuates', but *DOST* only approaches that with 'intend, make a prelminary move towards'; perhaps then 'gesture toward a meaning' would give the right sense.
304, l.17. *Marginal note*: Buchanan, Bk.X, fol.111, *'de statu publico, et regni administratione temere, ac liberius, quam opportebat locuti fuissent'*.
304, l.17. *(rashlie)*: What might appear rash in someone else might not be so in a Privy Councillor, according to A2, HP, p312, and 1633, p160.
305, l.18. *the Earle of Athol*: Walter Stewart, the eldest son of Robert II by Euphemia, the daughter of the Earl of Ross (see p339, ll.28-1).
305, ll.20-28. See McGladdery, pp8-9 for other ways in which James alienated the nobility than by warding.
305, ll.28-31. See Buchanan, Bk.X, fols.108v.-109, on James's remission of taxes, and Nicholson, p284-5.
306, l.14. *his twynnes*: 'Alexander and James' (HP, p313); see *SP*, I, 19.
306, l.19. *knight of the order*: of the Thistle (so HP, p313, insertion). *sayes the Manuscript*: Maitland, p60.
306, l.22. *Marginal note*: Boece, Bk.XVII, ch.3, and Holinshed, *SC*, p379, say only that he made William knight at baptism.
307, ll.3-4. *This was in the 1430 zeir... October*: i.e. the knighting of Douglas's son at the baptism. James's twins were born on the 16th October, 1430. All this in Hume's account would have taken place before the '2nd' warding in 1431.
307, ll.3-11. 1633, p162, HP, p313 and 1644, p138, omit 'betwixt the tent and sixteine of' and the repetitious 'for sa they differ... this solemnitie endit', and HP and 1633 insert a paragraph on Henry VI's overture to exchange Berwick and some

other English territory in return for the Scots' dissolving of the Auld Alliance, an overture succesfully resisted by Douglas in the name of loyalty. *Marginal note*: Holinshed, *SC*, pp379-80; Maitland, p60. Maior, Bk. VI, ch.13; Buchanan, Bk.X, fol.111; Boece, Bk.XVII, ch.3. *this solemnitie*: i.e. the Earl's witnessing the baptism of the King's twins and the knighting of the infant William Douglas.

307, l.26. *Marginal note*: Maitland says nothing of Douglas's engagment in France.

307, l.28-308, l.1. *It is attributit... slane in the Blak friers*: A marriage contract between the Dauphin and Margaret Stewart was sealed in 1428, though the marriage did not take place till 1436 (Nicholson, pp289-90). The 5th Earl seems to have been engrossed in Scottish politics from the return of James, anyway, and not to have returned to France. He would not have been absent when the King was murdered (see p308, ll.32-33). *Lewis the ii*: Louis XI.

308, l.2. *Patrik Grame*: Boece, Bk.XVII, ch.9, and Buchanan, Bk.X, fols.113-115, speak of Robert Graham, and also HP, p315, but at this point all the texts follow A. See Buchanan, Bk.X, fols.113-115 for Robert Graham's grievances in the face of the King's predatoriness, and Nicholson pp320-23. Sir Robert Graham and Sir *Robert Stewart*, grandson and heir of Walter, Earl of Athol, were the leaders of the assassins. In Bk.X, fol.113, Buchanan says that Robert Graham's brother, Patrick, married Euphemia, grandaughter of Robert II, by whom he had a son Malise (cf. *SP*, VI, 214-15). Hume probably confused the names from this source.

308, ll.3-5. See Buchanan, Bk.X, fol.112v-113, for Athol's schemings, also Nicholson, pp322-24.

308, ll.14-15. *ane bairne of sixe zeirs old*: 'or seaven' (HP, p315). Six, according to Nicholson, p326.

308, l.33-309, l.15. HP, p315, and 1633, p163, say that Douglas insisted on a second trial of the Earl of Athol, which convicted him, a conviction that the Papal legate, Aeneas Sylvius, praised for its impartiality; HP adds that Robertson of Struan got lands for handing over Robert Graham. What follows ('and was (as some think)... present or not' [ll.33-15]) is altered in HP to fit the Earl's being in Scotland to insist on the trial, the doubt about the year being omitted.

308, l.35-309, l.1. *tent of Marche 1437*: 25 March 1437 (Nicholson, p326).

309, ll.4-8. See *Buchanan*, Bk.X, fol.115v. Boece, Bk.XVII, ch.7 (1536), ch.9 (1531), has 1436. James I was murdered on 21 February, 1437, 1436 Old Style.

309, ll.18-19. *he was not regardit*: he was in fact made Lieutenant General perhaps after the death of the Earl of Angus, October 1437 (McGladdery, p12).

309, ll.21-22. *bot the Chrichton and the Levistoun made Chanceller and Governour*: Sir William Crichton was made Chancellor by 10 July, 1439, after Douglas's death on 26 January, 1439. Alexander Livingston of Callendar was made Keeper of Stirling Castle but not Governor (McGladdery, p16).
309, ll.22-23. *Our wryters*: Buchanan, Bk.XI, fol.116, anyway.
309, l.27. *I refer me*: i.e. 'I refer to the impartial judgement of the reader in the light of the following considerations'. McGladdery, p12, says that after James II he was next in line to the throne.
310, ll.21-23. *the Earle of Marche*: James I had deprived the Earls of March of their earldom in 1435, rejecting the pardons given them for their wars on Robert III (*SP*. 111, 277). *the Earle of Angus*: William, 2nd Earl of had died in October 1437 (*SP*, I, 175). *the Earle of Cassils*: John Kennedy of Cassillis escaped abroad into exile after warding by James I (Nicholson, p320).
310, ll.31-32. *wherein kythit it vnder the lait king*: Crichton had been master of James I's household and sheriff of Edinburgh; Livingston, on the other hand, rose during the minority of James II (McGladdery, p16).
311, l.13. ^Chrighton the first Chancellor in Scotland^ has been inserted in the margin.
311, l.30. *to his owne house*: the Threave 'built by himself in Galloway', according to HP, p317. Douglas, as Lieutenant General does not seem to have been a particularly effective head of government, but this is not withdrawing from affairs as Hume would have it.
312, l.34-33, l.26. Buchanan, Bk.XI, fol.117-17v, has the story of the Queen Mother's coming to Livingston with James, Crichton's proposal to Douglas and his reply. See also Boece, Bk.XVIII, fols.357-358 (Pitscottie, I, 16-17). *skrimars zokit togeather*: A2 and all other texts follow Buchanan, Bk.XI, fol.117v, who speaks of fencers (*gladiatores*). Priscilla Bawcutt comments, 'There exists a good Scots verb, *scrim, skrim,* much used of fighting, with senses, "skirmish, dart at aggressively" (cf. Holland, *Howlat,* l.67; Dunbar, *Abbot of Tungland*, l.123; also *CSD*: *scrim*, v. "beat, strike vigorously"). *Scrimars* would thus be an agent noun formed from this verb, and would roughly correspond both to vernacular "fencers" and Latin "*gladiatores*". Cf. also French *escrimeur.*'
314, ll.10-11. *not a profitable speiche*: Buchanan, Bk.XI, fol.117v., says that he spoke more freely than prudently ('*magis libere, quam utiliter*'). McGladdery, p17, treats the story of Crichton's and Livingston's being driven together by Douglas's speech as an invention of the later chronicles.
315, ll.11-12. *calling as the Macedonians a spaid a spaid*: See Plutarch, *Apophthegmata,* 17B, and *OED* 'spade, 2.a' for a note on Erasmus's giving currency to a mistranslation of Plutarch's

'*skaphe*' by '*ligo*'.
316, l.2. *of ane*: i.e. 'of any'; redundant, as the revisers felt since the course of the course of Livingston and Crichton is already said to be as treasonable as possible.
316, l.6. *sayes our writers*: Buchanan, Bk.XI, fol.118.
316, ll.4-5. *1439*: 1432 (1633, p167); 1438 (HP, p320, and 1644, p143). A is correct according to Fraser, I, 420, in spite of funerary monument in St Bride's Church, Douglas, transcribed p350, l.29. *of a hote fever*: he died of the plague, according to McGladdery, p15. *Marginal note*: Buchanan, Bk.XI, fol.118.
317, l.1. *generouse naturall*: HP, p321, 1633, p168, and 1644, p144, find evidence of his generosity in his free answer to Crichton and in his treatment of Lord Kennedy over the lands of Stewarton, evidence rather of generosity in Hume, at least with regard to his second example.
317, l.8. *locum tenens Regis Scotiae:* Douglas was made Lieutenant General of Scotland on the death of James I, possibly after the death of the Earl of Angus (McGladdery, pp12-14), a fact surprisingly omitted by Hume, especially in view of this epitaph.
317, l.10. *tricesimo secundo*: he died in 1439.

The Life of William, 6th Earl of Douglas (A, pp351-381)

1439-1440

1633, pp169-181, follows A2 in the main with a few insertions.

HP, pp322-336, follows 1633 closely, though in some ways more ceremonious and bland. David, William's younger brother, is called 'Sir David' and the outburst against Crichton and Livingston is severely reduced (pp366-367).

1644, pp144-156, follows 1633 more closely than usual, though rephrasing, with some specific traces of A. It ends with a Latin epitaph and an English translation, both in verse.

Buchanan, with the 1574 continuation of Boece, Bk.XVIII, behind him, supplies Hume with his story. But even more than with the last life, Buchanan stands in the way of celebratory history here. For him, Douglas , 'though of excellent promise if his education had been equal to his rank','had no prudence; he was young, wavering, corrupted by flatterers, and guided by parasites' (Bk.XI, fols.118, 119; Aikman's translation, II, 123, 126). What solid grounds Buchanan had for his judgement, or Hume in turn for his that, on the contrary, Douglas, though youthful, was prudent, high-spirited and sweet-natured, it is useless to inquire. Hume works up a picture of an innocent victim of wicked politicians and the life is less a narrative than a rhetorically charged meditation on events. Though Hume's moral scheme divides good from evil in an improbably clean cut way, the reflections on moral shadiness are interesting. The theme of mutability, introduced in its saturnian aspect in the last life, takes on imagery of the crooked and monstrous. And the writing is enlivened with copious adages and grim jesting.

McGladdery, the most recent historian of James II's reign, does not pay much attention to the story of the Black Dinner, and thinks it probable that James Douglas of Abercorn, William's uncle, Gross James, the next Earl of Douglas, was behind the murder, in this at odds with Fraser, I, 441-42. At no point does her book cite Hume as an authority for its narrative or analysis of events.

320, l.29. *the Livingstoun being Governour*: keeper of Stirling Castle, not Governor, as Hume persistently calls him.
321, l.12. *the Lord of Lorne*: Robert Stewart. Neither McGladdery, p117, nor *SP*, V, 3, records his warding and there is no note of it in *APS*. *his brother William*: HP, p324, 1633, p170, and 1644, p146, have Sir James Stewart, correctly. Sir James Stewart, the Black Knight of Lorne, married the Queen Mother, Joanna. See Boece, Bk.XVIII, fol.359v. (Pitscottie, I, 26).
321, l.15. HP, pp324-325, and 1633, pp170-171, have a clumsy insertion about the Queen in prison and the marriages of her daughters by James I. 1644, p146, omitting the material about the daughters, makes a neater insertion.
321, ll.8-31. For the events noted, see Buchanan, Bk.XI, fol.118v..
321, ll.31-32. *the dyce is changit*: 1644, p146, retains this phrase, but 1633, p171, and HP, p325, follow A2's 'the case is altered'.
321, l.32. *gotten the Durk*: Metaphorically, Crichton had got the advantage; literally, perhaps in the scuffle he had got hold of the one dirk between himself and Livingston. I can find no other instance of this saying.
321, l.33. *he will pairt the pray over again*: Possibly an allusion to Aesop's fable of the Lion and the other beasts, in which the Lion gave himself all four portions of the prey; see 'the Lion's share' in Brewster's *Dictionary of Phrase and Fable.*
322, l.3. *Neid hes no law*: 'Need hes na law' (Fergusson, 649); see also Tilley, N76 and Whiting N51; also cf. '*necessitas feriis caret*' ('necessity knows no holiday'), Palladius, *De re rustica*, I, 6, 7, ed. J. C. Schmitt (Leipzig, 1898).
322, l.6. *he hes gotten ane meiting mides dishe*: Taking 'meiting' as a 'counter' or 'check', this would mean metaphorically that Livingston has met a check in his scheming; metaphorically perhaps that he has been stopped in the middle of enjoying his

meal (of the King and Queen Mother).
322, l.7. *bowis his banie hart*: 1644, p146, has 'boney' and I should like to think that A reads 'banie', a strange expression here for 'stiff'; 1633, p171, has, however, 'bonnie', an irony of the sort Hume frequently allows himself with Livingston and Crichton, and this may be the more plausible reading. 'Banie' is not recorded in *DOST*. HP, p325, has 'hautie'.
322, l.9. HP, p325, and 1633, pp171-172, say that the reconciliation in St Giles was achieved through the mediation of Henry Leighton, Bishop of Aberdeen, and John Innes, Bishop of Moray. 1644, p146, abridges this information.
322, l.10. *a Clerke play*: 'a play composed or acted by clerks' (*DOST*), often used derisively; other texts have 'a stage play'.
322, l.16-323, l.6. HP, p326, and 1633, p172, abridge this speech in much the same way; 1644, p147, abridges rather differently. Hume's account of what was said is based in a general sort of way on the speeches Buchanan gives to Livingston and Crichton, Bk.XI, fol.119-19v.; see also Boece, Bk.XVIII, fols.361-62 (Pitscottie, I, 35-39).
323, ll.9-10. *opportet mendacem esse memorem*: 'a liar had better have a good memory' (Quintillian, *Institutio Oratore*, IV, 2, 91). Cf. Fergusson, 17.
323, l.9. *Marginal note*: *Igitur veluti antea pravo studio certavimus, uter nostrum honoribus, e auctoritate auctior esset, ita in posterum contendamus, uter moderatione, et iustitia alterum antecedat* (Buchanan, Bk.XI, 119v.).
323, ll.18-19. *when the fox preaches tak tent to the henis*: HP, p326, omits. Cf. Fergusson, 707, 'Quhan the Tod preaches, beware of the hens', and Whiting, F605, and Tilley, F56.
323, l.28. *Marginal note*: Buchanan, Bk.XI, fol.119..
324, ll.4-5. *mot in their eye*: Matthew, 7, 3.
324, ll.12-13. *their Holydays name*: *OED*, cites Greene and Lodge's *Looking Glasse* for 'holiday terms', meaning playful names of abuse, which does not fit well here, unless we suppose a sort of feast of misrule at which rudeness is part of the licence; HP, p327, and 1633, p173, omit; 1644, p148, retains.
324, l.15. *they most have muffils that wald take sik a Cate*: cited in *DOST* under '*muffil*'. I can find no other instance of this saying.
324, ll.16-29. *Indeid... France*: For Buchanan, Bk.XI, fol.118, all this is evidence of Douglas's insolence. HP, p327, has pasted in a note specifying the friendship with James Hamilton of Cadzow, noting his advice to James the 9th Earl at the siege of Abercorn.
324, ll.28-29. *Malcolme Lord Fleminge*: of Cumbernauld, was beheaded at the Black Dinner. *Sir Johne Lauder of Bas (or Hotoun)*: There were Lauders of both Bass and Hatton; the Lauders of Hatton, at least, were apparently allies of the Douglases

(see p461, l.1). Boece, Bk. XVIII, fol.360, Maitland, p64, and Leslie, Bk.VIII, p192, speak of Alan, not John Lauder; Buchanan, Bk.XI, fol.118, speaks of John. According to Fraser, I, 409-10, 425-26, it was William, 8th Earl, who tried to have himself invested; the 6th Earl succeeded as a matter of course to the title, if not to the revenues. So the expedition may not have taken place.
324, l.33-25, l.6. *he had al his affairs... Earle and Duk*: Fraser, I, 425, cites the parallel case of the Earls of Crawford to argue that in holding court like this Douglas followed the pattern among great magnates. *Marginal note*: Holinshed, *SC*, p386.
325, l.5. *Marginal note*: Boece, Bk.XVIII, fol.359v.; Buchanan, Bk.XI, fol.118.
325, ll.7-9. HP, p327, and 1633, p173, omit the talk of Douglas's age, but not 1644, p148; *1439*: or 1438 according to 1644, p148. 24 November, 1439, according to Fraser, I, 427.
325, l.14. *iappit*: the context requires the sense of 'vexed', but *DOST* and *OED* give only 'tricked, seduced'. There is, however, a ground notion of Douglas's virtues making a fool of his enemies' designs.
325, l.17. *contrepoyson*: HP, p327, and 1633, p173, follow A2's 'contrepoise'; 1644, p148, follows A.
325, l.18. *the skine of a lion*: Erasmus, *Adages,* LIL to LV, 100, trans. M. M. Phillips. ed. R. B. Mynors, *Collected Works* (Toronto, 1982), I, 111, 66, refers to Lucian's tale of the ass who disguised himself in a lion's skin until he was discovered. See also Tilley, L319: 'If the lion's skin cannot the fox's shall'.
325, l.20. *Marginal note*: Buchanan, Bk.11, fols.117v-118.
325, l.24. *betwixt hands*: 'between stooles' (1644, p148); 'between both' (HP, p327, and 1633, p173). *DOST*'s 'at intervals' (under '*hand*', 7,e) does not fit the sense required as well as these revisions.
326, ll.2-3. *ane Isle of Louchloumond callit Marin*: Inch Murrin
326, ll.3-12. Alan Stewart of Darnley was killed on 20 September, 1438. Sir Thomas Boyd was killed by Darnley's son Alexander, 7 July 1439. These murders had to do with pressing a claim for the earldom of Lennox. Alexander, Lord of the Isles, was also involved with the Lennox claim but the reasons for the murder of Sir John Colquhoun of Luss, 15 September, 1439 are not clear (McGladdery, pp14-15, and Nicholson, pp327-28). Hume is not saying that Douglas was behind these disturbances but that when they arose he encouraged trouble on his own lands. Buchanan says these troubles were supposed to be encouraged by Livingston, who was supposed to be in secret correspondence with Douglas, (Bk.XI, fol.118v). Archibald, the 5th Earl, died on 26 June, 1439, an argument at least against William's being in any way associated with the first outrage.
326, ll.15-16. *their factes were interpretit to be his allowance*: according to Buchanan everyone knew that Douglas was the

source of all these disorders (Bk.XI, fol.120).
326, ll.16-17. *a Convention at Edinburgh*: No complaints are recorded in *APS* at any Parliament about William, 6th Earl, nor was there any Parlaiment at Edinburgh during his tenure of the earldom.
326, l.17. *Marginal note*: Buchanan, Bk.XI, fol.118-118v, 119v.-120.
Pp326, l.33-327, l.30. Livingston's plot and letter are close to Buchanan, Bk.XI, fol.120.
327, l.6. *stay the Decreit*: delay or stop their decision from taking effect (a legal phrase).
330, l.7-331, l.6. Crichton's hospitality and speech are drawn from Buchanan, Bk.XI, fol.120. Maitland, pp68-70, has a different speech.
331, ll.10-16. *Venemous... ages; Lo a beast... hart of it*: HP, p331, omits with the result that the siren is a man transformed into a beast. *Cokatrice*: a basilisk, i.e. a reptile with venemous glance or breath; but see *OED* article on 'basilisk'.
332, ll.2-4. *Abner... Joab*: Joab killed Abner treacherously as an act of private revenge without the King's being party to it (2 Sam. 3). There is a rough analogy between the innocent James II and David and between the wily Crichton and Joab.
332, l.7-333, l.2. Hume follows Buchanan, Bk.XI, fol.120-120v. For Buchanan, however, the boy is incautious and his speech petulant, while Hume manages to make him trusting and his speech evidence of understanding beyond his years.
334, l.14. *sayes our histories*: Boece, Bk.XVIII, fol.363v. (Pitscottie, I, 45).
334, ll.18-27. *Nather... interteining him*: HP, p333, omits; *a Bulles head*: ^*Teste de veau*^ inserted in the margin. *a tryme ruise and ane vnhonest*: 1633, p178, and 1644, p153, follow A2 in preferring the ironic 'honest', and lest we miss the point the reviser has written in the margin of A ^*Ironicos*^, a Greek adverb given a Latin spelling.
335, ll.8-9. *to that the wryters are contraire*: Boece and Buchanan suggest the murder was planned by Crichton
337, ll.8-9. *to eik an zit the Comble of their wickednes is...* : i.e. 'to add a "yet", an "even more", to the heap of their wickedness is...'.
337, l.12. HP, p334, adds rather inconsistently with its general toning down that the Crichton and Livingston were fitter counsellors for Nero and Domitian than for a Christian prince.
338, l.12-339, l.13. *as indeid... as indeid*: all other texts follow A2 in omitting.
338, ll.12-29. In 1428 James I summoned a Parliament at Inverness and arrested 50 of the magnates as they arrived, including Alexander, *Lord of the Isles*, whose grandmother, had been married to *Sir Walter Leslie*, Earl of Ross (d. Feb. 1381/82).

Their daughter and his mother, Margaret or Mary, married Donald, Lord of the Isles. As she survived until 1435 or 1436 as Countess of Ross, Bower, Bk.XVI, ch.15, from which Hume draws here, anticipates Alexander's accession to the Earldom of Ross, though Nicholson, p315, says that he had proclaimed himself Earl before that (see notes to Bower, vol.8, pp355, to *Isles*, and 362, to *countess of Ross*). *Ad turrim etc.*: the verses are in Bower Bk.XVI, ch.15, and translated by Watt, 'Let us take the chance to conduct this company to the tower with care/ for, by Christ's death, these men deserve death'. *Marginal note*: should read Maior, Bk.VI, ch.12. The list of magnates is given in Major, (who makes a better job of it than Hume) from Bower, Bk.XVI, ch.15; I am indebted to Watt's notes for identifications. *Angus, Dufe*: a mistake for Angus Dubh or Mackay; *Kennedies*: Kenneth Mor, perhaps a Mackenzie chief; *Johne Rosse*: probably the Rose or Ross lord of Kilravock; *William Leslie*: not identified; *Angus of Morton*: Angus de Moray, said to be lord of Culbin. ^It wold seeme to be Angus Makonell or els Angus, Morton^ has been written in the margin and scored out; *Mackeinzies*: in Bower, MacMachan, said to be Mathieson of Lochalsh.

339, l.21. *be the same that he is great*: i.e. 'just by the fact that he is great'.

339, l.29-340, l.6. *Alwyse vthers... great service*: 1644, p155, omits. HP, p335, and 1633, p180, having omitted the passage on James I's possibly having shown a bad example in killing nobles, alter 'Alwyse vthers... James the first' and here suggest that James may have taught an evil lesson, only to retract the suggestion.

340, l.13-341, l.21. *Zit I can hardlie... our Chronologie*: Against this passage, marked in the margin by two crosses, ^Looke if all this between the two crosses be not to be left out, as unnecessary, be only repetitions of what hath been largely said alredy^ has been inserted. HP, p336, and 1633, p181, omit the passage; 1644, p155, omits as far as l.16 ('at leist') and abridges the remainder. *Marginal note*: The quotation is from Buchanan, Bk.XI, fol.120v. *what count we may make of our Chronologie*: i.e. 'how far we may trust the accepted datings'.

341, l.25. *Maior*: Bk.VI, ch.18, fol.CXLIv.

342, l.16. *Marginal note*: Buchanan, Bk.X1, fol.118.

342, l.26. 1644, p152, ends with funerary verses in Latin and English.

The Life of Gross James, 7th Earl of Douglas (A, pp381-389)

1440-1443

1633, pp183-186, follows A2 generally.
HP, p337-341, follows 1633, with occasional additions and corrections.
1644, pp157-160, follows 1633, abridging here and there, and adds a funerary couplet in Latin and English.

In the lives of Gross James and of his sons, Hume looks for romantic conduct and makes his story one of feud between the Douglases and the courtiers. Gross James fails miserably by romantic standards (if he were behind his nephews' murder, revenge would not be in his mind) and Hume is not interested in the unromantic political power that he wielded. He accepts Boece's and Buchanan's unfavorable picture the better to bring out the contrast with those true Douglases, James's sons. James's fatness is perhaps an implicit metaphor for Hume of possessions so great that they become unmanageable.

343, l.7. *fathers brother*: James, 7th Earl, was in fact William, 6th Earl's great uncle, and brother of Archibald Tyneman. *Marginal note*: Holinshed, *SC*, p387.
343, ll.8-9. *Balvennie*: Gross James was known as Lord of Balvany (in Banff) before he was made Earl of Evandale in 1437 (Fraser, I, 431). *Evindail*: Evandale, Dumfriesshire. *4. Duk of Turain*: in 1448 William, 8th Earl of Douglas, was refused the Dukedom of Touraine on the grounds that it had been granted only to the heirs male of the body of Tyneman. This would mean that James and his son William had no claim to the title, which had reverted to the French Crown (Fraser, I, 409-10, 425-26; Nicholson, p331).
343, l.13. *Beatrix*: actually Margaret Douglas, the Fair Maiden of Galloway (see below, p388, l.22; McGladdery, p24).
343, l.16. *Annandaile*: Annandale in fact reverted to the Crown (McGladdery, p24).
343, l.18. *had to wyfe Beatrix Sinkler*: this daughter of Henry Sinclair was his second wife. His first, a daughter of Robert, 1st Duke of Albany, died without issue.
343, ll.18-19: *it is not set downe, to try we must consider*: 'which of the Earls of Orcknay it is not sett downe. To finde it, wee must consider' (HP, p337, the most explicit of all the revisions).
343, 20-344, l.9. Hume gets the Sinclair pedigree wrong (see *SP*, II, 332-36, and VI, 564-71). No William Sinclair married the king

of Denmark's daughter, Florentina. Egidia Douglas, daughter of the Lord of Nithsdale, married Henry, 2nd Earl of Orkney. Their daughter, Beatrix, married Gross James. Summarily *SP* says that the first William married Agnes Dunbar, in this agreeing with Hume; their son Henry married Alice Fenton; and theirs, William of Roslin died with the Good Sir James in Spain. He had a son William, who married Isabella, daughter of Malise of Strathearn, Orkney and Caithness. Their son Henry became first Earl of Orkney. He married Jean, daughter of Walter Halyburton. To him, Henry succeeded as 2nd Earl and married Egida Douglas. Their son William became Chancellor and Earl of Caithness.

343, ll.25-27. *This Henries sone past with Good Sir James Douglas... callit Sir William*: See p124, ll.22-23, note.

343, l.30. bot this mans *tyme is lang before*: a puzzling remark omitted in all other texts.

344, ll.3-5. *Now this James his wyfe can not have bene this Sir Williams daughter for then was scho his awne sister daughter*: In fact, if Gross James had married the daughter of William Sinclair, Hume's 7th person, it would have been also his great grand uncle's illegitimate son's great grand daughter that he married, according to Hume's genealogy. If, as Hume prefers and *SP*, VI, 571, has it, he married the daughter of Henry Sinclair, he married, according to Hume's genealogy, his great grand uncle's illegitimate son's grand daughter. In fact he married his illegitimate brother's grand daughter, his grand niece.

344, l.18. *neice to King Robert*: 'neere of kinne to King Robert' (HP, p338, 1633, p184). John Dunbar, Earl of Moray, had married the sister of Robert III.

344, ll.15-20. Archibald became Earl of Moray 'by rather dubious means' (McGladdery, p24). Gross James secured an entail through the younger daughter, to whom Archibald was married. See below, p372, ll.7-10, and note.

344, ll.21-23. *Hugh efterward made Earle of Ormond*: his lands were mainly in Inverness and Buchan.

344, ll.23-24. *Johne... Lord of Balvenie*: see below, p372, ll.22-24.

344, ll.24-25. *Henrie was Bishope of Dunkelden*: see note to p391, ll.15-32. Fraser, I, 444-45, thinks Henry and George are the same. George continued to live in a ghostly way in Hume's pages: see his calling Hugh 'George' below p372, l.22, etc.

344, l.27. *as our Chronicles writes*: not Boece, anyway.

344, l.29-345, l.1. *his foure daughters*: *Margaret* actually married Henry Douglas of Borg, a brother of James Douglas, Lord of Dalkeith (Fraser, I, 445). *Beatrix* in fact married William Hay, 1st Earl of Errol, Constable of Scotland (concerning her supposed marriage to Lord Aubigny, 1633, p184, adds that John Stewart Duke of Albany was son to the Countess of Bouloigne); HP, p338, adds further information about Alexander Stewart, her

supposed husband. *Jennot* indeed married Robert Fleming, first Lord Fleming of Cumbernauld, and *Elizabeth* may, as HP, p338, maintains in a correction to what originally ran as the other texts, have married Sir John Wallace of Cragie. Fraser, I, 446, says there is no proof of this marriage: see also note to p384, ll.24-25.
345, ll.6-7. *Beatrix Douglas callit the fair Maden of Galloway*: actually Margaret Douglas, the sister of William, 6th Earl of Douglas (McGladdery, 24).
345, ll.12-17. See Buchanan, Bk.XI, fol.120v., for the objections of other branches of the Douglas clan; also Maitland, p74, and Boece, Bk.XVIII, fol.364 (Pitscottie, I, 47-48).
346, ll.3-4. *Augustus Caesar*: the ultimate source of this comment on Augustus, probably mediated through the reflections of another historian or political moralist, who has escaped my search, may be Putarch, *Moralia*, 207D, trans. Frank Cole Babbitt, vol.III: '[Augustus] learned that Alexander, having completed nearly all his conquests by the time he was thirty two years old, was at an utter loss to know what he should do during the rest of his life, whereat [he] expressed his surprise that Alexander did not regard it as a greater task to set in order the empire which he had than to win it'. Augustus's actual drive to expand and his moderation in doing so may be gathered from M. Cary and H. H. Scullard, *A History of Rome to the Reign of Constantine*, 3rd ed. (London, 1975), p388: 'In making the Roman boundary coterminous with the Danube, Augustus made a greater addition to Roman territory than any Roman conqueror before or after him... in the long run his policy of extending the Empire to certain well-considered limits, and no further, was fully justified by its results'.
346, l.28. *Marginal note*: Maitland, p74.
346, l.28-347, l.4 This account of the marriage is drawn from Buchanan, Bk.XI, fol.120v. to which the *Marginal note* refers. According to McGladdery, p35, the marriage was not brought about till 1443, the year of Gross James's death.
347, l.4. *Some wryte*: Buchanan, Bk.XI, fol.120v.
347, ll.9-10. *Anent the actions... no particulars recordit in histories*: in 1405 he burned Berwick, and in 1406 killed the escort of James, heir to the crown (Nicholson, p225-26). He seems to have been a vigorous and able politician and schemer.
347, l.14. *Marginal note*: Buchanan says nothing about his not pursuing the business of revenge.
347, ll.17-18. *warden of al the Marches*: see Nicholson, p225.
347, l.19. *Vthers wryt*: Buchanan presumably. *Marginal note*: Buchanan, Bk.XI, fol.120v., may be cited in support of his not being so much wicked as slack in pursuing wrongdoers.
347, l.24. *sayis the Manuscript*: Maitland, p74.
347, ll.26-27. *or 1444*: all other texts omit, and the epitaph in St Bride's Church says James died in 1443 (below p387). Fraser, I, 442-43, says that he died on 25 March, 1443. See headnote to the

Life of William, 8th Earl of Douglas.
347, l.30-348, l.1. 1644, p159, abridges the list of titles. *Avach*: Avoch, Black Isle. *Edirdoun*: Edeydoun (1633, p186, HP, p340); Edderdor (Fraser, I, 437); perhaps Edderton, near Tain. *Brachtin*: Broughtoun (1633, p186, HP, p340); Brachly, Inverness (Fraser, I, 437). *Botherny*: Bocharm, Banff (Fraser, I, 437). *Murchlach*: Murthly, Perthshire. *Rattray*: in Buchan. *Duffus*: in the shire of Elgin (Fraser, I, 437); *Evindail*: see note top381, l.8. *Albasher*: probably the Alvas-schir 'in vic. Elgin' named in *RMS*, II, no.49 (probably the parish of Alves, with 'sher' derived from the Gaelic 'sgìre', for parish suffixed). On 11 May, 1426, James I confirmed a gift from Archibald, Lord of Douglas and Galloway to his brother James of this holding. Since Archibald Tyneman and his son James had been killed at Verneuil on 17 August, 1424, this was either a posthumous confirmation of a gift of Tyneman's to his brother Gross James or of Archibald, 5th Earl of Douglas's to his brother James for the benefit of unspecified heirs.
348, l.9-349, l.2. A slip in the Latin suggests that Hume cannot have had a hand in revising A. 1644, p160, translates the epitaphs and appends a funerary couplet in Latin and English on 'Jacobus crassus' 'To be a *Douglas*, and be grosse withall,/ You shall not find another 'mongst them all'. 'The yeir of God M,CCCC.XLIII the XXV day of Merche erll James Douglas deit at the castell of Abercorn, to the takin thai said he had in him four stone of talch [tallow] and mair' (Auchinleck, p35, cited McGladdery, p161).
348, ll.12-13. *Gallovidiae:* other texts add the missing 'a Lidalia' or'Lidaliae'. *Dominus de:* other texts supply the blank with 'Balvenia'.
348, l.14. *Magnus Wardanus Regni Scotiae*: James was Warden of the Marches under Robert III (Nicholson, p225).
348, l.17. *quadringentesimo*: 1633, p186, 'quadragintesimo', a slip.
348, l.21. *Dominae:* other texts have 'Domina', correctly.
348, ll.30-31. *praedicti Domini Jacobi successit*: other texts have '*praedicti Domini Jacobi qui successit*', a more regular reading.

The Life of William, 8th Earl of Douglas (A, pp389-471)

1443-52

1633, pp187-222, follows A2 closely with more small omissions than additions.

HP, pp342-385, follows 1633 closely with a few corrections and additions.

1644, pp161-194, is closer to A than to 1633.

The narrative is drawn mostly from Buchanan (who leans heavily on the 1574 continuation of Boece, Bk.XVIII) with a scattering of additions from Maitland's MS history of the Douglas family and at least one sentence and a few details taken from Holinshed (who also follows Buchanan).

Buchanan's history of the early reign of James II is taken up with the Douglases. In spite of his theories about tyrants and the duty of aristocrats to counter excesses of monarchical power, he accepts the blackening of the Douglases and the palliation of James's unscrupulousness by the chroniclers. For him, William is an insolent overmighty subject, Crichton, Livingston, and Kennedy, Bishop of St Andrews, are by no means evil counsellors and the King is provoked to his treachery by the Douglas's impossible behaviour. Hume, though he can not entirely make out otherwise, does his best by blackening the courtiers and by various pleadings (some special) to palliate and excuse Douglas's offences and to present him as more imprudent than wicked. Hume was a redoubtable arguer; this, perhaps his most deeply meditated life, shows that to appear vigorously as an advocate does not necessarily recommend one as a judge. The theme of this life is how justice and power should be combined, the theme also of his dialogue about tyranny with the eighth Earl of Angus.

In McGladdery's history of *James II*, the political scene is vastly more complex than what Buchanan and, following him, Hume, show. Douglas is only one among other players, and James, like his father, asserts his authority more aggressively and predatorily than Hume's idea of a monarchy, served and counselled by great noblemen, can quite take in. It is also clear from her account that the 8th Earl, far from withdrawing from a political scene that disgusted his aristocratic nature, pursued factional politics with considerable success.

Hume's chronology is very unreliable. Thomas Thomson in a book of MS notes in the National Register of Archives (Scotland) RH 13/20), suggests a particular difficulty in Hume's account. Gross James's tomb says that he died on the 24th day of March, 1443. That would now be reckoned 24 March, 1444, and would make the early events of William the 8th Earl's earldom, as recorded by Hume, take place before Gross James's death. If he died, as *The Auchinleck Chronicle* says (see note to pp348-49, ll.9-2, above), on the 25th March, 1443, that would mean that he died in 1443 early enough for a possible chronology to be constructed for William's holding of the earldom. See also Fraser, I, 442-43.

350, ll.8-9. *5 Duk of Turain*: see note to p381, l.8.
350, l.11. *his Gudshire*: Tyneman was his grandfather in Hume's

erroneous reckoning instead of his uncle.
350, l.17. *Marginal note*: Buchanan, Bk.XI, fol.120v. on marriage to his cousin.
350, ll.20-22. *conveinit his hail freinds and dependars at Dumfreis*: possibly a reference to his setting down the laws of the Marches in writing in the presence of his freeholders in 1448, noted in Fraser, I, 462. *Marginal note*: The relevant pages are missing from Maitland.
350, l.30. *of Douglas*: 'and Jedburgh-forrest' (HP, p342).
350, l.33. *as second in the Kingdome*: 1644, p161, applies this, to William, 8th Earl.
350, l.33-351, l.2. *the lordshipe of Galloway*: Galloway was acquired by Archibald the Grim by gift of David II and by purchase from Thomas Fleming, Earl of Wigtown. Archibald the Grim did acquire the *Lordshipe of Bothwel* by marriage. Galloway was inherited, without Annandale, which reverted to the Crown, by Margaret, the Fair Maid of Galloway and sister of William, 6th Earl, married to William, 7th Earl of Douglas.
351, ll.8-18. 1644, p161, abridges the account of the other Douglas branches.
351, ll.11-13. *William Gudshire to the Earl of Angus... this Earl of Douglas Grandshire*: According to Hume's reckoning, William, 1st Earl of Douglas, would be grandfather to James, 3rd Earl of Angus (died, 1446) and father to Archibald the Grim, great grandfather (grandshire) to William, 8th Earl of Douglas. In fact, though the 1st Earl of Douglas was grandfather to the 3rd Earl of Angus, he was only cousin (illegitimately) of Archibald the Grim, the great grandfather of William, 8th Earl of Douglas.
351, ll.13-14. *Earle of Mortoun and Lord of Dalkeithe*: see note to p344-45, ll.29-1. The son of James, 3rd Lord of Dalkeith, became 1st Earl of Morton only in 1458.
351, ll.16. *Dumlanrige*: see p275, ll.30-32.
351, l.18. *vther sisters*: see p344-45, ll.29-1, and notes.
351, l.21. *be his wyfe Beatrix, the house of Crafurde*: see p205, ll.9-10, note. Margaret, the Fair Maid of Galloway, wife of the 8th Earl, was daughter of the 5th Earl and Euphemia Graham (McGladdery, p35), not of him and Maud Lindsay, as Hume thinks. See also Fraser, I, 420.
351, l.24. HP, p343, adds the Earldoms of William's brothers.
351, ll.26-28. *and that whereof...a short view of it*: i.e. 'a diligent reader may glean more about the friendship between the Lindsays and the Douglases from histories and even more from other sources (though I treat the matter briefly)'.
352, l.1. *the house of Angus and Morton*: there was no house of Morton before the Lords of Dalkeith were made Earls of Morton in 1458 (*SP*, VI, 354. The Black Douglases may have resented the success of the Red. McGladdery, p35, speculates that the Black Douglases may have worked against the marriage of James,

3rd Earl of Angus, to the King's sister Joanna. When James died in 1446, George, his brother, succeeded to the earldom and pushed the Angus interest vigorously at court.

352, ll.9-10. *(wha became indeid (but was not zit) his pairtie)*: Douglas according to Hume was reconciled with the King in 1444 (p359, ll.6-25).

352, l.13. *half brother*: uncle (HP, p343; a correction of 'half brother'). James Kennedy, was third son of James Kennedy of Dunnure and Mary Stewart, daughter of Robert III and earlier wife of George Ist Earl of Angus, who was grandfather to James and George, the Earls of Angus in question. Kennedy was therefore their half uncle (*SP*, II, 448-49).

352, l.26-353, l.3. See Buchanan, Bk.XI, fols.120v-121. for Douglas as the source of lawlessness. The Black Douglases were the ruling faction till 1449, when James II attacked the Livingstons, their allies against the Crichtons (Nicholson, pp358-71; McGladdery, pp32-34). Douglas would not be working against his own government, as we should have to believe if we accepted Buchanan's stories. *Johne Gorme of Athol*: John Gorm Stewart of Athol attacked Sir William Ruthven, Sheriff of Perth in 1443; they were both killed (Fraser, I, 456).

353, ll.4-7. *And thogh it had bene said sa to be his Enemies, they had done him now wrong, and more treacherouslie delth with him then to make sik report:* 'And though it had beene said so too, by his enemies, no force: they had done him more wrong, and more treacherously delt with him and his, then to make such a report' (HP, p344, and 1633, p188). Taking 'then' as 'then, at that time' and 'now' as 'as a result of what had gone before', the passage might mean, 'Even if the slander had been put abroad by his known enemies, that did not matter because the slander worked and putting the report abroad then now really damaged him and did so more treacherously than their other machinations'.

353, l.16. *Buchanan, Bk.XI, fol.120v*: has '*etsi non aleret non tamen satis acriter reprimeret*', of Gross James.

354, l.14-17. *and they that war able... be true vertue* i.e.'the Estates allowed men that were able for offices to take office, not by appointing them, but through these men's appointing themselves, who perhaps disdained the appointment of the Estates anyway as having no worth, for by the standards of true virtue we see no merit in their appointings'.

355, l.4-358, l.9. This reflection on authority and love, though dealing with Douglas's forfeiting the love of the people, glances almost as much at the King and his ill-treatment of the Douglas. Cf. *Apologia Basilica*, pp9-10.

355, ll.26-27. *Nothing is more populare; zea nothing is more profitable, then iustice, sayes al writers*: Buchanan anyway, Bk.X, fol.115v: '*nihil iusticia esse popularius'*.

357, ll.3-20. *whils they wald... to be favoured*: 1644, p164, follows A; A2 (followed by HP, p347, and 1633, p191) has, ^of the State to mak their inability to govern to be the better seen and made palpable to all men, The Earles connivence to broken men (as we tearme them) of the Borders/ some what more than was fitting/ did peece and peece empayre the Ancyent good Opinion generally held of that house (which they enherited with their heritage for many Ages together)/ furthering the plots of their Enemies against them/ and making their greatnes hitherto applauded of all/ to be suspected by their Soveran^.

358, l.10-359, l.25. According to Buchanan, Bk.XI, fol.121, it was not that Douglas had at last got a just king, but that popular hatred drove him to change his ways publicly. *1444*: The Douglas-Livingston faction proclaimed the King's 'majority' in a general council of 1444 (Nicholson, p340). James II properly entered politics, aged 19 with his marriage in 1449. *Marginal note*: Holinshed, *SC,* p387; Boece, Bk.XVIII, fol.364.

359, l.25. *sayes our wryters*: Boece, as above.; Buchanan, Bk.XI, fol.121.

359, l.28. *very casual*: i.e. his change was more a matter of appearance than of real conversion, for his former behaviour (apparently lawless) obeyed the same principles.

360, l.15. *whilk was a continuation of maners*: i.e. 'which was a continuation of his old ways'.

360, l.16-361, l.12. McGladdery (p28) suggests that there was probably an alliance between the Livingston and the Douglas factions against the Crichton one and again on p34 that Douglas probably regarded the Livingstones as potential allies during a period when he assiduously attended court.

360, l.29-363, l.11. See Buchanan, Bk.XI, fol.121, for this story of Douglas's raprochement with James, a raprochement that Buchanan describes as his taking advantage of the King's inexperience.

362, l.2. *Marginal note*: Possibly a reference to the pages missing in Maitland between those numbered 74 and 75.

362, ll.21-22. *put to the horne in a Convention halden at Stirling*: A General Council at Stirling declared Sir George and Sir William Crichton rebels, November, 1443 (McGladdery, p29).

362, l.24. *Johne Foster*: John Forrester of Corstorphine, chamberlain to James I and James II, was despoiled by Sir William and Sir George Crichton as a depender of Douglas. But it was Douglas himself who razed Barnton, Sir George Crichton's house. And it was after (not before) that attack that the Crichtons were proclaimed rebels (McGladdery, p29).

363, l.11. *Johne Earle of Mortoun*: probably James Douglas, 4th Lord of Dalkeith, made 1st Earl of Morton in 1457/58 (*SP*, VI, 354).

363, ll.11-12. *The Earle of Angus was the kings Cousin germane*: James, 3rd Earl of Angus, not George his brother (though Hume mistakenly makes out that he was his uncle in 1644, p210), was Earl at this time. His grandfather, George, 1st Earl of Angus, had married Mary Stewart, daughter of Robert III; James II was therefore cousin (germane) not to the 3rd Earl of Angus, but to his father (*SP*, 1, 18; Fraser, II, 39).

363, ll.14-15. *The Earle of Mortoun had married the Kings sister*: James Lord of Dalkeith had married Joanna, daughter of James I (*SP*, VI, 356).

365, ll.4-10. Buchanan, Bk.XI, fol.121v., approves of Kennedy's wisdom. With this approval of covert action compare Hume's condemnation of meeting fraud with fraud on pp412-13, ll.20-13. *the Bishope was the principal mover*: James Kennedy, who had been displaced from the Chancellorship, became leader of the opposition to the Douglas faction (Nicholson, pp340-41). For another view, see Dunlop, pp69-760.

365, ll.11-12. *Earl of Crafurde*: David Lindsay, 3rd Earl of Crawford (*SP*, III, 18-21). *Alexander Ogilvie of Innerwharitie*: Walter Ogilvie of Inverquharity or Inverarity (*SP*, IV, 522, and IX, 740).

365, l.14. *Marginal note*: Holinshed, *SC*, p387, merely mentions the harrying of Fife; it is Buchanan, Bk.XI, fol.121v., who mentions Kennedy's cursing, perhaps with a glint of Protestant malice.

365, l.19. *Maister of Crafurde*: Alexander Lindsay (*SP*, III, 21). Buchanan, Bk.XI, fol.121v., says the monks put Ogilvie in charge because the Master of Crawford was so insolent.

365, l.23. *the Earle of Huntlie*: Alexander Seton, made first Earl of Huntly in 1445 (*SP*, IV, 522).

366, ll.1-2. *especialie be the Cliddisdail men*: according to Buchanan they won by means of a dishonourable ruse. The battle took place on 23 January, 1445.

366, l.6. *Earle Bairdye*: His father having been killed, the Master of Crawford is now called the Earl. Alexander Lindsay, 4th Earl of Crawford, was known as 'Beardie' or 'Beard the best of them' and 'Tiger' for his ferocity; he also had a notable beard (Lord Lindsay, *The Lives of the Lindsays: A Memoir of the Houses of Crawford and Balcarres* (London, 1849), I, 134. I can make nothing of the scored out 'Bairdake' (?). The nickname is omitted by HP, p352, perhaps as too undignified.

366, ll.10-11. *whose doughter... the Earle of Douglas wyfe*: See note to p295, ll.9-10.

366, ll.25-26. *the Castle was renderit*: in July 1445 and Crichton returned to government, though not the Chancellorship (McGladdery, p33).

366, l.30-31. *Marginal note*: Buchanan, Bk.XI, fol.122. 'Our wryters' refers therefore to him; see also Boece, Bk.XVIII, fol.366 (Pitscottie, I, 57).

366, l.34-67, l.1. *he who is most strong wald seeme also most*

Innocent: a translation of what Buchanan, affirms, presumably sardonically, of Crichton (see marginal note). *Marginal note*: Buchanan, Bk.XI, fol.122. '*In omni enim certamine*' etc.
367, ll.5-6. *not so hurt as terrified*: 'not so much as terrified' (HP, p353); cf. Buchanan, Bk.XI, fol.122, '*magis perculso quam everso*, not that he was either.
367, ll.14-15. *but the Livingstoun leaps not so dry shode*: Quite apart from the false account of a supposed feud between Douglas and the Livingstons, Hume leaps forward here some years, in spite of the marginal note, to 1449 and 1450, when the King attacked the Livingstons possibly because he needed money to endow his wife, Mary of Guelders. Douglas, who had used the Livingston connection, evidently did not feel the need to stir for them (Nicholson, pp349-50, McGladdery, pp50-51).
367, ll.18-24. *Alexander Lord Livingstoun*: Sir Alexander Livingston of Calendar. *James and Robert Livingstons*: James Livingston, later Chamberlain and Robert Livingston, Comptroller. *Dauid Livingston*: of Greenyards. *Robert Bruce of Arthe*: of Clackmanan. *James and Robert Dundases*: Sir James Dundas of that ilk. The Dundases were suporters of the Livingstons. Robert Livingston, the Comptroller, was executed; Sir Alexander and James Livingston suffered forfeiture and temporary imprisonment, as also Bruce and the Dundases (McGladdery, pp49-50; Nicholson p350).
367, l.23. *Marginal note*: see notes above for right dates. Holinshed, *SC*, p389.
368, ll.11-12. *set downe in the Chronicles*: Boece, Bk.XVIII, fol.366v. Cf. Buchanan, Bk.XI, fol.122-122v. *what be gyltinese*: The correction, 'giltlesnese' is almost certainly correct; Buchanan's Livingston says that some of the charges against him concerned matters already pardoned, some, matters of which he was innocent. To make any sense of 'giltinese', we should have to suppose that confession of his crimes made a clean breast and in that sense purged him.
368, l.14. *Some coniecture*: who these are, I have been unable to discover.
368, l.21. *the second Parlament in the 1438*: James's second Parliament was in 1445, his first one in 1437 (*Acts of the Parliament of Scotland*, II). An act of the General Council of 13 March, 1438, at Stirling, against rebellious men (*APS*, II, 32) is probably meant. 1644, p170, has '1488' a misprint.
368, ll.27-28. *1447*: The Livingstons were executed in January 1450. Marie of Guelders was married to James in July 1449. *Marginal note*: Holinshed, *SC*, p389.
368, ll.29-30. *at whilk tyme the Chrichton is said to have bene forfaultit*: Crichton is said to have been Chancellor again by April 1448 (Nicholson p352), and at no time after the siege of Edinburgh do his goods seem to have been forfeited .

369, l.18. *ather of the Catoes*: M. Porcus Cato Censorius and his great grandson, M. Porcus Cato Uticensis.
369, l.23. *Cato callit censorius*: see Plutarch, 'Cato', *Lives,* XV, 3.
370, ll.28-30. *James Stewart*: given Hume's confused chronology, either Alan Stewart, Lord Darnley, killed by Sir Thomas Boyd, 20 September, 1438 (McGladdery, pp14-15), or James Stewart of Auchingowne, killed on 31 May, 1445, by Alexander Lisle and Robert Boyd (Auchinleck, p37). *Patrick Dumbar:* Archibald Dunbar, Earl of March, took Hails in East Lothian, Patrick Hepburn's castle (*SP*, III, 278-79). According to Buchanan Bk.XI, fol.122, Douglas was blamed for both these stirs. But only the capture of Hails was in Douglas's interest; Dunbar surrendered the castle to him (Dunlop, p77).
371, l.1. *Marginal note*: Holinshed, *SC,* p388; Boece, Bk.XVII, fols.365v.-366.
371, l.5. *Sir James Stewart*: had married the Queen mother and so was the King's step father. For his being forced to leave the country, see Buchanan, Bk.XI, fol.122. He was put to death by his captors, according to Auchinleck, p41, but according to McGladdery, p123, was still alive in 1454.
371, l.19. 1423: James I returned to Scotland in April 1424.
371, ll.22-26. In 1448, the younger Percy and Sir Robert Ogle burned Dunbar in May, the Earl of Salisbury, Dumfries in June and the Earl of Douglas and Hugh (not James), Earl of Ormond, Alnwick (Fraser, I, 462; Nicholson, p346, puts these events in 1449 after the Battle of Sark, but Auchinleck, pp39-40, and Boece, Bk.XVIII, fol.367 [Pitscottie, I, 61-62] agree with Fraser).
372, l.1-375, l.20. This interesting defence of Douglas's doing well by his family is written against Buchanan's accusations of greed, Bk. XI, fol.123, and Boece's, as above (Pitscottie, I, 62-65).
372, ll.4-14. *James Dumbar*: James Dunbar, Earl of Moray, died in 1429. Gross James arranged the marriage of Archibald to Dunbar's younger daughter, Elizabeth, and the entail that cut out Janet the elder daughter and her husband, James Crichton of Frendraught, son of Sir William Crichton, the Chancellor (Nicholson, p332). See above, p344, ll.15-20, and note. *Holinsyd cals him Johne*: I cannot find this in Holinshed. *Not the les that... the title belongit*: HP, p356, omits. Buchanan says that Douglas used his influence with the King to obtain Archibald the Earldom, against all laws of succession (Bk.XI, f.123).
372, l.22. *George (or Hugh)*: Buchanan says 'George', which is not consistent with the Latin epitaph in St Bride's Church on Gross James, quoted on p388. HP, p356, says Ormond is in the province of Kelso. In fact it is a hill in the estate of Ardmanoch in the Black Isle (McGladdery, p46, n.2; Nicholson p342). His lands (in Aberdeenshire and Invernessshire) were created from the patrimony of his sister in law, Margaret (McGladdery, p32). See above, p344, ll.21-23, and note.

372, ll.23-24. *Johne*: John Douglas, Lord of Balveny may have been a youth (see 'The Book of the Howlat', l.602; Fraser, I, 453); he possessed Balvenny and other lands in Banff. See above, p.344, l.23-24, and note.
373, ll.18-24. *and if ever it come... overmatchit with Enemies*: see 1644, pp172-73. The sense is 'even if friends one has advanced should outstrip one, as long as they remain friendly their success should not be grudged. And even if they should disappoint one's expectations in friendship, their success should still not be resented unless, of course, it should be combined with great wickedness, and perhaps not even then, rightly considered. After all being outstripped in this way is better than being overmatched by enemies, which can hardly be avoided if one stands alone without allies whose support one has cultivated'.
374, ll.23-24. *a mans riches... be brigandes*: Cf. Juvenal, Satire, X, ll.19-22.
375, l.2. *Pirrhus*: HP, p358, tells the story of Cineas, who by continually questioning Pyrrhus what he meant to conquer next brought him to say that after so many intended conquests he would live content; at this Cyneas asked why he could not be content with the moderate possessions he enjoyed. See Plutarch, 'Pyrrhus', *Lives*, IV, 229.
375, l.7. *Augustus*: see p346, ll.3-4.
375, l.31-382, l.23. This defence of Douglas is directed against charges advanced in Buchanan, Bk.XI, fol.123. It is anticipated to some extent by Maitland, pp75-76.
377, ll.26-28. *and of the number of these, that are bot amplifiet and augmentit for invy*: i.e. 'including among the charges that are false those that have been aggravated by envy'.
378, l.4-5. *the Cummings is comptit to be greatter*: before they were broken by Robert the Bruce, they were the most influential family in Scotland.
379, ll.9-10. *animus per se insolens*: Buchanan, Bk.XI, fol.123.
379, ll.15-18. *for it is historical only... (of whilk both we are skant)*: i.e. 'it is a matter of historical facts, which Buchanan, I hope, has found, he having had leisure and having looked through histories, two things rather lacking with me'. Hume probably means to cast doubt on Buchanan's exactness (Cf. pp381-82, ll.7-2).
379, l.26-380, l.19. It is not obvious what the stoical reflections on the mind as it own place and the universality of flattery have to do with defending Douglas from Buchanan's charges. Probably with the first, Hume wishes to raise an eyebrow with regard to Buchanan's report: if Douglas's dependers could not protect themselves from him by concealing their thoughts, he must have gone far indeed. With the second, probably he wants to defend Douglas by saying that flattery is so universal that there is nothing very special about his case. *Diogenes*: founder of the Cynics. See

Diogenes Laertius. *Lives and Opinions of Eminent Philosophers*, VI, 32, for the story about Diogenes the Cynic and Alexander, and VI, 40, for the story about the mouse as his parasite.
380, l.27. *out of doubt*: i.e. 'without doubt'.
381, 34-382, l.1. *I wate not... absolutlie*: Hume has Buchanan in mind.
382, ll.10-11. *Blew bairde*: the alias of Thomas Cheyne, captain in chief of the Kentish rising of January 1450 (see Isobel Harvey, *Jack Cade's Rebellion of 1450* [Oxford, 1991], pp64-66). *John Cade*: Jack Cade led a peasant rebellion that occupied London in 1450.
382, l.20. *Marginal note*: Buchanan, Bk. XI, fol.123-123v.
382, ll.27-28. *in this zeir*: the Battle of Sark took place on the 23 October, 1448.
383, l.4. *Marginal note*: Maitland's manuscript has nothing on Cumberland's being reduced to a wilderness, but Boece, Bk.XVIII, fol.369v. (Pitscottie, I, 72) has.
383, ll.6-7. *a verie great armie of 40000 men (as some wryte)*: a number not to be found in Buchanan or Holinshed but in Boece, as above.
383, ll.14-15. *the Earle of Northumberland*: In fact it was the son of the Earl of Northumberland at the time of the Battle of Sark in 1448, Henry Percy, Lord Poynings, who was in charge; he became 6th Earl of Northumberland in 1455 (*CP,* IX, 716; Fraser, I, 451).
383, l.17. *a gentilman onelie born... but in derision*: this account of Magnus with the Rid maine is not in Fraser but may be found in Boece, Bk. XVIII, fol.369v., Buchanan, Bk.XI, fol.123v. (who says nothing about his red beard) and Holinshed, *SC*, pp389-90. Boece, as above, calls him 'Ruffabarba', but Pitscottie, I, 73, thinks the 'main' is a hand.
383, ll.31-32. *The manuscript callis him Magnus with the rid baird*: Perhaps on the page or pages missing between pp74 and p75.
384, ll.3-4. *George Douglas Earle of Ormond (or Hugh as vthers cal him righter)*: See note to p417, l.5. Holinshed, *SC*, p389, gives the alternative names, Buchanan, Bk,XI, fol.123v. only George. In fact Hugh.
384, ll.9-11. *having passit... the water of Sark*: The Sark Burn now marks the boundary between England and Scotland. Percy must have retired after having crossed the Annan considerably to the West.
384, l.20. *Sir Johne Ponentarie*: 1644, p178, has 'Pennington', Buchanan, Bk.XI, fol.123v., 'Ponentonius'. The Sir Johne Ponintoun, taken prisoner later (p433, l.18) is the same man in Buchanan. He is 'Pennytoune' in Auchinleck, p40, and 'Peneintoune' in Boece, Bk.XVIII, fol.370, and Apmiroun in Pitscottie, I, 73. *Marginal note*: Holinshed, *SC,* pp389-90.
384, ll.24-25. *William Wallace of Cragie*: HP, p364, scores out

'William' and writes in 'Sir Johne', 'of whose house the famous Sir William Wallace was descended'. Wallace of Craigie is said by HP, p388, to have married Elizabeth, the sister of Ormond and Douglas (see note to p344-45, ll.29-1). *RMS, 1342-1513*, no.301, January 1449/50, has a Sir John Wallace of Cragy as witness of an indenture between Archibald Earl of Moray and James Douglas of Heriotmure to support the Earl of Douglas, so HP may be rightly corrected.

384, l.26. *the knight of Carlaverock callit Maxwel*: Herbert, 1st Lord Maxwell (*SP*, VI, 475).

384, l.28. *sayes the Manuscript*: perhaps on the pages missing between p74 and 75.

384, l.32-385, l.12. The reported speeches are from Buchanan, Bk.XI, fol.123v. See also Boece, Bk.XVIII, fol.370 (Pitscottie, I, 74-75).

385, ll.26-30. *The slaughter of this man... impression*: Holinshed, *SC,* p390, verbatim.

386, ll.6-7. *not to sell the beirs skine before he be slane*: Cf. 'Sell not the bear's skin before you have caught him' (Tilley, 132).

386, ll.11-13. *Sir Johne Ponintoune: see p384, l.20; Sir Robert Haringtoun*: perhaps the Jhon Herntoun of Auchinleck, p40. *Lord Percie*: See p383, ll.14-15.

386, l.33-387, l.14. The speech of the King is not in Buchanan but in Boece, Bk.XVIII, fol.370v. (Pitscottie, I, 76-77). HP, p366, and 1633, pp206-207, give the Earl of Douglas a courteous speech that manages to disclaim the faults that the King would fix on him by pardoning them.

388, ll.8-17. According to Nicholson, p347-48, Crichton along with others negotiated the match between Mary of Guelders and James II with Philip of Burgundy (her uncle, not brother). Philip the Good of Burgundy was the grandson of Philip the Bold, the son of King John of France, and in that way of the blood royal.

388, ll.17-20. After the King's marriage in 1449, Douglas associated with Crichton and Kennedy in James's government.

388, ll.24-25. *as it did aganes the Boyds*: Robert Lord Boyd went to Norway to arrange a marriage for James III with Margaret, daughter of Christian VII. While he was away, James struck at the Boyd ascendancy and Robert went into exile (MacDougall, pp80-81).

389, l.3. *Richard Colvin (or Melvin)*: 'Colvin' alone HP, p368 and 1633, p208; 'Colville', 1644, p180, and Buchanan, Bk.XI, fol.124. Richard Colville was killed on 20 April, 1449, The Colvilles were allied to the Crichtons by marriage (McGladdery, p57). *Marginal note*: Maitland, p76.

389, l.3-90, l.7. Buchanan, Bk.XI, fol.124, from whom the account of the Colville affair is taken, does not use the 'the some said one thing, some another' formula here (though he does elsewhere); he says that Douglas was praised only by flatterers.

390, l.18. *Jubile*: according to Buchanan, Bk.XI, fol.124, the ancient Jews remitted all debts every fifty years; by analogy, the Pope every fifty years remitted all spiritual debts, offering pardons on a grand scale, not however without earthly payment. Douglas set out for Rome in 1450 (McGladdery, p55).
390, l.18. *Marginal note*: Maitland, 96, so far from saying he went to Rome as a penance for murder, has it that Douglas went 'thinkand Scotland not sufficient to schaw his magnificence thairin'.
390, l.30. *Marginal note*: Boece, Bk.XVIII, fol.371; Holinshed, *SC*, p391.
390, ll.31-33. The list of attendants, without the particularizing of the Lauders, is given in Boece, Bk. XVIII, fol.371 (Pitscottie, I, 80), Maitland, p77, and Holinshed, *SC*, p391. *CDS,* p249, has an entry for April 25, 1451, Privy Seals (Tower), 29 Henry VI, file 2, a safe conduct for the Earl of Douglas and his brother James, Sir James Hamilton (of Cadzow), Sir Nicholas Campbell, William Lauder of Halton (or Hatton), and Alan of Lauder, Andrew Gray. There were no Lauders of Philorth or of Cromarty. Urquhart (of Cromarty), Saltoun, Seton, Oliphant, Forbes and Calder are not specified in the safe conduct. In Boece, Forbes is given as 'Froster' (Forrester).
391, ll.7-8. *gud services done be his avuncle at Baugé, and his Gudshire at dyvers tymes*: Hume, thinking Gross James a son of Archibald Tyneman, calls the latter William's grandfather and Archibald, the 5th Earl, his uncle (in fact his uncle and cousin, respectively).
391, ll.15-32. This passage should have made up Hume's mind that the Earl of Ormond was not called George (see notes to pp372, ll.22, and 384, ll.3-4). HP, p370, says that Gross James sent James to the Sorbonne with a view to his training for the bishopric of Dunkeld, but made him give over his claim to his brother Henry when Henry became close to the king and in a position to ask for a place. *He is said by the Manuscript in the lyfe of their father to have beene Bishope of Dunkel*: the relevant part of the life of Gross James is missing, but on p80 James, later 9th Earl, is said to have been intended for Bishop of Dunkeld. Buchanan's 'oversight' occurs in the place cited in the marginal note. *Marginal note*: Buchanan, Bk.XI, fol.124.
391, l.33. *Marginal note*: Maitland, p77.
392, l.7. *The Laird of Symontoun*: 'chief of the Dicksons' (HP, p371). The Dicksons had changed their names to Symington after the grant of the Barony of Symington in Robert Bruce's time (Fraser, I, 114). See pp61, ll.30-33, and 78, ll.20-28.
392, ll.28-33. The speech is out of Buchanan, Bk.XI, fol.124; see also Boece, Bk.XVIII, fol.371 (Pitscottie, I, 83). But the description of the motives behind it is all Hume's, Buchanan attributing it, not even to enemies, merely to 'some'.

393, l.33-394, l.2. *William Sinkler Earle of Orknay*: according to McGladdery, p56, William Crichton was Chancellor at the time (1451), though Buchanan, Bk.XI, fol.124, names Sinclair in that office. See note to pp343-44, ll.20-29, for the relation of Sinclairs and Douglases. William Sinclair was Douglas's uncle, not cousin; he had also married Elizabeth the daughter of Tyneman, his brother in law, who was already a remote cousin of his mother. Giles or Egidia Douglas, the daughter of the Lord of Nithsdale and mother of William Sinclair, was already in 3rd and 2nd degree of consanguineity with Henry, 2nd Earl of Orkney, his father (*SP*, VI, 570-71). *this mans gudshire*: Henry was the grandfather of William, the 8th Earl of Douglasr, but he was the father of 'this man', William 3rd Earl of Orkney, and 1st Earl of Caithness (*SP*, II, 332-36).
394, ll.2-9. *wha appearantlie... for the tyme*: the other texts follow A2 in omitting this passage.
394, ll.14-15. *be the instigation... during his absence*: Fraser, I, 467, agrees with Hume after discussing this contested point.
394, l.18. *Marginal note*: Holinshed, *SC,* p391.
394, l.20-395, l.10. McGladdery, p55, puts this invasion of Galloway down to James's attempt to enforce crown claims to the titles of Archibald Tyneman's widow, Margaret, on her death.
394, l.32. *Marginal note*: Holinshed, *SC*, p391.
395, ll.2-3. *the Castle of Lochmaben*: this was a royal castle, but McGladdery, p56, thinks it may have been manned by Douglas's men and that James may have wished to change the keepers.
395, ll.4-5. *the Castle of Douglas*: either Douglas Castle in Douglasdale or Craig Douglas on the Yarrow (Fraser, I, 467; McGladdery, p56).
395, l.25. *Annandail*: with the murder of William, 6th Earl, Annandale had passed to the Crown.
395, l.27. *Marginal note*: Holinshed, *SC*, p391.
395, ll.29-30. *Lieutenant general of the hail Kingdome of Scotland*: so Buchanan, Bk.XI, fols.124v-25, but according to McGladdery, p59, this is a misunderstanding of his being restored to the Wardenship of the Marches.
396, ll.1-5. *This not the les... forget it*: The sentence seems to need either 'howbeit he' of the revision or a 'zit' before 'could'.
396, ll.10-11. *gyding throgh sik surges to so peacible a port whatever dexteritie*: i.e. 'whatever dexteritie guided him through such surges to so peaceable a port'.
396, l.15-398, l.1. Buchanan, Bk.XI, fol.125, tells of Douglas's rash journey to England. McGladdery, p60, says that there is no evidence of Douglas's having used the safe-conduct issued by Henry VI and that he may have sent his brother James to negotiate the release of Malise Graham, one of the hostages for James I's ransom. Graham had a claim to the crown that might be made to look better than James II's and scandalously had not been

redeemed.
397, ll.13-14. *that conspiracie of the Duk of Zork*: Richard Duke of York, father of Edward IV (See E. F. Jacob, *The Fifteenth Century, 1399-1485* (Oxford, 1961), pp502-504..
397, ll.21-24. *to wit of lands... and so furthe*: 1644, p184, omits. George, 4th Earl of Angus, was offered lands in England by Henry VI (1644, pp215-16).
398, l.3. *our writers seem to say the contrare*: Buchanan, Bk.XI, fol.125, says that Douglas did plead to the King that restitution was his aim, but suggests that there was something deeper in his mind. See also Boece, Bk.XVIII, fols.84-85 (Pitscottie, I, 84-85).
398, l.4. *Marginal note*: Maitland has nothing on acquainting the King with his purpose in England or on the tokens being brought from the English to the Scottish Queen
398, l.9. *Marginal note*: Holinshed, *SC*, p391.
398, ll.14-15. *spoylit him of the office of Lieutenantrie*: Douglas was probably made Warden of the West and Middle Marches in 1451 after his return from Rome. It is doubtful if he was deprived of office before James murdered him. See McGladdery, p59; for Hume's account see Boece, Bk.XVIII, fol.372 (Pitscottie, I, 84).
398, ll.19-20. *restorit his ancient Enemie William Chrichton to the Chancellerie*: Sir William Crichton had been Chancellor since 1448.
399, l.3. *Marginal note*: Buchanan, Bk.XI, f.125.
399, l.17. *Marginal note*: Maitland, p79, has nothing about Crichton's providing against such an eventuality or being well attended or horsed.
399, ll.20-21. *Vthers*: Buchanan, Bk.XI, fol.125, gives this version of the attack on Crichton. *Marginal note*: Holinshed, *SC*, p391.
399, l.33-400, l.7. So far from retiring, Douglas at this point, according to McGladdery, p64, was afraid not to attend court after what had happened during his absence in Rome. Neither she nor Fraser mention Douglas's and Crichton's assaults on each other.
400, ll.10-32. See p366, ll.4-13. HP, pp375-76, on a page revising the earlier version, lists many more subscribers to this band, omits 'or rather renewit... this same Earle', expresses the tenor of the band more strongly and says that by it Douglas was enabled to put 40000 men in the field. *Earles of Crafurde and Rosse*: Alexander Lindsay, 4th Earl of Crawford (*SP*, III, 21) and John MacDonald Lord of the Isles and Earl of Ross (*SP*, V, 45-47). *her mother being a daughter of ane of the Earls*: see p295, ll.9-10, note.
400, ll.19-20. William, 1st Earl of Douglas, persuaded Robert II, to pardon James Lindsay, Earl of Crawford, for the murder of John Lyon (pp200-201); for help against Kennedy, see p365, and for the Fair Maid of Galloway, see note to p345, ll.6-7.
401, l.1. *Marginal note*: Buchanan, Bk.XI, fol.125.
401, ll.32-33. *Sir William Hereis of Tarrigles*: John Herries of

Terregles was alive in 1478, according to *SP*, IV, 403, which knows of no William of Terregles. Buchanan, Bk.XI, fol.125, says flatly that Herries detested Douglas's tyranny.
402, l.26. *within his bounds*: see note to p395, ll.25.
402, l.31. *Marginal note*: Holinshed, *SC*, p391.
402, l.33. *a pitieful mater*: Contrast,'*ea res cum atrox, ut erat'* (Buchanan, Bk.XI, fol.125v).
403, ll.10-12. *he might have convictit... his Enemitie*: i.e. 'got the Lord Herries convicted in some measure without dangerous courses for whatever he (Douglas) might have incurred by his enmity'.
403, l.15-405, l.1. According to Jenny Wormald, *Lords and Men: Bonds of Manrent, 1442-1603* (Edinburgh, 1985), pp151-152, the story of the tutor of Bombie was a fabrication of Pitscottie, I, 88-94, though Hume does not cite this source; so also Fraser, I, 471. See also McGladdery, pp136-37.
403, l.3. *Treive*: Threave, Galloway.
404, l.5. *Patrik Gray of Fouls*: Patrick, Master of Gray (*SP*, IV, 275).
404, ll.9-10. *somewhat of kine to the Earle*: on p462, l.4, he is said to be a cousin. How this might be does not emerge from *SP*, IV, 272-75.
405, l.18. *beistlines*: 1644, p188, has 'brutishnesse' which, with its suggestions of dullness or lack of spirit, comes closer to Buchanan's '*ignavia*' (Bk.XI, fol.125v.).
406, ll.2-3. *if he had send*: if he had delivered him to the King.
406, l.10. *factious inclyning*: following A2, HP, p379, 1633, p217, and 1644, p189, all have 'factions' (inclining the King's will); but 'factious' makes the better sense here and looks quite as plausible in the MS.
406, ll.29-30. *Zea his pleasour to be in what is right and himself obeyit*: A2, followed by HP, p379 and 1633, p217, fills out the elliptical construction ('Yea makes his pleasour to be in what is right and thinks himself obeyed when that is performed').
407, l.13. *a gentilman his freind*: William Lauder of Hatton (McGladdery, p65).
408, l.19. HP, p381, inserts the story of the Livingstone's beating back his nephew, James Hamilton of Cadzow, and only Douglas's page Lockhart of Lie being allowed to go in with him.
408, l.25. *Marginal note*: Maitland, p80.
409, ll.2-9. Douglas's modest reply is not in Buchanan.
410, l.1. HP, p381, adds that Lockhart slid over the Castle wall and spread the news that the King had murdered Douglas.
411, l.16. *Marginal note*: Buchanan, Bk.XI, fol.125v.
411, ll.17-18. *Maxime in Machivelisme*: see *The Prince*, 'How princes should honour their word', ch.XVIII. See *Apologia Basilica*, ch.4, sec.4, p121ff., for Hume's elaborated reflections on Machiavelli's discussion of promise keeping among princes.

411, ll.29-32. In Hume the divinity of kings, even if forfeited with difficulty, is dependent on the kings' not acting unjustly and so destroying the divine image of authority that they bear. *Marginal note*: Perhaps *Manuscr.* refers back to Crichton's speech to the 6th Earl in Maitland, pp68-70.
412, l.3. *Marginal note*: Holinshed, *SC*, p392, who dates the murder correctly as 1451, does not make Hume's point about authority.
412, l.15. *resolvit to quyt the Countrie*: According to McGladdery, p78, James's actions against the Douglases show that he had no attention of flying the country.
412, l.20-413, l.2. Cf. the earlier remark on p365, ll.6-10, about meeting covert methods covertly.
413, ll.1-5. *be allowit... base meanes*: 1633, p220, and HP, p383 follow A2 in omitting this too pointed limitation on kingly power; 1644, p192, makes it even more pointed ('unworthy of a King to stoupe to such unworthy and base wayes').
413, ll.12, 20. *Marginal notes*: Buchanan, Bk.XI, f.125v., a rendering of *'Si ne id quidem auderet, quid aliud superesse, nisi ut qui ad euum diem in fide perstitissent, aliquando tandem sibi consulerent.'*
414, l.1. *Marginal note*: Buchanan, Bk.XI, f.126.
414, l.19. In order to show that the murder was premeditated, 1644, p193, adds as a received tradition, the story about Hamilton's being beaten from the King's supper by his uncle so that he would not share in Douglas's fate (see note to p408, l.19). It does not sound as if 1644, were directly indebted to HP here.
414, ll.27-28. *but that... zit not as iniust; we never find as imputit to him*: i.e. 'we never find him charged with injustice in his revenge, only haste and violence'.
415, ll.21-22. *the 13 of Februar, 1452*: 22 February, according to McGladdery, p66.
415, ll.22-25. *the 1451 Fastingseven*: 'or Shrove Tuesday' (1644, p194); HP, p387, gives only 1451 as the date. *Maior*: Bk.VI, ch.18, fol.141v. *the Romane supputation*: begins the year in January; *the Compt of Scotland*: begins the year on Lady Day, 25 March.
415, l.28. HP, p387, adds in the margin that 'some report that his body was put in a blak coffin there in the Castell' (see p441, ll.5-16); 1644, p194, adds a couplet in Latin and an English translation.

The Life of James, 9th Earl of Douglas (A, pp472-512)

1452-88

1633, pp222-240, is close to A2 on the whole, with additions and small omissions. The revisions of A not only sometimes tone down Hume's Melvillian ideas about the monarchy but actually replace them with royalist pieties abut the divinity of kings. In places the muddled account of events suggests bad editing of this heavily revised life.

HP, pp387-420, is written throughout in a poor hand, differing from the standard one, and though for large tracts it follows 1633, in many places it departs from it, altering and recasting to fit the account of events in Ringan Dalyell's MS.

1644, pp194-211, follows A in the main rephrasing and cutting or adding on a minor scale.

A, 1633 and 1644 follow Buchanan (and behind him, Bk.XVIII of the 1574 edition of Boece) mostly for their narrative, though not for their view of events. For Buchanan, as for Hume, the chief business of the reign of James II is the crown's feud with the Douglases, but, unlike Hume, Buchanan thinks highly of James and of his councillors, and poorly of the Earl of Douglas, a rash and rebellious aristocrat. For Hume, the earl is an unfortunate but noble gentleman, a Douglas incapable of contending effectively and resolutely with his sovereign, in spite of the terrible wrongs that have been done to his family. And so Hume is able to bring his history of the Douglases as a family of loyal servants of their country and kings to a satisfactory sad conclusion. HP, depending on the Ringan Dalyell MS, makes it clear that at least at one point Douglas was very eager for reconciliation with the King and only prevented from it by the devious and hostile response from James. This implicit admission that the earl was not driven by irresistible demands of family honour against an immovable loyalty to his king is more in line with McGladdery's account of the reign than the other versions are. And it suggests for a moment the view of both McGladdery and Wormald that it was the King's aggressiveness and rapacity that brought about the quarrel with the Douglases, not the Douglases' insolence or the courtiers' malice.

416, l.16. *Chrichton*: HP, p387, adds 'the Lord Levingston'.
417, ll.10-11. *driven to sik point of dispaire, as to have left the Contrie*: see note to p412, l.15.
417, ll.13-15. *zitt had he... four brethrein*: Fraser, I, 480-81, doubts the story that the four brothers were present, noting that their absence would explain why they did not lay siege to the town immediately. See below.
417, l.19. HP, p388, citing the MS of Ringan Dalyell, schoolmaster of Dumfries, says that James, not George (see note to p391, ll.15-32) was designed for Bishop of Dunblane and trained

at the Sorbonne and that William, the 8th Earl, persuaded him to resign the title in favour of his brother Henry on his return from Rome. According to Nicholson, p359, James had been designed for the bishopric of Aberdeen, until it was thought better to declare him heir presumptive to William in 1447.

417, l.26-418, l.1. *according to... Longaville*: HP, p388, omits; 1633, p223, and 1644, p195, omit the titles to which James acceded. *Annandail*: see note to p343, l.16. *Duk of Turain*: see note to p343, ll.8-9.

418, ll.4-13. The account of the events following the murder of William is drawn from Buchanan, Bk.XI, fol.126. In Buchanan 'sent for their freinds... horrible a fact' is James's speech, and so it is given in 1644, p195; but in A, HP, p388, and 1633, p223, it is made part of the narrative of events.

418, ll.29-30. *draw his end*: 'draw his breath' (A2, HP, p389, 1633, p223).

P418, l.30. *Marginal note*: Buchanan, Bk.XI, f.126.

419, ll.3-4. *Twenty fyve of Marche*: Buchanan, Bk.XI, fol.126, has 27th March. HP, p389, adds that Douglas in this interim repared his castles of Douglas, Straven and Threave and that the King went to Fife. James Douglas returned to Stirling on the 17 March (McGladdery, p75) . *Hamiltoun*: Sir James Hamilton of Cadzow at this time.

419, ll.7-8. *ane il favored meire*: 'an ill-favoured spittle jade' (1644, p195).

419, l.14. *Marginal note*: Maitland, p81, has an account of the burning of Stirling but nothing about going to the Castle gate.

419, l.17. *Vthers wreite*: I have not been able to trace them.

419, l.22. *Marginal note*: Holinshed, *SC*, p392.

419, l.23-421, l.2. HP, p389-90, omits the reflection on Douglas's failure to lay seige to Stirling Castle. It explains Hamilton's interest (he had married Archibald 5th Earl of Douglas's widow Eupham Graham) and goes on to mention his second marriage to a daughter of James II. The story about the King's only being stayed from withdrawing to France by Bishop Kennedy's counsel is in Holinshed (see marginal note, below), but according to McGladdery, pp75-76, James had escaped to Fife.

420, l.22. *blasfemit*: i.e., 'reviled'. The MS is illegible, but Priscilla Bawcutt's suggestion, 'blasfemit', fits the sense and the letters that can be made out.

420, l.25. *Marginal note*: Holinshed, *SC,* p392. Maitland has nothing about the despair of the King or the counsel of James Kennedy.

421, l.6. *Earle of Angus brother uterine to this James Kennedie by their moter, daughter to King Robert*: see note to p352, l.13.

421, ll.14-17. *as fittist for him... preferment*: HP, pp389-390, and 1644, p196, omit.

421, ll.17-29. *There was also Johne... callit Margaret*: Joanna,

James II's sister was married on 15 May 1459 to James Douglas, recently raised from 4th Lord of Dalkeith to 1st Earl of Morton. Henry, his uncle, had married Gross James's daughter, the sister of the 9th Earl of Douglas (*SP*, VI, 351, 353, 354-56). These connections have no bearing on the 3rd Lord of Dalkeith's actions in 1452. *Holinsyde... sone to Banquho*: *SC*, pp246-48.
421, ll.22-23. *as also the Manuscript*: perhaps in the pages on genealogy missing at the beginning of Maitland's History. Pp81-82 say that the Lord of Dalkeith was friendly with King James and that that particularly angered the Earl of Douglas as a betrayal of kinship.
421, l.25. *also the Manuscript in the lyfe of Gros James*: perhaps in the pages missing in Maitland's History between p74 and 75. For Margaret Douglas's marriage to the Lord of Dalkeith, see p344-45, ll.29-1, and note.
422, ll.1-8. *laid seige to the Castle of Dalkeith*: Fraser, I, 481, doubts whether it took place at this time. *Patrik Cokburne*: Patrick Cockburn was keeper of the Castle from 1444 (Dunlop, p59). His lands are not named in the *RMS* or *ER*, and it may be that Hume is simply supplying contemporary families with distinguished forebears. HP, p390, gives a more circumstantial account of the seige of the Castle of Dalkeith and omits with 1633, p225, 'or rather Clerkington'.
422, ll.12-13. *Alexander Gordoun Earle of Huntlie his brother in law (or sister sone) whom he made Lieutenant*: an error. Alexander Seton of Gordon, 1st Earl of Huntly's mother was Elizabeth Gordon and his wives Egidia Hay and Elizabeth Crichton.
422, l.17. *the Earle of Crafurd*: Alexander Lindsay. See note to p366, l.6.
422, ll.27-28. *Johne Colesse of Bonnimoone*: See Boece, XVIII, fol.374. John Cullace of Balnamoyn, near Brechin. A 16th century Collace of Balnamoyne is mentioned in Fraser, III, 311. John Collace might be his ancestor. See Pitscottie, I, 98, note.
422, l.32. *Baronie of Ferme*: Fern, c. 7 miles East of Brechin.
423, l.2. *Marginal note*: Holinshed, *SC*, p392.
423, l.7. Buchanan Bk.XI, fol.126v., says that this and the following battles in the North East took place in Spring, HP, p391, that the Battle of Brechin took place on Ascension Day, 1451, 1633, p225, and 1644, p197, on Ascension Day 1453, and Holinshed *SC*, p392, on the 18th May, Ascension Day, 1452, a date accepted by McGladdery, p76, who thinks the battle might have more to do with a feud between Crawford and Huntly than with war between the King and the Douglases.
423, l.10. *Vruins*: Irvines.
423, l.13. *Johne Lindsay*: Sir John Lindsay, said to be the ancestor of the Lindsays of Pittairlie (*SP*, III, 20).
423, l.22. *Marginal note*: Holinshed, *SC*, pp392-393.

423, l.27. *demolishit their Castles*: HP, p391, specifies Innerwharitie and Bonnimoon (Inverarity and Balnamoyne in Angus).
423, l.33. Buchanan, Bk.XI, fol.126v., says that Archibald Douglas, Earl of Moray, had used every species of cruelty in his campaign. *coming to Elgen*: Forres in Pitscottie, I, 99-100 (not in Boece). No Elgin records survive for this period and Herbert B. Mackintosh, *Elgin Past and Present* (Elgin, 1914), p89, relies on Hume's account.
424, ll.4-5. *halfe done as Elgen was brunt*: I cannot find other instances of this proverb.
424, l.8. *the Drum of Pluscardein*: near Elgin.
424, ll.10-11. *forrowit his lands to witte... Bot the Earl of Murray finding them so skatterit*: The blank is in MS. 1633, p226, simply omits this passage so that it is the Earl of Huntly who 'invaded' and wins the battle, against the sense of the rhyme. HP, 391, says that the Earl of Huntly's men 'invaded' the Earl of Moray's army though positioned on the Drum, and were driven back into the Bog. 1644, p198, says that the Earl of Huntly tried to draw Moray from the Drum of Pluscarden by plundering his lands and that the Earl of Moray took advantage of the dispersal of his troops to defeat them. HP, p392, adds that in the end Huntly succeeded in driving Moray out of the North.
424, ll.14-15. *the Bogge of Dunkintie in the bounds of Pittindriche*: near Elgin.
424, ll.27-31. HP, p392, says that James bargained with Douglas to raise the siege of Dalkeith, and on pp393-395 (a passage confused with additions and deletions), gives the texts of an 'Appointment' signed by the Earl of Douglas and Hamilton of Cadzow on 28 August, 1451, and another undertaking at Lanark 16 January, 1452, in which Douglas renounces revenge for his brother's death (Cf. McGladdery, p81, who gives the date of 'the Appointment' as 28 August, 1452 and the Lanark band, January, 1453). These concessions were, however, met with delay and shuffling by the King so that Douglas (HP, p397) was exasperated into rejecting the course of conciliation, as he was in the other texts (A [pp426-27]).
424, ll.32-33. *convocats a Parlament to Edinburgh*: the parliament opened on 12 June (Nicholson, p483).
425, l.9. *Marginal note*: Buchanan, Bk.XI, f.126v; Holinshed, *SC*, p393.
425, l.11. *Beatrix*: i.e. Margaret, the Fair Maid of Galloway (see pp345, ll.6-7, and note).
425, ll.9-18. The forfeiture is not noted in *APS* but is said to have taken place in Auchinleck, pp10-11, 48-49.
P425, ll.24-25. *the Earle of Douglas... these thinges*: Holinshed, *SC*, p393, almost verbatim.
425, l.28. *Marginal note*: Holinshed, *SC*, 393.

425, l.33. HP, p396, says that the marriage was grudged by other branches of the Douglases and by bishop Kennedy, who counselled the overthrow of the Earl. As McGladdery points out (pp82-83) far from impeding the marriage, the King undertook by the Lanark Bond to support Douglas's proposed marriage to his sister in law. At this point the murder of the 8th Earl and the war on the Douglases had failed to gain the King anything.
425, ll.33-34. *ane ancient buik of the Douglases written in meitter*: There is no reference that I can make out to the Fair Maid of Galloway in Holland's 'Buke of the Howlat', which in any case was probably not written before the 8th Earl was murdered and the Fair Maid's statement made; see Felicity Riddy's notes pp.41 and 330, note to l.407, in Priscilla Bawcutt and Felicity Riddy, eds. *Longer Scottish Poems,* Volume 1, 1375-1650 (Edinburgh: Scottish Academic press, 1987). I have not been able to find another candidate for the ancient book written in metre.
427, l.7. HP, p397, gives Douglas an extended speech rejecting the King's offer and adding that he will send James Hamilton to England to negotiate for assistance.
427, ll.8-9. Hume has already used the 'some... some...' formula for the response to the 8th Earl's murder of Colville, p390, ll.2-4.
427, l.22. HP, p396, adds that the King was raising an army against Douglas and Crawford, which no doubt increased the latter's weariness.
428, l.2. *the gude offices done be his predecessors*: HP, pp397-398, adds to the account of Crawford's suing for pardon, which is drawn directly from Buchanan (see also Boece, Bk.XVIII, fols.375-76 [Pitscottie, I, 103-112]), the names of his predecessors who died fighting the English. Even in A, there remain traces of what in Boece is a story of repentance for sin, and this rather undermines Hume's sympathy for James Douglas's rebellion. Crawford in fact made his peace with the King in September, 1453, after Douglas had.
428, ll.19-20. *and restorit... and honour*: Sir Robert Gordon, *A Genealogical History of the Earldom of Sutherland* (Edinburgh: Constable, 1813), p.72, says the King gave Huntly, Brechin for the victory, which he exchanged for Badenoch. Crawford then got his land back on making peace with the king, but surrendered the hereditary sheriffship of Aberdeen to Huntly.
428, l.23. *Phinevin*: Finavon, Angus.
428, l.30. *some also wryte*: it is not likely that Hume had consulted Gordon's MS, which is dated 1630; the account is not in Boece, Pitscottie, Buchanan or Leslie, but in Holinshed, *SC*, p392.
429, l.4. *dieing of a hote fever in Phinevin*: 1633, p228, and HP, p399 add that he was buried in the Greyfriars of Dundee in the sepulchre of his ancestors.
429, ll.8-9. *sent James Hamilton of Caidzow, to Henrie of*

England: HP, p397, has already broached this matter and now, p399, brings it up again without back reference, an indication of the imperfect working of the new material into HP in this life. Negotiations occurred in 1452 before the Lanark Bond of 1453, and Hamilton renewed them in 1454, the price of support being homage by both Douglas and Hamilton to Henry VI. These may have been a reason for James's striking (McGladdery, p.80).
429, l.22-430, l.17. Buchanan, Bk.XI, fol.127, implies only that such terms were impossible, so that the reflection on Douglas's honest heart is Hume's. HP, p399 omits 'This being so honest... in that whilk followit' (ll.29-17).
430, l.21. Page **[491]** has not been numbered.
431, ll.6-7. *as sayes the Manuscript*: this is not what Maitland's History says or implies (p80).
431, l.14. *Vthers interpret it to be cowardice*: Buchanan; the word is 'ignavia' as in A2. *Marginal note*: Buchanan, Bk.XI, fol.127.
431, l.20. *Marginal note*: Buchanan, Bk.XI, fol.126.
432, ll.2-3. *by them that so heighlie respects that heigh place*: A2, followed by 1633, p230, and HP, p400, has 'those that do respect as duty *and* divinity enioynes the high place and person of these Gods vpon earth'. 1644, p202, like A, is drier about respect for kings. On this and 'heigh place', see Introduction, pxxxvii.
432, ll.27-28. *occasion representis not to explicate it self*: i.e. 'no opportunity presented itself for a resolving of the divided duty'.
433, l.9. *Marginal note*: Holinshed, *SC*, p394.
433, ll.11-13. *that he gave him his eldest daughter... neir to the Crowne*: In 1474, fourteen years after James II's death, Hamilton was given James II's sister Mary as second wife (Boece, Bk.XVIII, fol.377v. [Pitscottie, I, 122]; *SP*, IV, 352). *the Marqueis*: Given that A was written before the death of James VI in 27 March, 1625, the Marquis might be either James, 2nd Marquis of Hamilton (died 2 March, 1624/25) or James, 3rd Marquis.
433, ll.13-14. *vthers write... in Rosling*: Boece, Bk.XVIII, fol.377v. (Pitscottie, I, 121); Buchanan, Bk.XI, fol.127. *Marginal note*: Holinshed, *SP*, IV, 351. ^infra fol. 499^ has been inserted; but the information that Hamilton was warded in Roslin is not in Holinshed and the pagination does not accord with the obvious editions of other writers cited. There is nothing on fol.499 of A about Hamilton.
433, ll.15-16. *as he to whose... was imputit*: 1644, p202 omits, but says that Hamilton was released at the suit of the Earl of Angus. HP, p401, says that Angus used the argument about bloodless victory to obtain Hamilton's release.
433, ll.24-25. *a proclamation*: On 24 April, 1455, the Douglases were ordered to appear before the King on charges of treason. Forfeiture followed in the Parliament of June at Edinburgh.
434, ll.12-26. *In the 1455 zeir... so acceptable to al*: James was not present when his brothers were defeated at Arkinholme (on

the Esk, not Sark), near Langholm, 1 May, 1455, by a party of Southern lairds. *Marginal note*: Holinshed, *SC*, p394.

434, ll.12-19. *In the 1455 zeir... defait him*: HP, pp402-409, has a different account of affairs. It tells how on his journey south Douglas laid waste the lands of those who would not promise to stand with him on his return; how, called on to appear before the King's council and refusing, he, his brothers and mother, Beatrix Douglas, but not his wife (Margaret, misnamed Beatrix) forfeited their lands (the forfeiture is quoted on pp403-408). His wife's case was pleaded by John Stewart (she was only a woman) and she was given to him as wife [in 1460], Douglas having forfeited her by banishment (See p435, ll.23-28, below). According to Dalyell, as reported by HP, Douglas returned to Langholm (so also Fraser, I, 449), not Annandale as A says, and was defeated by Barclough (Buccleugh) and other landowners who had decided to take the King's side, not by Angus. It does seem, though, as Hume says on pp436-37, ll.22-2, that George, 4th Earl of, Angus, had a part in repelling a Douglas incursion in the East in 1557 (see McGladdery, p88). The two defeats of the Douglases are kept distinct (*as some wryte*) by Boece, Bk.XVIII, fol.378v. (Pitscottie, I, 127-28) and Holinshed, *SC*, p394, who say the victors in the second engagement were led by George Earl of Angus. Hume has confused the two defeats.

434, l.28. *Hugh Dean of Brichen*: see 1644, p232. 1633, p231, also talks of saying more about Hugh in the life of Archibald, Earl of Angus, an indication perhaps, among others, that it was planned to bring out the part on the house of Angus after the one on the house of Douglas, or perhaps an oversight on the part of the revisers.

434, l.31. *Lord of Carleil*: possibly Sir John Carlyle of Luce rather than his father, William Carlyle, Lord of Kinmont and Tortherwald (*SP*, II, 380-86). *the Laird of Johnstoun*: John Johnstone of Johnstone (*SP*, I, 237-38).

435, l.2. *Pittinane*: upon Clyde (1633, p231). Near Lanark. Sir William Fraser, *The Annandale Family Book of the Johnstones, Earls and Marquises of Annandale* (Edinburgh, 1894) I, xix, says he got the lands of Buittle and Sannoch after the capture of Threave, no mention of Pettinain.

435, l.12. *the fyft of June (or of August) and Marginal note*: the 9th of June according to Buchanan, Bk.XI, fol.127v. and *APS*, II, 42, 75-77.

435, l.13. *Marginal note*: Buchanan, Bk.XI, 127v.

435, ll.15-22. *This Beatrix... said actes*: the mother, Beatrix Sinclair was forfeited, not Margaret (Beatrix) Douglas according to the Act of Parliament of 5th August. 1455 (*APS*, II, 42, 75-77).

435, ll.23-28. On the Fair Maid's second marriage, see note to pp434, ll.12-19. *Marginal note*: Maitland, p88. *the nixt zeir*: that would be 1446, but the Fair Maid was married to John Stewart in

1460 (Fraser, I, 495).
435, ll.27-28. *Johne Stewart his half brother*: The son of James Stewart, the Black Knight of Lorne (see p371, l.5, and note) by Joanna (widow of James I) and consequently James II's half brother, was made Earl of Athol (*SP*, I, 440-42).
435, l.31. *Marginal note*: Buchanan, Bk.XI, f.127v; Holinshed, *SC*, p394.
436, ll.1-14. Fraser, I, 492, accepts that John Macdonald, Lord of the Isles and Earl of Ross, was stirred by the 9th Earl. In 1461 in the reign of James III, Douglas intrigued with him on behalf of Edward IV; in 1463, he led an unsuccessful rising (Fraser, I, 491, also Dunlop, pp221-26, 250).
436, ll.14-18. *Patrik Thorntoun and Johne Sandelands of Calder*: On 21 August *1451* Sir John Sandilands of Calder was killed by Sir Patrick Thornton, a Douglas henchman (Nicholson, p357). Given this confusion about dates, one wonder whether *Allane Stewart*: might be the Lord Darnley killed by Thomas Boyd in the 5th Earl of Douglas's time (see note to pp360-61, ll.24-29). The same confusion is to be found in Boece, Bk.XVII, fol.378 (Pitscottie, I, 126), and Holinshed, *SC*, p394.
436, l.20. At this point HP, p410, puts in that Douglas was enrolled in the order of the Garter in England.
436, l.22-437, l.2. *till efterwards... alyke on both sydes*: Fraser, II, 52, guardedly accepts this account of an expedition in retaliation for James II's invasion of 1456. 1457 would then be the correct date (see also McGladdery, p88). Nothing, however, is said about it in MacDougall, pp42-43, where James II's agressions and English retaliations are detailed. *Marginal note*: Holinshed, *SC*, p394, whose cited date, 1455, disagrees with Hume's 1457.
437, ll.3-5. *so effrayit... receivit by him*: McGladdery, p94, thinks the Lord of the Isles kept quiet for the rest of James III's reign.
437, l.14. *slane with the wadge of a great piece of artillirie*: James died of the wound he received from a fragment (*'particula machinae'* [Leslie, *De origine*, Bk.VIII, p298]) of a bursting gun.
437, l.18. 29 *September*: on 'the thrid sonday of August' [1460] according to Auchinleck, p57; interpreted by McGladdery, p130, as 3 August (rather than 17 August, the date of the third Sunday in that month). Nicholson, citing *Extracta ex cronicis Scocie*, Abbotsford Club (Edinburgh, 1842), p244, gives the same date.
437, ll.19-20. *the dissention betwixt the Kennedies and the Boyds*: In 1466 Lord Boyd seized the person of James III and held power against the Kennedys till 1469 (Nicholson, pp409-20).
438, l.3. HP, has already dealt with the garter but repeats the information here (p412).
438, l.6. *Earle of Arrandail*: Arundel.
438, l.7. *Nobilitas politica vel civilis*: by Robert Glover, (London, 1608), p171.
438, ll.15-18. *At whilk tyme... so ydle in England*: Douglas's

plans for invasion from England had been a source of anxiety since 1482 (Nicholson, pp495-96). The tyme would be 1483.

438, ll.16-18. *seimes a verie strange... in England*: omitted by HP, p412, and 1633, p233; this divagation should be in parentheses.

438, ll.18-20. *Alexander Duk of Albanie... being banisht*: According to HP, p412, Albany, fearing he would be executed like his brother John, Earl of Mar, broke ward and escaped to England (Nicholson, p485).

438, l.24. *the Magdalene day*: 22 July 1484.

438, l.29. *Musegrave*: The baron Musgrave at this time would be Richard, but *CP*, IX, 437, does not record his involvement in this engagement. *Burnishwarke*: Birrenswark between Ecclefechan and Lockerbie.

438, l.33. *Laird of Moussil*: John, Master of Maxwell, Steward of Annandale (MacDougall, p211).

439, ll.11-12. *ane brother of the Laird of Closburns*: Thomas Kirkpatrick, was laird of Closeburn, by Thornhill, Dumfriesshire, in 1470 according to the *RMS,* II, 1007, and may have been the brother of Alexander. Alexander Kirkpatrick was granted lands of Kirkmichael in Dumfriesshire on 2 October, 1484 (*RMS,* II, 1603).

440, l.3. *vpon the watter of Eie*: The lands of Kirkmichael are on the Water of Ae.

440, ll.7-8. *and gave... of Kirkmichael*: See above note.

440, l.9. *Marginal note*: Holinshed, *SC*, p404.

440, ll.10-11. *the Lairds of Cockpule and Johnstoun*: Cuthbert Murray of Cockpool and John Johnstone of Johnstone (MacDougall, p211).

440, ll.18-19. *He that may no better be, most be a Monke*: Perhaps a weak version of Tilley, D270: 'The devil was sick, the devil a monk would be; the devil was well, the devil a monk was he.'

440, l.27. *Couchrine*: Thomas Cochrane, favourite of James III, for which he was hanged at Lauder 1482 by peers, according to tradition led by Archibald Bell the Cat, 5th Earl of Angus (Nicholson, pp501-505).

440, ll.28-29. *the Earle of Angus*: Archibald 'called Bell-the-Cat' (see 1644, p206).

440, l.32-441, l.2. *Vthers... to be Lieutenant*: Boece, Bk.XVIII, fol.400.

441, ll.9-10. *as vthers say*: I have not traced them. As a possible explanation of the Black Coffer, Fraser, I, 494, cites *APS,* II, 230, concerning an inquiry into the recently killed James III's treasure.

441, l.15. *Marginal note*: Holinshed, *SC*, p407. This is his reply to the rebels not to the King.

441, l.16. A2 adds, ^This sayeth Holinsyde, But It is more likely that he meant by the black Coffer the blak Coffine wherein his brothers slaine bodie was kept/ which I am the apter to beleeve because there is no mention where it was buried/ And for that the sayeing in that sense is much more generous/ And that the thought of that Coffine did much more stick in his stomack (as we saye) and made a deeper impression in his hart, then the loss of all the moneys lands or honors that ever he had/. As did plainely appeer by all his demeanour in the avenging it^. HP, p414, and 1633, p235, follow A2. Holinshead, *SC*, p407, does not mention the black coffer and the speech.

441, ll.21-26. *beginning at... tyrannie*: this passage is grammatically a muddle. The passage, heavily revised, reads, ^beginning at the daies of the noble Sholto, but efter the 3, generation not mentioned for the space of 200 years till the first Baron of that house. Vide fol. 24. 26. 28. 30. Sholto grewe famous in the dayes of King Sulvathius, and in the yeare 767, fol.2. and this Lord W*illia*m father to Lord Hugh and maker of the Endenture for his sone Hughs marriage with the Lord Abernat*hies* [daughter], whose race we have hithervnto sett down by a continued lyne (who lived in the dayes of King William, Anno 1200). And hee was most remarkable for the rare love^. The revisions are sometimes illegible and cut off at the margin. The result of this revision is not more coherent than A and like the original, is historically wrong in attributing the disdain of English tyranny shown by William the Hardy, the 7th Lord of Douglas, to his grandfather William, the 5th Lord, who, moreover, lived in the days of Alexander III (the Indenture was sealed in 1259). In any event the whole passage, revisions and all, has been scored out as if beyond repair. I have supplied the ellipses. The folio numbers refer to the MS page numbers of A.

1633, p237, and HP, p415, pass over this botched passage with a neat reference to the negligence of historians; 1644, p206, equally neatly attributes the patriotism and disdain of the English to the Douglases as a family.

1633, pp235-237, has a long insertion, consisting of a ceremonious introductory paragraph and then the passage from the Preface (missing in 1633), pp11-13, ll.24-1 (*So manie, ... glorious Empyres*). After that, 1633 summarizes the four heads of the Preface under which the preeminence of the Douglases may be adduced and finally adds a paragraph on French and English honours to the house, including the Indenture of 1407 between Archibald Tynman and Henry IV, with an offer of lands between Trent and Humber, an offer some thought was renewed by Henry VI to William the 8th Earl; this indenture is in the hands of a Starkie, former servant of Robert Cotton the Antiquary. The material on the indenture is a muddle. 1633 itself, pp140-141, gives the indenture, which is about the ransom of Archibald Tynman and contains no offer of lands (see note to p275, l.4, below, and HP, p277). George, 4th (5th, by Hume's reckoning)

Earl of Angus, was offered lands between Trent and Humber for his services to Henry VI (1644, pp215-216). As for the remark about Starkie, it is clear that the Marquis of Douglas had not at the time of printing 1633 yet acquired the MS as he did later (see HP, p277). This passage in 1633 concludes (p237), 'The true transumpt of which articles, and indenture; may be seene verbatim in the following Tome of this storie'. 'The following Tome' could mean the present history of the house of Douglas if the whole passage had been carelessly lifted from its prefatory position. Or it could refer to a second tome consisting of the history of the House of Angus if we supposed that a second tome was planned and that the Angus and the Douglas transactions with the kings of England had become hopelessly confused in the mind of the editor.

HP, p415, has the same first paragraph as 1633 until the conclusion, where instead of undertaking to survey the main points of the greatness of the house of Douglas, it declares that the house of Angus became what the Douglases were; after that it passes to A (p441, l.19) but in the version of 1633, p237 ('Thus began...'). 1644, pp206-207, gives an abridged but coherent version of this whole muddled passage.

441, l.30. ^The iust account from Sholto, to this last Earle Is-721 yeares^ is written in the margin. *288 zeirs*: following A2's marginal note, HP, p415, and 1633, p237, say that it was 721 years from the death of Sholto.

443, l.4. *Marginal note*: perhaps Holinshed, *SC*, p394.

443, ll.5-9. *the last battle ... disconfite him*: the Earl of Angus was not at the Battle of Lochmaben, nor (*Marginal note*) does Maior say he was.

443, l.9. *Marginal note*: Holinshed, *SC*, p392; this citation refers to the men he could put in the field.

443, ll.18-21. *to have riden... from Durhame north*: See note to Preface, p24, ll.25-28, above.

444, ll.4-6. *were ever the siker... wassaledgis*: ^1[?] Section^ has been added to the *marginal note*. *zit since that house was put downe, Scotland hes done few valiant deids*: appears in Boece (1536: Bk.XIV, ch.8), not in 1531 or Boece's original (1574: Bk.XIV, fol.300).

444, l.27. *Earle of Wigtoun*: Archibald, 5th Earl of Douglas see p301, ll.5-12, 303, l.16ff..

445, ll.27-28. Holinshed, *SC*, p394, sees the hand of providence behind the triumph of James II and the fall of the Douglases.

445, l.28-446, l.4. *whilk had determinit... tint it indeid*: the passage is scored out and replaced with 'Which moved the Earle rather than he would attempt his vttermost against his Souerane, to the hazard of his person or his Croune, to cast himself and his owen estate awaye./ and to slipp that opportunity of fortune offerd him/. (Although thereby he hath incurred the imputation of

Cowardise and sluggishnes by the too sharp and wrongfull censure of some writers;)'. HP, p419, and 1633, p239, follow A2; 1644, pp208-209, follows A. *Marginal note*: Holinshed, *SC*, p394.

446, l.17. The following has been inserted: ^Ancyent house, and familie whose eminent greatnes and mathles vertues of the men, they so much envyed. And therfor drewe the Princes by there suttle persuasions to suppress the same, giving them to vnderstand that thereby their authoritie would become more free and absolut^. HP, p419, and 1633, pp239-240, but not 1644, p209, accept A2 in part.

446, l.23. *libertie*: 'authoritie' (A2, HP, p420, and 1633, p240), implies, as 'libertie' does not, that restraining the powers of the crown is bad.

447, l.2. HP, p420, and 1633, p240, add '*Vivit post funera virtus*' and 'Finis'. HP, p420 in a footnote says that Hugh, Dean of Brechin, son of Hugh, Earl of Ormond, was heir to James, but resigned his rights to Archibald Earl of Angus, 24 August, 1490 (see 1644, p232, where Hugh is said to be Dean of Buchan), and tables (pp421-435), life by life, the memorabilia of the house of Douglas; 'Finis' appears on p434.

1644, pp209-11, appends two Latin epitaphs with English verse translations and, by way of a graceful bridge to the History of the house of Angus, salutes to George, Earl of Angus, the Douglas who overcame the Douglas, also with English verse translations.

GLOSSARY

This Glossary is a list of hard words. Some of these are familiar words with unfamiliar spellings, some familiar words in unfamiliar senses. It is not an exhaustive word list or even an exhaustive list of Scots forms used by Hume. Normally it is assumed that the reader will cope with single consonants where modern spelling doubles them and with standard Scots spellings such as, for instance, 'ei' where modern English uses 'ea', or 'ai' where modern English has 'a' + consonant + 'e'. Verbal nouns have been counted as derivatives of verbs unless they are the only form that verb takes.

abassing *v, pres p* subduing 62/27, 167/6
abbassien *n* monastery 255/31
abbatie *n* monastic foundation 18/2, 39/33, 255/35
able *adv* perhaps 148/8
abstract *v* withdraw 402/12, 402/13
abstraction *n* absence, withdrawal 307/23
abuilzaments *n* equipment 219/30
accesse *n* addition, accession 350/27
accom(p)t *n* account 49/16, 56/10, 390/35
accord with *v* make terms with, come to an accord with 32/30,
account *n* esteem 20/21, 27/24
account *v* hold in acount, esteem 46/12, 208/12
acquissance *n* acquaintance (probably a slip for 'acquentance') 190/28
acresse *v* acrue, increase, add 215/1, 324/22, 428/15
addicted *v, pp* devoted 401/3
address *v* prepare (a meal) 80/26
adebtit *v, pp* indebted 253/28
adhibite *v* use, employ 369/3, 377/22,
adminicle *n* aid, support 140/13
admonish *v* give notice of 211/9, 426/7; warn 308/26
adoe *n* trouble, concern 78/30, 216/26, 261/10
advert *v* notice 356/31, 373/11
advertis *v* to let know 61/2, 67/3, 220/28
af *adv* off 280/32, 399/10, 416/26
af *prep* out of, 296/13, 321/23; away from, 362/9
affamish *v* starve 116/14
affect *v* be drawn to, love, inclined 410/16, 432/17, 442/6
affectit *v pp* effected 445/25
affectat(e) *v* aim at, desire 45/36, 141/35, 375/3
affectation *n* desire 251/1
affection *n* desire, passion 156/6
affray *v* frighten 230/34, 237/28
afore *prep* before 371/31
aforehand *adv* in store 361/25; 'keipe himself aforehand' survive 442/11
ag(g)r(ieance *n* agreement, 300/3, 315/33, 320/25
agains, agans, aganes, aganis, 113/2, 383/8, 429/26
air *n* heir 283/3, 343/13, 417/28

allanerlie *adv* only, alone 323/4
alledgeance *n* allegation, assertion 16/13, 28/3 64/36
alliay, allya *n* alliance 123/28, 130/26
allowance *n* consent 299/25
allvterlie *adv* absolutely 439/34
allya *n* see alliay
allya *v, pp* allied 301/21 (doubtful reading)
allyated *v, pp* allied 22/marg. 58/7
Alman *n* German 27/22
als *adv* as 71/27, 117/4, 220/20
alsweil *adv* as well 107/26
altogidder *adv* altogether 27/1, 192/3, 380/1
alway(e)s, alwise, alwyse *adv* in any case 250/24, 334/21, 435/23
amandement *n* amends, reparation 356/26
amend *v* rectify 308/32
anent *prep* concerning 12/29, 20/29, 66/24
aneugh *adv* enough 92/36, 107/7, 141/16
angel *n* a gold coin first issued by Louis XI 282/21, see note
apardone *v* pardon 408/22
apparance, apparence *n* probability, apparentness 315/29, 411/8, 441/1
appardon(e) *v* pardon 126/27, 361/23, 370/13
apparand, aparant, appearand, appeirand, appeirant *adj* apparent (as in 'heir apparent') 193/13; apparent, likely, probable, to all appearance 264/23, 359/29, 396/28, 435/18
arbeletriers *n* arbalester, crossbowmen 212/23
arbitrage *n* arbitrament, decision 62/5
argentine *adj* of silver 40/33, 41/29
ascryve *v* ascribe, attribute 271/28
aservil *v* enslave, render servile 373/28
assail *n* assault 149/32
asseige *v* besiege 153/32, 223/7 assertion 16/13, 28/3, 64/36
assignais *n* assignees 102/12
assist to *v* be present at 74/10, 197/7
astrict *v* bind 197/12
ather *conj* either 195/213, 240/16, 319/22
attend *v* wait for 283/27
attendance *n* waiting upon in service 5/9, 35/18, 402/12
auantcouriers *n* advance guard 223/24
auantguard(e), avantgarde *n* vanguard 91/29, 263/8, 289/18
avant *n* vanguard 184/7
aventure *n* chance 287/24; risk,346/25
avuncle *n* uncle 262/19, 295/18, 352/24
awen, awne *adj* own, 131/12, 374/11, 379/9
awner *n* owner 359/9

bailzerie *n* a district administered by a baillie, instead of a sherrif 365/20
bailzie *n* baillie, steward 392/7
baird *n* beard 109/31, 383/27; **in baird** in defiance 111/16
bairnlines *n* childishness 331/32, 340/27
bait *v* ?bathe 341/17
baitting *v, pres p* beating (as in a hunt), scouring in pursuit 99/18
bake *adv* back 33/19, 46/1, 84/9
balcode *n* scrotum 269/13
band *n* league, bond, 38/16, 120/16, 131/2
bane *n* bone 320/20
banie *adj* boney, 322/7, see note
banket *v* banquet 21/15, 334/9,

336/9
barme *adj* **barme horse** pack horse, 132/36
base, bass(e) *adj* 'of bass age', in his minority 26/7; base 372; illegitimate 22/27, 127/2
bat(t)le, bat(t)el *n* battle line, array 268/29, 290/4, 385/14; troop, battallion 422/21
be *prep* by 183/23, 184/25, 376/9
beam *n* bar (heraldic?) 41/29
beare *v* state, witness 16/35, 183/23, 487/8
begoude, begouth *v, pt* began 260/25, 281/8, 292/18
behalf *n* matter, concern 403/4; **in his behalf** as regards him 52/23
beistliness *n* dullness, lack of spirit 405/18
bellies *n* bellows 297/24, 360/26
beseiking *v, pres p* beseeching, 68/36
besouth *adj* south of 251/27
beteach *v* 'to commit or consign (to God or the devil)' (DOST) 241/12
bethrowhit *pp* betrothed, 251/13
betrouthit *v, pp* betrothed 259/22
betwixt hands *adv. phrase* 325/24, see note
big(e) *v* build 228/22, 401/18
birk *n* birch 98/12
blasfemit *v, pp* reviled 420/22
blenk (of) *n* gleam of comfort 148/9, 158/5
boldned *v, pp* swollen, 9/33
bot *conj* but, 20/25, 350/26, 445/28
brangle *n* broil, confusion 412/15
brangle *v* embroil, confuse 150/11, 263/8, 387/31
bravado *n* offer of battle, 286/17
brea *n* brae, hill 165/22
break, breik, brek(e) *n* break 38/14, 193/7, 253/4
breik *n* breeches 269/18
brigandies *n* brigandages, armed robberies 204/9, 215/22
brige *n* bridge 245/8, 275/29, 280/29
broik, brooke, bruik *v* brook, put up with, enjoy possession of 63/6, 263/2, 297/3
bru(i)t *n* report, fame 4/32, 140/31, 211/3
brunt *v, pt* burned, 102/28, 199/31, 210/17
buittis *n* boots 219/29
bulwarke *n* rampart 165/13
bund *v, pt* bound 114/23, 130/26, 150/11
bussie *adj* bushy 88/5
bussines *n* bustle, busyness 113/4, 332/10
but(t)e *n* aim, end 151/2, 205/13, 322/20
but(t)ie(s); butis *n* booty 24/28, 133/23, 199/2
by *prep* at **by times** betimes, occasionally 29/10; against 376/10, 378/17
byd(e) *v* await, wait for 165/8, 367/10, 370/3

cadger *n* carrier 85/13
calcule *v* reckon, calculate 17/22
campe volant *n* 'a little army of horse and foot, that keeps the field and is continually in motion' (*OED*) 116/16
cantrop *n* caltrop, a trap or perhaps an iron ball with spikes 96/6
captiver *n* one who keeps someone in prison 298/11
careful *adj* laborious, 9/12
caressed *v.pp* made much of 168/16
cariage *n* conduct 37/14, 39/27; load, baggage 165/25, 254/25, 290/2
cassen, cassin *v, pp* estimated 368/27, 435/32; stored, heaped on? rendered void? 376/30;

cast 85/8, 207/33, 434/2
casual *adj* accidental, incidental? 359/28, see note
casuality *n* incidental source of income 350/23
catastrophe *n* end 206/23, see note
cause *n* case 214/16
cense *n* tax, 57/34
censure *n* judgement 8/6, 293/19
chainezie, chanzie *n* chain 259/5, 428/30
choise *v* choose 24/1, 350/22, 387/25
choke *n* point of encounter (military; see OED, 'shock') 289/19
choyse *v, pt* chose, 346/24
circumvein *v* circumvent 330/17, 340/29
ciuile, civile *adj* secular 9/1; civilised, lawful, law abiding 16/15, 29/11, 398/33
clame *v* 155/25, see note
cleik *n* hook 88/20
clerke play *n* 'a dramatic representation of a religious subject by the clergy' (OED) 322/10
cleugh *n* gorge 98/11
coft *v, pt* bought 250/30
cognoissance *n* cognisance, heraldic bearing 41/20
cognosce *v* make a judicial inquiry into 360/32
collect *v* 'gather by reasoning' (DOST), calculate, 204/18
com(me)d *v, pp* came, 22/6, 344/10, 346/2
com(p)t *n* account, estimation, 386/8 415/25
comble *n* heap 374 (cf, DOST: 'combill')
commone *n* debt ('a quyt common', a settled debt) 94/1
commove *v* move (with grief) 245
compeir(e) *v* appear, present oneself 66/1377/23, 424/34
complo(i)t *n* plot, conspiracy 32/10, 66/23
compone *v* make payment for, compound for 181/8
composition *n* **by composition** on terms 85/fn, 89/24
comt see **com(p)t**
conceit *n* idea, notion, imagination, 38/28, 148/18, 250/30
concredit *v* entrust, commit 107/33
concur *v* come together, coincide 91/12, 96/8, 99/2
condescend *v consent* 248/7, 248/15
conducit *v, pt* brought together, 188/22
conduct *n* leadership, command 25/11, 280/11
conductor *n* leader, manager 205/4, 214/7, 280/6
conduit *n* leadership 133/19, 140/1
confer *v* bring together, compare 12/19, 12/32
conforme *adj* according, in harmony 37/7, 40/22, 37/7, 40/22, 253/7
conqueis *n* conquest 115/28, 118/10, 164/3
conqueis *v* conquer, acquire 71/15, 115/9, 287/27
considerance *n* consideration 329/31
consonat *adj* consonant, in agreement 133/29
contemporaire *adj* contemporary 238/35
conterfitting *vbl n* counterfeiting 96/10
contrair(e), contrare *adj* contrary 91/24, 155/32, 198/3
contrar *n* contrary 388/5
contrarieing *vbl.n* opposing 70/13
contrepoyson *n* antidote 323/17

convenable *adj* appropriate 243/13
convictit *v, pp* prove guilty 403/10, see note
convocat *v, pt* convoked 424/32
convoy *n* protective escort 161/16; management of affairs 403/14
convoy *v* convey 151/11, 203/21, 404/20
couleurs *n* coulours (of rhetoric) considered as deceptive painting 9/20
count of *v* consider as of account 315/27
count with *v* compete in degree of relation (perhaps a slip for contend) 196/14
coustomable see customable
cowpe *v* overturn 321/25
craigis *n* rocks (but probably a mistake for 'creeks') 244/18
crapt *v, pt* crept 88/5
croppin *v, pp* crept 315/18
croude *n* fiddle, violin 233/18
crowne *n* an écu 282/31
cuile *v* cool 306/5, 356/29
curatoris *n* '[Those] appointed to take charge of the affairs of a minor, idiot, or legally incapable person' (DOST) 340/16
curious *adj* laborious, painstaking 19/24, 178/25 29/26
c(o)ustoumable *adj* usual 168/10, 230/11
customablie *adv* usually 249/23

daght see dow
danger *n* power of a lord etc 324/17, 334/30, 427/17
dar *v* dare 319/16
darrest *adj* dearest 401/12
de(a)lth *v, pt,pp* dealt 353/6, 360/4, 374/18
deal, deil *v* act, proceed, have dealings with 201/7, 296/6
debait *n* contention, competitive strife 29/10
debordit *v, pp* unrestrained, exceeding all bounds 376/6
deboursed *v, pt* disbursed 105/26
deboutit *v, pp* expelled, thwarted 260/18, 321/20
decern(e) *v* determine, decree, appoint 135/20, 278/3, 383/8; discern 53/29, 377/9
decore *v* decorate, give dignity to 41/37, 43/12, 306/13
decreit *n* decree 292/7, 327/6
deduce *v* trace, follow, set down 197/24, 179/16, 228/11
deduction *n* descent, consecutive account 8/29, 16/10, 42/32; logical consequentiality 56/24
degast *n* devastation 116/13
degener *v* degenerate 35/27
deil *v* see 'deal'
delated *v, pp* accused 171/33
delt *v, pp* divided, dealt out (to others) 63/13
delyverly *adv* nimbly 88/29
demanteld *v, pp* dismantled, demolished 155/22
demerit *n* crime 61/1
demit *v* allow, let go 413/4
denunce *v* proclaim 253/32
deport *n* conduct, behaviour 183/18
deprehend *v* catch, take 122/32
descryve *n* describe 9/24, 42/1, 233/26
designe *v* designate, name 18/24, 298/31, 360/16
devise *n* invention, faculty of devising 131/2
diffide *v* mistrust, lack confidence in 91/19
diffidence *n* mistrust 198/4
dificil(e) *adj* dificult 336/33, 374/17, 414/31
digest *v* put up with, 'swallow' take in 172/8, 432/18
dignied *v, pt* deigned 141/16
dimisse *v* dismiss 155/13, 405/1,

425/23
dimit *v* let go, dismiss 94/27, 107/4, 269/31
discerne *v* show, distinguish 88/9
disgoust *n* vexation 64/27
disherise *v* disinherit 191/5, 277/23
dishonestie *n* shamefulness 416/30
displeasour *n* grief, sorrow 261/17
dispone *v* dispose 64/2, 68/26, 146/16
disposition *v* an assignation of property 181/33, 182/32
dispyse-worthie *adj* despicable 249/16
dissimuling *n* dissembling, dissimulation 202/23, 322/11
dittie *n* accusation, charge 328/3
document *n* proof 291/5
domage *n* damage 212/16, 216/27, 270/20
dotation *n* endowment 18/20
dote *n* dowry 22/31
double *v* **double it out** survive? 206/9 (see also 97/25, note)
doubteslie *adv* 205/29, see note
douce *adj* sweet 318/14
dow *v, pt* **daght** was able to 70/10
draghte *n* design 13/32
dreidence *n* fear 269/11
ducherie *n* duchie 351/3, 397/22
duging *v, pres p* drudging? worthless 190/8, see note
dukrie *n* duchy 25/1, 285/1, 307/12
dung(e) *v, pt, pp* beaten 61/19, 224/30, 339/23
durk *n* dirk 321/32

eafaldlie *adv* sincerely 374/13
eam *n* uncle 86/14
effect *n* effort (a slip?) 115/27, 117/12
effect *v* affect, have effects 296/24 **effrayit, effrayed** *v. pp* frightened 84/15, 437/3
eik *v* add 298/25, 337/8, 350/17
eike *n* addition 92/12
either *comp. adv.* more easily 115/16
eivine *v* 249/32, see note
enarmit *v, pt* armed 286/27
ende *n* breath 418/30
enorme *adj* inordinate 319/1, 326/29, 370/16
entalzit *v, pp* entailed 97/17
equal *adj* fair 361/19
equalie *adv* probably 347/26
erect *v* raise lands to a lordship 397/22
erection *n* raising possession to a lordship 17/25
escapad *n* escape 399/21
eshek *n* check 143/6
esperance *n* hope 35/34
ether *conj* either 134/35, 146/18, 337/26
ettil *v* intend 97/26
evanish *v* vanish 141/10, 148/16
event *n* fortune, outcome 84/27
evictit *v, pp* 'obtain or recover by a legal process or right' (DOST) 336/25
evident *n* document, evidence 17/17, 19/13, 287/34
execution *n* executive ability 415/16
exemed *v, pp* exempted 51/13
exoneration *n* discharge, fulfilment 191/27
exorable *adj* capable of being moved by entreaty 4426/23
expect *v* wait to see 260/17
experimented *ppl adj* experienced 386/18
expert *adj* experienced 75/26, 329/23
explicate *v* disentangle 432/28
exprobat *v* blame 334/20
exquisite *adj* recherché 351/26
extenuat *v* depreciate, disparage 113/32, 228/23, 292/9; extenuate 338/4, 341/1

extenuater *n* detractor 117/11
eyelish, eye list *n* grievance 73/1, 194/4, 197/27

fact *n* act, deed 326/6, 386/32, 411/10
faile *n* turf 96/4
failzeing *v, pres p* failing 390/28
fainzeing *v, pres p* feigning 164/25
fainzit *v, pp* feigned 333/34
faird *n* **face** paint 319/19, 337/23
falset *n* falsehood 72/16, 313/28, 314/29
fand *v, pt* found 216/4, 407/4, 314/29
farder *adj* further 85/29
farder *v* further 357/17
farnzeir *n* last year, 248 marg.
farrest *adj* furthest 285/5, 422/15
fastings ewin *n* Shrove Tuesday 87/25-26
faughen *v, pp* fought 229/17, 285/14
faughten *v, pp* fought 67/12, 439/3, 439/22
fault *v* err 375/22
fauxburgh *n* suburb 240/31
feckful, fectful *adj* effective, forceful 175/4, 373/33, 375/15
feckfullie *adv* cogently, forcefully 374/22
fectful see 'feckful'
feid *n* enmity 315/27, 329/13, 403/19
feikles *adj* weak, valueless 249/34
feilding piece *n* field piece 262/34
feinzit, feinzed *v, pp* feigned, false 275/9, 407/19
fermerer *n* farmer 395/5
fich *v* fetch 215/14
fitmen *n* foot soldiers 220/19, 223/29
fivere *n* fever 204/14
flaike *n* hurdle 113/11
flakons *n* flagons 164/26
foranent *prep* over against 111/24, 268/13
foreseine *v, pp* warned, moved by foresight 399/18
forfa(u)ltit *v, pp* subjected to forfeiture 195/21, 368/30, 435/14
forfaultor, forfaulture *n* forfeiture 19/33, 270/23, 368/25
formal *adj* exact with regard to outer form 47/27
forra(i)ne *adj* foreign 151/31, 207/34, 436/22
forrane *n* foreigner 306/22
forranner, forrenner *n* foreigner 87/18, 289/6
forrow(e) *v* make a foray, ravage 101/19, 135/21
fortunat *adj* dealt with by fortune 294/26
fortvne *n* happen 401/24
fough(t)en *v, pp* fought 70/31, 165/26, 264/6
fourt *adj* fourth 26/19, 43/37, 51/5
foussie *n* ditch 96/4, 163/13
fra *prep* from 276/17, 295/21, 408/19
frack, frak *adj* forward, bold 74/31, 149/13, 421/30
fraudful *adj* deceitful 155/25
fraudfulnes *n* deceit 108/15
fraughtit *v, pt* freighted 244/19
fray(e) *n* alarm 83/26, 83/31, 360/61
freind *n* relative 305/1, 372/3 372/29
fremde, fremmed *adj* strange, unusual 52/21; foreign 118/5
fremedlie *adv* strangely 55/29
frequent *adj* crowded 222/4
frivile *adj* idle, frivolous 315/16
froward *adj* refractory, perverse 106/23
fund *v, pt* found 141/27
furde *n* ford 82/31
furrow *n* foray raid, 187/15

furrow *v* make a foray, ravage (see forrow) 362/32, 402/16, 424/10
furrower *n* one sent out in advance to seize provisions or quarters 384/15, 436/28
furth *adv* out, beyond, forth 133/3, 197/26, 385/23
futstop(pe)s *n* footsteps 204/4
fyft *adj* fifth 176/8, 275/20, 435/12

garnish *v* furnish, equip 158/16
garnison *n* garrison 163/1, 238/1, 285/28
gat(e) *v, pt* got 247/10, 371/2, 435/5
gat(t)e *v* get 71/10, 72/29, 84/2 ('gatte' is the best reading of a word that heas been heavily tinkered with; cf. DOST 'gait', 'gayt')
gatten *v, pt* got 338/19
geir *n* goods 323/12, 362/23
generouse *adj* noble 317/1
ghast *n* guest 336/28
gif *conj* if 133/fn 6
girth *n* sanctuary 336/22
glaif *n* glaive, a kind of halberd 199/14
glomming *n* dusk 439/4
glosit *v, pp* flattered, spoken with specious falsity 315/3
gone *v, pt* come 285/26
good father *n* step father 371/6
grable *v* grapple 273/24
grandshire *n* great grandfather 351/13
gratful *adj* gratifying, pleasing 356/26
gratifie *v* please 284/23
gratuit *adj* gratuitous 381/13
gree *v* agree 320/12
greif *n* passion, fury 112/24 385/23
greiting *n* weeping 305/36
grit *adj* great 221/3; *compar*
gritter 197/12
gudame *n* grandmother 129/37
gudbrother *n* brother in law 197/1, 265/5
gudfather *n* father in law 195/19
gudshir(e) *n* grandfather 130/1 301/25, 351/11
guidon *n* pennant 221/29
gyder *n* manager, governor, controller 352/21, 389/25

hability *n* ability 99/3, 114/27
hail(e) *adj* whole 205, 224, 358
haililie, hailily, hailylie *adv* wholely 85/20, 132/1, 166/6
hairshipe *n* armed raiding, plundering 405/17
halden *v, pt, pp* held 118/26, 152/27, 387/22; **taine halden** taken hold 430/7
hale *n* hall 89/2
hammiet *adj* home bred 295/24
hant *n* haunt 81/26
hanting *n* haunting, frequenting 200/28, 341/11
hard(e) *v, pp,* heard 284/34, 383/25, 386/5
hardie, hardy *adj* bold 58/16, 59/9, 60/22
hardilye *adv* boldly 319/17
hartfullie *adv* with all one's heart 319/17
harting *n* encouragement 148/4
hartlie *adj* heart felt 279/15
haynous *adj* heinous 405/108
he(a)ry *v* harry 210/17, 376/13, 420/24
heast *n* haste 79/25
heastie *adj* hasty 84/2, 254/23
heaving *pres p* having 83/20, 91/4, 187/3
heig(h)lie, hieglie *adv* highly 240/8, 267/6, 284/34
heigest *adj* highest 12/15, 26/1, 31/15
hereditaire *adj* hereditary 234/19, 442/8
heretrix *n* female inheritor 59/28, 129/31, 197/20

hery see **he(a)ry**
hidlings *n* hiding places 75/13
hinder ***n*** hindrance 115/29, 391
hinging *v, pres.p* hanging 165/14, 419/7
hithertils *adv* hitherto 16/9
holydays name *n* abusive, but ?real name 324/2, see note
honest *adj* commendable 327/31
honestie *n* honour done, respect, trust 193/14
hosting *vbl.n* campaigning, making war 312/18
hundreth *adj* hundred 17/6, 45/9, 227/16
hurde *v* harbour 357/6

iappit *v, pt* dashed, vexed 325/14, see note
ilk *adj* same (name) 263/21, 288/6; each 312/26, 322/30
illustrat *v, pp* adorned 12/26, 30/20, 30/27
illustre, jllustre *adj* illustrious title page, 4/13, 16/2
illustred *v, pp* made illustrious 22/3
imbrulzie *v* embroil 314/6
impairt *v* give a share 164/31
impare *adj* uneven, unequal 41/18
importun *adj* importunate 93/25
impression *n* charge, onset 385/30, 422/22
impyre *n* rule 122/1
in maritagium *adv. phr* by way of dowry 183/20
inadvertisance *n* inadvertence 159/34
incontinent *adv* immediately 281/8, 285/13, 384/5
inconvenient *n* difficulty, trouble 170/27, 192/16, 354/13
indifferencie *n* impartialitie, disinterestedness 403/1
indignit *adj* indignant 281/19 (DOST 'indignat')
indomaging *n* injuring 330/33
infeft *v* invest with heritable property 105/34
infeft(e)ment *n* investment with heritable property 105/31, 251/26, 347/33
ingenuosment *n* ingenuity 172/16
ingyne *n* wit, mind, spirit 169/19, 172fn.11
inhabilitie *n* incapacity 212/10, 248/26
inique *adj* iniquitous, unjust, injurious 70/14, 293/20, 364/11
iniquitie *n* injurious action 19/15, 64/12, 65/3
inland *adj* from the inlands, the central parts of the country 384/27
inlands *n* the central parts of the country 13/34
innuat(e) *v* hint 293/29, 325/5
inought *adj* enough 408/19
insist *v* continue urgently, persevere 2/27, 225/23
interest *v, pp* damaged, injured 193/5, 390/6
interpone *v* introduce, add to 408/11, 408/15
interteine *v* maintain 347/20, 353/18
intrait, intreat *v* treat 158/32, 169/35
intreit *v* entreat 200/15
intrese *n* interest 201/33
intromet *v* interfere, handle property of another 362/26, 394/10, 395/35
intruse *v* push someone into an office to which he has no right 205/15
invtile *adj* useless 27/3
invy(e) *n* grudge, ill will, jealousy 173/30, 326/32, 346/8
invy *v* grudge 373/19
invyers *n* ill wishers 384
invyfulnes *n* jealousy, grudging 373/1

invyous *adj* subject to envy or grudge 374/29
inward *adj* intestine 30/5

joukit *v, pp* bowed down, humbled (themselves) 324/2
journey *n* military expedition 248/30, 278/4, 283 marg.

kaist *v, pt* cast 88/20
keipe himself a fore hand,
ken *v* know 120/1, 168/9; ?acknowledge 324/11
kinred, kinrid, kynred *n* kindred 301/9, 353/9, 399/8
kist *n* chest 313/2
kittle *adj* ticklish, difficult 346/11
knigh(h)ede, knigh(h)ode *n* knighthood 21/12, 26/2, 92/13
knowe *n* knoll 224/2
kyndelie *adj* showing family feeling 431/22
kyndnes *n* natural affection, friendship, acknowledging of family ties 370/20, 372/29, 374/12
kynred see **kinred**
kyth *v* show, reveal 218, 346, 416

laick, laik(e) *n* lack 138/7, 264/13, 431/14
laick, laik *v* lack 11/14, 164/16, 387/11
laid *n* load 85/4, 84/7, 84/9
laidner *n* larder 81/20
lape *v, pt* leapt 88/28
laying one's (ac)count that *adj phrase* calculating that 84/34, 214/24
leafe *v* leave 97/14
leif(e) *n* leave, permission to leave 91/2; the paying of one's respects on leaving 149/26 (see 'lofe or leif')
let *v* hinder, *prevent* 420/2
lethernes *n* lethargy, sluggishnes 432/5, **lithernes** 432/21, 446/6
lettin *v* let 335/4
ligue *n* league 338/16, 266/33 366/7
limitating *vbl.n* limitation, 375/6
limmer *n* scoundrel 330/34
lipned *v, pt* trusted, 134/30
lippener *n* truster 336/29
lippening *n* trust 333/16
lithernes *n* see **lethernes**
lofe *n* honour, praise 149/26 'lofe or liefe', see note
longsome *adj* tedious 42/36
lourd *adj* grave, 375/31
louse *v* loose 70/3, 114/24, 395/31
louth *adj* loath, averse 428/10
ludification *n* trickery, deception 211/23
luke *n* luck 77/17
lustre *v* make illustrious, embellish, adorn 294/21
lyings af *n* withdrawals 300/20

magnanim(e) *adj* high souled, noble 298/26, 315/9
magnanimitie, magnanimity *n* high spirit, greatness of soul 90/28, 124/5, 315/26
magnificence *n* liberality 272/10, 324/24, 342/20
magnifike *adj* munificent, noble 169/31
ma(g)nifiklie *adv* nobly splendidly, 261/5, 280/18, 330/13
malapertnes *n* presumptuousness 392/31
malheur(e) *n* misfortune 167/22, 3351/34
man *v* must 415/14
maners *n* ways 320/25
manifiklie see **magnifiklie**
maniure *v* tend 337/29
marashis , mar(r)es(s)es *n* marshes 82/32, 223/7, 424/15
mase, masse *n* mace 225/19, 240/16
mawing *v, pres p* mowing 424/25

mayne *n* mainland 75/34
meane *adj* inferior 325/26, 353/33, 444/18
meane *n* (horse's) main 383/30
meane *n* means 292/33
mediocritie *n* moderation 345/30
meeting *n* requital 342/23
meikle *adj* much 207/11, 356/27, 369/9
meikle *adv* much 80/7, 277/19, 403/31
meikle *n* much 75/27, 120/13, 156/14
meine *adj* inferior 282/15
meine *n* 'by the meine' in the meantime 76/17
menagit *v, pt* managed 140/12
mercat *n* market 84/33, 419/12
merche *n* march, boundary, border 210/29, 219/6, 254/10
mervel *v* wonder 259/30, 413/9; **it mervels** it surprises 252/24
mid(e)s, midis, myds *n* middle, midst , 98/8141, 148/8, 225/3; **midds and meines** ways and means 95/30
mid(e)s *adv* in a middle position, impartial, 289/10; in the middle of ('in mides dishe'), 322/6, note
mides man *n* intermediary, mediator 431/9-10
militare *adj* military 207/22 234/17
mint at *v* hint at 304/8, see note
miscontentment *n* grievance, discontent 388/30
mishant *adj* evil 319/17, 339/29
mishantnes *n* wickedness 318/15
mishantrie *n* wickedness 335/21
misken *v* ignore, spurn 359/31; mistake 360/14
misknaw *v* ignore, mistake 91/7, 97/12
mister *n* need 375/15, 377/21
mitigate *v* appease 327/3
moe *adj* more 291/9, 326/28, 373/23
moit *v, pt* must 322/6 (should, might, *DOST)*
monument *n* record 179/13, 296/30, 428/30
most *v* must 346/15, 354/30, 365/6
mott *v, pt* might 165/1
moveables *n* movable property 15/24
moyen *n* intermediary 367/12; means 72/8, 313/2; power, influence 351/30, 388/16, 410/2; mediation 270/16, 403/24
muffils *n* gloves 324/15
mute *v* utter 70/17
myndes *n* mines, tunnels (perhaps a slip for 'mynes') 163/13

nar(r)est *adj* nearest 79/28, 179/35, 436/32
nather *adv* neither 233/34, 402/8, 432/16
nather *conj* neither, nor 233/34, 402/8, 432/18
nather *pron* neither 324/9, 432/23, 441/6
natural *n* nature, disposition 153/4, 317/1, 318/13
naughtie *adj* wicked 119/30
nephew *n* grandchild 195/32; nephew 238/30, 253/12
nether *conj* neither 321/21, 340/16, 432/10
nippit *v, pt* **nippit obliquitlie** criticized by hints 315/21
nixt *prep* next 68/5, 93/20, 478
nolt *n* cattle 88/12
nor *conj* than 196/18, 199/27, 296/2; would that, grant 241/13, 342/6
note *n* reproach 342/12
notified *v, pt* noted, observed 137/4
notoriouslie *adv* publicly, in a way known to all 443/25
noysome *adj* annoying, harmful

216/31
nynt *adj* ninth 128/5, 417/30

obiect, object *v* put in the way 235/11; accuse, charge 26/24, 328/30, 336/25
oblique *adj* perverse 217/15
obliquitlie *adv* slantwise, indirectly 315/22 (see **nippit**)
oblish *v* oblige 354/6, 400/19, 404/31
obnoxious *adj* liable to punishment 364/32, 412/26
obtein, obtine *v* obtain 130/2 130/21, 133/8
official *n* 122/33, see note
oppoision *n* opposition (a misspelling?) 193/25
oppone *v* oppose 206/3, 327/5
or *prep* before 358/9
oraison *n* oration 322marg.
outbrading *v, pres p* upbrading 194
outpass *v* surpass 55/12
outpassing *vbl n* way out, escape 32/26-27
outrance *n* **at outrance** at or to the bitter end, mortal (of combat) 85/28, 221/24
outward *adj* distant 359/30
overshote *v, pt* went beyond bounds, ran into excesses, erred 381/1
overslip *v* escape 158/24
overtake *v* undertake, take in hand 12/4
overvail *v* veil over, conceal 9/10
ovirlayde *v, pt* overwhelmed 272/34
ovirseen *v, pt* connived at 58/4
oy *n* grandchild 18/18

painfulnes *n* carefulness, painstaking 114/26
paise *n* pace 110/35, 222/14
pansing *v* think, consider 312/25, 425/25
parbroulzie *v* confuse, perplex 445/10
parbulzerie *n* confusion, disorder, broil 207/34
partage *n* portion, share 345/10
partialitie *n* plausibility 54/24, see note. (Not *DOST* or OED in this sense)
particular *adj* individual, private 315/1, 406/9, 429/27
particular *n* private interest 339/27, 364/1, 410/6
particularitie *n* private interest 370/15
partaker *n* supporter, partisan 57/15, 403/22
Pas(c)h *n* Easter 282/2, 346/34
pat(e) *v, pt* put 160/32, 238/8
peil(e) *n* tower, fortified house 143/3, 423/21
perfyting *v, pres p* fulfilling, accomplishing 105/25
period *n* end 66/10
persue *v* prosecute, sue 404/4
pertine *v* belong 218/18, 267/5
pillule *n* pill 70/15
plaid *v* plead 358/4
plainlie *adv* forthrightly 253/5, 303/22
pleining *v, pres p* complaining, blaming 300/14
plent *n* complaint 116/3
plentuous *adj* aggrieved, injured, complaining 327/16
politike *n* politician 146/35
port(e) *n* gate (of a castle or town) 60/30, 165/25, 246/1
potent *n* a powerful person 56/8
pous *v. trans* push, press, advance 5/10, 24/9, 405/5
pousser *n* partisan, supporter 57/13
poysonable *adj* poisonous, 325/16
poysonablenes *n* poisonousness 331/14
preiss, preise *v* endeavour, press forward 103/31, 319/9, 337/21

prejudge *v* treat prejudicially 191/11, 293/32
preoccupy *v* get in first 427/27
prescrive , prescryve *v* command, order 164/32, 435/8
presentlie *adv* immediately 119/22, 223/9
pretendit *v, pp* claimed 252/23, 309/28, 413/5
pretension *n* claim 13/30, 195/12, 196/21; intention 32/11
pretermit *v* omit, pass over 426/17
prevein *v* forestall, anticipate 168/11, 218/30, 384/8
privatie *n* privacy, secrecy 407/14
probation *n* proof 16/13
proces *n* judicial process, trial 336/24
procurator *n* agent 361/15
promoved *v, pt* promoted, 26/9
pronephew *n* great grandson 195/33
prophetie *n* prophecy 226/22
propone *v* propose, intend 139/22, 190/22, 191/28
prove *n* proof 386/34
proye *n* prey, booty 212/2, 215/35, 234/3
punchon *n* cask 81/14
pupil *n* 'a person below the age of legal puberty, viz. a boy under 14 or a girl under 12' (DOST) 287/25
purchased *v, pt* procured (to be), got (to be)101/5

quavis *n pl* bogs 424/15
quhat *interrog pron* what 408/7
quhatsomever *adj* whatsoever 68/22
quhyte, quyte *v* quit 77/29, 271/44
quite *n* 97/24, see note
quyot , quyit *adj* quiet 81/24, 83/33, 332

raid *v, pt* rode 324/18, 402/21
rander *v* surrender, give back 154/7, 155/1, 429/33
rathest *adv* soonest 82/17, 107/33
ratirit *v, pp* retired 279/24
rear oy *n* great grandson 195/33
reave *v* plunder, take by force 72/6, 296/13; **reft** *pt* plundered 254/29
recept, receyt *n* shelter, harbouring 78/25, 203/4, 395/2
recherche *n* study, investigation 4/20, 5/7, 9/27
recompensation *n* compensation, reparation 243/1
recreat *v* revive, refresh 242/27, 437/3
rede *v* rid 302/27, **red** *pp* 314/3, 388/32
redactit *v, pp* reduced 159/12, 277/28, 383/4
reede *n* raid 278/19
reedefiet *v, pp* rebuilt 246/3
refel *v* refute, rebutt, give the lie to 222/34, 228/30, 260/13
refer *v* reserve for later treatment 309/27
reft *v, pt* see reave
regardit *v, pp* esteemed 269/12, 284/20, 309/19
regne *n* reign 285/18
regrate *v* regret 340/32
reif *n* robbery, plundering 402/30
reik *n* smoke 110/2
reive *v* rob, plunder 72/19, 381/4
reiven *v, pp* riven, torn 269/18
relent *v* slacken, cool 306/5
remaine *n* stay 275/6
remass *v* amass 90/5
remeid, remede *v* remedy 327/8 411/21, 413/23
remembring *v, pres p* puting in mind of 350/12

remit *v* lay aside 64/5
rencounter, renco(u)ntre *n* military engagement, encounter 221, 271, 228; chance? 14/13, 30/6, 66/2
rencounter, rencountre *v* encounter, meet in war 233/7, 281/30, 436/26
renge *v* set in order 71/21
renomme *n* renown 28/7, 29/20, 35/8
renommed *v, pp* renowned 4/13, 11/27, 28/18
report *v* get for oneself 94/14, 240/27
represent *v* present 432/27, see note
reproved *v, pp* blameworthy 45/8, 66/23
reputing (how) *v, pres p* considering (how) 73/30
requyre *v* inquire, question 145/29
resave *v* receive 92/11, 203/15, 278/25
reset *n* refuge, reception 77/17, 275/16
reset *v, pp* received, harboured 368/22
respectiuelie *adv* with due consideration of the circumstances 142/11
retein *v* retain 15/1, 175/22, 215/16
retined, retined, *v, pp retained* 123/3, 216/22
reval *v* devalue 292/9
rid *adj* red 39/2, 383/27, 402/29
roofe *n* see note to 70/8
ruge *v* tug, **reiving and ruginge** practise robbery 427
ruk *n* hay rick 100/7
rulzeon *n* a shoe of undressed hide 114/20
rung *v, pt* reigned 18/16
ryce *n* twigs, brushwood 98/16
ryp(e) *v* reap 6/20, 60/37, 189/22
sa(i)kles *adj* not liable to penalty, innocent 298/17, 419/22fn
saccaginge *v, pres p* plundering 110/4
sad(e) *adj* heavy 117/26, 225/29
saiglie *adv* sagely 298/8
sailz(i)e *n* assault, sally 136/4, 241/3
sam(e)in *adj* same 100/20, 134/10, 433/9
sam(e)in *pron* same 15/17, 409/19, 421/24
sattil, sattle *v* settle 170/18, 190/18, 401/18
sauld *v, pt* sold 282/20
savtie *n* 280/24, 367/13
sc(k)alad(e) *n* escalade, an attack using scaling ladders 163/9, 187/27
sche *pron* she 344/12 **scho** 209/18, 344/5
schote *v, pp* expelled 95/3
sclaverie *n* slavery 193/8, 208/2 215/32
scrimar *n* fighter, duelist, skirmisher 313/26 see note
seasinge *n* sasine, seisin, 'the act... of giving possession of feudal property, orig. by symbolic delivery of earth and stones'(DOST) 105/31
seazit *v, pp* seised, in feudal possession of 177/7
secours(e) *n* help 61/11, 162/34, 217/4
secretaire *n* secretary 200/20
seige *v* besiege 133/31, 214/32
seik *adj* sick 284/17
sek *n* sack 84/31
selfnes *n* self-serving, selfishness 372/35
seller *n* cellar 81/6
sen *conj* since 44/11, 296/30, 342/10
sence *conj* since 261/6, 393/16
sensyne *adv* since 193/7, 250/1
sevint *adj* seventh 26/16, 277/27,

287/3
sext *adj* sixth 57/2, 161/28
shaw(e) n show 211/14, 430/28
sheil *n* hut, hovel 440/5
sher(r)es(c)hipe *n* office of sheriff 168/12, 170/3, 185/7
sic *adj* such 205/22, 266/34, 385/22
sik(e) *adj* such 69/16, 269/33, 369/3
siker *adj* sure 175/7, 444/4
siklik , siklyke *adv* likewise 176/29, 300/12, 304/18
sindrie *adj* sundry 8/8, 162/9, 245/18
sindrie *n* sundry 168/24, 169/8
singular *adj* single, 154/30, 159/26, 278/20302; exceptional, 171/27, 324/33, 342/22
singular *adv* singularly, exceptionally, 324/33
sinisterlie *adv* prejudicially 304/13
sinistrous *adj* unfair 283/13
sixt *adj* sixth 417/32
skaking *v, pres p* shaking 221/30
skat(t)er *v* scatter 227/10, 244/8
skembels *n* shambles, slaughter-house 334/34
sleiprey *adj* sleepy 97/28
sleuth(e) *n* sloth, carelessness 95/32, 211/5, 288/9
sloutful *adj* slothful 199/27
solist *adj* solicitous 224/20
solist *v* solicit 153/13
sommerlie, summerlie *adv* summarily 24/18, 204/28
sound *v* appear, 353/7; 'sound to', it, accord with, 368/20
spaite *n* flood 72/7; press, crowd 174/27
sparit *v, pres* omitted 253/3
specialitie *n* particular specification 397/18
spous *v* espouse 410/8, 411/5
spoyle *v* deprive, plunder 199/30, 420/12, 426/12
spulzie *n* spoil 362/29, 384/30, 386/15
spunke *n* spark 333/14
stainzie *n* stain 193/9
staitlie *adj* splendid? belonging to the state 35/8
statish *adj* political, belonging to the state 35/19
stawe *v, pt* stole 322/5
stay *adj* steep 165/22
stay *v* withstand, stop 109/34, 200/6, 327/6
stead ***n*** stead, profit, service 373/12
steadable *adj* serviceable 438/10
steir *v* stir 397/30
stirage *n* commotion 444/28
stoke *n* stock 175/21, 176/13, 310/22
stone *n* testicle 269/14
stoode *n* collection of mares kept for breeding 363/2
stoppes *n* steps 204/4
stowen *v, pp* stollen 362/14
straik *v* spread, smear 315/5
straik(e), strake *n* blow, stroke, kick 218/17, 230/28, 248/19
strait *n* defile, narrow place, 2237/18
strait(e), strate *adj* narrow, strict 32/23, 80/5, 82/31
straite *v* straiten, press hard 61/7, 112/18, 116/14
straitnes *n* narrowness 281/6
strake *v, pp* see **streike**
strange *adj* strong 238/5
stranglie *adv* strangely?, strongly? 335/18
streike *v*; *pp* **strake** strike 72/28 (conjectural reading); 81/14, 149
streinzeing *vbl n* extorting 368/26
strenth(e) *n* stronghold 89/22, 142/26, 283/23
strict(e) *adj* narrow, tight 98/11, 110/37
stroike *n* stroke 154/21

strooke *v, pt* struck 241/7
struken *v, pp* of a battle, fought 270/9
stur(r)e *n* strife 253/1, 290/33
sturde *v, pp* stirred 286/23
subrogat *v, pp* substituted in an office 251/10
subscryve *v* subscribe 18/12
succes(se) *n* result, the way events fall out, luck 184/9, 204/2, 216/28
succumbe *v* give up, withdraw from an enterprise 5/8
suddentie *n* sudden happening 254/22
sufferable *adj* able to endure 324/10
sufferance *n* endurance 113/21
summerlie see **sommerlie**
suppone *v* suppose 190/31, 290/32, 302/30
supputation *n* reckoning 415/23
surmissing *vbl n* accusation 281/14
suspense *n* doubt 252/14
sustein *v* sustain 216/24, 223/32
sut(t)e *v* petition, court 84/21, 206/5, 370/33
sute *n* suit 370/4
sutter *n* petitioner 206/4
swa *adv* so 83/29, 91/24, 112/25
swart(e) *adj* dark 33fn, 240/23
sweir *adj* reluctant, loath 153/14
swyre *n* squire 154/30
syse *n* jury 336/24
syser *n* assiser, juryman 181/6

taiken *n* token 330/15, 334/13
tailzie *n* entail 149/11, 183/1, 183/27
tailzie *v* entail 283/3, 343/14
taine *v, pp* taken 174/2, 420/7, 430/7
tairge *n* targe, shield 175/7, 444/4
tasker *n* labourer 79/12
taucherles *adj* dowryless 298/16
teast *v* taste 401/29
temerare *adj* bold 32/14
tent *adj* tenth 18/10, 176, 337
tent *n* care 323/18
tesmonie *n* testimony 272/21 (a slip?)
then *conj* than 196/10, 214/5, 215/24
thesaurer *n* treasurer 162/33, 367/21
thesauririer *n* treasury 166/27
thir *pron* these, those 14/14, 310/29, 315/19
tho(u)ght *conj* though 92/1, 337/28, 432/20
thorter *n* obstruction, trouble 264/11
thorter *v* thwart 43/31, 66/2
thraw out *v* **threwe** *pt* extort 335/27
thraw *v* **threw** *pt* wring, 335/27, 388/1; thwart, 335/26
thrawart *adj* adverse, opposed 359/34
threttie *adj* thirty 17/6, 24/23, 280/29
threw *v, pt* see thraw
thrid *adj* third 397/20, 417/30, 435/30
thrid *n* **third** 22/16, 56/1, 182/6
thrist *n* thirst 154/79, 166/17
throgh-light *n* clear light 224/18
throughlie *adv* thoroughly 12/29
throw *v* extort, compel (see 'thraw out') 96/23, 272/3; wring, twist 388/1 406/6
throwing *vbl n* compulsion 360/10
thus way *adv* thus 91/6
tierce *n* third part 182/10
tigue *n* twig scion, 35/12
tint see 'tine, tint'
tinsel *n* loss 169/16
titulare *adj* titular 188/25
to *adv* too 210/26, 259/6
to(e) name *n* nick name 59marg., 258/fn10
tocher, toucher *n* dowry 120/9, 201/9, 251/15

tone *n* tune 95/15
tort *n* wrong, injury 392/3
touch *n* stroke of satire 11/15
towardnes *n* docility 126/3
traictie *n* treaty 66/20
trait(te) *n* touch (in a picture) 58/18; mark 42/33
traitable *adj* tractable 318/13
traittie *n* treatise, volume title page, 8/20; entreatie 291/20
transact *v* negotiate, arrange 382/22
transumpt *n* copy 183/22
travel *n* labour, pain 54/21, 299/21, 385/3
treasor *n* tressure 201/13, see note
treatise *n* treaty 210/23
tresor *n* treasure 166/30
tresorrer *n* treasurer 171/30
tresure *n* stock, funds 39/10
trie *n* wood 87/33
trif(f)ils *n* trifles 217/10, 304/7
troublance *n* troubling 311/1
tryne *n* train 324/20
tryst ***n*** appointed meeting 326/5
turk *n* infidel 124/32, 244/30
tutor *n* guardian of a legally incapable heir in the absence of the father 401/27, 403/17, 404/19
tutorie *n* tutelage, guardianship 97/18
twelft *adj* twelfth 247/6
tyne *v* lose 258/5, 355/32, 420/12; *pt* **tint, tynt** lost 258/13, 445/4, 355/27
tyst *v* entice 72/20

valiantise *n* valour 91/26, 255/13, 291/6
val(l)iancie *n* valour 159/26, 292/1
vassalage, vassalege *n* gallant exploit 225/14, 240/23
veille *n* calf 334/21
verse *n* article (of belief or instruction) 369/15
vertue *n* quality, virtue, preeminent manliness, force 233/22, 240/104, 387/1
vespe *n* wasp 331/13
vestit *v, pp* invested 177/7
vindicative *adj* vindictive 370/16
viuelie *adv* vividly 213/29
vivers *n* victuals 75/2, 103/68, 118/6
vmbeset *v* beset, attack on all sides 173/2, 389/16
vmquhil, wmquhil *adj* former, the late 15/12, 425/30, 436/3
vnabled *v, pp* disabled 240/23
vnapparant *adj* improbable 398/6
vnappeirand *adj* improbable 86/35
vnaquent *adj* unacquainted 393/18
vnaware, vnawars *adv* **at vnaware, at vnawars** unawares 399/23, 399/32
vnbeing *v, pres p* not or without being in some condition 399/20
vncouth(e) *adj* strange, unknown 335/19, 336/18; foreign 39/16
vndermyndit *v, pp* undermined 174/19
vnforesein *v, pp* not foreseeing 418/18
vnfreind *n* enemy 352/3
vnkyndnes *n* enmity, acting against ties of kinship and natual affection 374/3
vnmendableness *n* the quality of not being able to mend one's ways 265/5
vnnaturalitie *n* unnaturalness 297/4
vnquyetit *v, pt* disturbed 436/21
vnrefragable *adj* irrefraeable, incontrovertible 289/9
vnreprobable *adj* unblameable 415/1

vntymouslie *adv* inopportunely 316/10
vnware *adj* unwary 332/21
vogue *n* ('in vogue'), in prevalent acceptance 202/27; vigour? 351/16
voluntary *n* choice **of voluntary** voluntarily 278/5
voluptie *n* pleasure 64/26
voyage *n* journey 414/21
vsurpator *n* usurper 143/22
vsurpit of *v, pp* taken over by 269/23
vterine *adj* sharing the same mother (but not father) 421/6
vttermest *n* utmost 89/32
vyldnes *n* vileness 381/20

wadge *n* wedge 437/14
waird *n* fate, weird 232/18; prison 338/18
wait, wate *v* know 272/6, 353/28, 373/22
wal, wale, walle *n* wall 87/35, 175/8, 245/26
wande *n* stick 113/11
war(e) *adj* wary 120/32, 260/6; **a war(e)** aware 184/5, 380/23
ward(e) *n* prison 301/7, 303/7, 307/10
ward *v* imprison 300/18, 321/9, 338/29
ward *n* part of battle array 422/34
warreful *adj* martial 39/22, 63/24
wassaledge *n* gallant exploit 444/6
wate see 'wait'
wawe *n* wave 76/35
way *adv* away ('way carying') 63/31
waycuming *n* departure 213/20
wean *v* suppose 148/8
weast *adj* idle 375/28
weirds *n* fates 63/8
weshel *n* vessel, ship 163/28
wey *v* weigh 379/14, 381/marg.
what *adv* partly (introducing alternatives: 'what... what...) 189/7, 307/21, 308/17
whidder *conj* whether 101/33
while as *conj* while 14/7, 171/8, 283/27
whils *adv* sometimes 227/19, 300/16, 323/10
whils *conj* while 202/20, 210/26, 432/15
whinger *n* a short stabbing sword, dagger 409/29
whither *conj* whether 307fn.10
wight *adj* courageous 127/19
window *v* winnow 377/13
winne *v, pp* won 168/2
wit *v, imp* know 177/1
witter *n* token, mark 221/29
wmquhil see 'vmquhil'
woore *v, pt* bore the attack of 80/3
wraik, wrake *n* ruin 140/17, 301/2, 401/23
wrangous *adj* unjust, wrongful 147/11, 298/13
wrongouslie, wrangouslie *adv* wrongly, unrightfully 239/6, 247/8, 353/24
wreath *n* wrath 192/28, 201/25
wreke *v* wreck, ruin 258/19
wyce *n* vice 250/6

ympe *n* shoot, scion 338/29

ze *pron* ye 319/12, 322/9, 340/29
zea *adv* yea 316/12, 321/10, 374/18
zeild *v, pp* yield 322/4, 359/31, 403/8
zeile *n* zeal 255/34
zeir *n* year 316/4
zit *adv* still 302/26
zit *conj* yet 65/2, 315/33, 409/10
zoke *n* yoke 151/28
zomane, zomens *n* yeomen 199/13, 234/9
zoung *adj* young 343/11
zouth *n* youth 316/11, 318/12

zow *pers pron* you 14/35, 226/15, 409/11; **zour, zowrs** *gen* your(s), 4/12, 6/21, 198/13
Zul *n* Christmas 134/12

INDEX OF PERSONS

The end notes are indexed only for those names to which there is no direct reference in the text. When 'n' is added to a page number, the number refers to the end notes for that page.